# THE TRANSFORMATION OF POSITIVISM

# THE TRANSFORMATION OF POSITIVISM

## Alexius Meinong and European Thought, 1880–1920

*David F. Lindenfeld*

UNIVERSITY OF CALIFORNIA PRESS

BERKELEY · LOS ANGELES · LONDON

University of California Press
Berkeley and Los Angeles, California

University of California Press, Ltd.
London, England

© 1980
The Regents of the University of California

Printed in the United States of America

Library of Congress Cataloging in Publication Data

Lindenfeld, David F
    The transformation of positivism. Alexius Meinong
    and European thought, 1880–1920

    Bibliography: p.
    Includes index.
    1. Meinong, Alexius, Ritter von Handschuchsheim,
1853–1920.  2. Philosophers—Austria—Biography.
3. Europe—Intellectual life.  4. Philosophy,
Modern—19th century.  5. Philosophy, Modern—20th
century.  I. Title.

B3309.M24L56    193    79-65775
ISBN 0-520-03994-7

1 2 3 4 5 6 7 8 9

TO MY PARENTS

# CONTENTS

# PREFACE

This book is an essay in intellectual history of a rather traditional sort. It dwells for the most part on philosophical ideas rather than on the political or social factors which may have shaped them or influenced their dissemination. The fact that I have written it in this way does not mean that I believe all intellectual history should be so done, or that such factors are irrelevant to explaining the changes in European thought and culture at the turn of the century—indeed, I have sought to bring them in as background. There seems to be little point, however, in explaining the patterns of thought of an age in terms of social history until one has a more accurate descriptive notion of what those patterns actually were. The primary purpose of this study is to try to clarify these patterns. It seeks to modify somewhat the traditional picture which historians have held of European thought in the late nineteenth and early twentieth centuries.

The most appropriate means for presenting this material seemed to me to be an intellectual biography of a figure whose ideas and development were representative of these neglected trends; I chose the Austrian philosopher Alexius von Meinong. I should add that the book is in no way intended to be a comprehensive exposition of Meinong's philosophy. This has already been done by J. N. Findlay in his book *Meinong's Theory of Objects and Values* (Oxford, 1963) in a way that can scarcely be bettered. Neither is this study a critical analysis of Meinong's thought, except insofar as such considerations serve to illuminate his historical significance.

The encouragement and support which I received from a great many people in this project have indeed been gratifying. My advisers for the dissertation on which the book was based were Leonard Krieger and George Stocking. Both contributed not only valuable criticism, but also a great deal of tolerance in letting me develop my own approach. Paul Ricoeur also read parts of the manuscript: his insights were most helpful and his enthusiasm a source of great satisfaction. The research abroad was done under a grant from the Foreign Area Fellowship Foundation. The staff at the Universitätsbibliothek in Graz, particularly Dr. Maria Mairold, offered generous assistance. A special word of thanks should go to Professor Rudolf Haller of the philosophical institute at the University of Graz. His patience with my initial gropings in Meinong's philosophy was truly invaluable. The friendliness and fine-working atmosphere of the institute made my stay in Graz a most enjoyable one.

Since the time of the dissertation I have received helpful comments and criticism from several sources, particularly from Professors John Baker and Karl Roider in the philosophy and history departments at Louisiana State University, respectively. Maurice Mandelbaum also read the manuscript and gave valuable advice.

In the footnotes and Bibliography I have cited English translations whenever possible. I have, however, read most of the works cited in the original languages.

D.F.L.

*Baton Rouge, Louisiana*
*1978*

# ABBREVIATIONS

GA      *Alexius Meinong Gesamtausgabe.* Edited by Rudolf Haller, Rudolf Kindinger, and Roderick M. Chisholm. 7 vols. Graz: Akademische Druck-u. Verlagsanstalt, 1968–.

GS      *Wilhelm Dilthey Gesammelte Schriften.* 18 vols. Stuttgart: B. G. Teubner, and Göttingen: Vandenhoeck and Ruprecht, 1914–1977.

Kalsi      Meinong, *On Emotional Presentation.* Translated by Marie-Luise Schubert Kalsi. Evanston: Northwestern University Press, 1972.

HR      René Descartes, *The Philosophical Works of Descartes.* Translated by Elizabeth S. Haldane and G. R. T. Ross. 2 vols. Cambridge: Cambridge University Press, 1968.

LTC      Meinong, "The Theory of Objects." In *Realism and the Background of Phenomenology*, pp. 76–117. Edited by Roderick M. Chisholm, translated by Isaac Levi, D. B. Terrell, and Roderick M. Chisholm. Glencoe: The Free Press, 1960.

SE      Sigmund Freud, *The Standard Edition of the Complete Psychological Works of Sigmund Freud.* Edited by James Strachey, Anna Freud, et al. 24 vols. London: Hogarth Press, 1966–1974.

# INTRODUCTION

During the closing years of World War I, Sigmund Freud delivered a paper which contained his estimation of the importance of psychoanalysis in Western intellectual history. According to Freud, the advances of science had dealt three severe blows to man's self-esteem: the first had been the Copernican theory, which had unseated man from his assumed position at the center of the universe; the second had been Darwin's theory of evolution, which had robbed him of his sense of superiority to animals; the third was psychoanalysis, which demonstrated that *"the ego was not master in its own house."* [1] In Freud's view, his own discoveries were probably the most devastating of these three, for they in fact contained two separate attacks on man's self-love. On the one hand, psychoanalysis had shown that man was often at the mercy of his instincts; his conscious thoughts were often shaped by forces from within over which he had no control. The importance of the instincts amounted to a significant limitation on human freedom to choose between different courses of thought and action. On the other hand, this limitation was based on another more fundamental one: the deficiency of human self-knowledge. Consciousness was also hampered by its lack of information from the unconscious; instinctual conflicts manifested themselves deviously, through symbols and rituals, rather than directly through thoughts. Even the most intelligent could not hope to gain complete knowledge of their own minds. [2]

There was nevertheless a paradox in Freud's formulation: the

---

1. Sigmund Freud, "A Difficulty in the Path of Psycho-Analysis," trans. Joan Riviere, in *The Standard Edition of the Complete Psychological Works of Sigmund Freud*, ed. James Strachey, Anna Freud, et al., XVII (London: Hogarth Press, 1955), 143; 139–141; hereafter cited as *SE*.

2. *Ibid.*, 142f.

blows to human self-esteem and ultimately to the powers of reason were brought about by the very extension and deeper penetration of these powers in the forms of an ever-advancing psychological science. Freud's faith in the power of science to liberate man alternates with his doubts about man's capacity for self-mastery and self-knowledge. In the same paragraph in which he chides us for overestimating our consciousness, he admonishes us to "learn first to know yourself! Then . . . perhaps, you will avoid falling ill in future [sic]."[3] To be sure, Freud was aware of this paradox, and sought to overcome it by arguing that only when reason was freed from the illusions of its own omnipotence could it contribute to the betterment of the individual and of mankind. The greatest obstacle to progress, then, had not been the irrational forces within us, but our own unrealistic assessment of the power of reason itself. Once man had gained knowledge of his own irrationality, he could use that knowledge to overcome it.[4]

Such an ambivalent attitude towards human reason and its capacities for knowledge was not unique to psychoanalysis. Indeed, it may be said to characterize in general those various attempts to apply the standards of modern science to the study of man which have acquired the label "positivism." Although the term customarily refers to a more or less definite group of figures, including Comte, J. S. Mill, Spencer, Mach, Avenarius, and the Vienna Circle of logical positivists headed by Schlick and Carnap, it is also used more broadly to apply to any thinker or movement which seeks to imitate the rigor of natural science in philosophy, the social sciences, or history. It is not difficult to find in the programmatic statements of the positivists expressions of the same ambivalence: the belief that the key to the advancement of knowledge is the awareness of the limits of knowledge. Comte, for example, spoke in 1829 of the positive stage of a science as distinct from the more primitive metaphysical stage in the following way:

> In the final, the positive state, the mind has given over the vain search after Absolute notions, the origin and destination of the universe, and the causes of phenomena, and applies itself to the study of their laws—that is, their invariable relations of succession and resemblance.[5]

3. *Ibid.*, 143. Similar waverings can be found if one compares such works as *The Future of An Illusion* with *Civilization and Its Discontents*, written within two years of each other; see *SE* XXI, 38, 48, and 87f, 145.

4. *Ibid.*, 49, 56, 142f.

5. Auguste Comte, *The Positive Philosophy of Auguste Comte*, trans. Harriet Martineau, 2 vols. (London: John Chapman, 1853), I, 2.

Similarly, Spencer opened his comprehensive system of the sciences in 1864 with a disquisition on "The Unknowable," in which he saw an end to the age-old quarrel between science and religion. "A permanent peace will be reached," he wrote, "when Science becomes fully convinced that its explanations are proximate and relative, while Religion becomes fully convinced that the mystery it contemplates is ultimate and absolute."[6] In a very different context, Moritz Schlick launched the logical positivist journal *Erkenntnis* in 1930 with an article entitled "The Turning Point in Philosophy," in which he claimed that there were "no questions which are in principle unanswerable, no problems which are in principle insoluble. What has been considered such up to now are not genuine questions, but meaningless sequences of words."[7] Most commentators on positivism have agreed that it can be characterized as much by what it denies as by what it affirms— though not all would go as far as Leszek Kolakowski in summarizing it as "a collection of prohibitions concerning human knowledge."[8] An apparently essential feature of positivism, then, is its critique of illusions that go under the name of metaphysics. The grounds for this critique lie in the assumption that the human mind is unable to grasp ultimate truths or things in themselves—a position derived from the empiricist theory of knowledge which antedated positivism itself.

Freud's sketch of intellectual history is indicative of another trend in positivist thought that reaches beyond psychoanalysis: the tendency for the pessimistic implications of the positivist critique to predominate in the twentieth century. Given the fact that positivism invoked the dual expression of man's strengths and weaknesses that went back to some of the earliest humanistic texts of the Renaissance as well as the writings of Locke and Hume, the balance has shifted perceptibly in favor of the weaknesses. This has been manifested in a number of ways.

For one thing, it became increasingly difficult to reconcile the notion of individual freedom of action with the belief that human be-

6. Herbert Spencer, *First Principles*, 4th ed. (New York: D. Appleton and Co., 1896), pp. 109–110.

7. Moritz Schlick, "The Turning Point in Philosophy," trans. David Rynin, in *Logical Positivism*, ed. A. J. Ayer (Glencoe: The Free Press, 1959), p. 56.

8. Leszek Kolakowski, *The Alienation of Reason*, trans. Norbert Guterman (Garden City: Doubleday and Co., 1968), p. 9. For a less negative summary, see Maurice Mandelbaum, *History, Man and Reason* (Baltimore: The Johns Hopkins Press, 1971), pp. 10–11, 376.

havior was governed by rigorous scientific laws. This tension has been discussed in detail by Talcott Parsons with respect to the social sciences, and more recently by Gerald Izenberg with respect to psychoanalysis itself.[9] For another, the whole assumption that scientifically precise reasoning was at all relevant to issues of norms for human conduct was called into question. This can be seen by contrasting the positions of Comte and Spencer with that of Schlick. The earlier positivists shared a belief that scientific inquiry was advancing in a more or less steady direction from the simpler aspects of nature to the more complex. According to Comte, the scientific method was first established in astronomy and physics in the seventeenth century, but in the nineteenth was moving to encompass chemistry and physiology, which in turn would provide the basis for the study of man proper through sociology. Comte explained this cumulative process through his law of three stages that each science passes through: the theological, the metaphysical, and the positive. As a given science moves into the positive stage, it provides the lasting foundations for the more complex sciences to move through the same cycle. In Spencer, a similar hierarchy is justified by appeal to the theory of biological evolution. When the sciences of man were thus eventually established, the rules of morality and action could be derived. This was the basis for Comte's positivist religion. Spencer, for his part, could characterize the data of morality as "the generalizations furnished by biology, psychology and sociology which underly a true theory of right living."[10]

By contrast, the logical positivists based their critique of metaphysics and their views on ethics on utterly different grounds. They did not draw on the advances of empirical science for their theories, but rather on the new developments in deductive logic of Russell and Whitehead in the *Principia Mathematica* and of Wittgenstein in the *Tractatus Logico-Philosophicus*. They saw these new techniques as marking a revolutionary break with the past—not simply the culmination of technical progress in logical notation but, in Schlick's words, "the insight into the nature of logic itself."[11] This insight was that logic tells

9. Gerald Izenberg, *The Existentialist Critique of Freud* (Princeton: Princeton University Press, 1976), Ch. I, p. 183.

10. Spencer, p. xv.

11. Schlick, p. 55. It is such statements by the logical positivists that make Jürgen Habermas' characterization of positivism in his *Knowledge and Human Interests* (trans. Jeremy Shapiro; London: Heinemann Educational Books, 1972) misleading. On the one hand, Habermas correctly points out that positivism bases its position on the finality and incontrovertibility of "the facts" (p. 89). On this point Schlick would agree: for

us nothing about the world itself; rather it is concerned purely with the formal properties of the language we use in talking about the world. From this starting point, the Vienna Circle drew several conclusions which differentiated their type of positivism from earlier types. First, a philosophy which sought to be scientific by virtue of rigorous logical analysis did not make statements about the world directly; rather it consisted of analyzing the language of science and of other supposedly philosophical disciplines such as metaphysics and ethics in order to clarify the meaning of their statements. Thus philosophy was no longer based on the results of science, but rather constituted a way of reflecting on scientific expression. Second, if it could be shown that a given statement, even if logical in form, had no concrete referent in the empirical world, then it could be dismissed as meaningless and not worth talking about. The statements which fell under the axe of this critique included not only those of metaphysics, but also the normative statements of ethics. The best that scientific reasoning could do in relation to ethics was to describe the actual, empirically verifiable conduct of individuals and their motives. Ethics, according to Schlick, thus became absorbed into psychology.[12]

Such a contraction in the range and applicability of positivism undoubtedly helps to account for the fact that the word itself carries a bad connotation for many educated people today, and seems to be a less desirable version of secular humanism than existentialism or Marxism, for example. Positivism connotes for many an abdication from the important questions regarding man; the sacrifices it makes in the name of precision make it unacceptable. Or, alternatively, positivism seems to imply reductionism: that the higher qualities of human life could be explained away in terms of physical or biological laws, as the nineteenth-century positivists often attempted to do.

This study will be concerned with the question of how and why this narrowing occurred. It will seek to trace the changes that took place in positivist thought between the time of Spencer and the time of Schlick and Carnap.

---

him, the criterion for what constitutes meaning is the empirically verifiable fact. But Habermas also maintains that this position is arrived at by generalizing ex post facto from the results of science, thus shutting off any prospect of reflecting critically on scientific activity itself (pp. 4–5, 89). This would not apply to logical positivism, as the passage from Schlick demonstrates.

12. Schlick, "What is the Aim of Ethics?", trans. David Rynin, in *Logical Positivism*, p. 263. Kolakowski attributes this feature to positivism as a whole (p. 7), but it does not apply to most of the nineteenth-century positivists; see Mandelbaum, p. 376.

It may seem to some readers that this ground has already been well-covered by intellectual historians and historians of philosophy—the lines of transition and influence are already well known. One could point, for example, to the movement known as empiriocriticism of Mach and Avenarius, which flourished from the 1880s to the First World War, as the decisive link between evolutionary and logical positivism.[13] Certainly there is a good deal of truth in this argument. The members of the Vienna Circle looked to the empiriocriticists as their predecessors; moreover, the ideas of Mach and Avenarius represent a clear step in the direction of emphasizing the critical aspect of positivism. Mach and Avenarius made their impact by pointing out the imprecisions in meaning of traditional scientific concepts of the nineteenth century, such as those of physical atoms, force, and causal law, as well as of such commonsensical concepts as the self. According to the empiriocriticists, such concepts could be analyzed into the more precise and observable notion of sensation. Sensations constituted a common ground, as it were, for the data of physics, physiology, and psychology.

Nevertheless, empiriocriticism still breathed the air of nineteenth-century positivism. Mach and Avenarius based their critique of established concepts on the advances of empirical science. They argued that their system was justified on biological grounds: the most successful adaptation of the human mind to its environment was to find the most economical means of formulation; this the notion of sensations represented. Mach also cited the work of Fechner in psychology and of Avogadro in chemistry as providing the stimuli to his thought.[14] Certainly the synthesis of physics and psychology would not have been possible without the new advances in nerve physiology of the 1850s and 60s.

More importantly, however, it is clear that logical positivism had other roots besides that of empiriocriticism: the analysis of language and its relation to symbolic logic, which plays such an important role in the later movement, is not to be found as a major theme in the writings of Mach and Avenarius. For this one must turn to the work of

13.   Nicola Abbagnano, in his article on positivism in the *Encyclopedia of Philosophy*, ed. Paul Edwards (New York: Macmillan, 1967), VI, 414ff, makes a useful distinction between three types: the "social" positivism of Comte and the Utilitarians; the "evolutionary" positivism of Spencer; and the "critical" positivism of Mach, Avenarius, and Pearson. Abbagnano does not discuss logical positivism in detail, however..

14.   John Blackmore, *Ernst Mach* (Berkeley: University of California Press, 1972), pp. 27–30.

Wittgenstein and Russell, and to the German philosopher Gottlob Frege, who influenced Russell strongly and who brought to bear some of the new technical developments in symbolic logic to philosophical questions.

It is not these technical developments in themselves which will be the central focus of this book. Rather we shall view them in terms of the light they shed on developments in European thought as a whole during the years preceding World War I—a period full of radical change in virtually every area of intellectual and cultural expression. One has only to think of psychoanalysis, Einsteinian physics, atonal music, expressionist and cubist art, and the new methodologies in social science. Not without reason has this period been called one of intellectual revolution.

It is possible to see amongst these new developments a broader conception of the human mind and its capabilities which seems to be opposed to the development of positivism. This interpretation has been stressed by H. Stuart Hughes in his seminal book *Consciousness and Society*. Concentrating on social thought, Hughes argues that major figures such as Weber, Dilthey, Bergson, and Sorel sought to expand the notion of human consciousness to include the irrational aspects of experience. In so doing they rejected analogies to mechanistic laws of human behavior or biological determinism that often colored the writings of the nineteenth-century positivists. Inasmuch as their inquiries involved epistemological questions, they tended to emphasize the role of intuition in addition to strictly rational knowledge, and argued that knowledge based on such intuition need not be less valid or "objective" for being so. Hughes' label for these important developments, however, is "the revolt against positivism," a label that is misleading in a number of respects. First, as he himself admits, some thinkers such as Freud and Durkheim shared these concerns while remaining steadfastly within the positivistic tradition through the use of mechanistic or biological analogies.[15] Second, many of the figures he leaves out because of their peripheral connection with social thought also broke with these analogies but remained committed to the ideal of philosophy as a rigorous science. These figures would include not only Russell and Frege, but also philosophers of science such as Heinrich Hertz and Ludwig Boltzmann. These figures were concerned with investigating the phenomenon of human language, with explor-

15. H. Stuart Hughes, *Consciousness and Society* (New York: Random House, Vintage Books, 1958), p. 37.

ing relationships between logic and language in general, as well as the bearing of these linguistic phenomena on philosophical questions. Thus the narrow positivism of the Vienna Circle had its roots in a much broader version of positivism that flourished at the turn of the century. One can just as easily talk of a revolt within positivism during this period as a revolt against it.

Moreover, these two strands were not unrelated. This can be seen by looking at the ideas of Franz Brentano and Edmund Husserl, two of the leading figures in the new phenomenological movement. Brentano and Husserl were positivists in the broad sense; that is, they were committed to a strictly scientific philosophy. They too were concerned with language and its relation to experience. But they also sought to take into account the less rational types of human cognition and how these were reflected in language. Husserl, for example, was able to influence strongly one of the figures who was supposedly against positivism, namely Dilthey. And phenomenology was later to lead to existentialism—a form of philosophy very much opposed to positivism. The concern with language at the turn of the century, then, represents a watershed in European thought, an important source of currents that led to the twentieth-century versions of both positivism and anti-positivism.

It is these considerations which led me to choose the Austrian philosopher Alexius von Meinong (1853–1920) as the central subject of this book. At first glance, Meinong might seem a most unpromising candidate for such a subject. Other figures, such as Russell or Husserl, were certainly better known and had greater influence. Meinong spent the bulk of his academic career not in a major center of intellectual life such as Vienna or Prague, but in the remote provincial capital of Graz; apart from a small following of students, he never achieved a lasting reputation in the German-speaking world. His written works were forbidding, not because of an obscure or difficult terminology— in this respect he was refreshingly different from such better-known philosophers as Kant, Hegel, or Heidegger—but because of his preoccupation with detailed investigation of seemingly minute problems rather than with building grand and bold syntheses. Not surprisingly, this style won him a more appreciative audience among English and American philosophers. But beyond philosophy and psychology, his name remains virtually unknown.

If Meinong nevertheless deserves the attention of intellectual historians, it is as a pivotal figure who participated in a number of divergent trends in European thought which have since emerged as distinct or even opposed. Specifically, Meinong exerted a decisive influence on Bertrand Russell in the early 1900s, helping him to formulate the doctrines which were later to lead to logical positivism. At the same time, Meinong adopted many ideas from his teacher of philosophy at Vienna, Franz Brentano, and thus shared many ideas in common with Husserl and the phenomenologists. One can thus see in Meinong's thought a linkage between positivist and non-positivist thought. In addition, Meinong has a place in the history of experimental psychology as a precursor of Gestalt psychology, a movement which constituted another attempt to develop a world view on strictly scientific grounds.

Finally, I would not have devoted so much space to Meinong if I did not believe that he had something distinctive to contribute to the issues raised by the positivist tradition. Meinong's way of conceptualizing the relationship of language, experience, and meaning was broad enough to account for both the scientific and intuitive aspects of consciousness and discourse—without lapsing into a crude mechanism or determinism on the one hand, or retreating to the narrow definitions of logical positivism on the other. Though he was not the only figure to propose such a common conceptual framework at the time—Husserl and the Gestalt psychologists were others—he succeeded in avoiding some of the pitfalls to which they eventually succumbed. His philosophy allowed in principle for the development of a more humane positivism in which the balance between the greatness and the limitations of the human intellect can satisfactorily be struck.

This balance, I believe, constitutes Meinong's principal historical significance. This may seem dubious to historians who would look for some sign of influence as an indication of his importance. But I would argue that it is precisely by way of contrast to the more influential intellectual trends before World War One that his significance emerges. For it is not too much to say that the dominant intellectual movements, whether popular or restricted to an elite, betokened a deep crisis of coherence in humanistic thought and values, a crisis which manifested itself in the increasing pessimism of intellectuals, and which anticipated in some ways the anti-humanistic doctrines of Russian communism and of fascism.

The contours of this crisis may be briefly described as follows: in the late nineteenth century, secular humanism in some form was spreading to the middle and lower classes in Western Europe as part of the process of modernization. Social historians have confirmed the insight of Nietzsche that, as a historical and cultural phenomenon, religion was no longer a vital force in the lives of many Europeans.[16] But the same process which spread these doctrines also undermined them. The liberal emphasis on the dignity of the individual became increasingly threatened by an urban and centralized society. The spread of the industrial revolution in Western Europe gave rise to a greater uniformity of life which offset the gains in leisure time afforded by the increase in material goods. It is no coincidence that the popular evolutionary philosophies that accompanied this change were opposed to liberal individualism. This was true of the Monism of Ernst Haeckel, a biologist who preached a conciliation of evolution and pantheism reminiscent of Goethe, as well as of the related notions of Marxist dialectical materialism that were then current.[17]

These evolutionary views nevertheless still embodied some conception of man as a rational animal, even if this reason was not revealed as much in individual actions as in the logic and purposiveness of collective human history. On the other hand, there were also prominent philosophers and literary figures who rejected this sort of reason in the name of spontaneity or some set of intangible spiritual values. But many of them, such as Langbehn, Barres, D'Annunzio, and Sorel, frequently turned also to mystical collectivistic notions that left the individual no more free and unique than before.[18] These thinkers may also be seen as humanists, but in a different sense: they started from the premise, originally developed by the romantics, that the differences among individuals and cultures were more fruitful than their similarities, and that any universal laws governing human behavior were suspect. The successors of the romantics in the late nineteenth and early twentieth centuries carried this premise to relativistic conclusions. Of all the intellectuals of this persuasion, it was Nietzsche

16. Edward Tannenbaum, *1900* (Garden City: Doubleday, Anchor Press ed. 1976), pp. 163ff.

17. On Haeckel, see Daniel Gasman, *The Scientific Origins of National Socialism* (London: Macdonald, 1971), pp. 33, 44; on Marxism at this time, see George Lichtheim, *Marxism*, 2nd ed. (New York: Praeger Publishers, 1965), p. 258.

18. Henry M. Pachter, *The Fall and Rise of Europe* (New York: Praeger Publishers, 1976), p. 76. Historians have tended to overestimate, I think, the popularity of the revolt against modernity and the protest against scientific ways of thinking before World War One. If one compares the book sales of a typical work of this genre, Langbehn's *Rembrandt als Erzieher*, one finds it sold 150,000 copies between 1890 and World War Two. By contrast, Haeckel's *The Riddle of the Universe* sold 300,000 copies between 1900 and 1914 (though admittedly the former appealed primarily to German readers, while the latter had an international audience). See Fritz Stern, *The Politics of Cultural Despair* (Garden City: Doubleday, Anchor Books, 1965), pp. 199–200; Tannenbaum, p. 239.

who developed this brand of humanism to its most consistent extreme: a world in which human differences prevail over similarities is a world in which conflict, struggle, domination, and submission are inevitable.

In between these poles of rationalism and irrationalism stood thinkers such as Durkheim, Weber, and Freud, who were committed to exploring the irrational dispassionately with the tools of reason. Their explorations, however, did not lead to an unqualified reaffirmation of liberal humanism, but to a highly ambivalent and frequently gloomy appraisal of the prospects for individual self-fulfillment in contemporary society. There was too often an adversary relationship between the two.

Meinong, by contrast, offered a philosophical framework in which the rational and irrational aspects of human existence could be given their due without requiring this adversary relationship. Meinong acknowledged that experiences involving the emotions and the will were irreducible to rational judgment and ideation but were nevertheless not entirely divorceable from these. Values might vary from individual to individual or from group to group, but they were still related to objective nature and the universal causal sequences that prevail there.[19] Meinong recognized, as did most of his contemporaries, the subjective element in science and all human cognition, but he did not see this as negating the existence of an objective natural order of things, which our cognition may never fully apprehend but may at least approximate. It is this belief in the reality of objective truth that constitutes Meinong's metaphysics and provides, I believe, a deeper meaning to the term "positivism" than the one usually associated with it. For despite the fact that many positivists and their critics alike have defined the label in terms of scientific *method*—that is, of applying uncritically the accepted methods of natural science to the study of man and eliminating metaphysics in the process—one may say that most positivists have carried with them an implicit metaphysics in spite of themselves. That metaphysics can be summarized in the notion that there is a determinate order in the natural universe and that man is a part of that order. To apply scientific methods to man is to affirm that human truth is a part of natural truth, and that the answers to social and ethical questions—such as the proper spheres of freedom and authority—must come from our understanding of the proper relation between that part and the whole. Meinong

19. See below, Chapter Seven.

affirms this while still allowing for a realm of human spontaneity and creativity which can never be adequately described in terms of causal laws. This, I would suggest, is an alternate sort of humanism to that provided by Marxists and others who believe in a logic of history. Marxism all too frequently emphasizes the unlimited power of man to transform nature through economic activity, in disregard of any limits placed on this activity by non-human natural laws. It is also different from any sort of humanism that rests its case on the plurality of human types and the relativity of values. It is impossible to illustrate here how Meinong steers between these positions; the proof, I trust, will come in what follows.

That both the Marxist and the irrationalist types of humanism have spawned totalitarianism in this century is a matter of historical record. It is equally obvious that a positivistic humanism, in the hands of an uncontrolled elite of experts, could lead to the same result; that possibility has been explored in fiction by anti-utopian writers such as Huxley. But a philosophy which integrates the presuppositions of natural science with those of the humanities, without subordinating one to the other, could at least provide the hope that there are alternatives to such a technocracy. In this, as I hope to show, lies Meinong's achievement and significance.

# PART ONE

*Background*

# I

# THE TREATMENT OF MIND IN
# THE EMPIRICIST TRADITION

The problem of placing Meinong within a recognized tradition of European philosophy offers little initial difficulty: in an autobiographical sketch, written late in life, Meinong labels himself an empirical thinker.[1] His first two philosophical works were studies of Hume, and both included extended analyses of Berkeley and Locke as well. The broad outlines of Meinong's empiricist heritage are evident in his own self-characterization:

It has always been far from me to begin my research work with far-reaching preconceptions, but rather to be led forward, so to speak, by the facts them-

---

1. Alexius Meinong, *Selbstdarstellung*, in *Alexius Meinong Gesamtausgabe*, ed. Rudolf Haller, Rudolf Kindinger, and Roderick M. Chisholm, Vol. VII (Graz: Akademische Druck-u. Verlagsanstalt, 1978), p. 4. Hereafter this edition will be cited as *GA*. The passage reads as follows: "It seems to me now that, if I have found myself forced to emphasize especially the extra-empirical side of knowledge and help it to its rightful place, I have nevertheless remained, if not an empiricist, at least an empirical thinker in the sufficiently broad sense of the term." According to the narrower definition of empiricism implied here, the only *objects* of knowledge one could have would be one's own experiences. The "broad sense," on the other hand, would be one which claims that all knowledge arises from experience. By the narrower standard, Meinong is not an empiricist, and recent scholarship on John Locke has tended to exclude him on the same grounds. See R. S. Woolhouse, *Locke's Philosophy of Science and Knowledge* (New York: Barnes and Noble, 1971), p. x; J. L. Mackie, *Problems from Locke* (Oxford: The Clarendon Press, 1976), p. 204. But it would be absurd, on this ground, to exclude Locke from the *historical* tradition we label "empiricism." Nor, on the same ground, should we exclude Meinong.

selves, striving above all to observe carefully, and also . . . to seek out what
the resulting line of investigation might offer. There is little trace of the sov-
ereignty of the intellect over the facts in such a procedure.[2]

One may note the emphasis on observation, the respect for the facts
as opposed to grand metaphysical speculation, and the sense of the
limits of knowledge. In addition, Meinong held the empiricist view
that conscious experience is central to human knowledge, and that all
true knowledge stems ultimately from what is incontrovertibly given
in experience.

This tenet has been one of the prime characteristics of positivism as
well.[3] It is also clear that Meinong identified such habits of investigation with positivism in a broad sense:

An exact determination of the area of work . . . a necessary modesty in immediate goals, a careful reserve, but in return a security in the gradual approach to these—these are the aims by which the philosophy which war-
rants the name of *scientific* philosophy may be recognized.[4]

It would nevertheless be mistaken simply to identify empiricism
with positivism. For one thing, positivism does not refer to a tradition,
properly speaking. It is rather a label for a number of thinkers who
shared similar doctrines or outlooks without necessarily having influenced each other (there is little evidence, for example, of the impact
of Comte and Spencer on Schlick and Carnap). For another thing, not
all empiricists can neatly be classified as positivists, much less vice-
versa. An example of the former, as we shall see, would be Locke; an
example of the latter would be Comte. In order to understand Meinong's achievement and his role in the transformation of positivism
which occurred at the turn of the century, it will be necessary to examine the empiricist tradition further and to identify its points of over-
lapping with and divergence from positivism. For it was within the
framework of these divergences that Meinong and his generation
made their distinctive contributions.


## 1. THE ATOMISTIC MODEL

Meinong inherited from his empiricist predecessors a definite
notion of the composition of the mind and how it worked. It was

2. Meinong, *Selbstdarstellung*, *GA*, VII, 4.
3. Habermas, p. 74.
4. Meinong, *Über philosophische Wissenschaft und ihre Propädeutik*, *GA*, V, 23.

Locke who had established this notion; indeed, Meinong once called Locke the "Aristotle of psychological analysis"—though the word "psychology" did not come to be used to describe this model until well after Locke's time.[5] According to this notion, a person's mind consists primarily of a number of distinct, nugget-like experiences called "ideas" or "presentations."[6] Locke's own use of the term "idea" was notoriously inconsistent, and scholarly opinion is divided as to what he meant by it.[7] For a long time, scholars thought of a Lockean idea as basically akin to a physical object—that is, as an entity or "thing" lodged within the mind—with certain properties wherein ideas resembled physical objects.[8] It is known that Locke embraced an atomic or corpuscular theory with regard to physics, that he was a close friend of Robert Boyle and an admirer of Newton, both of whom were also physical atomists.[9] This view would put Locke squarely within the domain of positivism, arguing for a philosophy based on analogies to natural science. On the other hand, there is also abundant textual evidence that Locke saw mental ideas as more analogous to human language than to physical objects. This interpretation has attracted scholars more recently, reflecting the interest of twentieth-century philosophers in language in general. According to this view, Locke was less interested in the intrinsic *properties* of ideas than in their *function* as vehicles of knowledge. The importance of ideas, in this view, lay in the fact that they *represented* objects in the world for us,

5.  Meinong, *Hume-Studien II: Zur Relationstheorie*, in *Abhandlungen zur Erkenntnis-theorie und Gegenstandstheorie, GA*, II. The word "psychology," though in use by the end of the seventeenth century, originally meant "science of the soul," a notion foreign to the atomistic model. Probably the first empiricist to use the term "psychology" was David Hartley in the late eighteenth century.

6.  John Locke, *An Essay Concerning Human Understanding*, ed. Peter H. Nidditch (Oxford: The Clarendon Press, 1975) Book II, ch. i, no. 1 (hereafter cited as II, i, 1). The first modern philosopher to use the term "idea" in this sense—as opposed to some extra-mental essence, as Plato had done—was Descartes. Indeed, the term still has this double meaning; for example, "the idea of a university" does not refer to any particular human experience. In German, the word for idea (Idee) never underwent this psychological modification. Kant was later to express outrage that such a concept could refer to sense-data. The Germans substituted the word Vorstellung, which is usually translated as "presentation." More recently, the word "representation" has come increasingly into use.

7.  Woolhouse, pp. 34–37; A. D. Woozley, Introduction to Locke's *Essay* (Cleveland: The World Publishing Co., Meridian Books, 1964), p. 34.

8.  *Ibid.*, pp. 25, 29.

9.  See Maurice Mandelbaum, "Locke's Realism," in *Philosophy, Science, and Sense-Perception* (Baltimore: Johns Hopkins Press, 1964); Woolhouse, pp. 113–114.

much as a symbol such as a word represents an object or concept. Particularly persuasive in this context is the final section of Locke's *Essay*, where he divides the sciences into three types: physics, ethics, and logic, or the science of signs. The study of ideas falls under the third, not the first, because an idea is a type of sign.[10]

Some of the confusion in this debate undoubtedly stems from the fact that these two uses of the term "idea" are not mutually exclusive; one can describe the mind *both* from the point of view of its intrinsic properties *and* from the point of view of its role in some larger human activity such as knowing or communicating. And while Locke's contribution in the latter area has justifiably aroused recent interest, it should not blind us to his legacy to the thinkers of the late nineteenth and early twentieth centuries, where the physical analogies to mind were of greater concern. For there was one feature of Locke's ideas which had a great influence at that time and cannot be explained by seeing ideas as analogous to signs: their permanence and indestructibility. Languages change; words grow obsolete or alter their meaning. Locke recognized as much when he claimed that the choice of a linguistic sign to represent an object was arbitrary; hence the differences between languages themselves. But ideas, once they enter our minds, stay with us for the rest of our lives:

> When the Understanding is once stored with these simple *Ideas*, it has the power to repeat, compare, and unite them even to an almost infinite Variety, and so can make at Pleasure new complex *Ideas*. But it is not in the Power of the most exalted Wit, or enlarged Understanding, by any quickness or variety of Thought, *to invent or frame one new simple* Idea in the mind . . . nor can any force of the Understanding, *destroy* those that are there. The Dominion of Man, in this little world of his own Understanding, being much what the same, as it is in the great World of visible things; wherein his Power . . . reaches no farther, than to compound and divide the Materials, that are made to his Hand; but can do nothing towards the making the least Particle of new Matter, or destroying one Atome of what is already in Being.[11]

One feature of the atomistic model which was positivistic, then, was the notion of constancy of ideas over time. As a result of this view, Locke describes simple ideas as maintaining their identity while combining into complex ones, just as in the physical world common-sense

10.   Locke, IV, xxi, 4; Woozley, pp. 30f.

11.   Locke, II, ii, 2; see also Ernst Cassirer, *Substance and Function*, trans. W. C. Swabey and M. C. Swabey (Chicago: Open Court Publishing Co., 1923; reprint ed., New York: Dover Publications, 1953), pp. 330–331.

objects such as tables and chairs are combinations of discrete atoms. The distinctiveness of this model can be seen by contrast to, say, William James's notion of the stream of consciousness, where the contents of consciousness lose their identity as they merge or blend with one another.[12] It is also distinct from the "organic" model of, say, physiology, where living cells change, die, and are replaced while the organ of which they are a part remains the same.

A second positivistic characteristic of the atomistic model was a tendency to reductionism—that is, to derive all ideas from a single homogeneous type. This was rarely as explicitly stated as the notion of constancy; indeed, most of the empiricists distinguished between several types of mental elements—Locke's "ideas of sensation" and "ideas of reflection," or Hume's "impression" and "idea." But in the latter case, as with many of Hume's successors, the distinction between such types was not one of kind, but of degree of intensity. Hume's *Treatise* opens as follows:

> All the perceptions of the human mind resolve themselves into two distinct kinds, which I shall call *impressions* and *ideas*. The difference betwixt these consists in the degrees of force and liveliness, with which they strike upon the mind, and make their way into our thought or consciousness.[13]

Simple ideas are thus copies of sense impressions or traces which sensation leaves behind. For this reason, one can divide and analyze the contents of the mind into these basic units without fear of distortion. The pervasiveness of this tendency may perhaps be gauged by showing the absurd lengths to which some empiricists were willing to stretch it. James Mill, for example, could claim that "Brick is one complex idea, mortar is another complex idea; these ideas, with the ideas of position and quantity, compose my idea of a wall."[14]

The tendency toward reductionism was also evident when the em-

---

12. William James, *Principles of Psychology*, 2 vols. (New York: Henry Holt and Co., 1890; reprint ed., New York: Dover Publications, 1950), I, 239. James sharply criticizes the notion of constancy of ideas over time on pp. 230–236.

13. David Hume, *A Treatise on Human Nature*, ed. L. A. Shelby-Bigge (Oxford: Clarendon Press, 1896), p. 1. See also James Mill, *Analysis of the Phenomena of the Human Mind*, 2d ed., 2 vols. (London: Longmans, Green, Reader and Dyer, 1878; reprint ed., New York: Augustus M. Kelley, 1967), I, 52. This edition contains editorial footnotes by two other prominent empiricists, John Stuart Mill and Alexander Bain. Bain's commentary elaborates further the distinctions between sensations and ideas. Aside from degrees of intensity, the other main difference, according to Bain, is that sensations are objective, a part of the physical world, while ideas are subjective—that is, purely mental (*ibid.*, pp. 62ff).

14. *Ibid.*, p. 115.

piricists turned their attention to the question of the coherence and
organization among separate ideas. How were ideas combined and
grouped? Locke's answer had to do with certain active faculties or operations, which acted upon the ideas of sense, combining them to
form complex ideas, separating these to form abstract concepts, and
comparing them in order to yield relations. Locke's catalogue of operations included perception, retention, and volition as well as combination, abstraction, and comparison.[15] For all his polemicizing against
innate ideas, these operations themselves were in fact innate and not
derived from sensation.[16] In this sense, operations and ideas constituted two heterogeneous dimensions of mind. Hume's approach
was quite different. Although he did not deny the presence of such
faculties as memory and imagination, he argued that the mind was
structured primarily according to the "principle of association," which
he described as a "gentle force" rather than an active operation.[17]
This force came into play when the ideas themselves manifested certain relationships, namely "*resemblance, contiguity* in time or place, and
*cause and effect*."[18] Later empiricists such as Hartley removed the faculties; James Mill reduced Hume's three principles to one: contiguity
of time and place. When sensations occurred together, they gave rise
to association.[19] Thus in Mill the structure of the mind was determined entirely by the structure of the external stimuli which prompted the ideas; the mind was passive, the environment active.

It is true that by the middle of the nineteenth century these reductionistic tendencies had abated somewhat, thanks largely to the famous *Logic* of John Stuart Mill, which appeared in 1843. Mill reacted
against the harshness of his father's doctrine just as he recoiled from
the harshness of his personality and educational methods. In his autobiography Mill tells us how he was led to reexamine some of his
father's precepts at the time he was pulling out of his mental depres-
sion.[20] This led the younger Mill to reintroduce some of the heterogeneity of ideas and mental processes that his predecessors had sought
to eliminate. Mill objected to his father's contention that complex
ideas *consisted* of simple ones. It would be wrong to say that a sensation

15.   Locke, II, i, 4; vi, 2.
16.   Noam Chomsky, *Language and Mind* (New York: Harcourt, Brace and World,
1968), p. 70.
17.   Hume, p. 10.        18.   *Ibid.*, p. 11.        19.   Mill, pp. 106ff.
20.   John Stuart Mill, *Autobiography* (Indianapolis: Bobbs-Merrill Co., Library of
Liberal Arts ed., 1957), pp. 101–104.

of white was made up of the sensations of the colors of the spectrum; white appears in consciousness to be just as elementary as blue or green. Rather, one could say that the sensation *resulted from* the action of the different light-waves on the retina.[21]

Moreover, such a process was but a special case of a type of causation that was present in other sciences as well, such as chemistry. Mill contrasts two different types of causation, the mechanical and the chemical. In the mechanical case, such as in physics, the causes of a complex event may be broken down into partial causes (as in the case of two forces acting on a body from different directions). In the chemical case, the partial causes do not add up to the complex cause: the combination of hydrogen and oxygen to produce water gives a substance qualitatively different from the original two elements. Mill underlines the significance of his distinction as follows:

> This difference between the case in which the joint effect of causes is the sum of their separate effects, and the case in which it is heterogeneous to them; between laws which work together without alteration, and laws which, when called upon to work together, cease and give place to others; is one of the fundamental distinctions in nature.[22]

Also, the younger Mill reintroduced a plurality of laws of association: resemblance and intensity were restored to the picture as well as contiguity.[23]

Nevertheless, John Stuart Mill remained true to his father's views in one crucial respect: the laws of association were the sole means of explanation of how the structure of the mind is formed. We are passively dependent on our sensations, which in turn are receptacles for stimuli from the environment around us. The grouping of objects in that environment thus determines the association of one sensation with another. There is no active principle in the mind which modifies these stimuli in any significant way. In this sense, Mill's empiricism was still reductionistic compared to Locke's. In this respect, too, Meinong and many of his generation were to break with earlier empiricists; they introduced active mental operations back into their model of the mind, as Locke had originally maintained. Meinong was

---

21. John Stuart Mill, *A System of Logic, Ratiocinative and Inductive*, 3rd ed. (London: John W. Parker, 1851), II, 425.

22. *Ibid.*, I, 376–77.

23. *Ibid.*, II, 424. For a full discussion of Mill's changing interpretation of the laws of association, see Edwin G. Boring, *A History of Experimental Psychology*, 2nd ed. (New York: Appleton Century Crofts, Inc., 1950), pp. 228–229.

consistently opposed to the notion that the mind consisted of one sort of entity, as well as to the laws of association as the sole organizing principles of experiences.[24]

## 2. THE ANALYTICAL APPROACH

Closely related to the atomistic model was a certain assumption about method which the empiricists shared: that the best way to describe a complex topic, say the human mind or the properties of gross physical bodies, was to break it down into its simpler conceptual elements or "parts" and describe these separately. Presumably the global properties of such complexities as the "self" or "personality" of a human being or the arms, legs, or seat of a chair would in time emerge from such partial descriptions, without falsifying these properties unduly.

The advantage of such an approach was, of course, precision— "clarity and distinctness" in the words of Descartes, the elimination of any vagueness or doubt as to whether a given property belonged to an object or not. The empiricists were not hesitant to advocate this approach in the study of moral questions as well. Here, for example, are two passages from Locke and Hume:

> *Justice* is a word in every Man's Mouth; but most commonly with a very undetermined loose signification: Which will always be so, unless a Man has in his Mind a distinct comprehension of the component parts, that complex *Idea* consists of. . . .[25]

> We must have an exact knowledge of the parts, their situation and connection, before we can design with any elegance or correctness. And thus the most abstract speculations concerning human nature, however cold and unentertaining, become subservient to *practical morality*; and may render this latter science more correct in its precepts, and more persuasive in its exhortations.[26]

The peculiar weight and significance of the analytical approach may perhaps best be appreciated by contrasting it with an opposing view which, though not part of the empiricist tradition proper, has nonetheless claimed the allegiance of scientifically oriented thinkers on repeated occasions. This is the view that one should not describe the parts of a complex whole separately, for doing so inevitably dis-

24. Meinong, *Selbstdarstellung*, *GA*, VII, 30–38; "Phantasie-Vorstellung und Phantasie," *GA*, I, 210–230, esp. 226.
25. Locke, III, xi, 9.     26. Hume, p. 621.

torts the subject. Each part is shaped in its peculiar quality by the whole to which it belongs; thus taking each part in isolation will never lead to a proper description of global properties. Among the adherents to this "holistic" approach who claimed to be scientific in some sense were Goethe, Hegel, and, I believe, Freud—despite the label "psychoanalysis."[27] One of the most thorough articulations of this opposing view came from the Gestalt psychologists in the early twentieth century. A classic example was given by Wolfgang Köhler in his introduction to Gestalt psychology.[28] Köhler asks us to visualize two different objects: a mechanical system such as a steam engine, and an electrical system such as a complex circuit. In the former, the parts of the system (the walls of the cylinder and the piston) are quite rigid; they channel the molecules of water and steam in a determinate direction. Here it is possible to analyze the water or steam into its constituent molecules, note their positions, and predict what will happen to the whole. In an electrical system, on the other hand, the situation is different. An electrical charge will immediately distribute itself throughout the circuit; any change in the density of any part will affect the whole. Thus, Köhler claims, it is impossible to describe the flow of electricity in this apparatus in a piecemeal fashion, unlike the case of the steam engine. The Gestalt psychologists' description of the human mind, of course, is like that of an electrical rather than a mechanical system.

Such comparisons may reflect unfavorably on the empiricists and on Meinong; the reader may suspect that the analytical approach cramped their thought, prevented them from seeing relationships and patterns which greater intellects such as Hegel or Freud grasped. While not trying to settle such questions at this stage, I wish merely to

27. Freud's clinical method could more properly be labeled "synthesis." It consisted not in isolating the separate parts of the mind, but of showing the insufficiency of such analysis in our sense. Such a concentration on parts was in fact a sign of repression: "Forgetting impressions, scenes or experiences nearly always reduces itself to shutting them off. When the patient talks about these 'forgotten' things he seldom fails to add: 'As a matter of fact I've always known it; only I've never thought of it.' . . . In the many different forms of obsessional neurosis in particular, forgetting is mostly restricted to dissolving thought-connections, failing to draw the right conclusions, and isolating memories." (Freud, "Remembering, Repeating, and Working-Through," SE, XII, 148f.). Freud's description of dream formation also precludes an analytical description in which the elements of the dream retain their identity. Rather, they undergo "distortion," "condensation," and "displacement" (Introductory Lectures on Psycho-Analysis, SE, XV, Chs. IX, XI).

28. Wolfgang Köhler, Gestalt Psychology (New York: Horace Liveright, 1947; reprint ed: New American Library, Mentor ed., 1959), p. 64.

point out that such faults, if they exist, cannot easily be laid at the door of the analytical approach itself. For this approach has also been found applicable to relations and patterns. One defender of the analytical approach, the philosopher of science Ernest Nagel, claims that Köhler's examples can be refuted. The patterns of distribution among electrical particles in a field or circuit can also be broken down into constituent "parts," though the analysis is considerably more complicated than that of the steam engine example. Not only would the particles and their positions have to be known, but also their velocities and the "initial and boundary conditions under which they occur."[29] Köhler's fallacy consisted in assuming that the ways in which the field as a whole influences the behavior of individual particles—the conditions under which such particles will change—cannot be described at a microscopic level. To do so would, of course, involve the separate description of "parts" which are fundamentally different in nature from the physical particles themselves: velocities and "boundary conditions." In other words, the parts in this case are heterogeneous, not homogeneous. A defender of the analytical approach might admit that one could "add" such parts to obtain a description of the whole, but only in the ambiguous sense that one could add apples and pears.[30]

We can thus see that the analytical approach does not demand a commitment to reductionism as defined earlier. Indeed, there may be a significant sense in which the formulations of natural science *demand* such heterogeneity and exclude homogeneity. If one thinks of the concept of velocity, for example, which is at the root of much of classical physics, one finds it described as a relation between two heterogeneous variables, distance and time, which are not measured in terms of the same units. One does not reduce miles or kilometers to hours or minutes, or vice-versa. But this does not prevent the relational concept of "miles per hour" from standing on its own, or indeed from functioning in turn as a building block for other relational concepts, such as acceleration, gravity, or kinetic energy.

While it is not our purpose to speculate whether all scientific statements involve reference to such heterogeneous parts, the point has a definite bearing on the historical relationship between empiricism and positivism. For one of the most controversial and difficult prob-

---

29. Ernest Nagel, *The Structure of Science* (New York: Harcourt, Brace and World, 1961), p. 396.
30. *Ibid.*, pp. 381ff. Nagel gives eight different common uses of this ambiguous phrase ("the whole is equal to the sum of its parts").

lems within the empiricist tradition was the handling of such abstractions as mathematical relations, or of any concept that was not clearly tied to sensation. The empiricists, we have noted, were suspicious of vague abstract concepts; their preference for analysis was part of their campaign for greater precision. But not all thinkers in the seventeenth century who were committed to analysis distrusted abstractions in the same way. Analysis also had its place among rationalists such as Descartes. Yet Descartes' interpretation of the analytical approach contrasted sharply with that of Locke, Berkeley, and Hume on one crucial point. One need only compare Locke's analysis of the idea "justice" cited above with Descartes' analysis of the idea "wax." For Locke, the complex idea of justice was analyzed when "the precise collection of simple ideas" was laid bare. For Descartes, such a complete collection would be a hindrance to clarity and distinctness rather than a help. In his analysis of wax, most of the parts are transient and changing. If we take the wax fresh from the hive, it still has the smell of honey; but this evaporates. If we put it next to a candle, it changes its texture. None of these component ideas, derived from the senses, help us to understand what wax really is. This can be done only through a single component, the essence of wax, or wax-ness, which is given not through the senses, but through the intuition of the mind.[31] Such an essence is, of course, an abstraction from the actual, changing qualities of wax; because it is not based on observation, it stands outside empiricism. It is no coincidence that it was developed by a mathematician, for as Descartes' use of analysis elsewhere indicates, such abstractions are necessary in order to ensure that qualities can be put into a series and measured. If all the parts of a complex idea were given, there would be no guarantee that these ideas would belong to the same conceptual order.[32] Descartes' interpretation of the analytical approach is also evident in his rejection of physical atomism, for mathematical analysis involved the assumption not only that one could divide a whole into parts, but that one could do so ad infinitum. Physical atoms, however, were not infinitely divisible.[33]

Now Locke in his *Essay* was sympathetic to such abstractions as used in mathematical demonstrations. It is certainly clear that he awarded

31.    René Descartes, *Meditations on First Philosophy* in *The Philosophical Works of Descartes*, trans. Elizabeth S. Haldane and G. R. T. Ross, (Cambridge: Cambridge University Press, paperback ed., 1968), I, 154f. Hereafter cited as HR.

32.    Descartes, *Rules of the Direction of the Mind*, HR, I, 14–19.

33.    Descartes, *The Principles of Philosophy*, HR, I, 264.

such demonstrations an important place in leading to certain kinds of knowledge, particularly in questions of morality.[34] But Berkeley and Hume detected the difference between this attitude and the bulk of the empiricist program. They realized that such abstract ideas were not on par with the other ideas of sensation and reflection. Hume formulated the objection in such a way to show that this use of analysis was incompatible with the atomistic model:

> Whatever objects are distinguishable are also different. For how is it possible we can separate what is not distinguishable, or distinguish what is not different? . . . But it is evident at first sight, that the precise length of a line is not different nor distinguishable from the line itself; nor the precise degree of any quality from the quality.[35]

This argument would also apply to Descartes' essence of wax; it is not distinguishable from the shape, color, and smell of wax. It occurs together with them in the form of permanent, indestructible ideas, and there is no point in separating them. There are thus no abstract ideas, only concrete ones.

This idea continued into the nineteenth century in the hands of James and John Stuart Mill, and here the younger Mill did not reject the reductionistic tendencies of his forebears but carried them further. John Stuart Mill's innovation was to explain away abstract reasoning such as occurs in logical deductions in terms of empiricist principles. If there are no abstract general ideas, then reasoning does not fundamentally concern itself with deduction from general propositions. Rather, we normally reason from particular experience to particular experience. If, in the course of such reasoning, we should make a general statement, it is valid only as an *induction* from the cases we have already observed; it has no a priori validity independent of experience. Thus, to use a favorite example of logicians, the statement "all men are mortal" is a conclusion drawn from our observations of particular people who have died. To conclude further that "the Duke of Wellington is a man, and therefore mortal" is merely to repeat a step made in the initial induction—not a new deduction, as most logicians had claimed.[36] Similarly, a mathematical statement such as "$2 + 2 = 4$" is a generalization drawn from seeing two concrete objects grouped with two other concrete objects. The importance of induction is also supposedly consistent with Mill's own adopted label for his position: nominalism. He denies that we really possess ideas

34. Locke, IV, iv, 6–7; xii, 7–8.
35. Hume, pp. 18–19.  36. Mill, *System of Logic*, I, 209, 229.

for such general concepts as "human mortality" or those signified by plus or minus signs. These are merely names for attributes of particular objects, and are represented in the mind by *parts* of concrete ideas that are selected out by attention (for example, "mortality" as part of "the Duke of Wellington").[37]

It was with respect to the status of such abstract concepts that the scientific philosophers at the turn of the century took issue with Mill. Bertrand Russell, for example, confessed:

> I first read Mill's *Logic* at the age of eighteen, and at that time I had a very strong bias in his favor; but even then I could not believe that our acceptance of the proposition "two and two are four" was a generalization from experience. I was quite at a loss to say how we arrived at this knowledge, but it *felt* quite different from such a proposition as "all swans are white," which experience might, and in fact did, confute. It did not seem to me that a fresh instance of two and two being four in any degree strengthened my belief. But it is only the modern development of mathematical logic which has enabled me to justify these early feelings and to fit mathematics and empirical knowledge into a single framework.[38]

Meinong, too, in his earliest works in the 1870s and 1880s took issue with the nominalism of Hume and Mill, arguing for the autonomy of abstract concepts and relations, and even claiming that Mill's position was inconsistent: to admit inductive generalizations is to say that these *are* separable from the particular experiences that form their basis.[39] By so emphasizing the non-sensory aspects of experience and inquiry, the empiricists of Meinong's and Russell's generation were able to bring their tradition closer to an increasingly mathematical practice of science.

### 3. THE INTROSPECTIVE CRITERION

Neither of the two themes discussed so far is concerned with the empiricists' central question: what is knowledge? How does one tell when a person knows something, as opposed to having a mere opinion about it, or as opposed to guessing? Their answers all hinged on a single phenomenon: the immediate awareness we all have of our

---

37. Stuart Mill, *An Examination of Sir William Hamilton's Philosophy*, 3rd ed. (London: Longmans, Green, Reader and Dyer, 1867), pp. 365, 377.

38. Bertrand Russell, *Portraits from Memory* (New York: Simon and Schuster, Clarion ed., 1956), pp. 124–125.

39. Meinong, *Hume-Studien I: Zur Geschichte und Kritik des modernen Nominalismus*, *GA*, I, 62–65. For further discussion, see below, Chapter Four.

own mental states. Whatever else we may doubt or be ignorant of, we know with certainty that we are thinking a particular thing or feeling a particular way at a given time. In this respect, the empiricists' treatment of knowledge was close to Descartes' invocation of "I think" (*cogito*) as the first premise of his philosophical system. As Locke put it:

> 'Tis the first Act of the Mind, when it has any Sentiments of *Ideas* at all, to perceive its *Ideas*, and so far as it perceives them, to know each what it is, and thereby also to perceive their difference, and that one is not another. This is so absolutely necessary, that without it there could be no Knowledge, no Reasoning, no Imagination, no distinct Thoughts at all. By this the Mind clearly and infallibly perceives each *Idea* to agree with it self, and to be what it is; and all distinct *Ideas* to disagree, i.e. the one not to be the other: And this it does without any pains, labour, or deduction; but at first view, by its natural Power of Perception and Distinction.[40]

This passage contains several far-reaching claims. Firstly, all mental acts are conscious; whenever we have an idea, we perceive it (Locke makes it clear elsewhere that this is his meaning).[41] Secondly, consciousness consists of two parts: the idea itself and the act of perceiving it. Hence the name "introspection" or "inner perception," as the later empiricists of the nineteenth century called it. Thirdly, this inner duality is the basis of all knowledge. More specifically, only when we are aware of our own ideas and the connections between them, can we be said to know.[42] Locke's own label for such knowledge was "intuitive," following Descartes.[43] In showing how it served as the basis for all other knowledge, Locke outlined three different "degrees" of knowledge, of which this intuitive type was the highest. The next highest degree was "demonstrative" knowledge, the sort contained in

40.  Locke, IV, i, 4. In i, 2 he defines knowledge more pointedly as "the perception of the connection and agreement, or disagreement and repugnancy of any ideas." But since in this section he includes the agreement of an idea with itself, it would seem to include all states of awareness of our own ideas.

41.  *Ibid.*, II, i, 19; xvii, 9.

42.  To equate knowledge and thinking in this way may seem to be an unduly restrictive way to construe knowledge. If Locke means what he says, then I would not know my own name when I am not thinking of it. But the introspective criterion can easily be translated so as to apply to this broader use: I can be said to know something if I *could* call forth the appropriate idea to my immediate awareness. This still would exclude certain uses of the term "knowledge," such as the knowledge that is found in books.

43.  Locke, IV, ii, 1; see Descartes, *Rules*, HR, I, 7. On Locke's indebtedness to Descartes, see Woozley, p. 46.

mathematical reasoning and logical proofs. We may ordinarily accept such proofs and the conclusions derived from them, says Locke, but only when we understand each step of the reasoning—that is, when we are aware of the idea of that step—can we be said to know it. Thus intuitive knowledge must accompany demonstrative knowledge. The last degree of knowledge runs a poor third: the "sensitive" knowledge of the outside world. We may be certain of our ideas, but this is no guarantee for the existence of real physical bodies or other persons. Nevertheless, Locke is convinced that our knowledge in this area is also certain and based on immediate intuition: one has only to compare the mere thought of being burned by fire to the actual experience of being burned by it.[44]

Once again, the empiricists after Locke in the eighteenth century tended to apply the introspective criterion in an increasingly reductionistic manner. While Locke still held to a limited knowledge of objects outside of experience, Berkeley questioned such knowledge. He did believe, however, that our ideas were ultimately caused by God, of Whom we could have knowledge.[45] His position is usually labeled idealism. Hume believed that we have knowledge only of our own mental states; this position later became known as psychologism.[46] Hume for one was aware of the humbling implications which his doctrine might have on human self-love:

> The *intense* view of these manifold contradictions and imperfections in human reason has so wrought upon me, and heated my brain, that I am ready to reject all belief in reasoning, and can look upon no opinion as more probable or likely than another. Where am I, or what? From what causes do I derive my existence, and to what conditions shall I return? Whose favour shall I court, and whose anger must I dread? What beings surround me? and on whom may have I any influence, or who have any influence on me? I am confounded with all these questions, and begin to fancy myself in the most deplorable condition imaginable, inviron'd with the deepest darkness, and utterly deprived of the use of every member and faculty.[47]

Rather than give up in despair, Hume concludes that a philosophy suited to the human mind cannot entirely be based on certain reason.[48]

This narrowing of the scope of knowledge also had its implications for the changing relationships between empiricism and positivism; it

44. Locke, IV, ii, 14; on demonstrative knowledge, see ii, 2–13.

45. George Berkeley, *A Treatise Concerning the Principles of Human Knowledge*, ed. Colin M. Turbayne (Indianapolis: The Liberal Arts Press, 1957), pp. 97f.

46. Hume, p. 189.        47. *Ibid.*, pp. 268–269.        48. *Ibid.*, pp. 270–271.

was, in fact, another source of divergence between the two. Locke, for one, would surely have resisted the label had it been available in the seventeenth century, for he stoutly denied that the method of physics was applicable to the study of moral and social questions. Physics was based on "sensitive" knowledge, the third degree, while morality was based on "demonstrative" knowledge, the second degree. Since the latter was so inferior, it had to be buttressed by experiments, which could only lead to "judgment and opinion, not knowledge and certainty."[49] Hume also opposed empiricism and science, but for just the opposite reason: certain knowledge was so restricted in range that any science of man must be based on experiment and the probabilistic reasoning associated with it. And Kant, while reacting against Hume, still upheld a strictly scientific philosophy on non-empiricist grounds. If reliance on experience led to skepticism rather than certainty, then the way to a scientific metaphysics was to look at the conceptual presuppositions of scientific theory that were independent of experience. Kant explicitly took exception to the psychology of his day, based as it was on the introspective criterion.[50]

On the question of the nature and limits of knowledge, however, the nineteenth-century empiricists retreated somewhat from the skepticism of the eighteenth century. The more optimistic conclusions of the Mills and Alexander Bain were perhaps typical of a more confident age. Their position is usually labeled phenomenalism, and consists in the view that we can ascertain the existence of physical objects, if not their properties or qualities as they are in themselves. But we can nevertheless know something about these objects beyond the fact that they exist, namely as they are relative to us—that is, through their appearances. Paradoxically, the arguments for this position departed considerably from the introspective criterion. John Stuart Mill, in his *Examination of Sir William Hamilton's Philosophy*, polemicized against Hamilton's attempt to combine phenomenalism and introspection. Rather than the "introspective method," Mill proposed the "psychological method" of ascertaining the origin of and evidence for our belief in reality.[51] This was based on the laws of association. When certain ideas are conjoined in our sensations constantly (for example,

49. Locke, IV, xii, 10.

50. On Hume, see Eugene F. Miller, "Hume's Contribution to Behavioral Science," *Journal of the History of the Behavioral Sciences* VII (April 1971), 158f. On Kant and introspection, see Theodore Mischel, "Kant and the Possibility of a Science of Psychology," *The Monist* LI (1967), 600f.

51. Mill, *Examination*, pp. 170ff, 219–221.

a given color with a figure or surface), we may judge them to be more than mere sensations present to consciousness, but "permanent possibilities of sensations." These possibilities are not, strictly speaking, always conscious, but are in our minds even when we fail to notice them (for example, we could be focusing our attention on the color and ignoring the figure or surface). Also, we can posit these "possibilities" as existing in the outside world, relative to us. The justification for making this considerable leap is that such permanent possibilities occur when the conditions and circumstances surrounding them are constant. To give Mill's own example:

> I see a piece of white paper on a table. I go into another room. If the phenomenon always followed me, or if, when it did not follow me, I believed it to disappear *e rerum natura*, I should not believe it to be an external object. I should consider it as a phantom—a mere affectation of my senses: I should not believe that there had been any Body there. But, though I have ceased to see it, I am persuaded that the paper is still there. I no longer have the sensations which it gave to me; but I believe that when I again place myself in the circumstances in which I had those sensations, that is, when I go again into the room, I shall again have them; and further, that there has been no intervening moment at which this would not have been the case.[52]

The criterion for belief has thus shifted in Mill from the awareness of my own state of mind to the circumstances surrounding that state. In this manner, Mill anticipated in a primitive way one of the major aspects of the transformation of positivism that occurred at the end of the nineteenth century: the dissolution of the dualism of the mental and physical to the common categories and circumstances underlying them both. For the plausibility of Mill's argument rests on our willingness to accept the premise that any "permanent possibility of sensation" can exist indifferently as a state of mind of which we are not entirely aware and as a state of affairs in the physical world. In either case, its characteristics are the same. Although not explicitly stated by Mill, the same premise was worked out later by such figures as Mach, Russell, and Gilbert Ryle.[53] According to these thinkers, to divide the events of the world into "mental" and "physical" is a false system of classification. Significantly, too, Edmund Husserl was to level the same criticism of Cartesian dualism in developing his pure phenomenol-

52. *Ibid.*, p. 222.
53. Ernst Mach, *The Analysis of Sensations*, trans. C. M. Williams and Sidney Waterlow, 5th ed. (1906) (Chicago: Open Court Publishing Co., 1914; reprint ed., New York: Dover Publishers, 1959), pp. 13–14, 17, 22; Russell, *Portraits From Memory*, p. 145; Gilbert Ryle, *The Concept of Mind* (New York: Barnes and Noble, 1949), Ch. 1.

ogy.[54] This revolt against dualism, then, was a characteristic feature of twentieth-century philosophical thought.

It was also a feature of which Meinong was not entirely representative. True, we shall see him moving away from an exclusive reliance on the introspective criterion and, along with other thinkers of his generation, developing a new set of categories for talking about the interrelationships between the mental and the non-mental. But, unlike most of his contemporaries, Meinong did not see these new categories as supplanting the old ones, but as an elaboration of them. This difference was at the root of Meinong's exclusion from the ranks of the "pure" phenomenologists and had something to do with his increasing distance from analytical philosophy and Gestalt psychology as well.

### 4. Positivism in the Mid-Nineteenth Century

The word positivism itself is a nineteenth-century invention. It was first used by St.-Simon and given wider currency by Auguste Comte. The notion that all of human knowledge could be ordered according to scientific principles was reinforced by the advent of new natural sciences such as chemistry and biology, as well as by the belief in the possibility of a science of man which had taken shape in the Enlightenment. But these new developments did not necessarily strengthen the ties between empiricism and positivism. In the 1820s and 1830s, Comte and Mill were simultaneously and independently working out their systems by which the old and the new sciences could be united in a single theoretical framework. Although Mill acknowledged the similarities of Comte's work to his own, differences were also evident. In Comte's hands, as later in Spencer's, positivism was to move further away from empiricism on certain crucial points.

Let us first examine Mill's views on the social sciences. For him, the basic science which was to provide the foundation for the others was psychology. Just as the laws of association provided the grounds for a belief in the lawfulness of the physical world, so could they yield up the laws of society upon proper analysis. Mill claimed that an intermediate science between psychology and sociology would have to arise for this purpose: ethology. It would deal with how differences between individuals and cultural groups are shaped by their environments, which provide the stimuli for their respective sensations:

54. Edmund Husserl, *The Crisis of the European Sciences and Transcendental Phenomenology*, trans. David Carr (Evanston: Northwestern University Press, 1970), p. 79.

A science of Ethology, founded on the laws of Psychology, is therefore possible; though little has yet been done . . . towards forming it. The progress of this most important but most imperfect science will depend on a double process: first that of deducing theoretically the ethological consequences of particular circumstances of position, and comparing them with the recognized results of common experience; and secondly, the reverse operation; increased study of the various types of human nature that are to be found in the world. . . .[55]

The notion that this derivation can work betrays Mill's continuing atomism as applied to society. He wrote: "Human beings in society have no properties but those which may be derived from, and may be resolved into, the laws of the nature of individual man."[56] For this reason, Mill's approach to ethology is strictly reductionistic—ethology is not analogous to chemistry, but to physics.[57]

Comte, on the other hand, rejected the social atomism of the empiricists as well as their emphasis on psychology. To him psychology was an inexact science, thanks to the vagueness of introspection.[58] It would eventually be replaced by a completely developed physiology, while sociology would become the basic science of man. This was consistent with Comte's views on the hierarchy of the sciences. He posited an ascending scale of five basic sciences, each of which deals with a special and more complex case of the preceding one: thus astronomy deals with the motion of the planets, and then physics treats of inorganic phenomena on any one planet. The third science in the hierarchy is chemistry, which deals with combinations of certain physical bodies, organic and inorganic. Physiology, the fourth, again presupposes the laws of chemistry but is limited to certain other combinations that have the properties of life; and sociology, or "social physics," deals with the most special and complicated case of life, namely man.[59] The name "social physics" is misleading: the laws of sociology are anything but those of the inorganic sciences. On the contrary, Comte was thoroughly committed to the principle of heterogeneity: each step on the ladder presupposes the previous ones, but because of its greater complexity has different laws of its own. Surprising as it may seem, this view is a direct consequence of Comte's definition of positivism as a unified method for all the sciences. Comte saw a science as becoming positive when it discards metaphysical entities and deals exclusively with the invariable relations of similitude and succession among phenomena.[60] But if the phenomena themselves are of

55. Mill, *System of Logic*, II, 446–447.    56. *Ibid.*, p. 454.    57. *Ibid.*, p. 474.
58. Comte, I, 11–12.    59. *Ibid.*, pp. 26–27.    60. *Ibid.*, p. 2.

different orders, the relationships at different levels will not be of the same type. The simpler phenomena of the inorganic sciences lend themselves to mathematical analysis and to the precision which this demands; the complex phenomena of life and society will not do so. "Thus," Comte writes, "organic phenomena are less exact and systematic than inorganic; and of these again terrestrial are less exact and systematic than those of astronomy."[61] Sociology, being the most complex, is least susceptible to mathematical analysis. At this end of the scale, indeed, the analytical approach is inappropriate. "There can be no scientific study of society," Comte claims, "either in its conditions or movements, if it is separated into portions, and its divisions are studied apart."[62] For this reason, Comte opposed such schemes as those of Laplace to predict social behavior on the basis of the principle of gravitation, as well as the new science of political economy, which treats only a fraction of that behavior out of the context of the whole.[63] Comte would doubtless also be opposed to the pretensions of political science insofar as it attempts to predict the consequences of political action.[64] The appropriate positive method for sociology is that of *history*, which seeks to establish similarities and succession among its phenomena.[65] It is this application of the positivist method which yields Comte's famous historical law of the three stages: that all sciences pass from a theological to a metaphysical to a positive stage.[66]

Comte's positivism, then, rejected all three of the tenets which the empiricists generally considered to be scientific: atomism in psychology, the analytical approach, and introspection. The position of Herbert Spencer with respect to these issues is not as distant, but still significantly different from that of Mill. Spencer also dissociated himself from the analytical approach. In his own words:

> Every thought involves a whole system of thoughts; and ceases to exist if severed from its various correlatives. As we cannot isolate a single organ of a living body, and deal with it as though it had a life independent of the rest;

61. *Ibid.*, p. 29.     62. *Ibid.*, II, 81.

63. *Ibid.*, I, 16–17; II, 62–63. Comte exempts Adam Smith from his condemnation of economics, on the grounds that he attempted no system, but merely conducted empirical analyses of social phenomena.

64. *Ibid.*, II, 90.

65. *Ibid.*, pp. 105–106, 110. In addition to the "social dynamics" of history, Comte also posits a "social statics," which resembles current sociology more than the latter. For Comte, however, social statics is less interesting and important than social dynamics (p. 127).

66. *Ibid.*, pp. 158ff; I, 2–3.

so, from the organized structure of our cognitions, we cannot cut but one, and proceed as though it survived the separation.[67]

Spencer accepted the introspective criterion to a greater extent than Mill.[68] Psychology does have a place in his pantheon of the sciences. Compared to Comte, he was more favorable to atomism, at least insofar as the relation of individuals to society is concerned. Yet he rejected one basic aspect of the atomistic model, both in his psychology and his sociology, that had characterized empiricism from Locke to Mill: the principle of constancy over time. On the contrary, according to Spencer, consciousness is characterized by change:

> It is admitted on all hands that without change, consciousness is impossible; consciousness ceases when the changes in consciousness cease.... Consciousness is not simply a succession of changes, but an *orderly* succession of changes—a succession of changes *combined* and *arranged* in special ways. The changes form the raw material of consciousness; and the development of consciousness is the *organization* of them.[69]

This theory is consistent with Spencer's famous law of evolution, which runs through all the sciences: the tendency for phenomena to move from homogeneity to heterogeneity or complexity.[70] Unlike Comte, Spencer presented his hierarchy of sciences as the result of a unified causal theory. Paradoxically, however, there is much less differentiation among the sciences in Spencer's scheme. His chapters are full of illustrations drawn promiscuously from diverse areas to illustrate the same point. The evolution from homogeneity to heterogeneity, for example, is illustrated by the division of labor in economics, the multiplication of languages in philology, and the greater detail in nineteenth-century art compared to that of the ancient civilizations. Spencer could even write in 1867 that human progress was exemplified in the tendency of modern art to become more realistic and true to life.[71]

By the turn of the century, such thinking was beginning to be regarded as too loose by thinkers committed to positivism. The theories

---

67. Spencer, p. 137.        68. *Ibid.*, pp. 142–144.

69. Spencer, *The Principles of Psychology* (New York: D. Appleton and Co., 1896), II, Pt. 1, pp. 291–292.

70. Spencer, *First Principles*, pp. 370–371. In leading up to this conclusion, however, Spencer finds it necessary to posit the "persistence of force"—that the units of force at all levels must remain constant (p. 198). This seems to contradict his principle that consciousness can only be known through its changing states.

71. *Ibid.*, pp. 389–390. On this contrast between Comte and Spencer, see Mandelbaum, *History, Man and Reason*, pp. 89–90, esp. n. 32.

of Comte and Spencer had sacrificed a certain degree of precision that was the goal of the analytical approach in the attempt to subsume all the sciences under a single overarching scheme. To the later generation of positivists, such attempts were becoming increasingly elusive. Russell, for one, confessed that he had hoped to write a synthesis of his work in logic and in social thought—but the synthesis never came.[72] The challenge of positivism at the turn of the century was rather to deal with the increasing complexities of science and its human and social implications without compromising on rigor and precision. The movement to which Meinong belonged began in the 1870s and 1880s with a return to the more pristine aspects of empiricism: a renewed commitment to atomism, analysis, and introspection. Only gradually, in the course of the 1890s and 1900s, did they reformulate these principles to free themselves of their limitations.

It may seem surprising that this renewed empiricism had such strong roots in Austria, and that much of the work toward the transformation of positivism originated there. One tends to associate philosophy in German-speaking lands with philosophical idealism such as that pursued by Kant and Hegel. Indeed, the German philosophers from the 1850s on tended to confront the issues raised by positivism by turning to Kant as a point of reference (Ueberweg's *Geschichte der Philosophie*, a standard work in German philosophy, lists no less than seven Neo-Kantian schools in Germany at the turn of the century).[73] But Kant's position, that scientific knowledge consists primarily in what we impose upon nature by our minds, rather than in properties and relations that are independent of us, never gained a sympathetic hearing in Austria. This deserves an explanation, which will be the subject of the next chapter.

72. Russell, *Portraits*, p. 57.
73. Friedrich Ueberweg, *Ueberwegs Grundriss der Geschichte der Philosophie*, ed. T. K. Oesterreich (Basel: Benno Schwage and Co., 1951), 13th ed., IV, xiv.

# II

# POLITICS AND
# PHILOSOPHY
# IN AUSTRIA IN THE
# LATE NINETEENTH CENTURY

At first glance, the world of philosophical empiricism would seem to have little to do with the world of fin de siècle Austria. At a time when the middle classes seemed to be rejecting reason and science in favor of the ineffable mysteries of art, poetry, music, and drama, and when political leaders were gleefully rejecting the hope of any reasonable solution to Austria's nationality problems, what possible importance could be attached to the abstract meditations of a careful and cautious philosopher?

Yet, as scholars have recently come to recognize, the mood of Austria at the turn of the century eludes any simple characterization. The incredible variety of intellectual and cultural expression in Austria has been thoroughly documented by William M. Johnston in his comprehensive history, *The Austrian Mind*. Psychoanalysis, Marxism, the music of Mahler and Schönberg, the estheticism of Klimt and Hofmannsthal, the almost militant positivism of Mach and the later Vienna Circle existed together in some "unlikely symbiosis."[1]

---

1. William M. Johnston, *The Austrian Mind* (Berkeley: University of California Press, 1972), p. 163. Johnston achieves his comprehensiveness at the cost of some artificiality of grouping his seventy-odd figures. Meinong, for example, finds a place in the section entitled "Bohemian Reform Catholicism," a movement with which he had

It will be the task of this chapter to explain how one of these strands, namely a peculiar kind of empiricism and positivism, took root in Austria under the same conditions that fostered many of the intellectual attitudes so different from it. Moreover, by investigating what was distinctively Austrian about this empiricism, we can perhaps understand how it helped to father such divergent trends as logical positivism and phenomenology. For although empiricism was not unique to Austria, in no other country did it lead to such unexpected and creative results.

## 1. THE POLITICAL AND INSTITUTIONAL SETTING

The role of political and institutional factors in determining the course of Austrian philosophy can hardly be overestimated. Ever since the mid-eighteenth century, policy in schools and universities, including curriculum and professorial appointments, was directly in the hands of the imperial bureaucracy. Inasmuch as philosophy was largely an academic discipline, it was thus subject to state regulation. This regulation followed a certain general pattern that was set during the ten-year reign of Austria's most energetic ruler, Joseph II (1780–90). Through some seventeen thousand laws and decrees, Joseph left his mark on Habsburg government in ways which persisted through the nineteenth century. His method of reforming the state was to a great extent that of confronting the clergy and nobility. Though Joseph himself was a devout Catholic and far from being anticlerical, he did seek to destroy the autonomy of the church and subordinate it to state regulation. In order so to overhaul the established order, he vastly expanded the ranks of the bureaucracy, into which he sought to integrate the clergy. Joseph succeeded in instilling in many of his new civil servants a sense of loyalty to the empire as a whole rather than to any particular class or interest group, as well as a commitment to peaceful reform through governmental initiative. Yet his measures failed to bring about the changes he desired, mainly because they were so drastic and radical. Joseph's decrees included the secularization of monasteries, the suppression of local tribunals, and religious toleration. The task of enforcing these and other regulations was sim-

---

nothing to do. Johnston makes the connection by claiming that Brentano and his students were philosophizing in a Leibnizian tradition. While it is certainly possible to draw parallels between Leibniz and Meinong, there was no "tradition" established in terms of influence. There are only eleven references to Leibniz in Meinong's collected works.

ply too tremendous and the unenlightened ways of the populace too firmly entrenched; the bureaucrats could often do little more than inspect or spy on the local authorities to see that imperial decrees were executed.

Joseph's legacy to Austria in the nineteenth century was thus a mixed one. On the one hand, the enlightened attitudes of his bureaucrats persisted among many; "Josephism" became synonymous with reform from above and eventually prepared the foundations of Austrian liberalism.[2] On the other hand, the resistance Joseph had aroused also persisted and gained influence during the reign of Francis I (1792–1835). The fact that Joseph had brought the clergy into his bureaucracy assured the influence of a conservative faction at the highest levels of the state.[3] In this way, factionalism and secrecy became enduring features of state life, shaping, among other things, the dissemination of ideas. The official body, the Studienhofkommission, decided what textbooks were to be used in the schools and what intellectual trends were to be promoted in the universities. Since administrative deliberations took place behind closed doors, it was easy for factional struggles to merge with personal feuds and vendettas. A good example was the fate of the early nineteenth-century philosopher Bernard Bolzano, who became recognized only in the twentieth century as a precursor of contemporary views. Bolzano, a priest and a Josephist, was relieved in 1819 of his teaching position on charges of heresy. In fact, he had incurred the enmity of a rival philosopher named Jacob Frint, who had greater influence on the Studienhofkommission, and whose textbook Bolzano had refused to use.[4] Given such pressures, many professors sought to gain personal influence with the officials themselves (Freud and Mach were later to advance their own causes in this way).[5] The general atmosphere of decision-making has been well described by Johnston: "Secrecy shrouded transaction of

2. Fritz Valjavec, *Der Josephinismus* (Munich: Verlag von R. Oldenbourg, 1945), p. 127; William J. McGrath, *Dionysian Art and Populist Politics in Austria* (New Haven: Yale University Press, 1974), p. 10.

3. There is some difficulty in attaching a precise label to this group. Valjavec sees it as descended from Josephism, though representing a more moderate variety than the radical, deistic strain that was also present (p. 35). Eduard Winter, on the other hand, in *Der Josefinismus und seine Geschichte* (Brünn: Rudolf M. Rohrer Verlag, 1943), identifies it as a party of "restoration," opposed to the Josephists (p. 282).

4. Johnston, p. 275.

5. Ernest Jones, *Sigmund Freud: Life and Work*, 3 vols. (London: The Hogarth Press, 1953), I, 377f; John T. Blackmore, *Ernst Mach* (Berkeley: University of California Press, 1972), p. 152.

public business, fomenting rumors of conspiracy and of sentimental adventure to explain even the most routine events. . . . In an atmosphere of half-truths, temporizing sustained the empire." [6]

This situation had several consequences for the development of philosophy in Austria that set it apart from developments in the other German states. First, philosophy had been a subordinate subject in the universities in the eighteenth century and remained so under Joseph and Franz. The philosophical curriculum served as a general preparation or "propadeutic" for the "higher" faculties of medicine, law, and theology; it was thus a subject to be taught, not a subject for scholarship. [7] Second, the centralized nature of the Austrian educational system prevented innovation at a time when intellectual life in the rest of Germany was undergoing a revival in the hands of such luminaries as Goethe, Schiller, Kant, and Hegel. This revival arose in large part because of the very multiplicity of German states and the lack of a single bureaucracy for all of them. It was in provincial universities such as Göttingen and Jena, rather than at Berlin, that much of the new learning arose in the late eighteenth century; only later, thanks to the reforms of von Humboldt, did these innovations spread to Prussia itself. In Austria, however, these new currents continued to play a subsidiary role. The anti-intellectualism of Francis I was evident from his remark to the university professors, "I have no use for scholars but only for good citizens." [8]

As a result, the idealism of Kant and his successors never penetrated Austria to the same extent as the rest of Germany. The Studienhofkommission rejected the Kantian philosophy in 1798 as too difficult. [9] It is significant that this decision was made by a Josephist, for the suspicion of Kant was shared by Josephists and anti-Josephists alike. Even for the former, Kant's philosophy, with its doubts about the actual concrete existence of the world as created by God, was too far removed from the true Catholic religion. Any reconciliation between faith and the enlightenment had to take place on the basis of realism rather than idealism (this was true of Bolzano as well). [10] The official textbooks of the early nineteenth century, reflecting the philosophies of Christian Wolff and Friedrich Heinrich Jacobi, held to

6. Johnston, p. 38.

7. Roger Bauer, *Der Idealismus und seine Gegner in Österreich* (Heidelberg: Carl Winter Universitätsverlag, 1966), p. 23.

8. Henry Schnitzler, "Gay Vienna—Myth and Reality," *Journal of the History of Ideas*, XV (1954), 105.

9. Bauer, p. 22.     10. *Ibid.*, pp. 13, 26ff, 43–44.

this point of view.[11] At the same time, this realism proved to be quite congenial to the development of empirical disciplines. The medical faculties in Vienna had a full complement of scientific subjects by 1848.

The intransigence of the government in all areas during the age of Metternich also had its effect on the popular culture of the middle classes. Theatre, art, and novels all reflected political indifference and a flight into an inner world of fancy. The music of Schubert and the plays and stories of Grillparzer both reflected this attitude, which came to be labeled "Biedermeier."[12]

It was only after the Revolution of 1848 that scholarship in the humanities and social sciences began to flourish. Despite the failure of the revolution, the administrators in the area of education during the 1850s were basically Josephist.[13] They not only created new university positions in the philosophical faculty but also improved secondary education to correspond to the German Gymnasium, thereby relieving the universities of their preparatory work for medicine, law, and theology. The Austrian high schools did, however, include more science than their German counterparts; also, philosophy was incorporated into the high school curriculum, serving the "propadeutic" function that it had served in the university previously. Thus Austria continued to have an "official" philosophy, which was promulgated in the high school textbooks and also taught in the new university chairs. The Josephist officials continued to be skeptical of German idealism; Hegelians were persecuted in Austria in the 1850s.[14]

The philosophy that best seemed to fit Austria's requirements, in the eyes of the administrators, was that of Johann Friedrich Herbart (1776–1841). Herbart had been Kant's successor at Königsberg, but had remained safely realistic in his own system. His views had much to recommend them. He had written on pedagogy, and had discouraged an excessively authoritarian teaching method based on memorization alone; the more humane classroom that he encouraged was congenial to the outlook of the Josephists. Moreover, Herbart rejected the emphasis on historical evolution and dialectic, which had seduced so

11. *Ibid.*, pp. 24, 62ff.    12. Johnston, pp. 19ff.

13. Winter, pp. 477, 483. Josephism did not prevail in the other sectors of the new government; it sought instead to arrive at an accommodation with the papacy through a concordat, which went against the Josephist attempt to subordinate the church to the state. See also Valjavec, p. 85.

14. Johnston, p. 285; Friedrich Paulsen, *Geschichte des gelehrten Unterrichts*, 2 vols.; 3rd ed. (Berlin: Vereinigung wissenschaftlicher Verleger, 1921), II, 482, 486.

many German students into dangerous political activity. His view of the mind and its relation to the world was basically static. In addition, Herbart's views on God were compatible with the Austrian Catholic tradition. Herbart had defined God as a "Real Being . . . a personal Essence outside of the world, [whose being] can be concluded from the perceivable purposefulness in the world."[15] Finally, the Herbartian philosophy was certainly more congenial to science than its predecessor. His model of the mind was based on three factors: experience, metaphysics, and mathematics. Ideas were subject to mathematical laws, so that the increase in intensity of one idea must be balanced by a decrease in another, in order to maintain an equilibrium (when an idea so "sinks" in intensity it is "repressed"—a Herbartian term that found its way into the high school textbook used by the young Freud).[16] This harmony between science and theology seemed to fit the melioristic attitudes of the middle class in the 1850s and 1860s. If the work of the popular novelist Adalbert Stifter is any indication, science was seen to work in harmony with ethics and esthetics in contributing to the development of the individual.[17]

By the 1870s, however, Herbartian philosophy had lost much of its appeal. Perhaps its static qualities no longer seemed to be applicable to a period that contained so much dramatic change: the unification of Germany, the Ausgleich, and the economic boom in Vienna followed by the crash of 1873. Whatever the reasons, philosophy at the University of Vienna was recognized to be at a low point during this decade.[18] It was Meinong's teacher, Franz Brentano, who reversed this situation dramatically.

## 2. THE CAREER OF FRANZ BRENTANO (1838–1917)

Although associated with Austria for much of his career, Brentano's origins were south German. He was born into a distinguished

15. Quoted in H. Holtzmann, "Der Religionsbegriff der Schule Herbarts," *Zeitschrift für wissenschaftliche Theologie*, XXV (1882), 67.

16. Jones, I, 410.

17. See Carl E. Schorske, "The Transformation of the Garden: Ideal and Society in Austrian Literature," *American Historical Review*, LXXII (1967), 1290, 1297.

18. Brentano's inaugural lecture at Vienna was entitled "On the Causes of Discouragement in the Philosophical Domain." His diagnosis was that students had become disillusioned with philosophical systems and their lack of generally accepted axioms, the impossibility of confirmation of its theories, and the lack of practical applicability. ("Über die Gründe der Entmutigung auf Philosophischem Gebiete," in *Über die Zukunft der Philosophie*, ed. Oskar Kraus, Leipzig: Felix Meiner Verlag, 1929, p. 92.)

literary family; his aunt and uncle, Bettina and Clemens Brentano, had been important figures in the romantic movement. His father, Christian, wrote many religious pamphlets, and his younger brother Lujo was to become a renowned economist and a winner of the Nobel prize. In his youth, Franz had shown a great mathematical gift and had decided to become a mathematician. But a deep religious crisis at the age of seventeen led him instead to turn to philosophy.[19] For the young Brentano, philosophy and religion were closely intertwined; two years after receiving his doctorate he was ordained as a priest in 1864. By this time, he had formulated a grand mission in life: it seemed to him that the philosophy of his day was in decline, due to the overly speculative orientation of the Hegelians, and could only be redeemed through the exactness and precision of science.[20] In 1866 he received an appointment at the University of Würzburg, and among the theses he defended as part of his appointment was that "the true method of philosophy is none other than that of the natural sciences."[21] As was later the case at Vienna, Brentano gained the reputation of being an outstanding teacher; his lectures were always filled to overflowing.[22] Nevertheless, his mixture of theology and philosophy met with no little suspicion among his colleagues—to them he seemed a "Jesuit in disguise." When he defended his views in public, however, his brilliance and logical acumen won over the most skeptical.[23]

Around the year 1870, however, Brentano experienced another religious crisis. He found that his mission was at variance with the authoritarian views of the Catholic Church itself, a conclusion that was reinforced by the proclamation of papal infallibility in that year. This new conviction led to his leaving the priesthood in 1873. Brentano did not as a result become irreligious, however; he continued to believe in the existence of God and the immortality of the soul. It was under these circumstances that the liberal minister of education in Austria, Karl Streymayr, called Brentano to a professorship in Vienna in 1874 (despite some opposition from the cardinal) to revitalize philosophy

Meinong reached a similar conclusion in his *Über philosophische Wissenschaft und ihre Propädeutik*, *GA*, V, 16.

19. Antos Rancurello, *A Study of Franz Brentano* (New York: Academic Press, 1968), p. 3.

20. See Karl Stumpf, "Franz Brentano," in *Franz Brentano*, ed. Oskar Kraus (München: Oskar Beck, 1919), p. 90.

21. Brentano, "Theses," in *Zukunft*, p. 137.

22. Stumpf, pp. 90–91.      23. Rancurello, pp. 5ff.

there. His professorship met with the same enthusiastic response among students that he had received in Würzburg; for example, Freud was drawn to his lectures for four semesters, the only ones outside the medical faculty that he attended.[24]

Brentano was ideally suited to his new post for several reasons. First, the realism of Catholic philosophy was also characteristic of him. He was one of the sharpest critics of Kant of his day, and saw the whole critical attempt of Kant—and of his own Neo-Kantian contemporaries—not as a sign of philosophical renewal against skepticism and scientism, but as a sign of an advanced stage of philosophical weakness and decline. He called Kant's synthetic a priori ideas "blind prejudices,"[25] and reacted especially strongly against Kant's compartmentalization of scientific knowledge and belief in God, freedom, and immortality; any final beliefs founded on such a broken structure were unnatural and literally incredible (*ein unglaubliches Glauben*).[26] Brentano, by contrast, was an avowed empiricist. He maintained that by careful observation and closely reasoned inductions one could move from experience to those self-evident and absolutely certain truths that characterized theology and metaphysics.

Second, Brentano's position vis-à-vis the church suited the needs of Austrian liberals, who were experiencing their heyday in the 1860s and 1870s. The defeat of Austria in the war with Prussia and the division of the country into Austria and Hungary, each with its separate parliament, gave the German liberals a greater role in the Austrian half than they had experienced before. They were able to dominate the political scene temporarily, until the various non-German nationalities were to make their numerical superiority felt. The liberals represented business and professional interests, and their political views were correspondingly more adventurous than those of the Josephist bureaucrats. Much of their program was directed toward securing of civil rights and reducing the influence of the church. Under the liberal ministries of Auersperg (1867–1870 and 1871–1878), the power of the church in education was diminished and freedom of scientific investigation was guaranteed. Brentano's identification of the philosophical and scientific methods, combined with his commitment

24. Philip Merlan, "Brentano and Freud—A Sequel," *Journal of the History of Ideas*, X (1949), 451.

25. Brentano, *Die vier Phasen der Philosophie und ihr augenblicklicher Stand* (Stuttgart: Verlag der G. G. Cotta'schen Buchhandlung, 1895), pp. 31f.

26. *Ibid.*, p. 27.

to religion outside the traditional institutions of the church, provided the ideal support for the liberal program.

But the political power of the liberals was severely limited from two sides. The middle class could not penetrate the upper echelons of the bureaucracy; these were still reserved for aristocrats. Moreover, they could not represent the aspirations of the non-German nationalities in the Austrian half of the empire. Numerically, they were outnumbered by Czechs, Poles, and Slovenes; in 1879, Auersperg was replaced by the emperor's friend, Count Taaffe, who drew his support from a coalition of these non-German nationalities (the "Iron Ring"). Meanwhile, the younger generation of middle-class Viennese began to reject the values of their elders; influenced by irrationalist thinkers such as Schopenhauer and Nietzsche, they were repulsed by the narrowness of vision of liberalism. Some of them, such as Victor Adler and Georg von Schönerer, traveled to the new mass political movements of the radical left and right.[27] Other members of the wealthy middle class found their way to the cultivation of an increasingly apolitical and esthetically oriented set of values, as they had done in the "Biedermeier" period.[28]

The remarkable aspect of Brentano's years at Vienna is that he combined the appeal of estheticism and irrationalism in politics with a respect for scientific reasoning and method in philosophy. His affinity with the former lay in his personal style in the lecture-hall. Like Lueger and Herzl, the demagogic spokesmen for Christian Socialism and Zionism respectively, Brentano held a peculiar sway over his audience. No one who has written of Brentano's lectures has failed to comment on the impact of his personality and his emotional appeal. Husserl spoke of his "elevated and artistic style . . . [he] spoke in the supple, low, veiled tone, accompanying the speech with priestly gestures, and stood before the youthful student as a seer of eternal truths and as a herald of a world above heaven."[29] An obituary in 1917 contained the following description,

> Brentano was surrounded with a romantic magic; the wonderful image framed this scion of the romantic Brentano dynasty of poets and thinkers. The luxuriant black hair, the full, black beard which framed the pale face made an all the more obscure impression, given the silver shimmer of gray

27. McGrath, *Dionysian Art and Politics*, pp. 1ff, 73.
28. Schorske, "Transformation of the Garden," pp. 1303f.
29. Edmund Husserl, "Erinnerungen an Franz Brentano," in Kraus, *Brentano*, p. 154.

which overlay the black . . . the strange quality of the face, which could belong to no one but a philosopher, poet, or artist, were the coal-black eyes of Brentano, which, always lightly veiled, had a quite peculiar, weary, fanciful expression to them.[30]

Yet Brentano never allowed this charismatic element to dominate the content of his philosophy, which remained a model of logical clarity. And it was Brentano, too, who wrote a book called *Psychology from an Empirical Standpoint*, who corresponded with John Stuart Mill, and who campaigned vigorously—though unsuccessfully—for a laboratory in experimental psychology at Vienna.[31]

The vicissitudes of liberalism in Austria were also reflected in Brentano's personal fortunes. In 1880, he became engaged to a wealthy and beautiful ex-Jewish patrician, Ida von Lieben. This engagement soon found opposition, however, because it was against the law of the state for an ex-priest to marry. When his request for special permission to marry was denied, he resigned his professorship and Austrian citizenship. He remained at the University as an unsalaried lecturer (Privatdozent), hoping that he might be promoted again after a number of years.[32] This hope proved to be unrealistic, however; the ministry evaded his petitions and those of the faculty, never giving Brentano a clear answer. Finally, in 1894, after the death of Ida, he left Austria in despair, full of bitterness against the officials who had treated him so ungenerously. His public speech to this effect, "My Last Wishes for Austria," contained a plea for a more humane bureaucracy, greater protection for civil liberties, and a peaceful solution to the nationalities problems. The speech set off a renewed controversy between liberals and clericals.[33] Brentano never held an academic post again, but lived in Florence until World War One; he then moved to Zurich, where he died in 1917.

In Vienna, no one tried again to forge theology and empirical science into a single philosophical discipline. The faculty decided that there should be two separate philosophical chairs, one for the philosophy of natural science, the other for the philosophy of the human studies. It was Ernst Mach who filled the former post with great distinction; the second was filled by a man of lesser qualities, Friedrich

---

30. Quoted in Alois Höfler, "Franz Brentano in Wien," *Süddeutsche Monatshefte* (May 1917), p. 320.

31. Brentano, *Meine letzten Wünsche für Österreich* (Stuttgart: Verlag der J. G. Cotta'schen Buchhandlung, 1895), pp. 33ff.

32. *Ibid.*, p. 12.

33. Kraus, *Brentano*, p. 108.

Jodl.[34] Nevertheless, Brentano's influence on Austrian philosophy was still strongly felt; if anything, it increased after he had left Vienna. By the turn of the century his students filled major chairs at virtually all the German-speaking universities in the empire. His influence in Prague was especially strong; there, some of his most devoted followers under Anton Marty formed an intellectual circle to which Franz Kafka belonged for a time.[35] In addition, Brentano's students included Thomas Masaryk, the later president of Czechoslovakia and at that time a professor of philosophy in the Czech university in Prague, as well as Kasimir Twardowski, a leading figure in Polish philosophy. In Germany, his views were felt primarily through Husserl, the leading figure in phenomenology, but also through Karl Stumpf, the director of the prestigious psychological institute in Berlin. Even in Vienna, the later logical positivists were to credit Brentano and his students with a partial role in providing the background for their movement.[36]

One can say, then, that Austrian empiricism emerged as another "orphan of liberalism," like estheticism and the mass political movements, which it resembled in some respects and from which it differed in many others.[37] Its distinctive position was in its attempt to blend a respect for hard science with a respect for the imaginary and intangible. It is to Brentano's synthesis that we must first turn.

### 3. BRENTANO'S IDEAS

Because of his underlying commitment to the scientific method in philosophy, Brentano may be labeled a positivist in the broad sense of the term. He shared with Comte, Mill, and Spencer the optimistic belief that science was progressing from the study of the simpler aspects of nature to the more complex, from the inanimate matter of mathematics, physics, and chemistry to the living matter of biology and physiology, and finally to the study of man himself.[38] It was easy

34. Blackmore, p. 152; Johnston, p. 182.

35. See Peter Neesen, *Vom Louvrezirkel zum Prozess* (Göppingen: Verlag Alfred Kümmerle, 1972). Neesen explores the possible influences of Brentano's philosophy on Kafka's writings.

36. Rudolf Haller, "Ludwig Wittgenstein und die Österreichische Philosophie," *Wissenschaft und Weltbild*, XXI (1968), 77.

37. See Janik and Toulmin, *Wittgenstein's Vienna* (New York: Simon and Schuster, Touchstone ed., 1973), p. 48.

38. Brentano, *Psychology from an Empirical Standpoint*, trans. Antos C. Rancurello, D. B. Terrell, and Linda McAlister (New York: Humanities Press, 1973), pp. 24f.

to give a materialistic interpretation of such a view, which reduced all human qualities to physical ones, and one popular writer, the German Ludwig Büchner, gave voice to it in his book *Energy and Matter*, which went through fifteen editions between 1855 and 1884.[39] Most of the leading thinkers of the period found more sophisticated alternatives than the reduction of all the laws of life and society to those of physics. But significant differences remained even among these thinkers, particularly as to the role of psychology in the ascending scale of sciences. This question centered to a great extent around the ambiguities of the introspective criterion. Comte had dismissed psychology because of the vagaries of introspection, and had looked to sociology as the fundamental human science. Brentano, on the other hand, sided with Mill in claiming that psychology held the key to the social sciences. For Brentano, psychology was superior to the physical sciences because it was based on the complete certainty of "inner perception"; it was the "science of the future."[40]

Brentano was anything but naive in his defense of introspection, or "inner perception" as he called it. By the 1870s, the Kantian objections to it had become well known and were revived by the Neo-Kantians such as Friedrich Albert Lange. Brentano dealt thoroughly with Lange's criticisms and with those of Comte. He recognized, along with them, the need for some stable basis of comparison from one inner perception to another. This led him to distinguish clearly between two things: the *criterion* of certainty of our own experience on the one hand, and the *methods* of observation that derive from it on the other. Inner perception itself does not constitute a method, according to Brentano. As he put it, it can never become observation per se.[41] If we try methodically to observe an emotion such as our anger, the anger itself diminishes. Inner perception—the state of having the anger, so to speak—is rather the source of legitimacy for the methods of observation actually used. To observe our experiences, we must compare them with each other, either through memory or in an experimental situation. But for the comparison to be valid, we must at least be certain that the emotion we experience at a given moment is anger and nothing else. This is assured by inner perception.

As for methods of observation, Brentano was remarkably tolerant. He advocated the newly established experimental psychology, which had grown out of physiology and empiricist philosophy, though he

39.  Ludwig Büchner, *Kraft und Stoff*, 15th ed. (Leipzig: T. Thomas, 1883).
40.  Brentano, *Psychology*, pp. 10, 25.      41.  *Ibid.*, pp. 29ff.

found its applicability to be overestimated.[42] It was based mainly on the Weber-Fechner law, which provided a method of measuring the relations between mind and body. This law stated that changes in physical stimuli were regularly related to changes in sensation, though there was considerable controversy as to how these measurements were to be interpreted. Brentano's notion of psychology, however, extended beyond the narrowly circumscribed area covered by the new law. For him, observation and comparison of data could also include the behavior of others—their facial expressions, their written testimony (as in autobiography), and also the comparative observation of children and adults, of different cultures or ethnic groups, or of pathological cases to normal ones. Brentano's methodological pronouncements thus anticipated the variety and scope of modern psychology.[43]

Brentano also remained committed to the analytical approach. The first task of psychology was to describe the basic psychic elements, just as describing the basic physical elements was the first task of chemistry.[44] Only when such elements were established, Brentano claimed, could we go on to induce the laws of succession and change that bound them together. Indeed, Brentano saw these two steps as two different branches of psychology, which he called "descriptive psychology" (or "psychognosie") and "genetic psychology" respectively, comparing them to anatomy and physiology.[45] Proper analysis was not only important for psychology, however; it also provided the basis for Brentano's metaphysical and theological enterprises. Once the basic types of mental states are properly understood, we can induce from them the laws of logic, the structure of ethics and esthetics, and proof of the immortality of the soul.[46] Psychology for Brentano thus pointed in two directions: not only to the social sciences but to the whole of philosophy as well. Herein lay, I believe, the basis of Brentano's reputation as a revitalizer of philosophy in his own day.

From a contemporary point of view, most of Brentano's ideas regarding introspection and analysis were in themselves neither particularly original nor distinctively Austrian. Many of the scientific philosophers of the day in Germany shared similar assumptions, albeit with different emphases. Wundt, Fechner, Lotze, and von Hartmann

---

42. *Ibid.*, pp. 66ff.     43. *Ibid.*, pp. 36ff.     44. *Ibid.*, p. 46.

45. Brentano, *Letzten Wünsche*, p. 34; Roderick M. Chisholm, "Brentano on Descriptive Psychology and the Intentional," in *Phenomenology and Existentialism*, ed. Edward N. Lee and Maurice Mandelbaum (Baltimore: Johns Hopkins Press, 1967), p. 2.

46. Brentano, *Psychology*, pp. 230f, 261f, 25.

all sought a metaphysics based on the results of science.[47] Wundt also saw psychology as being more than experimental; it was to be the foundation of his Völkerpsychologie, the Psychology of Peoples, which comprehended the study of societies as well. Yet Brentano's reputation as a philosopher today soars above his German contemporaries named above; so does his role in the history of philosophy, as the precursor of phenomenology and as related to modern linguistic philosophy. This difference stems from Brentano's originality with respect to his conception of the mind itself: his rejection of the atomistic model as analogous to physics. His ideas in this area are associated with the name "intentionality."

According to Brentano, the mind cannot be properly understood by viewing its constituent experiences in terms of a set of properties, but only in terms of their *relationships* to other things. If, for example, I am in the presence of a physical object such as a horse, the atomistic model would describe my mental state in terms of some entity in my mind that corresponds to this object. The intentional model would describe it as an act of being consciously directed to the object itself— that is, being aware of it. For Brentano, all consciousness has this "quasi-relational" character.[48] All consciousness is consciousness of *something* other than itself. "In presentation, something is presented, in judgment something is affirmed or denied, in love loved, in hate hated, in desire desired, and so on."[49] This direction to an object is what Brentano called intentionality, a name he derived from medieval philosophy, but the meaning of which was quite his own.[50]

This intentional model of the mind differed from the atomistic model in one important respect: the relation of "being directed to something" was not a causal relation. True, one could explain some mental states causally. If, for example, my idea of a horse occurs when I was actually seeing a horse, I could invoke the chain of physical processes whereby the light rays reflected from the horse's body strike my retina and are translated into nerve-impulses which somehow give rise to an idea in my brain. But such a description of awareness is circuitous and complicated when compared to what is directly evident to inner perception: my being aware of a horse. Furthermore, the causal chain does not describe what happens when one imagines a horse, or

47. Uberweg, IV, 347, 294, 297, 304, 307, 334f.
48. Brentano, *Psychology*, p. 272.     49. *Ibid.*, p. 88.
50. See Herbert Spiegelberg, *The Phenomenological Movement*, 2d ed.; 2 vols. (The Hague: Martinus Nijhoff, 1969), I, 41.

thinks of a mythical horse such as Pegasus. In these cases, which are obviously related in some way to the case of seeing a horse, there are no evident physical processes one can point to: one at best can hypothesize that something neurophysiological is taking place. Indeed, only an intentional psychology can tell us directly what the difference between seeing a horse and imagining a horse is: the difference resides in the different ways we have of relating to a given object. These ways of relating, these types of awareness, are the basic phenomena of psychology itself—that is, not "horse" as opposed to "pony," but "seeing" as opposed to "imagining." Mental phenomena are thus called *acts* rather than *contents*:

> Every idea of presentation which we acquire either through sense perception or imagination is an example of mental phenomena. By presentation I do not mean that which is presented, but rather the act of presentation. Thus, hearing a sound, seeing a colored object, feeling warmth or cold, as well as similar states of imagination are examples of what I mean by this term. I also mean by it the thinking of a general concept, provided such a thing actually does occur. Furthermore, every judgment, every recollection, every expectation, every inference, every conviction or opinion, every doubt, is a mental phenomenon. Also to be included under this term is every emotion: joy, sorrow, fear, hope, courage, despair, anger, love, hate, desire, act of will, intention, astonishment, admiration, contempt, etc.[51]

It was on this basis that Brentano criticized the Weber-Fechner law, as measuring contents rather than acts. Also, from this definition of mental phenomena, Brentano concluded that all such phenomena are conscious, and he defends the view that there are no unconscious mental phenomena at some length. Thus Freud's polemicizing against philosophers who sought to deny the unconscious certainly had Brentano as a prime target, since many other prominent philosophers, such as Hartmann, Fechner, and Herbart, had already rejected this proposition.

Brentano's actual classification of mental phenomena was based on his view that we can relate to objects in one of three ways. The three fundamental classes of mental acts are: (1) ideas, that is, the acts of the senses such as seeing, hearing, as well as fantasizing; (2) judgments, the acts of accepting or rejecting an object as true or false, such as recognizing that the horse which I see exists, whereas Pegasus or a horse that I imagine does not; (3) feelings, or the acts of loving and

51. Brentano, *Psychology*, pp. 78–79.

hating, as when a horse which I see does something that makes me angry.[52] Brentano goes to great lengths to argue why *this* classification is the correct one, that is, how it describes all mental events in a way that older models, such as the atomistic one, cannot. For example, he claims that the empiricists from Locke to John Stuart Mill all failed to grasp the distinctiveness of judgments. For them, judgments were merely a connection of two ideas, as in Locke's awareness of agreement or disagreement, or in Hume's relations of association. But the judgment "This horse exists" shows no such connection; thus, argues Brentano, it must be generically different from an idea or presentation itself.[53] It is obvious, however, that a judgment presupposes an idea; I cannot accept or reject the existence of a horse without being aware of a horse, either through the senses or through the imagination.[54] Similarly, loving and hating presupposes having such ideas. Brentano argues, less convincingly, that feelings such as love and hate also presuppose judgments, so that there is a hierarchy among the three types of acts.

Although the notion that all experiences presupposed ideas betrayed a certain remnant of the atomistic model, Brentano interpreted this notion in an entirely new way. He arrived at a different notion of the structure of the mind—of how individual mental states were related—than that held by the earlier empiricists. In contrast both to Locke's view that ideas were connected by mental operations, and to Hume's view that they were related by association, Brentano claimed that mental acts exhibit certain *logical* relationships between themselves. Judgments and feelings presuppose ideas, i.e., are impossible without them. In other words, once the psychic elements are properly understood, certain self-evident relations between them emerge as intuitively obvious. The components of mind exhibit certain formal properties that are independent of the particular sense-data which enter it; these data are not the proper subject matter of descriptive psychology in the first place, being contents rather than acts. In the light of this distinction, the earlier versions of psychic coherence, such as association, did indeed appear physicalistic, because ideas were associated on the bases of the properties of contents, such as similarity or contingency in space and time. Even Locke's notion of mental operations was different from Brentano's notion of mental acts, for these operations of combining, comparing, and abstracting

52. *Ibid.*, pp. 197ff.     53. *Ibid.*, pp. 205ff.     54. *Ibid.*, pp. 266f.

worked on the ideas themselves, rather than being directed to non-mental objects.

In Brentano's view, it was the presence of such self-evident relationships that made psychology such a rich source of insight for other philosophical disciplines. For example, the nature of judgment according to the intentional model had implications for logic. The fact that judgments are all acts of accepting or rejecting the existence of something meant that all logical propositions can be reduced to two basic types: propositions that assert, and propositions which deny, existence.[55] Similarly, much of the material of ethics can be derived from proper understanding of the psychical phenomena of love and hate. Admittedly, not all knowledge is based on such internal, self-evident relationships of mental acts; the perception of external, physical objects is still a matter of inductive probability, to be established by experiments; so is induction concerning the existence of God. But Brentano differed sharply from other empiricists such as Hume and John Stuart Mill, who claimed that all self-evident propositions were ultimately derived from repeated observations of physical phenomena, that is, from sense-experience.[56] In this respect, Brentano was closer to Locke, who admitted demonstrative knowledge based on ideas.

In sum, Brentano's distinctive contribution to philosophy was to claim that consciousness, when scrutinized in the light of an appropriate conceptual model, revealed a richness of structure that could provide the tools and insights for the study of man and for a new rigorous philosophy. For all his championing of experimental psychology, Brentano's own work was primarily philosophical. His persuasiveness stemmed from the consistency of his model and from his ability to exploit relationships between abstract concepts, not from any new empirical discoveries. To deny, as Brentano did, that psychology was concerned with causal relationships such as stimulus-response, or that mental contents such as sensations were the legitimate subject matter of psychology, seemed to reduce the bulk of psychological research in his own day to peripheral status.[57]

55. *Ibid.*, p. 231.

56. See the reference to Brentano's unpublished lectures in Chisholm, "Brentano's Descriptive Psychology," *Acten des XIV internationalen Kongresses für Philosophie* (Wien: Herder, 1968), p. 165; Stumpf, "Brentano," in Kraus, p. 100.

57. For a comparison between Brentano and Wundt in respect to their relation to experimental psychology, see Edward Bradford Titchener, *Systematic Psychology: Pro-*

The significance of the intentional model lay rather in its anticipation of one of the main theoretical perspectives of twentieth-century thought: the study of meaning and symbols. There is an unmistakable family resemblance between intentionality and the notion of symbol. Brentano's definition of psychic phenomena shares a common feature with the dictionary definition of symbol: their distinguishing characteristic is their being related to something else. A further common characteristic is that causality does not adequately describe an intentional or a symbolic relation. In the words of Suzanne K. Langer: "The age of science has begotten a new philosophical issue, inestimably more profound than its original empiricism ... the edifice of human knowledge stands before us, not as a vast collection of sense reports, but as a structure of *facts that are symbols*."[58] Symbolic facts, like mental facts, pertain to human beings. They belong to a different order than do the facts of physics and chemistry. The logic of "objects" of human consciousness and language is totally different from that which applies to physical bodies. From the point of view of intentionality, for example, a unicorn is as much an "object" as a real animal. The fact that unicorns do not exist does not in any way hinder us from referring to them in a precise way; indeed, we must do so when we judge that they do not exist. The intentional use of the term "object" is thus quite different from the common-sense use in such phrases as "objective reality."

The close relationship between language and the intentional model of the mind occupied many of Brentano's students, including Meinong, Husserl, and Anton Marty in Prague, as well as Brentano himself. At the same time, it highlighted one element of instability within the framework which led to a break between Meinong and Husserl on

---

*legomena* (New York: Macmillan, 1929; reprint ed., Ithaca: Cornell University Press, 1972), pp. 10, 20f. Paradoxically, however, these conceptual differences did not prevent Brentano's students from making fundamental contributions to experimental psychology. Karl Stumpf's Tonpsychologie is a case in point—though Stumpf preferred to think of his work as phenomenology, not psychology. On the question of Brentano's influence on psychology, see Frank Wesley, "Masters and Pupils among the German Psychologists," *Journal of the History of the Behavioral Sciences*, I (1965), 254. This account is to be preferred to that of Joseph Ben-David and Randall Collins, "Social Factors in the Origins of a New Science: the Case of Psychology," *American Sociological Review*, XXXI (1966), 456. Ben-David and Collins also draw a genealogy of masters and pupils which contains inaccuracies: Stumpf was a student of Brentano; Witasek and Benussi were students of Meinong, not of Stumpf.

58.  Suzanne K. Langer, *Philosophy in a New Key* (Cambridge: Harvard University Press, 1942), p. 21.

the one hand and Brentano and Marty on the other. This concerned the uncertain status of the "object" to which conscious acts were directed. For if intentional psychology was to be the foundation from which new investigations in logic, epistemology, and ethics were to spring, the question of what this object of consciousness *was* could not be easily dismissed. On the one hand, it would seem that, if such objects were to include such diverse entities as physical, imaginary, and mythical horses, it would be wrongheaded to call such objects real. Brentano's original claim was that they had a special sort of existence, which he called "intentional inexistence." Objects which had intentional inexistence were neither physical bodies nor mental entities in the sense of being ideas contained inside the mind. Rather, they were a third type of being, independent of the mind but produced by it whenever an act was directed to it. Thus Pegasus would have intentional inexistence insofar as anyone thought about it for a given stretch of time.[59] But such a notion had its problems—it provided, for example, a very awkward description of the cases in which we actually are aware of something physical. For if we are aware of a horse that is actually in front of us, we are hardly thinking of another "intentionally inexistent" horse that is not physical.[60] Such problems led Brentano in his later life to reject the notion of "intentional inexistence," and to embrace a more conventional realism. For a number of reasons, however, this solution was unsatisfactory to many of Brentano's students, including Husserl and Meinong. The result was that both these thinkers used the intentional model to shed light on the ontological status of the "imaginary" or "nonexistent." Meinong in particular succeeded in exploring the close relationships between our commonsensical notions of reality and the awareness of nonexistence and possibility, as we shall see in detail later. He could claim both that philosophy had often suffered from a "prejudice in favor of reality," and also that liberation from such a prejudice was entirely true to the empiricist tradition.[61]

It was at this level that Meinong succeeded in bringing together the positivist concern with rigor and exact analysis with the themes of

59. Chisholm, "Brentano on Descriptive Psychology," p. 8.
60. *Ibid.*, p. 11.
61. Meinong, "Über Gegenstandstheorie," *GA*, II, 485; This work has been translated by Isaac Levi, D. B. Terrell, and Roderick Chisholm in *Realism and the Background of Phenomenology*, ed. Chisholm (Glencoe: The Free Press, 1960), pp. 76–117. Subsequent references will refer to the *Gesamtausgabe* and translation, with the latter cited as LTC.

imaginative literature and social thought of the day. For the question
of the "objectivity" of "subjective" thought, and the interest in consciousness as the locus for exploring the extent and limits of human
reason were, as we have seen, some of the major themes of European
thought as a whole at that time. The fact that he approached these
questions as a scientific philosopher was by no means as unusual for
Austrian thought of the day as has often been assumed. One can
point, for example, to the economic theories of Brentano's colleague
at Vienna, Carl Menger, whose modifications of classical economics
resembled those of Brentano with respect to the psychology of stimulus-response. Menger redefined the concept of economic value as
something not simply attributable to a physical object (such as a scarce
commodity), but as a conscious judgment about the meaning of that
object. Value, like Brentano's intentionality, had both a subjective and
an objective component.[62] In addition, there is persuasive evidence
that the fascination of many Austrian intellectuals and esthetes with
the irrational was not opposed to science: Freud's belief that psychoanalysis was a science bespeaks the same conviction. So, too, does the
reception which Brentano's successor, Ernst Mach, received when he
arrived at Vienna. Mach, though equally committed to positivistic philosophy, was admired by the Viennese literati such as Hofmannsthal
and Bahr: just as they were seeking to dissolve the notion of the "self"
into the finer subtleties of individual, momentary experiences, so
Mach was preaching that the "self" was unscientific and must give way
to a multiplicity of individual "sensations."[63] The sensitivity to feeling
and nuance which set the artist and poet apart from the rest of society
was assuredly a theme of European literature that was by no means
unique to Austria. One thinks of the poetry of George, Rilke, Mallarmé, as well as the novels and short stories of Mann, Hesse, and
Proust, to name a few. But only in Austria, to my knowledge, did a
work appear in which the sensitive individual is a scientist and mathematician: *The Man Without Qualities* by Robert Musil. Musil had begun
his career as a mechanical engineer, went on to study experimental
psychology under Stumpf, wrote a dissertation on Mach's epistemology, and came close to accepting an academic position in Graz under
Meinong in 1909. After some hesitation, he decided not to come, because, in his words, "my love of artistic literature is no less than my

62.  Carl Menger, *Grundsätze der Volkswirtschaftslehre*, in *The Collected Works of Carl
Menger* (London: London School of Economics and Political Science, 1934), pp. 86–88.
63.  Blackmore, pp. 155, 187.

love of science." [64] In his novel, Musil expressed this admiration in the following manner:

> Modern research is not only science but magic, a ritual involving the highest powers of heart and brain, before which God opens one fold of His mantle after another, a religion whose dogma is permeated and sustained by the hard, courageous, mobile, knife-cold, knife-sharp mode of thought that is mathematics. [65]

64. Musil to Meinong, Jan. 18, 1909, Meinong *Nachlass*, Universitätsbibliothek Graz, Carton 50, No. 4405.

65. Musil, *The Man Without Qualities*, trans. Eithne Wilkins and Ernst Kaiser, 2 vols. (New York: Capricorn Books, 1965), I, 39–40.

# III

# MEINONG'S LIFE AND CAREER

Alexius von Meinong, Ritter von Handschuchsheim, was born in 1853 in Lemberg in the province of Galicia, now a part of Poland. As his name indicates, his background was aristocratic, but his world was far removed from the court life of the upper nobility. His family was made up mostly of civil servants, priests, and military officials, and belonged to the Beamtenadel, a part of the lower aristocracy. Meinong's grandfather had emigrated from southwest Germany in the last quarter of the eighteenth century, and his father had a long career in the Austrian army.[1] At the age of fourteen he had fought for the monarchy against Napoleon, and in 1859 he had served in the war with Italy as a major general. Meinong tells us significantly that his father raised him in the "spirit of the Josephist style of life"—which meant that "we children never saw in our title, which we had hardly been aware of, any natural privilege."[2] He remained true to this sentiment throughout his life; his works and letters all bear the name Alexius Meinong. While Meinong's own choice of vocation was unusual for his family, it is noteworthy that his only son Ernst also chose a military career.

There was another influence, however, which undoubtedly shaped his mature outlook as much as his family environment: the city of Vienna. For at the age of nine, Meinong left Lemberg to study there

1. The main biographical sources are Meinong's own *Selbstdarstellung*, part of which is translated by Reinhardt Grossman, *Meinong* (London: Routledge and Kegan Paul, 1974), pp. 224–236; Ernst Mally, "Alexius Meinong," *Neue österreichische Biographie*, ed. Anton Bettelheim et al. (Vienna: Almathea Verlag, 1935), VIII, 90–100.

2. Meinong, *Selbstdarstellung*, *GA*, VII, 4.

privately, which he did for six years. He completed his education with two years at the Academic Gymnasium, one of the city's finest schools, and at the University of Vienna.[3] Meinong lived in Vienna for a total of twenty years, from 1862 to 1882, and thus experienced the period of the liberals' dominance and the beginning of their decline. It is likely that Meinong's separation from home at such an early age led to one of his most consistent and distinctive personal traits: his independence of mind and insistence on going his own way, regardless of fashion. When his father wanted him to study law, he wanted to study music (which remained a lifelong avocation; Meinong was a cellist and amateur composer). By the time he entered the University of Vienna at the age of seventeen, however, he had decided to study history instead, and graduated with a dissertation on Arnold of Brescia. His independence is clear from his first encounter with philosophy, which was his minor subject: he plunged into the study of Kant entirely on his own, without the aid of commentaries or lectures.[4] The academic year 1874–1875 was one of change for Meinong: he first turned to economics under Carl Menger, whose important analysis of economic value was later to influence Meinong's general theory of values. In early 1875 he decided to devote himself to philosophy and asked Brentano to be his tutor. Meinong confessed that he felt overshadowed by Brentano's magisterial personality, and that his own need to preserve his independence prevented him from becoming as close to his teacher as other students, such as Stumpf, were able to do.[5] Meinong never acquired the charisma that Brentano possessed in his lectures; nor did he take on his teacher's sense of mission in philosophy. Meinong later resisted becoming too closely identified with Brentano's thought, and kept his distance from Brentano's other students who followed the teacher's ideas more closely. (The same was true of Thomas Masaryk, one of Meinong's closest friends during these years. The correspondence between the two lasted until 1904.)[6] At the end of his life, nevertheless, Meinong properly acknowledged his enormous intellectual debt to Brentano. Aside from the specific ideas which Brentano bequeathed to his student—such as intentionality— Brentano influenced Meinong in a number of general ways. It was Brentano who probably directed him to Hume and the other British empiricists. Meinong's two *Hume Studies* were the result—his first ma-

3. *Ibid.*, p. 5.    4. *Ibid.*    5. *Ibid.*, pp. 5–6.

6. Meinong, *Philosophenbriefe*, ed. Rudolf Kindinger (Graz: Akademische Druck-u. Verlagsanstalt, 1965), pp. 1–17.

jor works. Meinong kept in close contact with contemporary British
philosophy and reviewed issues of the British journal *Mind* for the
German *Philosophische Monatshefte* in the late 1870s.[7] He further inherited Brentano's distaste for the Kantian tradition in philosophy:
he remained opposed to epistemological idealism, and avoided put-
ting his ideas into Kantian form.[8]

Underlying these affinities was a deeper trait, Brentano's most important legacy to Meinong: the empirical "scientific" method of philosophizing. Meinong's writings are stylistically much like Brentano's:
we find the same respect for experience, the same blend of observation and argument, the same delimitation and precise definition of
philosophical questions and tasks.[9] There was, however, an important
difference between Meinong's intellectual goals and those of his
teacher. While Brentano sought to reconcile scientific philosophy with
religion and metaphysics, Meinong pursued scientific philosophy as
an end in itself. Religion played no significant role in his thought or
life. Moreover, he distrusted philosophies which claimed to establish a
Weltanschauung or sought sweeping answers to the great philosophical riddles.[10] The same "modesty" also differentiated him from Husserl, who used similar methods in the pursuit of far more ambitious
and lofty, if secular, philosophical projects.

Needless to say, Meinong's philosophical style was also worlds apart
from that of estheticism, despite his own musical inclinations; his
analyses remained dry and unemotional to the end of his life. Some of
his friends even chided him for being insensitive to matters that could
not be expressed clearly and precisely, such as the greatness of Wagner's music.[11] While Meinong's choice of philosophical themes often
reflected his artistic interests, his approach to such topics as the psychology of fantasy and its role in creativity was one of dispassionate
analysis. This self-effacing, careful attitude is perhaps attributable to
Meinong's social background. It was as if he transferred the habits
and attitudes of the Josephist tradition in which he was raised to the
activity of scientific investigation. The civil servant who worked con-
scientiously but cautiously for progress and reform became the mod-

---

7. A very brief article by Meinong appeared in *Mind* itself in 1879. Entitled "Modern Nominalism," it sought to clarify a point in the *Hume-Studies* (*GA*, VII, 118).

8. Meinong, *Selbstdarstellung*, *GA*, VII, 57.

9. See Meinong, *Über philosophische Wissenschaft und ihre Propädeutik*, *GA*, V, 23.

10. Meinong, *Selbstdarstellung*, *GA*, VII, 43.

11. Von Ehrenfels to Meinong, Sept. 13, 1884, Meinong *Nachlass*, Carton 37,
No. 1207.

est scientist-philosopher in the slow pursuit of truth. Meinong often speaks about "service" to science.[12] When he attempted to justify his career in his letters, it was in terms of ideals like "honest, selfless work."[13]

Meinong's academic career bears all the outward marks of success. His first *Hume-Study* won him a position as Privatdozent at the University of Vienna in 1878. In 1882, he was called unexpectedly to a post as Extraordinarius at Graz, where he remained for the rest of his life (his promotion to Ordinarius came seven years later).[14] During the early years in his new position, Meinong showed himself to be a reformer and innovator within the academic profession. He was particularly concerned with the teaching of philosophy in the secondary schools and soon found an opportunity to express this interest. The philosophy curriculum in the Austrian Gymnasium came under fire shortly after Meinong came to Graz. In 1884 the Ministry of Culture and Instruction, the descendent of the old Studienhofkommission, decided to reduce the hours in philosophy from four hours per week in the seventh and eighth classes (the final two years) to two hours in the eighth—thus telescoping logic and psychology, which had been taught separately. The change undoubtedly reflected the low estimation of philosophy in the 1860s and 1870s. Meinong sought to defend the old system in the name of the new philosophy; his book on the subject, *On Philosophical Science and its Propadeutics*, appeared in 1885. The work is as much a manifesto of scientific philosophy itself as a defense of its educational value. Meinong argued that the educators had confused philosophy as a whole with the older speculative sort, and had mistakenly treated philosophy as unscientific and antiquated.[15]

Meinong's defense also reveals the degree to which he had assimilated liberal values as they applied to education. In a manner reminiscent of John Stuart Mill's *On Liberty*, he argues that uncertain or hypothetical material plays a positive role in training the mind—in opposition to the ministry's instructions, which contended that only finished results should be taught.[16] For this reason, he advocates the

12. Meinong, *Philosophische Wissenschaft, GA*, V, 7; *Hume-Studien II, GA*, II, 167; Meinong to Höfler, July 14, 1912, *Nachlass*, Carton 45, No. 2795.

13. Meinong to Hans Benndorf (draft), March 8, 1907, Meinong *Nachlass*, Carton 67, unnumbered.

14. Meinong, *Selbstdarstellung, GA*, VII, 6–7.

15. Meinong, *Philosophische Wissenschaft, GA*, V, 30.

16. *Ibid.*, pp. 44, 49ff, 183ff.

actual performing of psychological experiments in the schools, rather
than mere memorization of accepted theories. Similarly, he is committed to the discussion method in the teaching of philosophy, also at
the university level, and argues for the institution of seminars in philosophy, which were rare at the time.[17] Since there were no satisfactory textbooks for the newer scientific philosophy, Meinong collabor-
ated with his student and friend Alois Höfler (himself a Gymnasium
teacher) in providing a text in logic. Höfler later wrote a psychology
text of his own, in addition to a book of one hundred experiments for
use in schools (together with Stephan Witasek, another of Meinong's
students).[18] Indeed, Meinong's philosophy probably had considerable
impact on the teaching of philosophy: Höfler saw it as his mission to
spread Meinong's ideas "among the people"; another student, Eduard Martinak, participated in the sweeping reforms of the Austrian
educational system during the first Austrian republic after the War.[19]

Meinong's other achievements on behalf of his discipline included
the establishment of a psychological laboratory and a philosophical
seminar. Meinong had begun to do experimental work in Graz in
1886 on his own financial means and time. The project found a sympathetic reception among students, and in 1894 the Ministry agreed
to an annual subvention; Meinong could claim to have founded the
first psychological laboratory in Austria. Meinong began petitioning
for a philosophical seminar at Graz in 1892, and it was granted five
years later.[20]

It would appear from these data that Meinong led the life of a comfortable academic, uncomplicated by insecurity or upheaval, pursuing
his intellectual tasks with a minimum of disturbance. Meinong's concerns and attitudes seem far removed from the conflicts of nationality
and class, and from the mass political movements that troubled Aus-

17. *Ibid.*, pp. 77f, 144. At this time only Prague, Leipzig, and Göttingen could boast
a seminar or similar arrangement. See Friedrich Jodl to Meinong, October 30, 1892,
*Philosophenbriefe*, p. 51.

18. Alois Höfler, *Logik* (Wien: F. Tempsky, 1890); *Psychologie* (Wien: F. Tempsky,
1894); Höfler and Stephen Witasek, *Hundert psychologische Schulversuche* (Leipzig: Verlag von Johann Ambrosius Barth, 1899). The text edition of the *Logic* went through
seven editions by 1919; the *Psychology* went through seven by 1921; the *Schulversuche*
went through four editions by 1918.

19. Höfler, *Selbstdarstellung*, in *Die Philosophie der Gegenwart in Selbstdarstellungen*, ed.
Raymund Schmidt (Leipzig: Felix Meiner Verlag, 1921), II, 132; Eduard Martinak, *Psychologische und pädagogische Abhandlungen* (Graz: Leykam-Verlag, 1929), preface (unnumbered).

20. Meinong, *Selbstdarstellung*, *GA*, VII, 11.

tria during his lifetime. Until the War years, Meinong made no reference to political and social conditions in his published works.[21] His personal correspondence, however, reveals a more complex picture, one of increasing disillusionment with his environment. If Meinong had no inclination to enter into the irrational politics and culture of his day, the political and cultural situation in Austria nevertheless affected his career through the medium of academic politics, and thereby determined some of his attitudes. One of these, as we shall see, was anti-Semitism.

Meinong's years as a student coincided with the beginnings of radical German nationalism. The year after he entered the university at Vienna, the German Second Empire was founded, an event which inspired heightened nationalist sentiment among Austro-Germans. The radical student movement talked of Pan-Germanism, advocating that the Germans in Austria should eventually join the Empire. During his student years, Meinong fraternized with at least two German nationalist groups, the Burschenschaft "Rugia" and the Deutsche Leseverein, a nationalist student organization that was later dissolved for its radicalism.[22] The latter group contained such illustrious and diverse figures as Victor Adler, later the leader of the Austrian Social Democrats, Heinrich Friedjung, later a prominent liberal, Theodor Herzl, the founder of Zionism, and Freud. The diversity of political views that emerged from this movement makes it difficult to evaluate its effect. In any case, Meinong's activities were modest enough to free him from any suspicion of subversion so far as the government was concerned.[23]

When Meinong came to Graz in the 1880s, he emerged as a moderate nationalist. Like many other members of the professions, he was distressed at the tactics of Georg von Schönerer, the leading Pan-Germanist of the time. He joined a counter-organization designed to consolidate German nationalists of moderate persuasion, the German National Union, as distinct from Schönerer's Union of German Na-

21. In the autobiographical sketch, Meinong expressed his intention to stay far from party politics. *Ibid.*, p. 4.

22. See William J. McGrath, "Student Radicalism in Vienna," *Journal of Contemporary History*, II (1967), 183; Meinong *Nachlass*, Carton 60, No. 6268 (on the *Rugia*).

23. The routine report of the local police at the time of Meinong's first appointment in 1878 contains the phrase, "concerning his moral and civic behavior there is nothing disadvantageous to raise." Eybesfeld to Streymayr, April 25, 1878. Records of the *K. K. Ministerium für Cultus und Unterricht*, Meinong file, No. 2068. Österreichisches Staatsarchiv.

tionals. Meinong also supported a Burschenschaft in Graz, called the "Arminia," for the same reason: to oppose the "Stiria," which supported Schönerer. When the "Arminia" also turned to Schönerer, Meinong left it.[24] Meinong was also a member of the German School Union, a very large organization that ran German language schools in areas where such schools were not provided by law. Meinong did not take an active role in these organizations, however; by his own admission, he was too absorbed in his own work to do so.[25] After 1885, his correspondence shows no further evidence of political activity.

Such a small amount of political activity would not seem to be significant for Meinong's thought or academic life. Meinong himself certainly thought as much when he participated in these movements. To his surprise, however, he found that the Ministry of Culture and Instruction looked upon his affiliations with suspicion. Meinong had grown up in the days of German dominance; coming from a family that had always served the emperor, he was ill-prepared to be looked upon as a subversive. But the new minister of education under the Taaffe government, Baron Gautsch, was highly sensitive to the German nationalist movement, and would even propose in 1888 a parliamentary bill regulating a number of student nationalist groups.[26]

The tension between Meinong and the ministry arose over the issue of his promotion to Ordinarius. The Graz faculty had proposed his promotion in 1886, and sent it to the ministry for approval. Meinong assumed that this last step was a routine matter. But the official notice of promotion did not come, and was not to come until three years later. The ministry chose not to reveal to Meinong the reasons for the delay. He made several trips to Vienna to inquire, but to no effect. Whatever he found out about his case, he found out indirectly. In January 1887, a close friend in Vienna informed him that his uncle, a retired member of the ministry, had heard Meinong's name in connection with political agitation.[27] Meinong thereupon drew up a detailed account of his activities with the nationalist groups and sent it back to his friend, in the hope that it would get back to the ministry and clear his record.[28] This plan and similar ones had no effect.

The files of the ministry confirm the rumors of which Meinong

24. Meinong to Lothar Dargum [a friend from student days], January 17, 1887, *Nachlass*, Carton 36, No. 1093.

25. *Ibid.*; also Meinong to Jodl, February 28, 1889, *Philosophenbriefe*, p. 41.

26. Paul Molisch, *Politische Geschichte der deutschen Hochschulen in Österreich*, 2d. ed. (Vienna: Wilhelm Braumüller, 1939), p. 109.

27. Dargum to Meinong, January 14, 1887, *Nachlass*, Carton 36, No. 1061.

28. Meinong to Dargum, No. 1093.

heard. A police investigation prompted by Gautsch noted that Meinong was observed repeatedly at the Burschenschaft "Arminia" and that he had been named an honorary member.[29] The police also knew of his membership in the German National Union. Only after subsequent reports that Meinong had ceased visiting the "Arminia," and after repeated petitions of the faculty, was Meinong finally promoted in March of 1889.[30]

The situation was complicated by Meinong's activities in curriculum reform. His public criticisms of the plan to reduce the hours in philosophy had appeared also in 1886, and Höfler had completed the textbook in logic, with Meinong's collaboration, in the following year. When Höfler submitted the book for ministerial approval as an official text, he found himself confronted with a new procedure: two scholars would review the book first. Gautsch was evidently anxious that the new book not be offensive to conservative sensibilities.[31] As it was, approval did not come until 1890, and only in 1900 were the extra hours restored to the curriculum.

The psychological effect of this bureaucratic delay on Meinong was clear. As the affair prolonged itself, Meinong became increasingly suspicious; he interpreted the vagueness and slowness of the ministry as deception, hiding some personal intrigue against him. In his eyes the political issue had been merely a pretext.[32] He became pessimistic about his future and demoralized about his work. In 1889 he wrote to Jodl, "I can hardly expect a full professorship in Austria, and a mutually agreeable collaboration with the education officials is naturally also out of the question."[33] He found his duties increasingly burdensome, and by 1888 had decided to end his experimental work, seeing no prospect for its growth or support. Then, apparently without warning or explanation, the notice of promotion came. Within a year, he was married—to Doris Buchholz, whom he had met in Vienna many years before.

It was during these years that Meinong's relations with Brentano began to deteriorate. A number of events contributed to the separation of student and teacher. In 1887 Meinong attempted to secure an assistant professorship for his student and friend Anton von Oelzelt-

29. Gautsch to Franz Joseph, November 6, 1887, *Ministerium* records, Meinong file, No. 22474.

30. Gautsch to Franz Joseph, February 20, 1889, *ibid.*, No. 4009.

31. Höfler to Meinong, January, 1888, Meinong *Nachlass*, Carton 42, No. 1996.

32. Meinong to Dargum, *ibid.*, Carton 36, No. 1091; Meinong to Höfler, June 19, 1887, Carton 52, No. 4485.

33. Meinong to Jodl, February 28, 1889, *Philosophenbriefe*, p. 41.

Newin. Brentano had doubts about Oelzelt's competence and opposed his appointment.[34] More important, an intellectual difference arose between them. Meinong published an article in 1886, *Zur erkenntnistheoretischen Würdigung des Gedächtnisses* (On the Epistemological Valuation of Memory), in which he claimed that memory was a reliable source of knowledge, provided we recognize that such knowledge is probable and not certain. Brentano rejected the notion of probable knowledge.[35]

The actual break between the two was precipitated by an incident in which the ministry was involved. One evaluation of the *Logic* came from Anton Marty, a loyal student of Brentano, whom Meinong suspected of defending the master's ideas against all dissenters. It supposedly contained the following statement: "Höfler, seduced by Meinong, is guilty of deserting the correct doctrine."[36] The ministry instructed Höfler to keep the recommendations confidential, but he showed them to Meinong and made reference to it in a publication.[37] Meinong was infuriated by Marty's dogmatism; it was easy to move to the suspicion that Brentano and his loyal students had been conspiring against him, even in his own case for promotion. His anger and suspicion quickly spread to Brentano's other students. In 1890–1891 two books appeared—Stumpf's *Tonpsychologie*, Vol. II, and Husserl's *Philosophie der Arithmetik*—both dedicated to Brentano and both void of citations of Meinong's works. Meinong drafted a virulent letter to Husserl in "thanks" for his complimentary copy:

> If one day you too are to be guilty of "deserting the correct"—and this fate will hardly be spared you—when you then, for a while completely unsuspecting, find yourself belittled, distrusted, and persecuted without end, then your threads of patience and objectivity too will be stretched to the limit.[38]

34. Ehrenfels to Meinong, August 25, 1888, *Nachlass*, Carton 37, No. 1241.

35. Meinong's article is in *GA*, II, 185–213. Brentano's reference is in *The Origin of Our Knowledge of Right and Wrong*, trans. Roderick M. Chisholm and Elizabeth H. Schneewind (New York: Humanities Press, 1969), p. 83. See also Brentano to Meinong, February 15, 1886, *Philosophenbriefe*, p. 23.

36. So claims Höfler, "Franz Brentano in Wien," p. 324. Kraus denies it, *Franz Brentano*, p. 16.

37. Höfler, *Selbstdarstellung*, p. 131. He refers there to an article of his in the *Zeitschrift für österreichische Gymnasien*. The phrase also appears in Meinong's review of Franz Hillebrand's *Die neuen Theorien der kategorischen Schlüsse*, *GA*, VII, 200. Hillebrand was another loyal Brentano student.

38. Meinong to Husserl (draft), May 20, 1891, *Philosophenbriefe*, p. 96.

Fortunately, Meinong's temper cooled, and the letter was not sent.[39] Meinong and Husserl remained on cordial terms for a number of years, but Meinong had made a lasting enemy in Marty, and never resumed communications with Brentano.

Meinong's treatment by the ministry was not simply an anomaly; others had to wait even longer. The ministry dwelled on Freud's promotion for five years, between 1897 and 1902.[40] Brentano's "Last Wishes for Austria" give testimony to his own frustration and disillusionment while hoping for promotion between 1880 and 1894. Masaryk voiced similar complaints to Meinong.[41] Another case was that of a younger colleague of Meinong at Graz, Hugo Spitzer, who was promoted by the faculty to full professor in 1895, and did not receive official approval until 1904. Spitzer, too, turned his anger and suspicions on his colleagues, in this case Meinong's students, who had been promoted at Graz. Meinong wrote revealingly of Spitzer's case (and perhaps unintentionally of his own):

> Spitzer is still an associate professor, despite repeated suggestions for full professor. Why? One doesn't know exactly: a rumor that is difficult to check claims that he aroused clerical annoyance through a very inopportune hymn of praise to Büchner in his book on Darwinism that is over 20 years old; now he suffers the consequences. In any case these are out of proportion to this superannuated rashness. He himself is naturally very much out of sorts because of it; less naturally, his ill-humor has turned in the course of the years always more against me and my students, although I promoted his cause as well as I could. Since Martinak's promotion, he seems to have lost his inner equilibrium. . . .[42]

As for Meinong himself, the events of the 1880s surrounding his promotion left permanent scars. Despite his outward success, Meinong was still overready to suspect others of intriguing against him. This disposition soon led him to embrace anti-Semitism.

During the 1880s Meinong was not anti-Semitic; indeed, he went out of his way to oppose von Schönerer and the other "antisemitische

---

39. Meinong to Höfler, May 30, 1891, *Nachlass*, Carton 52, No. 4561. See Hans Schermann, "Meinong und Husserl," unpublished dissertation, Université Catholique de Louvain, 1970, p. 13.

40. Jones, *Freud*, I, 372ff.

41. Brentano, *Letzten Wünsche*, pp. 12ff; Masaryk to Meinong, July 29, 1896, *Philosophenbriefe*, pp. 15f.

42. Meinong to Hillebrand (draft), November 15, 1904, *Nachlass*, Carton 67, unnumbered.

Unkulturkämpfer," as he called them.[43] He even acted to bring a Jewish philosophy professor to Graz—Jakob Freudenthal, whom Brentano had recommended and who had been refused a position in Germany.[44] During the 1890s Meinong was increasingly concerned with placing his students in tenured positions—a task that was becoming increasingly difficult with time. The late nineteenth century had witnessed a sharp increase in the number of university students and graduates; by the 1890s this had led to a surplus of Privatdozenten. Between 1891 and 1901 the number in Vienna jumped by 45 percent; in Graz by 50 percent. The number of higher positions did not match this growth: the figures for Extraordinarii and Ordinarii combined for the same years are 13 percent in Vienna and 23 percent in Graz.[45] Given the competition for such positions, it was inevitable that Meinong's students would be competing with Jews. Although the student population in Graz contained few Jews—only 1.8 percent—the number in Vienna was much higher—23.5 percent in 1901. The Jewish assistant professors of philosophy in Vienna increased also; they included Richard Wahle and Wilhelm Jerusalem, both of whom joined the faculty in 1890–1891. In the later 1890s the first publications of Heinrich Gomperz, son of the distinguished historian of philosophy Theodore Gomperz and member of a wealthy Jewish family, began to appear.

We can point to a specific incident concerning appointments that seems to have triggered Meinong's anti-Semitism. In the fall of 1895, a position became vacant at the University of Czernowitz. With Meinong's influence, the faculty suggested two of his protégés (Ehrenfels and Martinak) and Spitzer, whom Meinong had recommended. There were rumors, however, that the ministry would name someone not on the faculty's list: Wahle, whom Meinong considered to be of inferior quality. In March of 1896, Wahle's appointment was announced. As usual, the reasons for the decision against the faculty's wishes were not made clear, and Meinong was left to speculate on his own. He concluded that the ministry wanted to do Gomperz and the Viennese Jews a favor.[46] This remark set the tenor of Meinong's anti-Semitic statements, which began to appear in his correspondence

43.  Meinong to Jodl, February 28, 1889, *Philosophenbriefe*, p. 41.

44.  Brentano to Meinong, December 12, 1883, *ibid.*, p. 21; Meinong to Freudenthal (draft), April 12, 1884, *Nachlass*, Carton 67, unnumbered.

45.  *Österreichisches statistisches Handbuch* (Vienna: Verlag der K. K. statistischen-centralcommission), published yearly.

46.  Meinong to Ehrenfels, March 26, 1896, *Nachlass*, Carton 38, No. 1312.

during and after the Czernowitz affair. The Jews represented an organized interest group, whose influence and craftiness were keeping conscientious and deserving persons like his students out of power.[47] In January of 1896 he referred to Max Dessoir, an assistant professor in Berlin as a "communal Jewish plant" (*communale Judenpflanz*),[48] and in November of 1896 he warned Ehrenfels, who had just been appointed at Prague—to Meinong's complete surprise— "not to mistake purely intellectual vigor for what is specifically Jewish shrewdness" among his students.[49] Meinong continued to hold anti-Semitic views, and felt that the quality of philosophy in Vienna was threatened by Jews. In some of his uglier letters, he opposed the prospect of the Marburg Neo-Kantians and Husserl coming to Vienna.[50]

Meinong's anti-Semitic utterances had a particular emphasis: they were almost exclusively directed against the Jewish intelligentsia. Mention of Jewish economic interests, or any identification of Jews with the Social Democrats is missing. We do, however, find a bizarre association of Jews, liberalism, and the Roman hierarchy. Meinong on one occasion calls Vienna the "culture-center for clerical-semitic, or, what amounts to the same thing, clerical-liberal philosophy."[51] It is thus impossible to associate Meinong with Christian Socialism, though the same general motives that impelled the educated middle classes of Vienna to forsake liberalism for Lueger's movement certainly held for Meinong's individual case.[52]

Throughout the 1900s, Meinong continued to harbor feelings that official Austria had passed him by—despite the objective successes of the laboratory, the seminar, and the curriculum reform. The fact that the Habsburg bureaucracy itself, whose attitudes and traditions Mein-

47. Meinong's argument was similar to that of Molisch (*Politische Geschichte der deutschen Hochschulen*, p. 134) that gentiles were willing to promote qualified scholars regardless of religion; Jews, on the other hand, seek to promote each other. Thus it is necessary to limit their growth. Meinong of course never shrank from using his influence at the faculty and ministerial level. The amount of fantasy in this picture may be gauged by the fate of the other Jewish Privatdozenten. Jerusalem was not promoted for sixteen years. Gomperz had published four works before receiving an assistant professorship in Bern in 1900; he came to Vienna in 1905 and did not receive tenure until 1920.

48. Meinong to Höfler, January 10, 1896, *Nachlass*, Carton 52, No. 4625.

49. Meinong to Ehrenfels, November 24, 1896, *ibid.*, Carton 38, No. 1319.

50. On the Marburg School, see Meinong to Höfler, March 5, 1914, *ibid.*, Carton 45, No. 2836; on Husserl, see Meinong to Höfler, September 26, 1914, *ibid.*, No. 2855.

51. Meinong to Ehrenfels, November 24, 1896, *ibid.*, Carton 38, No. 1319.

52. See Peter J. Pulzer, *The Rise of Political Anti-Semitism in Germany and Austria* (New York: John Wiley and Sons, 1964), pp. 178f.

ong shared so deeply, lay at the source of this alienation undoubtedly
accounts for the persistence of such feelings. In 1912 he wrote to
Höfler:

> I have just completed my 30th year in office (Amtsjahr) and am so immod-
> est as to think that these years in office have yielded more for "Austrian sci-
> ence" than those of some other colleagues. But the high [ministry of] in-
> struction officials have, during these 30 years, abstained from so much as
> lifting a finger as a sign of recognition of my activity.[53]

A few years later, recognition did indeed come: Meinong was elected
to the Austrian Academy of Science in 1914. The following year he
received a call to a chair at Vienna—a position he had long coveted.
By 1915, however, Meinong was sixty-two years old, and preferred to
remain in the less hurried surroundings of Graz.

Meinong also sensed his increasing intellectual isolation from the
predominant cultural trends. In his autobiographical sketch, he admitted that "the art of making what is popular even more popular,
and thereby becoming popular myself, has always been denied me."[54]
Indeed, his relative lack of influence when compared to contemporaries such as Brentano and Husserl surely is due as much to his style
in teaching and writing as to the content of his ideas. The recollec-
tions of the psychologist Fritz Heider may serve as typical:

> When I knew him he was in his sixties, a rather short man with a full beard.
> He was practically blind, yet a very efficient person, sober and well-orga-
> nized, and the lectures seemed to come out of his mouth ready to be pub-
> lished. After getting used to Meinong's talks, everybody else seemed sloppy,
> messy, and diffuse. During his lectures he stood behind the desk; he seemed
> to speak without emotion, the only interruption in the flow of words being
> an odd kind of snort when he was at a loss what to say next. . . . I confess
> that during my study with Meinong I was often irritated with Meinong's
> scholastic way of thinking. . . . It is only in the last years that I have realized
> how much I actually learned from him.[55]

Meinong's prose conveys the same impression: a mind of extraor-
dinary clarity and precision with a highly developed sense of detail
and a somewhat deficient sense of coherence. Meinong's work is almost entirely monographic; even his larger books are extended inves-

53.  Meinong to Höfler, July 14, 1912, *Nachlass*, Carton 45, No. 2795.
54.  Meinong, *Selbstdarstellung*, *GA*, VII, 58.
55.  Fritz Heider, "Gestalt Theory: Early History and Reminiscences," in *Historical
Conceptions of Psychology*, ed. Mary Henle, Julian Jaynes, and John J. Sullivan (New
York: Springer Publishing Co., 1973), p. 64.

tigations into narrowly defined topics—for example, *On Assumptions* (*Über Annahmen*), or *On Possibility and Probability* (*Über Möglichkeit und Wahrscheinlichkeit*). One of his major weaknesses, as we shall see, was his failure to update his older ideas in accordance with his new ones, so preoccupied was he with the subtleties of the individual topic at hand. One commentator, Gustav Bergmann, has summed up these characteristics as comprising Meinong's "diffuse style."[56]

The lack of comprehensive vision is most conspicuous when Meinong attempts to be programmatic—to define the nature of philosophy, or to articulate the relevance of his researches to philosophy or science as a whole. Philosophy was first and foremost a "group of sciences"—psychology, epistemology, logic, ethics, esthetics, metaphysics, pedagogy.[57] By the end of his life, Meinong admitted that he had been unable to find a clear unifying concept to characterize philosophy.[58] It is hardly surprising that Meinong's ideas should have failed to win adherents beyond his own circle of students, at a time when Husserl was articulating a much grander role for his brand of phenomenology.

Yet it would be an exaggeration to say that Meinong's thought lacked any systematic coherence, however difficult it may be to cull such a system from most of his individual works. The autobiographical sketch, written near the end of his life, gives a retrospective view in which the unity of his thought emerges clearly. The theory of objects, psychology, value-theory, and ethics all grow naturally out of the intentional model—that is, out of a definite view of the relationships between human experience and the world. In Findlay's apt simile, "It is strange . . . that Meinong's object-theory should have been regarded by some as a bewildering and tangled 'jungle': it resembles rather an old formal garden containing some beautiful and difficult mazes."[59] Likewise it is easy to underestimate Meinong's impact in his own day from the perspective of a more recent time: Heider tells us that Meinong's reputation overshadowed that of Husserl in the first decade of the twentieth century.

Nevertheless, the last years of Meinong's life present an unhappy picture. In 1915, his most valuable assistant, Stephan Witasek, died.

56. Gustav Bergmann, *Realism. A Critique of Brentano and Meinong* (Madison: University of Wisconsin Press, 1967), p. 342.

57. Meinong, *Philosophische Wissenschaft, GA*, V, 19.

58. Meinong, *Selbstdarstellung, GA*, VII, 14.

59. J. N. Findlay, *Meinong's Theory of Objects and Values*, 2d ed. (Oxford: Clarendon Press, 1963), p. xi.

Meinong had viewed Witasek as his successor in the laboratory and seminar, and the loss was great. Two years later, his only son, Ernst, who had become an officer in the Austrian army, lost an eye in combat in the War.

The War had aroused Meinong's patriotism, and led him to write on political issues for the first time. Although in 1915 he expressed hope that the War would not injure relations among scientists and intellectuals of various countries, the defeat of the Central powers and the terms of the peace treaties aroused his anger.[60] His autobiographical sketch of 1920 contains the following expression of his feelings:

> We old ones, who saw the splendor of the new German Reich rise and flourish, we, to whom old Austria was the beloved home of our youth and work, we carry with us to the grave the pain over that which is irremediably lost, together with the just indignation over the ill-will which has brought it down. We would have to seem disloyal to ourselves if we could do otherwise. . . . And we will also want to take with us to the grave the faith in the unbroken strength of the German people and in a future worthy of this strength.[61]

Meinong died soon after these words were written at the age of sixty-seven, a victim of cancer.

It is tempting to explain Meinong's intellectual development in terms of the social history of ideas. As an exemplar of a social type of intellectual, Meinong fits approximately Fritz Ringer's characterization of the "mandarin": a loyal state official by background and qualification, confronted by modernity in a way which affected him adversely, and reacting against its manifestations in the realm of abstract ideas.[62] (True, Ringer developed his model for German academicians rather than Austrian ones, and it would need certain modifications: the "modernity" that Meinong faced was due less to the pressures of industrialization than to the upsurge of non-German nationalists and Jews within the Habsburg Empire. Also, Austria lacked a strong Kantian tradition, which Ringer stresses in the German case.) One could point out that Meinong privately embraced anti-Semitism during the same years in which he developed the theory of objects; the latter

---

60.  Meinong, "Über die Wiederaufnahme der internationalen wissenschaftlichen zusammenarbeit nach dem 1. Weltkrieg," *GA*, VII, 274–276. The article contained answers on the part of intellectuals to an open question posed by the *Svenska Dagbladet* as to whether international cooperation would be renewed after the War.

61.  Meinong, *Selbstdarstellung*, *GA*, VII, 59–60.

62.  Fritz K. Ringer, *The Decline of the German Mandarins* (Cambridge: Harvard University Press, 1969), pp. 15ff, 82, 90ff, 298ff.

seemed to turn away from reality in allowing for entities which were independent of the mind and yet did not exist. Yet such an approach would both oversimplify and trivialize Meinong's thought. His beliefs that fictitious entities had objective status went hand in hand with his belief that real, actual objects also exist independently of the mind; his concern with fantasy and fiction did not lead him to question the existence of the real world, but is connected to his affirmation of it. Moreover, such a focus would not illuminate the historically significant aspects of Meinong's thought. In fact, Meinong's intellectual biography has its own internal dynamics; it is a story of his resolving the inconsistencies of his earlier works, carrying a given line of thought through to its logical conclusion, rendering explicit what was formerly obscure. This pattern applies most clearly to the origin, between 1899 and 1904, of his theory of objects, or Gegenstandstheorie—the achievement for which he is best known. Meinong's own comment on the development of Gegenstandstheorie is basically accurate: "I have done scientific work for years, actually decades, under the influence of my interests in the theory of objects, without having had the slightest idea of the nature of those interests."[63] It is this development in its clarity that reveals Meinong as a representative figure of the intellectual revolution.

63. Meinong, "Über Gegenstandstheorie," *GA*, II, 525–526; LTC, p. 114.

# PART TWO

*Meinong and
the Intellectual Revolution*

# IV

# THE PSYCHOLOGISM OF THE 1880s

In *The Structure of Scientific Revolutions*, Thomas Kuhn draws certain parallels between revolutions in science and politics. Just as political revolutions are triggered by new developments in society which render the status quo intolerable for a sizable number of its members, so scientific revolutions arise when some members of a scientific community see that new discoveries are incompatible with the prevailing paradigm. In both cases, too, the period that follows is marked by conflict—between competing conceptions of social order in one case, and of natural order in the other.[1]

Intellectual historians have tended to use the term "revolution" somewhat differently. One frequently talks of intellectual revolutions when a variety of thinkers who do *not* belong to the same community—say artists, philosophers, and social theorists—arrive at similar ideas. While such thinkers may influence each other across disciplinary lines, it is by no means necessary to assume such influence. The individuals may well have arrived at their ideas independently.[2] Thus, for example, one can talk of romanticism as an epochal change in Western thought because various writers, philosophers, artists, and composers in England, Germany, France, and elsewhere were responding to their world in similar ways—even if some of them repudiated the label "romanticism" itself (as Goethe did at one point). In short, intellectual historians stress the parallels between ideas as

1. Thomas Kuhn, *The Structure of Scientific Revolutions*, 2d ed. (Chicago: University of Chicago Press, 1970), pp. 92f.

2. See, for example, Hughes, p. 32; Gerhard Masur, *Prophets of Yesterday* (New York: Macmillan, 1961), pp. 210, 248; Jacques Barzun, *Darwin, Marx, Wagner* (Garden City: Doubleday, Anchor Books, 1958), p. 7.

often as not, whereas in Kuhn's scheme the crucial points are the differences.

Now the philosophical situation in Europe between 1880 and 1920 offers some formidable difficulties for the intellectual historian. This is because it lends itself to neither of these commonly accepted interpretations of "revolution," but combines the most perplexing features of both. On the one hand, within the academic community of philosophers there was a bewildering variety of philosophical movements, a characteristic of a revolution in Kuhn's sense. In contrast to the third quarter of the nineteenth century, which was dominated—on the continent, at least—by a faith in science, one is faced by 1910 with neopositivism, historicism, vitalism, pragmatism, realism, phenomenology. Neo-Kantianism, and Neo-Hegelianism. From this turmoil, two "paradigms" eventually emerged: analytical philosophy in England and Vienna, and phenomenology and existentialism in Germany and France. On the other hand, the participants in this philosophical revolution were not limited to the community of philosophers. One finds sociologists such as Weber, mathematicians such as Frege, and physicists such as Mach and Boltzmann making significant contributions to the debate, and at the same time continuing to affect the developments in sociology, mathematics, and physics respectively. Given this cross-disciplinary fertilization, it was next to impossible for any one figure to remain informed about all of these changes. Thus we find Bergson, for example, chastising natural science for thought patterns which the natural scientists themselves were in the process of discarding. At the same time, moreover, many of the specialized sciences such as psychology were in the process of emerging and forming their own institutions and channels of communication.[3] Many psychologists were thoroughly grounded in philosophy and contributed to it, but their specialized literature was increasing at such a rate that it became more and more difficult for a traditional philosopher to keep up with it. Similarly, few German and French philosophers were able to comprehend the algebraic formulas of Frege or Russell, or were interested in doing so. In sum, while it is true that intellectuals in philosophy, science, and social thought did share common concerns, they did not necessarily communicate with each other, and consequently did not always arrive at the same ways of formulating questions.

It is therefore futile to try to sum up the revolution in philosophy in a single formula. The best we can do is offer a typology. This should

3.  See Ben-David and Collins, pp. 453, 456f.

illuminate the dominant concerns and assumptions of thinkers in the different schools and communities, whether or not they succeeded in communicating with each other. For there were such concerns, and they transcended the traditional barrier between positivism and anti-positivism. In the next three chapters, I will present these issues and Meinong's relationship to them. To outline briefly, the revolution in philosophy proceeded along three different lines. (1) There was a tendency to carry the empiricism of the previous period further, to the point where it undermined the traditional theories in science and the humanities. (2) There was a tendency to distrust this very empiricism, and emphasize instead those ordering principles necessary to intellectual endeavor which could not be described in terms of human experience alone. (3) There were several attempts made to find a proper relationship between these two, between experience and an ordering principle. While it would be too simple to say that philosophy as a whole passed through this neat dialectical pattern, it is true that the second and third tendencies became more widespread and influential in the late 1890s and 1900s, though the first by no means died out. It is also true that several prominent thinkers tended to evolve from one to the next, among them Meinong. Meinong's thought touched the first and the third tendencies, with an emphasis on the first in the 1880s and on the third from the 1900s, with the 1890s as a transition period. Thus we can present Meinong's intellectual development in the context of each of these tendencies, and show how his grasp of the issues managed to integrate the opposing viewpoints of his contemporaries.

## 1. EMPIRICISM AND THE PHILOSOPHY OF SCIENCE: ERNST MACH

We have already seen the close marriage between empiricist philosophy and science in the mid-nineteenth century. At this time, philosophers usually followed the lead of the natural sciences. By the 1880s and 1890s, however, a different use of empiricism was becoming prevalent, namely that of criticizing the basic concepts of natural science itself. The traditional empiricist bias against abstractions could be directed against some of the most commonly accepted notions of physics, such as "force," "mass," and "atom." None of these notions was evident to introspection, or even observable by experiment. Yet most physicists, before the intellectual revolution, would have agreed that these concepts lay at the core of physics. Even Helmholtz, who was one of the first practicing scientists of the period to engage in epistemological reflections, admitted that the goal of science was to "refer natural phenomena to unchangeable attractive and repulsive forces."[4]

One of the first persons to express doubts as to whether science could explain all phenomena in terms of such concepts was the physiologist Emil Du Bois Reymond, whose lecture "On the Limits of Knowing Nature" (1872) went through eight editions in nineteen years.[5] Du Bois Reymond pointed out the contradictions between the theory and the practice of Newtonian mechanics: physical theory demanded indivisible unchangeable atoms; empirical observations revealed no such entities. He also doubted that the marriage of physics and introspective psychology performed by Fechner could ever lead beyond the investigation of the senses. Fechner had discovered a correlation between physical processes and experience, but had not offered an acceptable scientific theory to explain it. Du Bois Reymond asserted that a mechanical view of the world could never do so.[6] His only solution was summed up in the word *ignorabimus*; in other words, these are matters in which natural science, no matter how highly developed, will leave us in ignorance.

Not all scientists in the 1870s were willing to accept Du Bois Reymond's pessimistic conclusions, however—even if the alternative was a radical reformulation of the aims of physics. It was the physicist Gustav Kirchhoff who gave the classical statement of this alternative in his introductory lecture on mathematical physics:

> We are accustomed to define mechanics as the science of *forces*, and to define the forces as the *causes* which produce motions, or *strive* to produce them. Certainly this definition has been the greatest use in the development of mechanics, and still is useful in learning this science, if we illustrate it by examples of forces which are taken from the experience of everyday life. But it is burdened by the vagueness of the concepts of cause and striving, a vagueness from which they cannot be freed. . . . Given the precision which the conclusions of mechanics otherwise allow, it seems to me desirable to

4. Hermann von Helmholtz, Einleitung, *Über die Erhaltung der Kraft. Ostwald's Klassiker der exakten Wissenschaften* (Leipzig: W. Engelmann, 1889), I, 6f, quoted in Cassirer, *The Problem of Knowledge*, p. 86. See also Maurice Mandelbaum, *History, Man, and Reason* (Baltimore: Johns Hopkins Press, 1971) for a full discussion of Helmholtz's epistemology.

5. Emil Du Bois-Reymond, *Über die Grenzen des Naturerkennens: Die Sieben Welträtsel* (Leipzig: Verlag von Veit and Comp.), 1891.

6. *Ibid.*, pp. 40ff.

remove such obscurities from it, even if this is only possible through limiting its aims. For this reason I put forth as the task of mechanics to *describe*
the motions that take place in nature, and to do so completely and in the
simplest manner. By this I mean that it should be only a question of indicat-
ing *what* the phenomena are that take place, but not of determining its
*causes*. If we start from this viewpoint, and presuppose the presentations of
space, time, and material, we arrive through purely mathematical considerations at the general equations of mechanics. . . . The introduction of
forces is here only a means for simplifying the mode of expression, specifically for expressing equations in a few words. Without the help of this
name, it would be most awkward to render these equations through words.[7]

The contrast between Kirchhoff's and Helmholtz's statements is significant. For Kirchhoff, such concepts as "mass," "force," and "atom"
were the *means* by which observational facts may better be described;
for Helmholtz they were the *ends*, and as such represented the true
reality behind the phenomena. For Kirchhoff they were merely tools
by which scientists arrived at a more sophisticated understanding of
the phenomena themselves. In denying a second level of reality beyond observed appearances, Kirchhoff intensified and rendered
more consistent the empirical approach to scientific knowledge. He
also emphasized the tentativeness rather than the finality of the scientific enterprise:

It is at the outset quite conceivable that a doubt could persist whether one
description of a given phenomenon is simpler than another; it is also conceivable that a description of certain phenomena which today is doubtless
the simplest that can be given, can, with the further development of the science, later be replaced by an even simpler one. The history of mechanics
offers a multitude of examples to show that similar things have happened in
the past.[8]

It was the new positivist movement of Ernst Mach and Richard
Avenarius that worked out Kirchhoff's program in fuller detail, applying it to all the natural sciences. The two men, one a scientist and
the other a philosopher, in fact arrived at the same position independently (Avenarius had called his version "Empiriocriticism"), but each
recognized his view in that of the other. Both had been stimulated initially by Kant and his project of determining the necessary conditions
of scientific knowledge, but their conclusions were so different from

7. Gustav Kirchhoff, *Vorlesungen über mathematische Physik*, 2d ed. (Leipzig: B. G.
Teubner, 1877), pp. iii–iv.
8. *Ibid.*, p. 1.

Kant's that they did not identify themselves as Neo-Kantians.[9] Of the two, Mach's version had greater influence, and we shall discuss it here.

Mach's empiricism is exemplified in his distrust of metaphysics and his insistence that all abstract concepts be verifiable through observation. As did Kirchhoff, Mach went about unmasking the purely hypothetical elements in physics by investigating its history in *The Science of Mechanics* (1883). The most comprehensive statement of his reform of science came in 1885, in the book entitled *The Analysis of Sensations*; the basic ideas came to Mach much earlier, in the 1860s, and were heavily influenced by the new physiology and psychophysics of that day.[10] It was essentially in physiology that Mach found the means for subsuming all of the natural sciences under a single set of concepts, allowing for the simplest possible description. It was physiology that dealt with the mechanisms in the nervous system by which physical stimuli were transmitted to the brain. Thus all the data of physics could be translated into the concepts of body sensations: the properties of inanimate bodies could be dissolved into the colors, shapes, textures, and so on that affect the nervous system. Similarly, it was assumed that all mental states, such as feelings, fantasies, and acts of will, had some correlate in physiological brain-processes and could in principle also be translated into the same language. Thus, according to Mach, the facts of physics, biology, physiology, and psychology can all be described in terms of a common, homogeneous set of "elements" or "sensations." [11]

On this basis, Mach mounted a critique of the existing sciences and the ideas in them which could be considered superfluous. Among his targets were the notions of physical bodies themselves, be they ordinary common-sense objects of the layman or the invisible atoms of the physicist.[12] In both cases they were independent of the complex of sense qualities that affect us, and therefore unnecessary except as auxiliary concepts. They were aids to description, rather than objects of description. A similar argument could be made against the psychological concept of the ego; it too was just a relatively stable combination of more fundamental elements.

9.    Ernst Mach, *The Analysis of Sensations*, p. 367; *Richard Avenarius, Kritik der reinen Erfahrung* (Leipzig: Fues's Verlag, 1888), I, xii.

10.    Blackmore, pp. 15, 25, 30. Mach disagreed with Fechner's dualistic interpretation of psychophysical parallelism, and held that mind and body did not represent two different kinds of sensations. Fechner's negative reaction to Mach's views in the 1860s led him to postpone the writing of *The Analysis of Sensations* for twenty years.

11.    Mach, pp. 8f, 12.

12.    *Ibid.*, pp. 6, 311–312.

The reader will easily recognize the thought-habits of the empiricist tradition in Mach's work. The importance of the analytical approach is evident in passages such as this one:

> Thus, gradually, different complexes are found to be made up of common elements. The visible, the audible, the tangible, are separated from bodies. The visible is analysed into colors and into form. . . . The complexes are disintegrated into elements, that is to say, into their ultimate component parts, which hitherto we have been unable to divide any further.[13]

The notion of an "ultimate" part also reveals Mach's commitment to the atomistic model, despite his rejection of physical atomism. It must be admitted that this model was no longer strictly psychological, because sensations were neither psychical nor physical, but neutral: they were simply the appearances that were common to both.[14] Perhaps the most appropriate label for Mach's view is "phenomenalism." Also, Mach is unwilling to admit that even his sensations are constant and permanent (though in this respect he resembled Hume, whose thought he admired so much).[15]

Such a model would seem to render Mach vulnerable to the same objections that Kant had made to Hume: that a theory of science which is based upon such ephemeral entities as sensations could never adequately account for the theoretical aspects of science, such as its mathematical laws. Indeed, Mach's contemporaries among the Neo-Kantians were to raise precisely this point. But Mach was too experienced a practitioner of science to ignore the importance of mathematics, and he argued in fact that the relationships described by mathematical formulas *were* the constant features of science, not the elements of sensations (in the later editions of the book, Mach amplified this point considerably to prevent misunderstandings).[16] Certain elements occurred together or existed in "relations of dependency."

Mach proposed that the concept of causality in traditional physics could be translated into such relationships. To give an example, Newton's laws of gravitation supposed that bodies such as the moon were the cause of certain phenomena on earth, such as the tides. But this

13. *Ibid.*, p. 5.

14. Mach was emphatic in his later writings that he did not wish to imply a Berkeleyan type of subjective idealism, according to which the world consisted only of psychic phenomena. See Mach, *Populärwissenschaftliche Vorlesungen* (4th ed., Leipzig: Johann Ambrosius Barth, 1910), p. 239. (Lenin had identified Mach with Berkeley.)

15. Mach, *Sensations*, pp. 2, 331; on the affinity with Hume, pp. 46, 368. See also Hume, pp. 8, 204f.

16. Mach, *Sensations*, p. 331. The bulk of this section was added in 1900.

conception involved the awkward notion of "action at a distance." Mach suggested instead that we can assume that the space between the moon and the earth is filled with contiguous elements, so that an action or motion of one is transmitted to the one immediately adjacent to it. Thus a change in each single element is dependent on a change in the one next to it.[17] It was this criticism of Newton's empty space that inspired Einstein's general theory of relativity, though that theory did not accept Mach's atomistic solution.[18]

It was these relations, moreover, that differentiated one science from another. An astronomer, for example, would take a sensation of a light impulse and relate it to other sensations of light-impulses in different spatial positions; a physicist would relate it to sensations of shape, heaviness, and motion. But Mach was quite vague as to just what these different relationships were. The only "functional relationship" mentioned in the *Analysis of Sensations* is the relationship of dependency; his category of order was thus as monolithic as his category of material. Yet if the various sciences *were* actually different from one another, they must deal either with different relations between elements, or with a heterogeneous rather than a homogeneous set of elements to start with. It was on this ground that Mach's doctrine drew criticism not only from the Neo-Kantians, but also from other empiricists such as Wundt.[19] It was here, also, that Meinong was able to make a fundamental contribution: his second *Hume-Study* was a theory of relations, which sought to show the place of the various relational concepts in an empiricist context.

It cannot be said that Mach adhered to the introspective criterion with the same intensity with which he embraced analysis and atomism. His interest, for one thing, was not primarily in epistemology, but in the theory of science. Although he admitted the validity of psychological evidence based on inner perception, his discussion of sensations reveals that many sensations are not consciously perceived. The visual sensation of the color orange, for example, appears simple to introspection, but it is actually composed of a complex of physiological sensations in the retina which represent red and yellow.[20] If asked why

17. *Ibid.*, p. 89. This passage was also added, but Mach states that he originally enunciated the position in *The History and Root of the Principle of the Conservation of Energy* in 1872.

18. Albert Einstein, *Ideas and Opinions* (New York: Crown Publishers, 1954), pp. 286, 348.

19. Wundt, "Ueber psychische Causalität und das Princip des psychophyschen Parallelismus," *Philosophische Studien* X (1894), 57ff, esp. 59, 72.

20. Mach, *Sensations*, pp. 62, 67.

he would select this rather elaborate description of orange instead of the immediately evident data of inner perception, he would undoubtedly refer back to his task of simplifying the sciences by reducing the total number of concepts. This task did indeed imply a new criterion of truth, which represented one of Mach's most interesting contributions to philosophy. Mach called his principle of simplification the "economy of thought," and defended it ultimately on biological grounds.[21] All thought, including science, was a form of adaptation of the human organism to its environment, and thereby served the function of improving its chances for survival. The true science was the one that made the best possible adaptation—the one that had the greatest success in solving the riddles of nature. The simplest description met this standard because it represented a more efficient use of human mental energy. Thus the concept of sensations was to be preferred not because of its introspective evidence, but because of its usefulness: in fact, all concepts should be viewed in terms of their results. Mach was not hostile to abstract concepts viewed in this way; even the atomic theory had proven useful in the past. But one should not mistake a useful notion for a real thing. Mach's anticipation of pragmatism in this principle is clear, as was his influence on William James. The two corresponded for twenty-eight years, and Mach dedicated one of his books to James.[22]

Mach's role in the transformation of positivistic thinking may be summarized as follows: he succeeded in bringing positivism back into line with the empiricist tradition by stressing the atomistic model and the analytical approach which Comte and Spencer had both spurned. Unlike John Stuart Mill and Brentano, Mach interpreted these notions reductionistically: the homogeneity of elements is one of the most striking features of his thought. Like Mill and unlike Brentano, however, Mach did not value the introspective criterion so highly. His alternative criterion for valid knowledge was, in the final analysis, pragmatic. This, together with his rejection of dualism, ultimately vaccinated him against the skepticism that the empiricist tradition had led to in the eighteenth century. Mach saw his views as an alternative to Du Bois Reymond's "*ignorabimus*."[23] While his ideas surely served as a skeptical corrective to hidden metaphysical notions—be they the

21. *Ibid.*, pp. 49ff. Mach claims here that he anticipated Kirchhoff's program of simple description, having first stated the principle in 1871–1872.

22. Blackmore, pp. 126f. On Mach's own statement of the importance of use, see *Sensations*, pp. 322–323.

23. Mach, *Sensations*, p. 366. See also Mandelbaum, *History, Man and Reason*, p. 310.

concepts of physical atoms, or force in natural science, or the evolutionary laws of positivistic social thought—it cannot be said that skepticism was the end product of his thought.

Mach's influence, especially in the 1890s, was widespread among surprisingly diverse groups of intellectuals. Not only did he appeal to literati such as Hofmannsthal, Schnitzler, and Bahr, but also to socialists such as Victor Adler in Austria and Alexander Bogdanov in Russia, who saw in his theory a way of keeping Marxism in touch with the latest developments in science.[24] Mach himself did not shrink from the moral and social implications of his views. If children were educated to disbelieve in the reality of the concept of "force" or "ego," Mach claimed, much of the motivation for human struggle would be eliminated.[25] Perhaps for this reason, Mach was most deliberate in disseminating his views in secondary schools: he wrote a number of science textbooks and co-edited an educational journal between 1887 and 1898.[26] This activity brought him into sympathy with Meinong and Höfler, and with their attempts to introduce scientific philosophy into the schools (Mach recommended Höfler to replace him as co-editor of the aforementioned journal)—despite the fact that Mach did not adopt the intentional model.[27]

Through such activities, Mach managed to influence a whole generation of physicists. Einstein, like many of his contemporaries, was exposed to Mach's ideas at an early age, and admitted his indebtedness to the older scientist. In an obituary, Einstein went so far as to speculate that Mach would have discovered the theory of relativity himself, had he been younger when the controversies surrounding the speed of light were alive.[28]

Yet it was often only the skeptical side of Mach's views that made an impression. If younger scientists such as Ostwald, Boltzmann, and Einstein appreciated Mach's willingness to question accepted dogmas, they nevertheless drew back from his program of reducing all scientific concepts to sensations. The same was true of William James. Although he embraced Mach's notion that there is no duality between

---

24. Blackmore, p. 239.     25. *Ibid.*, p. 234.
26. *Ibid.*, Ch. X, esp. pp. 136, 137.
27. Höfler, *Selbstdarstellung*, p. 139. Mach's respect for Meinong is evident in his correspondence. He was willing to send Meinong a student who was interested in experimental psychology, and accepted some of Meinong's polemical remarks against him (*Philosophenbriefe*, p. 92).
28. Einstein, "Ernst Mach," *Physikalische Zeitschrift* XVII (1916), quoted in Blackmore, p. 255.

the psychic and physical, he could not believe that man's biological mental needs could be met by thinking of the world as composed of sensations only.[29]

While the Neo-positivists were turning empiricism against traditional science in order to reform it, others also were using the same tools to argue against positivism itself. The most striking example was the French philosopher Henri Bergson, who had not yet arrived at the grand metaphysical vistas of *Creative Evolution* that were to win him such fame. In his first major work, *Time and Free Will* (1889), Bergson argued that psychological atomism was a distorted, hypothetical view of the mind, just as Mach had raised similar objections to atomism in physics. In particular, the atomistic model failed to do justice to what Bergson called psychic intensity, the emotional nuance that is present in all our mental states, and ebbs and flows in a way that can be neither quantified nor verbalized.[30] Once the preconceptions stemming from outward experience are removed, inner experience reveals itself as a continuous, heterogenous flow of mental states, melting into one another in a way that could not be analyzed.[31]

The same concern with fidelity to immediate experience, unencumbered by speculative hypotheses, could be found in the early work of Wilhelm Dilthey. Like Mach, Dilthey had developed his basic ideas in the 1860s, but only began to achieve prominence in the 1880s. His influence in Germany was great, and it was decisive in eventually curbing the expansion of experimental psychology there in favor of a "humanistic" psychology.[32] Dilthey's project was to provide a firm epistemological basis for the Geisteswissenschaften without resorting to metaphysics. He too was inspired by Kant's critical examination of the presuppositions of science, but he maintained that Kant's results had only limited applicability: they were valid for the natural sciences, but not for the study of historical and social reality.[33] The material for such a critique was to come from inner experience, but experience of

29. Blackmore, pp. 117f, 193, 299, 171, 206, 127f.

30. Henri Bergson, *Time and Free Will*, trans. F. L. Pogson (London: Swan Sonnenschein, 1910; reprint ed., New York: Harper and Row, Torchbooks ed., 1960), pp. 8, 63ff, 219f.

31. *Ibid.*, p. 107.

32. Wolfgang Metzger, "The Historical Background for National Trends in Psychology: German Psychology," *Journal of the History of Behavioral Sciences* I (1965), 112.

33. Wilhelm Dilthey, *Einleitung in Die Geisteswissenschaften* (1883), in *Gesammelte Schriften* (Leipzig: B. G. Teubner, 1959), I, XVIII (hereafter cited as *GS*). For a discussion of Dilthey's relation to Kant, see Hajo Holborn, "Wilhelm Dilthey and the Critique of Historical Reason," *Journal of the History of Ideas*, XI (1950), 99f.

a sort that was inaccessible to the methods of experimental psychology. Dilthey called for a "descriptive and analytical" psychology as opposed to an "explanatory" one, which would begin with the immediately given rather than with a hypothetical construction such as atomism. Like Mach, Dilthey avowed that hypotheses had a place, but their value was only heuristic.[34] But unlike Mach, Dilthey's immediately given psychic reality was not a set of elements, but a complex of thinking, feeling, and willing that were bound together in a single coherence. While this complex could be analyzed, it would not yield a single, homogeneous set of results, such as Mach's sensations.[35]

No doubt the differences between Dilthey and Bergson on the one hand and Mach and Avenarius on the other outweigh their similarities, at least in the light of their subsequent influence. But the preoccupation with psychological or physiological concepts as the solution to the major problems in epistemology and the philosophy of science did seem to be a general trend in philosophical thought by the 1890s. It was not long before this trend would be recognized by other contemporaries.

### 2. MEINONG'S EARLY PSYCHOLOGISM AND HIS THEORY OF MENTAL OPERATIONS, 1877–1890

By the end of the intellectual revolution, the radical empiricism discussed above had acquired a new label: psychologism. It was used for the most part by its opponents, and often served to express a revulsion against any intellectual endeavor that was based exclusively on the limited, contingent aspects of human existence.[36] According to these critics, psychologism contained the germ of relativism; it barred the way to the true calling of philosophy, which was to deal with absolute and spiritual truths.[37]

As a polemical term, psychologism was used rather loosely. In its broadest sense, it referred to any doctrines that put psychology at the

34. Dilthey, "Ideen über eine beschreibende und zergliedernde Psychologie" (1894), GS, V, 169.

35. Dilthey, "Die Einbildungskraft des Dichters" (1887), GS, VI, 139; "Ausarbeitung der deskriptiven Psychologie" (c. 1880), GS, XVIII, 130.

36. The locus classicus of the polemic against psychologism is the first volume of Husserl's Logical Investigations of 1900. The term was first used in the early nineteenth century in a positive sense by Jakob Fries and Friedrich Beneke to oppose Hegelianism. See Nicola Abbagnano, "Psychologism," Encyclopedia of Philosophy, VI, 520f.

37. For a general statement of this theme in German thought, see Fritz Ringer, The Decline of the German Mandarins, pp. 296ff.

center of philosophy, as did those of Mill, Brentano, Wundt, and the early Dilthey. It could also refer to a more restricted position, namely that certain philosophical questions could be reduced to psychological ones. For example, John Stuart Mill had claimed that the laws of logic were merely a special case of the laws of psychology (a position quite different from Brentano's, who merely claimed that an understanding of psychology could illuminate logic from a new and more fruitful perspective). Another form of psychologistic reductionism was the epistemological view that the only objects we can know are our own mental states—the view of Hume. Mach's doctrine of sensations was not strictly speaking of this sort, because sensations were neither psychic nor physical, but neutral; but it lent itself easily to a psychologistic interpretation, and, in the eyes of its opponents, shared the same errors.[38] Indeed, the critique of psychologism could be directed against virtually any empiricist view.

It is in Meinong's development that we can see clearly the underlying assumptions and problems of empiricism and psychologism laid bare: the question of the role of abstract reasoning in a philosophy based on concrete and contingent experience, and the question of the proper relationship between wholes and parts.

Meinong gives a clear statement of his early psychologism in the opening chapter of his book *On Philosophical Science and its Propadeutics* (1885):

> Philosophy is not psychology, for the name [philosophy] designates, on closer inspection, not one science, but a whole group of sciences. These, however, are held together by their common membership in the field of psychic phenomena. This comes to light in the circumstance that either the subject matter of these disciplines is composed only of psychic phenomena, or . . . that psychic as well as physical facts are included in the scope of their tasks.[39]

In other words, Meinong embraced psychologism in the broad sense: psychology was the central discipline of philosophy. Logic, esthetics, the "sociological sciences (including ethics)," epistemology, and metaphysics all deal at least in part with the data of experience.[40] Presumably the only philosophical discipline that deals exclusively with psychic phenomena is psychology. But if Meinong avoided a narrow

38. Husserl, *Logical Investigations*, trans. J. N. Findlay, 2d ed., 2 vols. (New York: Humanities Press, 1970), I, 205.
39. Meinong, *Philosophische Wissenschaft, GA*, V, 19.
40. *Ibid.*, 19f.

psychologism in his programmatic statements, he did not always do so in his actual philosophizing. Rather, he tended to restrict epistemological questions to the area of psychology, claiming that we do not have sufficient evidence to apply them to a real physical world.[41] By his own later admission, he had never meant to subsume epistemology under psychology, but was not in a position to say why it should be independent.[42]

While Meinong thus followed Brentano in using psychology as the starting-point for all other philosophical distinctions, his psychology per se differed from that of his teacher at a number of crucial points. Meinong generally sought to bring the intentional model into harmony with the existing experimental psychology of the 1870s and 1880s by modifying some aspects of that intentional model in favor of the atomistic one. For example, Meinong interpreted the "intentionally inexistent" objects of Brentano as being actually *in* the mind, rather than being created by the mind. Meinong's name for these objects was "content" (Inhalt). Thus a mental state consisted of two factors, the act and the content. Acts included such psychic phenomena as seeing, judging, and feeling, as in Brentano. Contents consisted, naturally enough, of what was seen, judged, or felt. By so treating contents as being in the mind, Meinong reverted to the position that we can be certain only about our own experiences. To be sure, Meinong never seriously doubted the independent reality of physical objects—his early *Hume Studies* are full of references to them—but simply held that the epistemological questions that interested him could be exhaustively treated in the context of psychology alone—that is, as relationships between mental contents.[43] Thus the "content" for Meinong functioned in much the same way as the old atomistic idea: it met the introspective criterion in a way that physical objects did not. Meinong's later turning away from psychologism came when he saw this position as no longer adequate.

In addition, Meinong restored a place for causal relationships in his psychology. A sensation, for example, was "a simple idea of perception from peripheral stimulation."[44] As experimental psychology was

41. Meinong, *Hume-Studien II: Zur Relationstheorie*, *GA*, II, 38.

42. Meinong, *Über Annahmen* (1st ed., Leipzig: Johann Ambrosius Barth, 1902), pp. 196–197.

43. Meinong, *Hume-Studien II*, *GA*, II, 122, 128. See also Bergmann, p. 401.

44. Meinong, "Über Begriff und Eigenschaften der Empfindung," *GA*, I, 182, 171ff, 169, 131ff.

concerned with the causal relation between physical stimuli and mental processes, Meinong's psychology represents an accommodation between intentional and experimental psychology.

Likewise, Meinong disagreed with Brentano on the basic classes of psychic phenomena. Whereas Brentano had listed three—ideas, judgments, and feelings—Meinong added a fourth: desire or will.[45] This, too, was a feature of experimental psychology of the day, in that, according to Wundt, an act of will was the source of a motor response. Ideas and judgments were classified as intellectual experiences, whereas feelings and desires were classified as emotional ones. There was a further symmetry among these types, Meinong claimed, which stems from the fact that some of our experiences are *active* and others are *passive*. We experience some mental states as coming upon us, whereas others involve more mental exertion. Both active and passive experiences are nevertheless mental acts, not contents, so that "act" and "activity" should not be confused. Applied to the above typology, we may talk of ideas as passive intellectual experiences, and of judgments as active intellectual ones. Similarly, feelings constitute passive emotional experiences, whereas desires are active emotional ones.[46]

In addition, Meinong also posited certain processes or operations that did not fit this scheme. These included abstraction, comparison, and combination of ideas—a derivation from Locke.[47] These played an important role in his early epistemology, as we shall see. Finally, we may note that Meinong did not share Brentano's "horror of the unconscious," though he made no attempt to develop the notion of unconscious experiences systematically.[48]

The writings of Meinong's psychologistic period show his concern

---

45. Meinong, *Kolleg über Psychologie des Gemütslebens II: Begehren*, Meinong *Nachlass*, Carton 14, folder B, p. 5.

46. Meinong, *Selbstdarstellung*, *GA*, VII, 30–38. Meinong also had a counterpart to Brentano's "genetic psychology" which did not deal in the basic elements. He called it the "psychology of dispositions." While he lectured on this topic as early as the 1880s, his only published piece devoted to the subject was a short piece in a Festschrift for one of his students in 1919. (Meinong, "Allgemeines zur Lehre von den Dispositionen," *GA*, VII, 287–310). "Dispositions" covered such phenomena that manifested themselves over repeated instances and could be induced from directly observable phenomena. They would include such reactions as "fatigue," or "recovery." Such concepts seem to correspond to modern notions in psychology such as "extinction."

47. Meinong, "Beiträge zur Theorie der psychischen Analyse" (1894), *GA*, I, 382; *Kolleg über Psychologie*, Meinong *Nachlass*, Carton 13, folder A, Ch. i, sheet 10.

48. Meinong, "Empfindung," *GA*, I, 135.

for avoiding the skepticism engendered by Hume's version of empiricism. His two *Hume-Studies* are attempts to show how this result could be avoided.

From the very beginning of his career Meinong addressed himself to the problem of reconciling the theoretical and empirical elements of human inquiry. He always maintained that the dichotomy between rationalism and empiricism was unfortunate and misleading. He wrote:

> How could one come to demand of the empiricist that he be an empiricist in all and sundry matters—or of the rationalist that he never inquire into experience? Fortunately there have never been empiricists or rationalists of this kind on either side of the Channel.[49]

The two *Hume-Studies* were attempts to seek out the rational elements *in* experience—by pointing out the way in which the British empiricists resorted to these elements.[50] In the first study, he broaches the much discussed problem of abstract concepts and their status. Meinong claimed that many empiricists such as the Mills had shied away unduly from abstract concepts because they seemed too general or metaphysical,[51] and did not refer to individual, factual objects. Meinong argues that our concepts and ideas may be abstract and yet completely specific and individual:

> I speak of the cabinet-maker who produced my writing-table; I think only of *one* individual, but I have never seen him, and thus cannot possibly have a concrete presentation of him. If one considers presentations such as: the wisest of all men, the brightest of all stars, one will also not find a trace of anything concrete; but they are nevertheless individual.[52]

49. Meinong, *Hume-Studien II, GA*, II, 163. See also Rudolf Kindinger, "Das Problem der unvollkommenen Erkenntnisleistung in der Meinongschen Wahrnehmungslehre," in *Meinong-Gedenkschrift* (Graz: Styria Verlagsanstalt, 1952), p. 41.

50. Meinong's critical approach to the empiricists resembles that of T. H. Green, who wrote several long introductions to Hume's works in the 1870s. Both Meinong and Green addressed themselves to Locke and Berkeley as well as Hume, and both sought to point out the inconsistencies in the empiricists' thinking in order to sharpen their own views. Green also sought to uncover the role of relations in perception. See John Hermann Randall, "The Development of English Thought from J. S. Mill to F. H. Bradley," *Journal of the History of Ideas*, XXVII (1966), 236ff, esp. 238.

51. Meinong, *Hume-Studien I, GA*, I, 16, 18.

52. *Ibid.*, p. 24. Meinong, like Berkeley, separated the problem of abstract ideas from the problem of general ones. The two agreed that the generality of an idea is a function of its ability to represent other particular ideas (see Berkeley, *Treatise*, p. 12; Meinong, *Hume-Studien I*, p. 28). Meinong calls the relation of a general idea to particulars its "range" (Umfang).

Meinong's description of how we arrive at such concepts, as well as the other aspects of reasoning that cannot be reduced to sensation, stems from his heterogeneous model of the mind, in particular the notion of mental operations that act upon ideas. The three operations which are paramount are: abstraction, comparison, and indirect ideation (*indirekte Vorstellen*). The role of judgment is secondary in these early works; the emphasis is on the Lockean rather than on the Brentanoan aspects of the model—that is, on ideas and mental processes rather than on mental acts.

The first *Hume-Study, On the History and Critique of Modern Nominalism* (1877), dealt with how Locke, Berkeley, and Hume handled the question of generals versus particulars, abstracta versus concreta. Locke had admitted general ideas or concepts; his position is conventionally known as "conceptualism." Such ideas were the result of the ability of mental operations to separate or analyze certain attributes from the sense-data in which they were originally given. For example, we can, with some effort, form an idea of a triangle that is neither equilateral, isoceles, nor scalene. Berkeley, on the other hand, denied the existence of such ideas, on the grounds of the introspective criterion: he defied anyone to find such an idea in his or her experience. Locke's abstract idea of a triangle was in fact contradictory: one could not conjure up an image of a triangle that did not have a particular shape. Berkeley proposed instead that the only abstract general entities were words or names—the position of "nominalism."[53]

The underlying issues involved in this question will be familiar from the first chapter: the tension between certain aspects of the empiricist tradition. For if one attempts to pursue physical analogies with an atomistic model of the mind, in which mental contents are images or representations of what one supposes the physical world to be, then one imposes certain limits on the analytical approach.[54] One cannot abstract a concept from its concrete attributes, such as "tri-

---

53. *Ibid.*, pp. 4–6, 33. More recent critics such as Bergmann and Kenneth Barber have charged that Meinong himself was a "nominalist" because he was unwilling to admit universals as objective facts (Bergmann, pp. 357, 360; Kenneth Barber, "Meinong's Hume-Studies I," *Philosophy and Phenomenological Research*, XXX (1970), 551. Reinhardt Grossman agrees, but with a slightly different definition: the view that there are no *attributes* in an objective world. Reinhardt Grossman, *Meinong* (London: Routledge and Kegan Paul, 1974), pp. 1, 180. Both Bergmann and Grossman maintain that Meinong continued to hold these views after he had forsaken psychologism, and most of their arguments concerning his philosophy stem from this interpretation.

54. See Chapter One, pt. 2.

angle" from a particular shape, or "wax" from its texture or color, or "2+3=5" from a set of five ideas grouped in subsets of two and three. As long as empiricists chose to stress the physical analogy at the expense of the analytical approach, the legitimacy of their claim to be scientific philosophers could be questioned—and was in fact so questioned during the intellectual revolution—by those who identified scientific method with mathematical analysis.

Meinong's position on this issue in his early work was midway between Locke's conceptualism and Berkeley's supposed nominalism. He expounds it by drawing attention to certain emendations that Berkeley made in the second edition of the *Treatise*, in which he made an allowance for mental operations. Berkeley had written: "And here it must be acknowledged that a man may consider a figure merely as triangular, without attending to the particular qualities of the angles or relations of the sides. So far he may abstract, but this will never prove that he can frame an abstract, general, inconsistent idea of a triangle." [55]

Meinong focuses on the word "attending" in this passage, which he claims is the operation of abstraction. He defines abstraction as an activity "through which one or a number of presentations are separated or set off from a larger idea complex. There can be no talk of abstraction before such a complex is present." [56] Abstract ideas such as "triangle" thus do not occur except as parts of a concrete whole, such as a triangle of a particular shape. It is the presence of abstraction that allows us momentarily to separate out the parts. Thus analysis is possible, but its results do not have a lasting existence. As for Berkeley, Meinong asserts that he was not a nominalist after all because of this emendation, and that Hume, who denied such operations, was the first true nominalist. [57]

The second *Hume-Study* (1882) is entitled "Theory of Relations." Relations are another set of ideas that are not given immediately in sensation and are essential to abstract reasoning. Once again, Meinong develops his own position through a critical study of the empiricists, particularly Hume's classification of relations. Meinong shows that some relational notions are more basic than others, namely equality, similarity, difference, and contrariety or incompatibility. [58]

---

55. Berkeley, *Treatise*, p. 16, quoted in Meinong, *Hume-Studien I, GA*, I, 14.
56. Meinong, *Hume-Studien I, GA*, I, 11.
57. *Ibid.*, p. 35.
58. Meinong, *Hume-Studien II, GA*, II, 45–58. Meinong seeks to show that Hume's other classes of relations—namely identity, space and time, quantity, quality, and

Except for the latter, which is the result of judgment, these relations are products of a second mental operation, comparison.[59] We compare two ideas with two color-attributes, for example, and find them to be equal, similar, or different. Comparison is also a function of attention, as it shifts its view from one idea to another. Then the ideas of equality, similarity, or difference appear in consciousness.[60]

Such a view of relations would seem essential to explain any continuity of our knowledge over time, at least for an empiricist who rejected the laws of association as the main explanatory mechanism for mental coherence—as Meinong did. For if we have an idea of a red ball at one time, and a red house at another, why do we naturally apply the concept "red" to both? What leads us to believe that the "red" in one belongs to the same category as the "red" of the other? Meinong's answer is: we engage in the operation of comparison between the two objects, and find them to be equal or similar to each other. The resemblance of this position to Kantian idealism may be noted, insofar as the coherence and continuity of experience is imposed by the mind itself, rather than coming self-evidently from reality. Meinong recognized as much when he called these relations "ideal."[61] He believed that the knowledge of these relational ideas was a priori, valid independently of experience. In other words, the difference between the ideas of red and green, or the similarity between two shades of red, is evident immediately upon comparison. Although it arises from the experience of the two ideas that are compared, it does not depend on this experience for its truth. If this were the case, we should have to test it over a period of time by repeating the comparison.

Meinong was nevertheless too steeped in empiricism to adopt the Kantian position completely. In his subsequent development he sought to steer clear of the ultimate implications of this view. Meanwhile, even in the second *Hume-Study*, he stressed that not all basic relations were "ideal." There were also "real" relations, which included

causality—are either derivative of these basic relations or are not, properly speaking, relations at all. Meinong also restores the relation of "difference," which Locke posited but Hume discarded. Meinong's later comments on causality are noteworthy, because they coincide with Mach's notion of functional dependence. Hume had defined causality in terms of constant conjunction of ideas in time, and Meinong states that these are in turn functions of "difference" in units of time (p. 118). Findlay has noted that Einstein's relations of space-time can be inserted into Meinong's theory without any change in meaning (Findlay, *Meinong's Theory*, p. 132).

59. Meinong, *Hume-Studien II, GA*, II, 42.
60. *Ibid.*, pp. 41–42.    61. *Ibid.*, p. 142.

the connections between the mental states that are given to us in intro-spection—for example, the relation between act and content, or be-tween ideas, judgments, and emotional experiences. But relations be-tween physical events were not included.[62]

The second *Hume-Study* also contains the germs of Meinong's later non-psychologistic views. In the course of that work, Meinong devel-ops other characteristics of relations both ideal and real which are not necessarily connected to the mental operations that form them or to their status as ideas. The relation "difference between red and green," for example, is dependent on "red" and "green"; Meinong calls "red" and "green" *fundaments* of the relation.[63] This notion is of great im-portance to Meinong. A relation is not complete without its funda-ments. The idea of "difference" is not yet a relation, but only the "dif-ference between red and green." We can have an idea of "difference" in isolation to be sure, but it is an abstraction. Furthermore, funda-ments can endure without relations, but the converse is not true. Rela-tions are dependent elements; fundaments are independent. The fundaments may themselves be relations, but they in turn must have other ideas as fundaments, and such a series cannot go on ad infini-tum. The ultimate foundation of the structure must consist of non-relational ideas.

Meinong was to retain these ideas throughout his life; we can trace them from his early theory of relations to his later realism. Relations may not be divided into their fundaments without some loss of mean-ing; that is, relations and fundaments are not logically homogeneous. But relations depend on fundaments, because without them they would become inexcusably vague. "A relation without absolute funda-ments," in Meinong's own words, "would be a comparison in which nothing is compared."[64] The fundaments thus retain the constancy of the traditional atomic "idea." The proper relationship of complexes such as relations to simple constituents is one of logical dependence or presupposition.

This psychologistic theory of relations was better equipped to deal with some problems than with others. It implied, for example, a plau-sible account of fictitious objects that was in accord with common sense. A unicorn or a golden mountain was simply a combination of subjective contents of ideas. On the other hand, Meinong's theory was obviously at odds with common sense in respect to real objects, and Meinong explicitly addressed himself to this divergence. If evidence

62.  *Ibid.*     63.  *Ibid.*, p. 45.     64.  *Ibid.*, p. 44.

for belief in external reality is so untrustworthy, he asked, why then do most people persist in being realists?[65] Meinong felt that if his epistemology could not justify the belief in external reality, it must at least provide some account of how men come to hold it. At this point, Meinong turned to his third operation, that of indirect ideation, which is built on the relations of comparison.[66] We may briefly characterize indirect ideation as the attribution of properties to something unknown by way of its relation to something known. Suppose, for example, that I am seeing a painting that hangs on my living room wall. By the introspective criterion, I know that there is at present an idea of this painting in my mind. Suppose further that I now remember gazing at the painting yesterday. My memory may be deceptive; it does not deliver the immediate evidence of inner perception. But if I *compare* my present idea with my memory, I have no difficulty in discerning a similarity between the two. Moreover, assuming that my memory is in some degree accurate, I can say further that there is some similarity between the content of my present memory and that of my idea yesterday. This allows me to say something determinate about my previous idea: it stands in a relation of similarity to my present one. Now when I commonsensically attribute certain colors to the painting itself, I am indulging in the same kind of operation: I am asserting that the picture is in some way similar to the content of my idea.

The importance of indirect ideation in Meinong's work, both early and late, can hardly be overestimated. It serves several functions in describing how we employ abstract reasoning. For one thing, it leads us to the concept of identity. Meinong defines identity as "the property of a thing to be a fundament for several relations; assertions about identity are resolvable into assertions of relation."[67] To continue the previous example: I base my view that the painting on the wall is the same object that was there yesterday on the fact that the relations between the painting and my idea of it yesterday agree with those between the painting and my present idea of it. Meinong gives the following example:

Suppose someone wants to describe a person whom he associates with. He might say: he is as tall as I, has chestnut brown hair, etc. The speaker here establishes a relation between the height of X and his own height; both fundaments are known to him and the comparison can proceed as normal. Quite different, however, is the psychic state of the hearer, who does not

65. *Ibid.*, p. 145.　　66. *Ibid.*, p. 146.　　67. *Ibid.*, pp. 135f.

know X. He knows the height of the speaker, is informed of a relative datum, and is able to construct, so to speak, the other fundament from the one . . . given fundament and the relation.[68]

This is a case of an abstract individual concept, like the cabinet-maker who made the writing table. We arrive at all such concepts by indirect ideation.[69] Another use is in the treatment of continua that are not obviously divisible into discrete parts. If, for example, we are trying to decide whether a certain shade of color is a bright orange or a dark yellow, we are in effect asking: is this particular sector of the color spectrum more similar to orange or to yellow?[70]

Meinong made the further far-reaching claim that relative determination is at the root of all mathematical operations:

> The axiom: two quantities which are equal to a third must be equal to each other, is nothing but the general formulation of such a case. One sees at first sight that all of mathematics is occupied in the first place with cases of this kind, since it is of the greatest consequence for mathematics to attain the greatest possible generality and therefore independence from the special determinations of size or place.[71]

He was later to exploit this insight in his article of 1896 on Weber's Law, in which he defined all measurement as a comparison of parts (with the help of physical operations such as laying a ruler on the thing measured).[72] But already in the *Hume-Studies*, Meinong anticipated one of the major links between mathematics and philosophy.

Indirect ideation, then, was the culmination of Meinong's theory of mental operations, one which survived intact into his later, realistic period. The fruitfulness of this concept shows why Meinong was such an interesting atomist. For even within the confines of psychologism, Meinong developed implicitly what he was later to assert: we establish the qualities of a real, objective world by means of the relations and interconnections between elements. We build up a context of experiences, bringing in memories and relating them to our immediate experiences, and through such a context we extend our knowledge. In this respect, Meinong's epistemology resembles none more than Locke's. For Locke, too, saw the expansion of demonstrative knowledge to lie in our ability to establish relations between relations. Mein-

68. *Ibid.*, p. 83.
69. Meinong, *Hume-Studien I*, *GA*, I, 24.
70. Meinong, "Empfindung," *GA*, I, 126.
71. Meinong, *Hume-Studien II*, *GA*, II, 85.
72. Meinong, "Über die Bedeutung des Weber'schen Gesetzes," *GA*, II, 271.

ong pointed out that Locke's epistemology was essentially a continuation of his theory of relations.[73]

At the same time, Meinong's attempt to integrate empiricism and rationality laid bare some of the tensions within the empiricist tradition. One such tension was that between his use of the introspective criterion, which limited knowledge to the realm of the psyche, and his common sense, which he could not entirely suppress even in his scientific philosophizing. The tension was entirely explicit: as we have seen, Meinong described at some length the ways in which men apply concepts to physical reality, while at the same time denying that it was legitimate for them to do so. His interest in expanding the role of reasoning led him to a solution of this impasse that resembled that of Kant. Indeed, Meinong's emphasis on indirect ideation showed that the ideal relations, which is to say the products of comparison, were basic in accounting for our notions of the structure of the external world—however illegitimately. Meinong's final assessment of these commonsensical notions in the *Hume-Studies* was that they were useful fictions. He claims that physical objects have certain objective determinate properties which, if we *could* compare them to our ideas, *would* lead to similarity between them.[74] This doctrine of "As If" resembles remotely Kant's "regulative" use of reason, which was given wide circulation by Meinong's Neo-Kantian contemporary Hans Vaihinger.[75]

Underlying this tension between introspection and common sense lay a deeper one involving the three assumptions of empiricism that we have isolated. On the one hand, Meinong inherited a commitment to the atomistic model: it was evident in his demand that all relations presuppose fundaments: the "reds" and the "greens" underlying such higher-level concepts as "difference" and "similarity." Were this not the case, our talk of relations would contain an element of vagueness. And yet, when we go to look for these atomic parts, we find that we must analyze them out of our complex, changing introspective data: they are not immediately given to experience. We can only find "red" already embedded in a concrete complex idea: we cannot assume, as Locke did, that such ideas as "red" or "triangle" exist separately. To-

---

73. Meinong, *Hume-Studien II, GA*, II, 23.

74. *Ibid.*, p. 144.

75. If I understand Kant's concept of the regulative employment of reason correctly, its fictional aspect is the exact inverse of Meinong's, namely that our reason has such properties that, if objects *did* exist, they *would* conform to that reason. See Kant's analogy with a mirror, *Critique of Pure Reason*, trans. Norman Kemp Smith, 2nd ed. (New York: St. Martin's Press, 1964), pp. 533, 551ff, 698ff.

gether with Berkeley and Hume, Meinong rejected this assumption. To remain true to introspection, then, involves denying the precision that can only come from analysis. To arrive at such precise parts, we must ignore part of the data of introspection. In this respect, the discrepancy between empiricism and positivism persisted.

It is instructive to compare Meinong's handling of this tension with that of Mach. By emphasizing atomism and analysis while slighting introspection, Mach had brought empiricism and positivism closer together. According to Mach, the images of reality that appear in consciousness could in fact be analyzed and separated to conform to the elementary data of physics and physiology. Meinong opposed Mach's position in his article "On the Concept and Properties of Sensation" (1888), in which he sought to define the notion of sensation according to his hybrid model.[76] Meinong upheld the notion that ideas such as "red" and "orange" were indeed simple, as is evident to introspection, rather than compounds of light-waves or nerve impulses. Meinong did not deny the fact that color perception was explicable in terms of such physical or physiological facts, but he did deny that we actually *see* a compound when we see a color; if this were the case, we could analyze the components through the operation of abstraction, as we might do in a multicolored painting. But given the sensation of red per se, this operation fails us. Red, therefore, must be simple. The relation of light-waves or nerve impulses to this sensation is one of cause and effect, but not one of parts to whole.[77] On the other hand, Meinong was forced to see that this position meant that such "sensations" were at the same time concepts: for "red" and "orange" do not occur in consciousness divorced from other concrete attributes any more than does "triangle."[78]

It was during the 1890s that Meinong was forced to reconsider the problem of the relation of sensations to concepts, as well as the meaning of the concepts "whole" and "part." This confrontation was to lead him out of psychologism.

76. Meinong, "Empfindung," *GA*, I, 182, where sensation is defined as "a simple perceptual idea from peripheral stimulation." The latter notion is arrived at through a discussion of Wundt's interpretation.

77. *Ibid.*, pp. 131–135.

78. *Ibid.*, pp. 127–129. Moreover, Meinong further concedes that these concepts are formed not by abstraction, but by indirect ideation: we arrive at color concepts by comparing certain parts of the complex color continuum and finding them similar or different; only as a result of such comparisons do we start labeling the fundaments as the different colors.

# V

# THE REVOLT AGAINST

# PSYCHOLOGISM, 1890–1905

### 1. The Philosophy of Mathematics and Logic: Frege, Husserl, Boltzmann

Meinong's journey away from psychologism was made in response to two problems that confronted him in the 1890s. The first was the controversy over Gestalt qualities, which led him to examine the question of the relation of wholes and parts. The second was the status of nonexistence, a problem which appeared as an unexpected ramification of his theory of values, on which he published his first treatise in 1894. To appreciate the significance of these questions, we must first present the growing opposition to psychologism among philosophers and scientists in some detail.

The most common objection to psychologism was that it failed to give an adequate account of the objectivity of knowledge or thought. To relate all of philosophy to human experience was to chain it to something limited in space and time and therefore fallible and arbitrary. If psychologism had arisen as a healthy reaction against an overly speculative philosophy, it had in turn led to excesses of its own. It was in the area of logic and mathematics that these excesses were most conspicuous, and in which psychologism became especially vulnerable: the truth or validity of "$2 + 3 = 5$" obviously lies in something other than the association of the idea of two apples with the idea of three apples. If this is not evident to the reader, he need merely try to apply it to a more complicated addition: imagine the truth of "$999,999 + 1 = 1,000,000$" by picturing apples. Yet this would be the implication of John Stuart Mill's proposal that the laws of logic were a special case of the law of association.

One of the first thinkers to criticize this sort of psychologism was the mathematician and philosopher Gottlob Frege, who was still virtually unknown when he published his *Foundations of Arithmetic* in 1884. The book was an investigation of the whole concept of number, which practicing mathematicians had usually taken for granted. Frege stated his opposition to a psychologistic interpretation of number in the introduction:

> Sensations are absolutely no concern of arithmetic. No more are mental pictures, formed from the amalgamated traces of earlier sense-impressions. All these phases of consciousness are characteristically fluctuating and indefinite, in strong contrast to the definiteness and fixity of the concepts and objects of mathematics. It may, of course, serve some purpose to investigate the ideas and changes of ideas which occur during the course of mathematical thinking; but psychology should not imagine that it can contribute anything whatever to the foundation of arithmetic.[1]

As a child, one may learn arithmetic through the association of images, but to reduce all of logic to such a process is to return to such a childlike, primitive stage in the history of civilization:

> Often it is only after immense intellectual effort, which may have continued over centuries, that humanity at last succeeds in achieving knowledge of a concept in its pure form, in stripping off the irrelevant accretions which veil it from the eyes of the mind. What, then, are we to say of those who, instead of advancing this work where it is not yet completed, despise it, and betake themselves to the nursery, or bury themselves in the remotest conceivable periods of human evolution, there to discover, like *John Stuart Mill*, some gingerbread or pebble arithmetic![2]

Such statements must be seen in the light of Frege's proclaimed intellectual mission: to show the new relevance of mathematics to philosophy, thanks to the gradual convergence of mathematics and logic that had occurred, almost unnoticed, in the nineteenth century. A number of logicians (G. Boole, E. Schröder, G. Peano, and C. S. Peirce, among others) had been attempting to work out algebraic symbols to replace words in the traditional logical syllogisms. Frege was the first to propose that statements in arithmetic could be written in logical form, and developed a system of notation (Begriffsschrift) to do this.

---

1. Gottlob Frege, *The Foundations of Arithmetic*, trans. J. L. Austin (Oxford: Basil Blackwell, 1950), pp. v–vi[e].
2. *Ibid.*, p. vii[e].

Through such a system, any ambiguities that might dwell in ordinary words when used in logical reasoning could be eliminated. Although Frege did not himself accomplish this project, his work was revolutionary in that it provided the stimulus and many of the conceptual distinctions necessary to do so. By the 1920s, the results had transformed the empiricist tradition and brought about the most radical changes in logic since the days of Aristotle.[3]

How could such a revolution in logical notation affect other areas of philosophy and thought, such as the problems of epistemology? Frege did not shrink from exploring these implications, and we shall take them up in the next chapter. As for Frege's critique of psychologism, it extended to less obvious cases, such as the attempt to define abstract concepts in terms of mental operations. Our activities of attention and comparison are just as subject to whim and mood as the association of our ideas. In a review of another student of Brentano who had employed such a notion, Frege wrote in 1894:

> Inattention is a very strong lye; it must be applied at not too great a concentration, so that everything does not dissolve, and likewise not too dilute, so that it effects a sufficient change in the things. Thus it is a question of getting the right degree of dilution; this is difficult to manage, and I at any rate have never succeeded.[4]

The author in question was Edmund Husserl, and Frege's criticisms undoubtedly prompted Husserl to move away from the psychologism of his early *Philosophy of Arithmetic* to the "pure logic" of the *Logical Investigations* of 1900–1901. The first volume of this work was in effect an anti-psychologism manifesto, stating the case in the broadest possible terms. According to Husserl, psychology is an empirical science, and its laws apply to phenomena that occur together or follow one another in time. The law of association is just such a case. It says that when we experience the idea of two, followed by that of three, the idea of five will immediately occur to us. But his "law," like any empirical law, is merely probabilistic. I cannot predict with certainty that the idea of five will invariably follow the association. I can merely induce that such a sequence is likely.[5] Moreover, should I make an error in adding, presumably an association has also taken place. Thus the law

3. Michael Dummett, *Frege* (London: Duckworth, 1973), p. 8.

4. Frege, Review of Husserl's *Philosophie der Arithmetik*, in *Translations from the Philosophical Writings of Gottlob Frege*, trans. Peter Geach and Max Black (Oxford: Basil Blackwell, 1966), p. 84.

5. Edmund Husserl, *Logical Investigations*, I, 106.

of association provides us with no criterion for distinguishing true logical statements from false ones. More fundamentally, the propositions of logic and mathematics are not probabilistic; they admit of no exceptions, but are instead universally necessary. In short, they are deductive rather than inductive.[6] Therefore they cannot be derived from experience.

Such an argument was clearly directed against empiricism itself as applied to logic, as Husserl explicitly stated.[7] Empiricism led inevitably to skepticism and "subjectivism," in claiming that all truth was relative to some human, time-bound category. This danger was inherent not only in the notion that logic is a matter of individual experience, but also in the notion, held by some, that it was relative to the constitution of the human mind as such—meaning that logical truths are founded on mental habits that are common to mankind, regardless of cultural background. Husserl called this "species-relativism" or "anthropologism."[8] It would of course apply to any doctrine that sought to reduce logic to something "culture-bound," such as a set of linguistic conventions. As long as logic remained tied to such notions, it would be useless in leading to truly objective knowledge.

It was on this ground that Husserl extended his critique to include the Neo-positivist theory of the economy of thought. According to Mach and Avenarius, all conceptual thought was a striving for simple description, by subsuming the greatest number of empirical facts under the fewest concepts—and as such was a case of biological adaptation of the species. While Husserl admitted that such a principle was useful in the practical aspects of logic (for example, deciding whether to use one set of symbols over another), it was no substitute for the validation of deductive truths.[9] What appears to be "economical" is as subject to historical fluctuations as the laws of psychology are subject to changes in mood. It may have been more difficult and less "economical" to think of the world as round before 1492, given the data of common sense and science. But it was no less true. As Husserl put it: "The ideal validity of the norm is the *presupposition* of every meaningful talk of economy of thought, therefore it is no possible explanatory result of the theory of this economy."[10] Insofar as the principle of economy of thought was a pragmatic criterion of knowledge, Husserl's op-

6. *Ibid.*, I, 99.    7. *Ibid.*, I, 115ff.

8. *Ibid.*, I, 138. Husserl's term is "spezifischer Relativismus," which Findlay translates as "specific." It is clear from the context, however, that Husserl does not mean "specific" in the ordinary English sense of the term.

9. *Ibid.*, I, 204ff.    10. *Ibid.*, I, 209.

position to psychologism may be presumed to extend to pragmatism.

Husserl argued that although logic may be able to do without empirical science, empirical science could not do without logic. If philosophy was to provide a rigorous foundation for the sciences, then the categories and laws of logic—and their relation to human experience—must be explored to a much greater degree than even Kant had done.[11] Phenomenology, as we will see, was to provide an important step in this exploration.

During the same years that Husserl was working out his program, Mach's theory was coming under increasing attack from physicists themselves. Although they did not use the term "psychologism," many of their objections centered on similar—though not always identical—issues. The 1890s and 1900s were, in fact, rich years for the philosophy of science, which was undergoing its own "revolution" independently of the theory of relativity and quantum mechanics. Among the classics that appeared during this period were Heinrich Hertz's *Principles of Mechanics* (1894), Henri Poincaré's *Science and Hypothesis* (1902), and Pierre Duhem's *The Aim and Structure of Physical Theory* (1904). We cannot consider these works in detail, but will concentrate on those of one physicist who sought to refute Mach in his own terms: Ludwig Boltzmann, one of the most distinguished theoretical physicists of his day, a founder of statistical mechanics, and a defender of atomism.

The occasion for Boltzmann's criticism was the movement among physicists known as "Energeticism," led by the physical chemist Wilhelm Ostwald. Ostwald, who claimed to be following Kirchhoff's prescription of describing in the simplest manner, took up Mach's thesis that the atomic hypothesis in physics was unnecessary. But Ostwald went further than Mach: he boldly claimed that all the phenomena that atomism had purported to explain could be subsumed under the concept of energy. Ostwald presented his views in 1895 in a speech with the provocative title "The Overcoming of Scientific Materialism." It was energy, not matter, he claimed, that worked on the senses; the notion of bits of matter as the constituents of bodies was not only unobservable, but an anthropomorphism, an outmoded and simplistic image of what the world is like.[12]

11. *Ibid.*, I, 214f, 236ff.

12. Wilhelm Ostwald, *Die Überwindung des wissenschaftlichen Materialismus* (Leipzig: Veit and Comp., 1895), pp. 16, 22, 32f. For a general account of the changes in the philosophy of science at this time, see Cassirer, *Problem of Knowledge*, trans. William H. Woglom and Charles W. Hendel (New Haven: Yale University Press, 1950), Ch. V.

Ostwald's speech provoked a quick rebuttal from Boltzmann. In an article entitled "A Word from Mathematics to Energetics" (1896), Boltzmann pointed out the shoddiness of Ostwald's energy concepts in mathematical terms.[13] Although he did not deny Ostwald's goal of descriptive simplicity, he showed that the claims of the energy concept to serve such a description were premature. (Indeed, his work in the founding of statistical mechanics, together with Einstein's experiment on the photoelectric effect, eventually forced Ostwald to admit his error.)[14]

Boltzmann continued his offensive with two further articles in 1897 attacking Mach's conceptions directly, including his phenomenalism. Boltzmann argued in effect that the reduction of all scientific material to sensation was not really "economical" at all, since the mathematics involved in translating physical concepts into sensations was complicated and cumbersome.[15] Even in terms of Mach's own criterion, then, the doctrine of sensations failed. On this basis, Boltzmann went on to argue that epistemological realism, which admitted the objective existence of atoms, was preferable to Mach's phenomenalism (Boltzmann was possibly influenced by Meinong in some particulars of this argument).[16] At the same time, Boltzmann admitted, the doctrine of atomism itself was in the process of transformation. The phenomenalists had been correct in claiming that the previous view of atoms as hard, indestructible bits of matter had been outmoded by the developments in electromagnetic theory. Indeed, the old characteristic of permanence, which Mach had attacked particularly, had proved

13. Ludwig Boltzmann, "Ein Wort der Mathematik an die Energetik," in *Populäre Schriften* (Leipzig: Johann Ambrosius Barth, 1905), pts. A and B.

14. Cassirer, *Problem of Knowledge*, p. 103.

15. Boltzmann, "Über die Unentbehrlichkeit der Atomistik in der Naturwissenschaft," *Populäre Schriften*, pp. 147f.

16. Boltzmann, "Über die Frage nach der objektiven Existenz der Vorgänge in der unbelebten Natur," *Populäre Schriften*, pp. 172f. I base this conjecture on two facts: (1) There is a pointed similarity between a passage in Boltzmann's writings and that of Meinong with respect to the role that memory plays in leading to knowledge (Boltzmann, p. 132; see Meinong, *GA*, II, 204, 207f.); (2) Boltzmann was a professor at Graz in the 1880s and was on the faculty committee which recommended Meinong for promotion. The report, signed by Boltzmann and two other professors, reflects a familiarity with Meinong's second *Hume-Study*, the book on propaedeutics, and the article on memory (*Ministerium* Records, Meinong file, No. 400989). Meinong's correspondence reveals an informal conversation with Boltzmann on experimental psychology (Meinong to Höfler, March 10, 1886, Meinong *Nachlass*, Carton 52, No. 4463).

to be indefensible.[17] But, even admitting this fact, Boltzmann claimed that *some* form of atomism was absolutely necessary to natural science in its current form.

The core of Boltzmann's argument is most illuminating for understanding the transformation of positivism from Mach to Wittgenstein. It centered on Boltzmann's view of the role of atomism in differential calculus. Mach had claimed that atoms could be eliminated by describing the causal relations which emanated from them in terms of functional relationships, expressed in differential equations. Yet he had postulated "atoms" of his own, sensations, as the fundaments of these relationships. Boltzmann argued that no user of differential equations could do otherwise:

> On closer inspection, a differential equation is only the expression for the fact that one must first think of a *finite number*; this is the first precondition. . . . Thus if I declare the differential equation, or a formula which contains definite integrals, to be the most suitable model (Bild), I give in to an illusion if I think I have banished the atomistic idea from my thoughts; for without it the concept of limit is senseless [emphasis added].[18]

In other words, mathematical analysis presupposes atomism. So long as one is dealing in phenomena that require description in terms of differential calculus, one must suppose that such phenomena are composed of parts that can be treated separately. And conversely, atomism finds its meaning primarily in the context of the analytical approach, rather than in that of physical nature itself or psychology. It was precisely as a model that atomism was necessary.

Thus Boltzmann saved the theoretical notion of the atom before its usefulness had been confirmed by the quantum theory in the 1900s. It is important to note, however, that just as the new atomism of "subatomic" physics bore little resemblance to the old, so did Boltzmann's treatment of the atomistic model completely transform it. For Boltzmann concedes that atomism is first and foremost a theoretical tool, a requirement of mathematics rather than a fact of nature. Like the old psychological atom it provides a constant reference point, but differs from it because it is not caused by the physical object. It is, rather, a purely symbolic element.

In this way atomism for Boltzmann was a feature of the scientist's language rather than of his subject matter. Calculus must start with a

---

17. Boltzmann, "Unentbehrlichkeit der Atomistik," *Populäre Schriften*, p. 140.
18. *Ibid.*, p. 144.

finite number; but the choice of which number is up to the scientist or
mathematician. Whether his choice is correct depends on whether the
hypothesis he has framed is eventually confirmed. In this way, scientific knowledge contains both subjective and objective components:

> This mode of representation is characterized by the fact that at first we op-
> erate only with thought-abstractions, mindful of our task only to construct
> inner representation-pictures. Proceeding in this way, we do not as yet take
> possible experiential facts into consideration, but merely make the effort to
> develop our thought-pictures with as much clarity as possible and to draw
> from them all possible consequences. Only subsequently, after the entire
> exposition of the picture has been completed, do we check its agreement
> with experiential facts. We thus justify only afterwards why the picture had
> to be chosen in precisely this and in no other way; at the beginning we do
> not give the slightest hint about this. We shall call this method deductive
> representation.[19]

This passage makes clear that Boltzmann, despite his criticism of
Mach's subjectivism, nevertheless retained Mach's emphasis on "conventions" as the heart of scientific theories. And, as with Mach, the
validity of such conventions can only be secured in terms of their results. Mathematics, as a symbolic system, was in no "pre-established
harmony" with the world.

Seen together with the work of Frege and Husserl mentioned earlier, scientific philosophy during the intellectual revolution underwent a major shift in emphasis and interest: from epistemology to
logic and mathematics, from the question of "What can I know?" to
that of "How can I formulate?" It was this shift that removed such
philosophy further from the interests of the layman, as the relevance
of such questions to the crisis of humanism was not at all apparent.
But this is not to say that the epistemological questions through which
such concerns could be voiced had entirely disappeared, or that the
philosophers and scientists now ignored them. On the contrary, most
of them emphasized that the new philosophy of science did not at all

---

19. Boltzmann, "Die Grundprinzipien und Grundgleichungen der Mechanik"
(1899), trans. Rudolph Weingartner under the title "Theories as Representations," in
*Philosophy of Science*, ed. Arthur Danto and Sidney Morgenbesser (Cleveland: World
Publishing Co., Meridian Books, 1960), p. 249. In this article, Boltzmann points out the
similarity—and certain differences—between his view and that of Hertz. Boltzmann
does not subscribe to Hertz's view that theoretical models must conform to the "laws of
thought"; these may be relative to historical conditions. For a further discussion of
Hertz's important theory, see Janik and Toulmin, pp. 139ff.

impair the objectivity of scientific knowledge, but in fact insulated it from the skepticism that had sprung from the older empiricist tradition.

In Germany at least, the figure to whom these scientists and philosophers turned for inspiration on the question of objective and necessary truth was Immanuel Kant. The influence of Kant can be seen on practicing scientists themselves such as Hertz and Max Planck, as well as on philosophers who sought to interpret the new science in idealistic terms. The center of this latter activity was the Marburg School of Neo-Kantianism, founded by Hermann Cohen, and including as his students Paul Natorp and Ernst Cassirer. In the writings of Natorp, one finds the arguments against psychologism as early as 1883.[20] Cohen's work on the philosophy of science also followed the trend away from epistemology to logic, as the title of his systematic work, *The Logic of Pure Knowledge* (1902), indicates. Cohen emphasized that the freedom which the scientist exercises in his choice of theoretical concepts was an example of Kant's insistence on the spontaneity and creativity of reason, as opposed to the empiricists' emphasis on observation and experience. Indeed, Cohen claimed that science did not require an empirical "given" at all; its concepts were not abstractions from the concreteness of sensory experience, but products of the theoretician's active mind exclusively.[21] Cassirer went still further than his teacher and claimed that relations, so important in scientific theory, required no fundaments whatsoever, *contra* Meinong.[22] Such subjective choices were nevertheless made objective through the process of testing and of determining the application of such relations. On this matter, the Neo-Kantians departed from Kant: they denied that our knowledge of external reality was merely fictitious, but argued that science enables us to know nature in all its detail—precisely through the developed system of relations. In Cohen's phrase, "Idealism is the true realism."[23] Once again, the criterion for determining which relations were applicable to reality was pragmatic:

20. Marvin Farber, *The Foundation of Phenomenology* (Cambridge: Harvard University Press, 1943), p. 5.

21. Hermann Cohen, *Logik der reinen Erkenntniss* (Berlin: Bruno Cassirer, 1902), pp. 33, 68ff.

22. Cassirer, *Substance and Function*, p. 339. On the difference between Cohen and Cassirer on the need for fundaments of relations, see Dimitri Gawronsky, "Cassirer, His Life and Work," in *The Philosophy of Ernst Cassirer*, ed. Paul Arthur Schilpp (La Salle, Ill.: Open Court Publishing Company, 1949), p. 21.

23. Cohen, *Logik*, p. 511.

as Cassirer made plain, subjective theories are "objectified" by their results.[24]

One might ask of these idealistic interpreters whether the pragmatic criterion was any sure guarantee against skepticism—whether the fallibility of human cognition was decisively corrected by the collective judgment of the scientific community. What prevented Neo-Kantianism from being a form of "species-relativism"? The answer that the Neo-Kantians themselves gave was clear: the proof lies in the history of science and its unilinear progress. The goal of science has always been to find a unity of understanding, and any disagreements or uncertainties among scientists have always served as a means to this end (Max Planck stressed this point also in his attack on Machian subjectivism in 1905).[25] Cassirer's brilliant *Substance and Function* (1911), for instance, is full of such teleologically formed statements; for example: "The complete concept of thought thus re-establishes the harmony of being. The inexhaustibleness of the problem of science is no sign of its fundamental insolubility, but the condition and stimulus for its progressively complete solution."[26]

In this sense, these new, scientific Kantians followed the same path that the romantic and Hegelian post-Kantians had trod: the objectivity of knowledge is guaranteed by the fact that history is rational. In the work of Cassirer, such an assumption yielded a rich dividend for intellectual historians. Not surprisingly, some of Cohen's students also arrived at a Marxist position and became prominent Social Democrats (one of them, Kurt Eisner, became a radical and met his death as head of the Bavarian Republic in 1918).[27] Thus Kant, no less than Mach, served as a model for those who sought to refine socialism. The most prominent Marxist revisionists, Bernstein and Jaurès, both appealed to the philosopher of Königsberg to support their views.

As far as the philosophy of logic and mathematics was concerned, however, the Marburg Neo-Kantians failed to win an enduring following among specialists in this area. Most of these logicians, despite their awareness of the importance of relative conventions, could not accept the proposition that these conventions were so divorced from the empirically given as the idealists had claimed. Some other recon-

24.  Cassirer, *Substance and Function*, pp. 318f.

25.  Max Planck, "The Unity of the Physical World-Picture," trans. Ann Toulmin, in *Physical Reality*, ed. Stephen Toulmin (New York: Harper and Row, Torchbooks ed., 1970), pp. 21, 25.

26.  Cassirer, *Substance and Function*, p. 325.

27.  Lichtheim, pp. 290ff.

ciliation of idealism and realism was needed, one which would avoid the traps of the earlier psychologism. It was to the analysis of language itself that these philosophers—such as Frege and Russell—turned in order to meet this need.

## 2. The Revolt Against Psychologism in the Social Sciences: James, Weber, Dilthey

If the opposition to psychologism in the hands of the Marburg Neo-Kantians led to a celebration of reason, it could equally lead to an understanding of the limits of reason and a better appreciation of the irrational. Indeed, one source of opposition to psychologism in philosophy was a set of new developments in psychology itself, which emphasized the dynamic rather than the static aspects of mind. As long as psychology had shouldered the burden of answering the great philosophical questions we have about the world, it seemed imperative that the structure of the world be imbedded in the model of the mind. The psyche had to be a faithful microcosm, or as the Neo-Kantian Paul Natorp put it, a "second object-world, even a second 'Nature.'"[28] The pursuit of analogies to physics in psychology found here its justification. But the development of psychology itself in the 1890s, beyond the level of sensations, showed just how limited these analogies were.

No one was more perceptive in discerning this than William James. James pointed to the "psychologist's fallacy" in his *Psychology* of 1890.[29] This fallacy consisted in confusing the description of the object with the description of the mental state—a confusion that was bound to continue if psychology was to provide all the distinctions for logic, metaphysics, and other areas of philosophy. James wrote:

> Naming our thought by its own objects, we almost all of us assume that as the objects are, so the thought must be. The thought of several distinct things can only consist of several distinct bits of thought, or "ideas"; that of an abstract or universal object can only be an abstract or universal idea. . . . The thought of the object's recurrent identity is regarded as the identity of its recurrent thought; and the perceptions of multiplicity, of coexistence, of succession, are severally conceived to be brought about only through a multiplicity, a coexistence, a succession, of perceptions. The continuous flow of the mental stream is sacrificed, and in its place an atomism, a brickbat plan of construction, is preached, for the existence of which no good introspec-

28. Paul Natorp, *Allgemeine Psychologie* (Tübingen: J. C. B. Mohr, 1912), p. 16.
29. William James, *The Principles of Psychology*, I, 196–197.

tive grounds can be brought forward, and out of which presently grow all sorts of paradoxes and contradictions, the heritage of woe of students of the mind.[30]

James thus showed how the burden of psychologism had been connected to the atomistic model. The insufficiency of that model could only reinforce the arguments of Husserl and Frege that experience was fraught with vagaries. (Husserl in particular made great use of James's "stream of consciousness.")

Arguments against psychologism also found a prominent place among the founding fathers of sociology. Since psychology had been seen as the basis of social studies since the days of Mill, it is not surprising that this should be the case. Among the leading theoreticians of sociology, both Durkheim and Weber sought to show the autonomy of sociology while spelling out its relation to psychology. Very often, their lack of awareness of similar developments in the philosophy of natural science led to paradoxical results. For example, Durkheim is usually considered to be closer to the positivist tradition than Weber. But it was Weber's arguments that in fact more closely resemble the reinterpretation of positivism that was taking place at the same time. Durkheim's claim that "social facts" were independent of individual, psychological facts, is well known; but he sought to show this, in an article entitled "Individual and Collective Representations" (1898), by drawing analogies between psychology and sociology. Just as mental states are not reducible to the physiological sensations that make them up, but rather form a stream, so "collective representations" are not reducible to psychic ones but instead transform them through some causal process. The whole is greater than the sum of its parts.[31]

Max Weber, in his methodological writings, also attacked psychologism in the social sciences (as well as historicism, for which he is perhaps better known). For example, the fact that the law of marginal utility in economics had the same mathematical formula as the Weber-Fechner law in psychology had led some economists (including Lujo Brentano, Franz's brother) to argue that the former was merely a special case of the latter. Weber addressed a polemical article to this question in which he defined his view of the relation of psychology and the social sciences quite clearly:

30.   *Ibid.*, pp. 195–196.
31.   Emile Durkheim, "Individual and Collective Representations," in *Sociology and Philosophy*, trans. D. F. Pocock (New York: The Macmillan Co., The Free Press, 1974), pp. 2, 12, 26. Durkheim further claims that "individualistic sociology is only applying the old principles of materialist metaphysics to social life" (p. 29).

The law of marginal utility and every economic "theory" whatsoever . . . does not analyze the *inner* experiences of daily life into psychical or psychophysical "elements" ("stimuli," "sensations," "reactions," "automism," "feelings," etc.), but attempts rather to "understand" certain "adaptations" of the *external* behavior of man to a definite sort of conditions of existence that lie *outside* of him.[32]

The subject matter of economics and sociology, then, is not composed of that of psychology, but is defined in a different context. Weber elsewhere gives an example:

A category such as "pursuit of gain" simply does not belong in any "psychology." For the "same" pursuit of "rentability" of the "same" business enterprise can, in the case of two successive owners . . . go hand in hand with absolutely heterogeneous "character qualities." [33]

This is not to say that individual experience is irrelevant to sociology; one needs only to glance at his basic definition to convince oneself of the contrary:

Sociology . . . is a science which attempts the interpretive understanding of social action. . . . In "action" is included all human behavior when and in so far as the acting individual attaches a subjective meaning to it.[34]

Indeed, Weber claims that the individual is the basic "atom" of sociological analysis, not a collective object as with Durkheim.[35] The difference between psychology and sociology, then, is that certain aspects of experiences are placed by the sociologist in a different context—that of the behavior of others. In the formulation of this context, there is plenty of room for the theoretician of society to construct concepts with the same freedom and independence from empirical reality, as with the physical scientist. Weber's definition of the "ideal type," his theoretical model, is very close to Boltzmann's "deductive representation":

In its conceptual purity, this mental construct cannot be found empirically anywhere in reality. It is a *utopia*. . . .
It has the significance of a purely ideal *limiting* concept with which the

32. Max Weber, "Die Grenznutzlehre und das 'psychophysische Grundgesetz'" (1908), in *Gesammelte Aufsätze zur Wissenschaftslehre*, 3rd ed., ed. Johannes Winckelmann (Tübingen: J. C. B. Mohr, 1968), p. 393.
33. Weber, "Über einige Kategorien der verstehenden Soziologie" (1913), *ibid.*, p. 430.
34. Weber, *The Theory of Social and Economic Organization*, trans. A. M. Henderson and Talcott Parsons (New York: The Free Press, 1964), p. 88.
35. Weber, "Über einige Kategorien," *Gesammelte Aufsätze*, p. 439.

real situation or action is *compared* and surveyed for the explication of certain of its significant components.[36]

Weber acknowledges further that the only criterion for judging the appropriateness of ideal types is pragmatic.[37] Weber himself employed his method to arrive at a typology of different kinds of social order (traditional, bureaucratic, charismatic), based on a comparative application of his ideal types to different cultural situations.

Among the opponents of positivism, Dilthey also exhibited a certain distancing from psychology as the fundamental science of the Geisteswissenschaften in the late 1890s. In "The Origin of Hermeneutics" (1900) Dilthey emphasized another operation that is a necessary part of knowledge: understanding. He explained its role as follows:

> Inner experience, in which I become aware of my own states, can never alone bring my own individuality to consciousness. Only in the comparison of my self with others do I gain the experience of what is peculiarly mine. . . . The existence of others, however, is given us at first only in the facts of the senses, in movements, sounds, and actions given from without. Only through a process of imitating that which comes to the senses in individual symbols, do we complete the inner dimension. . . . We call the process in which we know something inward through a symbol which is given sensibly from without: Understanding (Verstehen).[38]

This process further requires a system for interpreting such symbols: hermeneutics, a discipline that originally arose in connection with romantic philology. The new dimension of the epistemology of the Geisteswissenschaften, then, involved coming to grips not only with one's own experiences but also with the objective expression of others. In dealing with the latter, Dilthey was led to a consideration of the relation of symbols to reality—the same problem that confronted the logicians who had rejected idealism. Dilthey clearly saw this new discipline as part of the basis for the Geisteswissenschaften.[39] It was only after reading Husserl's *Logical Investigations*, however, that Dilthey was to return to his systematic work of providing these foundations. His attraction to Meinong's work came somewhat later, probably shortly before his death in 1910 (an undated postcard in Meinong's papers

36. Weber, "'Objectivity' in Social Science and Social Policy," in *Max Weber on the Methodology of the Social Sciences*, trans. and ed. Edward A. Shils and Henry A. Finch (Glencoe: The Free Press, 1949), pp. 90, 93.

37. Weber, "Über einige Kategorien," *Gesammelte Aufsätze*, p. 429.

38. Dilthey, "Die Entstehung der Hermeneutik," *GS*, V, 318.

39. *Ibid.*, p. 331.

from Dilthey read in part, "You will find in me an attentive and grateful reader").[40] The attraction to both Husserl and Meinong is explained by the fact that in their hands, the analysis of language and its relation to objects was integrated with psychological insights, so that a coherent description of the relations between experience, language, and reality resulted.

### 3. Meinong's Overcoming of Psychologism: The Emergence of the Theory of Objects of a Higher Order, 1890–1899

Meinong's correspondence of the 1890s indicates that he was planning an extended, systematic work on epistemology and the theory of relations.[41] Such a work was never accomplished. Instead, Meinong found himself developing in a different direction, which eventually led to the theory of objects, and in which psychological considerations no longer predominated. Although he did not arrive at this theory until 1905, he managed by 1899 to formulate an intermediate position, one that grew out of his theory of relations. This was the theory of "objects of a higher order" (*Gegenstände höherer Ordnung*). With this position, he decisively put aside his psychologism.

The impetus for the change came from a former student and close friend of his, Christian von Ehrenfels. The life and personality of this remarkable man deserve a brief digression, for he provides an illuminating contrast to Meinong, both in his works and his character. Whereas Meinong was the narrow, exact scientific philosopher, Ehrenfels was the grand speculator, seeking a Weltanschauung through philosophy to replace his lost religious faith.[42] Meinong's life work isolated him from most of the cultural and political movements of his time, whereas Ehrenfels managed to dabble in many of them. He was an ardent Wagnerian and faithful pilgrim to Bayreuth; before he turned to philosophy he had studied composition with Bruckner. In the early 1890s he was in Berlin, writing dramas and contributing to the *Freie Bühne*, a new literary organ and theater group whose members included Gerhart Hauptmann.[43] In 1896 he became a professor

---

40. Dilthey to Meinong, n.d., Meinong *Nachlass*, Carton 36, No. 1120.

41. Meinong to Johannes von Kries, August 17, 1892, in *Philosophenbriefe*, p. 111.

42. Imma Bodmershof, "Christian von Ehrenfels, Eine Skizze," *Gestalthaftes Sehen*, ed. Ferdinand Weinhandl (Darmstadt: Wissenschaftliche Buchgesellschaft, 1960), p. 428. The author is Ehrenfels' daughter.

43. Ehrenfels to Meinong, March 30, 1890, in *Philosophenbriefe*, p. 70.

in Prague, where Kafka was one of his students. While there, he became involved in the concerns of social Darwinism (he was on friendly
terms with Houston Stewart Chamberlain). His solution to the problem of the survival of the fittest was refreshingly atypical: the way to
prevent racial decadence was via polygamy.[44] Ehrenfels' publications
in favor of a freer sexual ethic won him an ally and friend in Sigmund
Freud.[45] At the same time Ehrenfels respected Meinong's method of
philosophizing and learned a great deal from it. As one might expect,
Ehrenfels was quick to apply Meinong's psychology of fantasy to his
own esthetic speculations. In an article on the limits of naturalism in
art in the *Freie Bühne* he wrote: "As important as conscientious observation may be for certain branches of art, its life-element is the form-
giving [gestaltende] and ordering fantasy."[46]

The relation between teacher and student was by no means one-
sided; it was Ehrenfels who stimulated Meinong to publish some of
his most interesting work—not only in the theory of relations and
complexes, but also in his value-theory.[47] Ehrenfels' publications "On
Feeling and Willing" of 1887 and "On Gestalt Qualities" of 1890, both
heavily indebted to Meinong's lectures, led Meinong to articulate his
own ideas in print.

Of these two articles, the second was of greater historical importance. Not only did it win for Ehrenfels the reputation of being a fore-
runner of the later Gestalt psychology—an honor that Meinong's theory of objects of a higher order shared—but it also triggered a
controversy in the 1890s that anticipated many of the basic themes of
the later movements. It was through this controversy, in part, that
Meinong's development took place.

Ehrenfels' approach to the Gestalt idea was typical of his wide range
of interest. He takes the notion from Mach's book on sensations, develops it as an utterly scientific fact, and goes on, later in life, to apply
it to art and metaphysics. The classic example of a Gestalt quality is
found in Mach:

> If two series of tones be begun at two different points on the scale, but be
> made to maintain throughout the same ratios of vibration, we recognize in

44. Ehrenfels, "Sexualethik," *Grenzfragen des Nerven-und Seelenlebens*, IX (1908),
80–81. On Ehrenfels and Kafka, see *The Diaries of Franz Kafka, 1910–1913*, ed. Max
Brod, trans. Joseph Kresh (New York: Schocken Books, 1965), p. 229.

45. Jones, *Freud*, II, 51.

46. Ehrenfels, "Wahrheit und Irrtum in Naturalismus," *Freie Bühne* II (1891), 739.

47. See Meinong, *Psychologisch-ethische Untersuchungen zur Werttheorie*, GA, III, 5;
"Über Werthaltung und Wert," *GA*, III, 247; *Über Annahmen*, 2d ed. (1910), pp. 288ff.

both the same melody, by a mere act of sensation, just as readily and immediately as we recognize in two geometrically similar figures, similarly situated, the same form [Gestalt].[48]

A melody or a figure, in short, is greater than the sum of its parts by virtue of its form. What, then, was such a "form"? For Mach, the answer had been simple and reductionistic: like all else, it was a sensation, grounded in physiology. Ehrenfels does not commit himself to this interpretation, but he claims that even if it were true, it would be incompatible with reductionism: the fact that one hears the same melody even when all the individual notes are different indicates that the process in the brain which corresponds to the melody must be different from that which corresponds to a succession of notes. His formulation, however, does not presume any such physiological theory; the evidence for Gestalt qualities lies simply in "the similarity of melodies and figures when their tonal or spatial components are generally different"—which is a formulation akin to Meinong's theory of relations.[49] Ehrenfels nevertheless accepts Mach's contention that our awareness of such a complex quality is not the result of conscious abstraction or comparison, but is immediately given along with the notes themselves.[50]

Meinong was sufficiently taken by the Gestalt-quality to write an extended review article on Ehrenfels' work, entitled "On the Psychology of Relations and Complexes" (1891). His approach to the same idea was predictably more cautious. He weighed Ehrenfels' argument carefully against other possible interpretations, but concluded that Mach and Ehrenfels had uncovered an undeniable empirical fact.[51] He went on to develop the similarities of these Gestalt-qualities to his own relations: the Gestalt-quality of a melody is logically dependent on the individual notes, just as the relation of difference is dependent on fundaments; but in neither case is the quality reducible to these elements. Meinong was also aware that Gestalt qualities did not result from the same mental operations as relations. Nevertheless, Meinong could not at first part with his view that mental activity was essential to such higher-level qualities: in perceiving a melody, he claimed, we must at least "group" the notes together somehow. Otherwise they would merely appear as individual notes. Indeed, Meinong's initial distinction between Gestalt and a relation was that the former de-

48. Mach, *Sensations*, p. 285; see Ehrenfels' reference in "Über Gestaltqualitäten," *Vierteljahrsschrift für wissenschaftliche Philosophie*, XIV (1890), 251.
49. *Ibid.*, p. 258.     50. *Ibid.*, p. 287.
51. Meinong, "Zur Psychologie der Komplexionen und Relationen," *GA*, I, 286f.

manded a lesser degree of mental activity.[52] By 1894 he was to call them a special case of relations, so that one could divide a melody into two sorts of components: its fundaments and its relations, or, as Meinong now called them, its "founded contents" (*fundierte Inhalte*).

The awkwardness of interpreting such perceptually founded contents as the product of mental operations remained, however, and became a source of further problems, which presented themselves as the decade progressed. Meinong soon found himself faced with the more radical implications of his doctrine, implications that he was unwilling to accept. The confrontation came through an article entitled "On Fusion and Analysis" (1892) by Hans Cornelius. Cornelius was a young psychologist-philosopher in Munich, who claimed to be a follower of Mach and Avenarius and later wrote a psychology in which all metaphysical presuppositions were supposedly excluded.[53] Cornelius built his empirical psychology on Brentanoan lines, and his terminology and outlook were close to Meinong's. He also admitted that Gestalt-qualities were empirical facts. Cornelius differed from Meinong, however, in his interpretation of them. He claimed that the activity of attention did not simply *lead* to our ideas of founded contents, but actually *transformed* the contents as it moved from fundaments to founded content.[54] His main example was the musical chord, in which the notes that made it up were fused (this tonal fusion, or Verschmelzung, had recently been pointed out by Stumpf in the second volume of his Tonpsychologie). Obviously the notes and the intervals founded on them do not maintain their identity in a chord in the way that they do in a melody. If parts lose their identity in complex wholes, then any sort of analytical approach—even if not reductionistic—is invalid; a characterization of complexes by way of their dependence on parts misses the crucial point. Such a criticism would apply to any whole in which the parts seemed indistinguishably merged, in which they "fused" or "flowed" into each other.

The argument that wholes materially altered their parts seriously undermined the analytical approach, as well as its assumption that parts could be treated out of context without distortion. It was this argument that stood at the core of the later Gestalt movement (Cor-

52. *Ibid.*, p. 296.

53. Hans Cornelius, *Psychologie als Erfahrungswissenschaft* (Leipzig: B. G. Teubner, 1897), p. iii.

54. Cornelius, "Über Verschmelzung und Analyse," *Vierteljahrsschrift für wissenschaftliche Philosophie*, XVI (1892), 417.

nelius was teaching at Frankfurt when Wertheimer formulated his initial ideas on Gestalt in 1912). Meinong, meanwhile, felt compelled to answer Cornelius, and did so in "Contributions to the Theory of Psychic Analysis" in 1894. In it, he sought to reexamine the analytical approach and defend it against Cornelius's attack. His main contention was that such elementary contents as sensations are unchanged in quality regardless of whether they are treated in context or isolated. They are not changed by mental activity, and therefore the operation of abstraction can do them no violence.[55] To use Cornelius's example of tonal fusion: the notes and intervals of a chord are perfectly distinct, as are the sensations caused by them. They simply appear to be merged because we do not notice them—we do not direct our judgment to them. It is the task of analysis (attention) to bring these parts into awareness, in the same way that it enables us to "pick out" the sounds of individual instruments from an orchestra.

In his examination of Cornelius's objections, however, Meinong was forced to the conclusion that there were some cases in which analysis *did* alter the contents of sensations: these were cases where something appears simple to begin with, but turns out to be complex. For example, a single tone is composed of a series of overtones, but, unlike a chord, it appears in the form of a single sensation. To separate the multiplicity of overtones in a single tone requires a more complicated analysis than the previous sort, and Meinong maintains that the mental process materially alters the results: the overtone series we have at the end is qualitatively different from the simple tone at the beginning.[56]

But this concession to a holistic approach still left Meinong with the awkwardness that had come with his acceptance of Gestalt qualities in the first place. The "relations" given in perception, such as the intervals between notes, are not ordinarily products of rational conceptualization, through abstraction, comparison, and indirect ideation, as were the original relations. They do not seem to be products of the mind in the same sense that the concepts "difference" or "similarity" may plausibly be said to be. On the other hand, neither is an "interval" a straightforward physical phenomenon like a note. Unless one accepted the Machian viewpoint, such Gestalt qualities were categorically different from physical elements. Gestalt qualities, then, were neither

---

55.  Meinong, "Beiträge zur Theorie der psychischen Analyse," *GA*, I, 316ff.

56.  Meinong, "Analyse," pp. 347ff, 354, 359, 366. Meinong does not, however, accept Cornelius's formulation of the problem (p. 359f).

psychical nor physical. What *were* they? Meinong announces, in the article on analysis, that he would deal with this question in a future article, which was to be entitled "On Objects of a Higher Order."[57]

A second route by which Meinong arrived at a non-psychologistic view was through his theory of values. Meinong had already lectured on this topic in the 1880s, but since Ehrenfels had referred to his work in print, he felt it was necessary to publish his own views on the subject. The result was the book *Psychological-Ethical Investigations on the Theory of Value* (1894). The work differs from those of the Neo-Kantians on the same subject, based as it is on an analysis of the experience of valuing something, rather than on the role of value-judgments as a logical presupposition for scientific theory. Meinong's value theory parallels his views on relations; just as his theory of relations is intertwined with his psychology of thinking, so his theory of value is linked to his psychology of feeling—as in Brentano. An object has value only for an individual person, and the index of this value is his emotional attachment to it.[58] Nevertheless, values are not merely subjective. It is, for example, valuable for a schoolboy to learn how to write, regardless of whether the boy feels so inclined. In his treatment of the objective aspect of values, Meinong was indebted to the work of the Austrian school of economics, which he had encountered as a student and to which he referred briefly in the *Investigations*.[59] This school, under the leadership of Carl Menger, had suggested a definition of value that was similar to Brentano's definition of intentionality—a relation between a state of consciousness and an objective economic good. In Menger's own words, "Value is the meaning which a concrete good . . . acquires for us, when we are aware of being dependent on its being at our disposal for the satisfaction of our needs."[60] Meinong's definition is more general, but similar: "An object has value insofar as it has the capacity, for the person who is sufficiently oriented and normally endowed, to be the actual basis for supplying a value feeling."[61] As with the rest of his philosophy at this stage, his value theory was psychologistic in a broad sense: the capacity for supplying a value-feeling may be attributable to an object even when the feeling is not actually present (as in the example of the schoolboy);

57.  *Ibid.*, p. 375.
58.  Meinong, *Psychologisch-ethische Untersuchungen, GA,* III, 27.
59.  *Ibid.*, pp. 17, 21.
60.  Carl Menger, *Grundsätze der Volkswirtschaftslehre*, p. 78.
61.  Meinong, *Psychologisch-ethische Untersuchungen, GA,* III, 37.

but there is no other way to define value except in relation to such a feeling.

Not all types of feeling yield values, Meinong claims. Simple sensory pleasures, for example, are not yet directed to values. It is only when we derive pleasure from a fact about the *existence* of such an object that we can be said to value it. I may enjoy the taste of a fine French wine; but we do not call such enjoyment a value-feeling. What I value is the fact that there *is* such a fine wine.[62] Furthermore, my value-feelings are often directed to the nonexistence of objects. My value-feeling about a fine wine may be heightened by the fact that I do not possess it.

Such thoughts of nonexistent objects were quite incompatible with Meinong's epistemological psychologism, and it was shortly after the appearance of the *Investigations* that he became aware of it. In response to an objection by Ehrenfels, Meinong published a subsequent article in 1895, "On Valuation and Value," in which the notion of nonexistence is given greater prominence. The question at hand involved the determination of the intensity of a value-feeling. In order to determine this, Meinong now argued, it is necessary to take into account the feelings aroused by the nonexistence of the object as well as its existence. In Meinong's own definition, "The amount of value depends not only on the intensity with which the existence of the object is valuated, but also on the intensity with which its nonexistence is held to be not valuable."[63] But if such nonexistent objects are nothing but mental contents, how can we distinguish them from existent ones? For surely the mental content exists as a state of mind. What, then, does not exist? There was no way to answer this question within a purely psychological framework.

By 1896, Meinong had overcome these difficulties, though he did not expound them in print until 1899. The solution to both his problems came from another outside source: a book of another Brentano student, Kasimir Twardowski, entitled *On the Theory of Content and Object of a Presentation* (1894). Twardowski took Brentano's intentional model and reinterpreted it. His argument was that to describe an intentional mental state, one must posit not only a mental act and content, but also a non-mental *object*. These objects differ from contents in a number of ways, among them: (1) the predicates "existence" and

---

62. *Ibid.*, p. 28.
63. Meinong, "Über Werthaltung und Wert," *GA*, III, 337.

"nonexistence" apply to this independent object, and not to the content, thus a nonexistent wine would be an object; and (2) contents and objects differ qualitatively. The object "box" has the property of being cubical, but the content which represents that object in the mind is not.[64] Thus the old equivocation as to whether ideas resembled reality qualitatively or merely served as signs of reality was resolved by Twardowski in favor of the latter alternative.

In "Objects of a Higher Order" Meinong adopts both of these points. The first enabled him to render his new value theory consistent with his older psychology, by admitting that mental states sometimes cannot be properly portrayed without reference to some nonpsychological distinctions, such as the ontological one of existence and nonexistence.[65] Twardowski's second point enabled him to find a new place for relations, such as "similarity" or "interval":

> Think of the similarity of a copy to its original: both pictures exist. But to say that the similarity has existence next to and beyond them does violence to the facts, as every unbiased observer will see. . . . The similarity does not exist, but it obtains (besteht).[66]

Thus relations, being neither psychic nor physical, were given a special ontological status: one should say that difference *obtains* for red and green, the interval of a major third *obtains* for the tones *c* and *e*. These relations are not homogeneous with the elements, and we can tell them apart by seeing that the word "being" does not apply to them in the same way. Objects have being, which may be that of existing or obtaining (or "subsisting" as it is often called). Objects which obtain are ideal, and those which exist are real. The objects of a higher order include both the relations and the complexes into which they enter. They are "of a higher order" because they are based on fundaments, just as in the old theory.[67]

The advantages of this theory over the one Meinong held in the *Hume-Studies* were twofold. First, it gave the ordering principles represented by relations the autonomy they deserved. Meinong was now able to distinguish more clearly the *necessary* self-evidence of ideal re-

---

64. Kasimir Twardowski, *Zur Lehre vom Inhalt und Gegenstand der Vorstellungen* (Vienna: Alfred Hölder, 1894), pp. 30, 13, 31. Twardowski's work contains extensive references to Bolzano, so Meinong must have had a minimal awareness of Bolzano's work through it. Twardowski's positions are discussed in some detail in Findlay, pp. 9ff and Grossmann, pp. 48ff, so I need not elaborate on them here.

65. Meinong, "Über Gegenstände höherer Ordnung und deren Verhältnis zur inneren Wahrnehmung," *GA*, II, 381f.

66. *Ibid.*, p. 395.          67. *Ibid.*, p. 387.

lations, such as "red is different from green," from the *immediate* evidence of our awareness of ideas, as in "I see red." Once he grasped this distinction, the temptation to describe relations in terms of the mental operations that led up to them melted away. Admittedly, our idea of a relation is still formed by the process of comparison, but this merely describes how we arrive at the idea, not the relation itself. This idea is directed toward a relational object which obtains independently of us. In this way, Meinong's description of the psychology of relations changed its emphasis from the terms of the atomistic model to that of intentionality. Thus his new theory represents a shift away from the hybrid model he previously held. Second, the theory allowed Meinong's common-sense realism to breathe freely. Physical objects now actually existed, and their existence was relevant to philosophy. As for nonexistent wines or golden mountains, they exist only in the imagination, as a mental content. As Meinong now says, they "pseudo-exist."[68]

Let us now look back over the ground we have covered and try to show the relation between Meinong's break with psychologism to the breaks made by his contemporaries. Meinong was led to introduce the category of "object" into his philosophy partly as a result of the Gestalt controversy, which stiffened his commitment to the analytical approach, as well as to the autonomy of relations, a doctrine he had long held. But he found these commitments to be incompatible with the introspective criterion—that we could have knowledge only of our own ideas. For to claim that ideas were the sole objects of knowledge put such a heavy burden on ideas, as representing such diverse aspects of the world, that it eventually involved imputing contradictory properties to the ideas themselves. One possible solution to this problem had been that of Mach—to reduce ideas and physical objects to a single neutral level of elements. But Meinong sought to avoid this reduction while still retaining his commitment to atomism and analysis. The shift to intentional relationships enabled him to do this. Put another way, in order to do justice to the problems posed by empiricism, it was necessary for Meinong to assume a heterogeneity not only of mental categories (acts, contents, and operations), but also of ontological categories (existence and subsistence).

At the same time and independently, as we have seen, a similar transformation was taking place in the philosophy of science. In the hands of Boltzmann and others, the old physical atomism was break-

68. *Ibid.*, p. 373.

ing down, only to be redefined rather than discarded. The principle of constancy of units was seen as a necessary presupposition of mathematical analysis, although there was no compulsion to define such a unit in any one way—the definition was left up to the scientist. On this interpretation, analysis in the natural sciences was rendered compatible in principle with analysis in the social sciences in Weber's formulation. The emphasis on choice, it is true, lent itself to an idealistic interpretation which demoted the importance of experience and observation of "the given" at the expense of the organizing categories of the observer's mind. Such an interpretation, if it was to allow for the possibility of objective knowledge—still a basic commitment of scientists and scientific philosophers—presupposed a teleological view of history, namely that human events such as scientific discoveries had an order and purpose of their own.

The significance of Meinong's revolt against psychologism, along with that of Twardowski and Husserl, was that it provided an empiricist alternative to this interpretation. The intentional model provided the means to redefine the "given" objective world so that the relational categories of the observer did not appear to be arbitrary. This was done by recasting the basic atomic unit of analysis from an idea within the mind to an idea directed to an object—a unit of context, so to speak, more complex than the old mental atom. With the help of this model, the question of how we can know objectively, despite the subjectivity of our conventions, was treated in the context of how we can experience objects in general. Once this context was fully explored, the specific question of knowledge could find an answer, without depending on teleological assumptions.

### 4. MEINONG'S ANALYSIS OF TIME AND HIS REVISION OF THE INTROSPECTIVE CRITERION, 1894–1906

It would seem that any thorough rejection of psychologism would involve a rejection of introspection as the sole instance of knowledge. Paradoxically, however, the article "On Objects of a Higher Order" contains some of Meinong's strongest statements in defense of inner perception. Indeed, the article was written in answer to a polemic by Friedrich Schumann that Gestalt qualities were not evident to introspection.[69] It was only gradually that he came to reevaluate the

69.  Friedrich Schumann, "Zur Psychologie der Zeitanschauung," *Zeitschrift für Psychologie*, XVII (1898), 106–148, esp. pp. 121, 128ff.

introspective criterion and to narrow its scope, even though he had at his command all the necessary arguments in 1899. His revised views on the subject appeared only in 1906, in a book entitled *On the Foundations of Knowledge in Experience* (*Über die Erfahrungsgrundlagen unseres Wissens*). Meinong's change of thought in this area is a classic example of the leisurely tempo of his development. His fascination with detail led him to see only slowly the implications that his newer ideas had for his older ones.

Meinong was in fact led to revise the introspective criterion via an aspect of the very same problem that led him to overcome psychologism in the first place: the proper relation of wholes and parts. Specifically, Meinong had to deal with the question of how we are aware of such perceptual complexes that are extended in time, such as melodies. The question was important for the philosophical psychology of the 1890s, for Bergson and James had raised crucial objections to experimental psychology with respect to such processes. James specifically had pointed out the limitations of the older empiricist tradition in dealing with the relations between elements, claiming that one could only point to a *feeling* in consciousness of the connection among elements, rather than to any law of association or to any non-experiential categories such as Kant's.[70] James maintained that any awareness of a process involved a process of awareness—his famous stream of consciousness. Meinong, without citing James or Bergson directly, gave the analytical approach to the problem (his first investigations came in 1894, in the "Analysis" article).

The problem was this: given the fact that processes such as a melody or a motion can, like any complex object, be analyzed into parts (elements and relations), how is it that we immediately perceive them as a whole, without bothering to add them up in our minds?

A melody is clearly divisible into notes, and each of these occurs at a definite time. We also perceive each of these notes as discrete—we never confuse a melody with a chord, so any talk of "fusing" is out of place. Yet we still hear the melody as a complex, as a whole, and not as a sum of parts. His most succinct statement of the problem came in the 1906 book:

> Let us weigh the matter first in an artificially simplified case. A musical motive that consists of, say, four consecutive tones in ascending order is played in such an ideal staccato that each of them can be viewed as discontinuous

70. James, *Principles*, I, 244ff.

and momentary, divided from its neighbor by a distinct pause. . . . I do not grasp the motive if I apprehend the first tone and forget it, then the second tone and forget it: only when I apprehend all four tones at once do I apprehend the complex of them. Despite this simultaneity, of course, every tone must be apprehended in the correct time-relation to the others.[71]

Processes, in short, must be perceived "at the same time but not *as* simultaneous."[72] How is this possible? Meinong's answer consists of several stages. First, he draws a strictly deductive conclusion: the time-scale of the melody cannot be the same as the time-scale of the perception. The melody is clearly divisible into temporal units, but the perception is not. The unit of perception comprehends the melody as a whole. To use Meinong's terminology, the complex object is "distributed" with respect to time; the mental content is "undistributed"; and distributed objects can only be apprehended by undistributed contents.

If we attempt to distribute the latter—to analyze our mental state into parts—we lose our awareness of the melody. Such an analysis would alter the content itself, just as an analysis of a simple tone into its overtones would lose for us the awareness of the original tone. Thus the basic, indivisible unit of perception of a process is the process as a whole. In this sense, Meinong reaches the same conclusion as James, in claiming that the limits of analysis of conscious processes are different from the limits of analysis of objects.[73]

This much, Meinong says, is self-evident from the proper understanding of the problem itself. But other questions remain: What is the relation of the time of the undistributed perception to that of the distributed object? Are they simultaneous? If so, how can one perceive a whole that is not yet completed? Meinong's answer is that the perception cannot begin until all of the objective data are "in." In other words, each tone must produce a content which remains in the mind while the other notes are sounding. Thus if a melody lasts from $t^1$ to $t^4$, the perception of the whole cannot properly begin until $t^4$.[74]

Such an account may apply to the first time we hear an unfamiliar melody, but it is certainly a forced description of how we hear melodies that we know. It was on this point that Husserl, who also pursued the question of the consciousness of time, disagreed with Meinong.

71. Meinong, *Über die Erfahrungsgrundlagen unseres Wissens*, GA, V, 434. See similar discussions in "Analyse," GA, I, 375ff., "Gegenstände höherer Ordnung," GA, II, 445ff.

72. Meinong, "Gegenstände höherer Ordnung," GA, II, 451.

73. *Ibid.*, pp. 443f., 448. See James, *Principles*, I, 278.

74. Meinong, *Erfahrungsgrundlagen*, GA, V, 435.

Following James, he claimed that we begin to perceive the melody as soon as it starts, because each individual note overlaps with the next in consciousness, leading the mind forward, so that we are aware of the whole at any one point, not just at the end.[75] This interpretation would agree with the Gestalt theorists, in that the organization of the melody itself determines the relation of one note to the next, and that we therefore can be aware of the whole as it is taking place. The greater plausibility of this account is clear if one simply imagines a melody that is suddenly cut off before the end. Even a person who had never heard the tune would recognize its incompleteness. Meinong's description could not account for this fact.

This issue reveals an important facet of Meinong's changing thought: he had by no means parted company with atomism. For although he no longer admitted that the parts of an experienced complex were homogeneous, he nevertheless continued to hold that the tone sensations maintained their identity and were in no way qualitatively shaped by the relations that joined them together. Just as in Locke, each note was impermeable, unaffected by the others or by the totality of the melody, as the Gestalt theorists would have it. Even Husserl, who by no means rejected the analytical approach in general, recognized its inapplicability to such phenomena, and accepted the Jamesian notion of a stream. We shall see that these remnants of atomism affected Meinong's mature thought at a number of crucial points.

Meinong, however, draws an important conclusion from his description. If awareness of a process is not strictly simultaneous with it, but temporally adjacent, then inner perception is really a limiting case of memory.[76] Insofar as the evidence for certainty of introspection was based on the assumption of simultaneity of act and content, that assumption is no longer valid. It would apply at best to the momentary experience of a melody which began at $t^4$, but not to any extended experience of a melody that would last for a longer stretch of time.

Several comments are needed to explain Meinong's meaning at this point. First, Meinong had always held a definite idea of what "perception" was. It involved an idea and a judgment. It was not enough to

75. Husserl, *Zur Phänomenologie des inneren Zeitbewusstseins (1893–1917)*, ed. Rudolf Boehm, *Husserliana* (The Hague: Martinus Nijhoff, 1966), X, 227. Husserl read Meinong's article on objects of a higher order in 1904 (p. 217n). The influence of James is clear in many passages where Husserl refers to a "stream" (e.g., p. 75).

76. Meinong, *Erfahrungsgrundlagen*, *GA*, V, 436, 437; "Gegenstände höherer Ordnung," *GA*, II, 458ff.

have sensations in order to perceive—the touch sensations caused by my clothing, for example, or the fact that my feet touch the ground, are there, but I do not usually perceive them; in order to do so I must judge that they exist.[77] Secondly, Meinong had an equally precise idea of what "memory" was. It was also an idea and a judgment, both existing in the present but having as an object something in the past.[78] Thus, if a four-note melody is sounded at an objective time $t_1 - t_4$, but the undistributed perception of that melody can begin no earlier than $t_4$, then that perception is, strictly speaking, a memory of an event immediately past, and is not completely certain.

Now Meinong had arrived at an epistemological assessment of memory even in the 1880s, so that he had an alternative at hand to the introspective criterion. He admitted that we cannot completely trust our memory, but he maintained also that we cannot completely distrust it either. If we did, we could never know anything beyond the present moment and would have to resign ourselves to an impoverished Humean skepticism. Memory has a type of evidence of its own—not the sure-fire certainty of inner perception, but evidence for *presumption*.[79] If we remember something to have happened, in other words, it is *probable* that it did in fact happen, and this probability can be determined by the circumstances in which the memory and the event take place. One such circumstance of cardinal importance is of course the distance in time between the act of remembering and the thing remembered. The probability that we apprehend a melody correctly approaches certainty, though it reaches that certainty only with the occurrence of the final tone. Thus, the introspective criterion still holds good for momentary experiences, but not for processes, which, after all, comprise the bulk of our consciousness.[80]

Nevertheless, on this issue also, the continuities between Meinong's earlier and later thought remained strong: the introspective criterion was by no means eliminated, but only confined to its proper sphere. Meinong realized that there *are* those momentary experiences when we are aware of what we are thinking or feeling—experiences we usually call "reflective." I may suddenly realize how tired I am, or catch myself in the act of daydreaming, or, like Descartes, judge that I am

77. Meinong, *Erfahrungsgrundlagen*, 403–404; "Empfindung," *GA*, I, 119–120; "Phantasie-Vorstellung und Phantasie," *GA*, I, 231.

78. Meinong, "Zur erkenntnistheoretischen Würdigung des Gedächtnisses" (1886), *GA*, II, 190f.

79. *Ibid.*, p. 207; *Erfahrungsgrundlagen*, *GA*, V, 438.

80. *Ibid.*, 436.

thinking. Locke had claimed that such experiences were the highest degree of knowledge, and Meinong continues to accord it a high status. The difference is that Meinong no longer sees such inner perception as the basis for all other knowledge; it is merely one type of knowledge among others.

Meinong expressed the special status of such moments in his new intentional language: in these cases the object of my mental act is not something outside me, to which the content is directed, but is identical with that content itself. Thus the certainty of inner perception is based on this identity as well as on the simultaneity of act and content. He used the following schema to distinguish "outer" perception from inner perception:

$$1. \quad I_c J \qquad 2. \quad O^J \qquad \begin{array}{l} I = \text{idea} \\ c = \text{content} \\ J = \text{judgment} \\ O = \text{object[81]} \end{array}$$
$$\downarrow$$
$$O$$

The historical significance of such distinctions may appear to be miniscule indeed, but the issue in fact represents a watershed in the history of twentieth-century philosophy. For as the lines between continental phenomenology and logical positivism became clear around the time of World War One, the validity of introspective knowledge became a major point of divergence. The logical positivists came to argue that validity is to be sought in the circumstances in which an experience is verified, just as in an experiment under controlled conditions.[82] Husserl, on the other hand, insisted that it was to be found in introspective experience divorced from all surrounding conditions—on the fact that in introspection content and object are identical.[83] Meinong, by allocating to each type of knowledge a separate sphere of application, made it possible to maintain a bridge, so to speak, between the phenomenological and positivist movements.

81.  *Ibid.*, p. 440. An explanation follows on pp. 441f.

82.  Moritz Schlick, "Positivism and Realism," trans. David Rynin, in *Logical Positivism*, ed. A. J. Ayer (New York: The Free Press, 1959), p. 87.

83.  See Chapter Ten. On the contrast between Husserl and Schlick on introspection, see Husserl, *Logical Investigations*, II, 663.

# VI

# THE LINGUISTIC ANALOGY
# AND THE THEORY OF OBJECTS

## 1. LANGUAGE AND LOGICAL REALISM

Michel Foucault and others have pointed out that the innovations of the intellectual revolution pointed in two directions: toward
an increased understanding of the irrational on the one hand, and toward a deeper awareness of the formal workings of reason on the
other—in short, to Freud and Russell.[1] And just as psychoanalysis
assiduously avoided surrendering to the unconscious, but sought to
bring the new reality under the control of reason, so the philosophers
who used symbolic logic initially sought to avoid a surrender to nominalism, to the implication that the conventions of human reason were
the only reality. By the time of the First World War, there were three
different ways in which philosophers sought to reconcile their new
awareness of the importance of symbolic convention with their concern for the real or transcendent.

One of them was a frank embracing of metaphysics. While scarcely
innovative itself, metaphysics did provide for many a valid means
of interpreting the new sciences. One of the most distinguished philosophers of science itself, Pierre Duhem, avowed the necessity of
metaphysics as a complement to science proper.[2] The most popular
metaphysician of the day, Bergson, repeatedly emphasized that his

1. Michel Foucault, *The Order of Things* (New York: Random House, Vintage ed.,
1973), p. 299. Also Langer, p. 24.
2. Peter Alexander, "Duhem, Pierre Maurice Marie," *Encyclopedia of Philosophy*, II,
422.

doctrine of the *élan vital* was not anti-scientific, but was designed to harmonize the results of science with those of intuition. Both had a place in his theory of cosmic evolution.[3] And in England, the Neo-Hegelian Francis Herbert Bradley, whose "metaphysical essay" *Appearance and Reality* appeared in 1893, sought at least to refute the presuppositions of positivism on its own terms. Bradley argued that a philosophy that sought out the diversity of the world, as given in appearance, inevitably ended in self-contradiction; the only alternative was to turn to the underlying, unified reality that was behind it. (In one of his most famous criticisms he attacked the empiricists' attempt to escape this impasse through a theory of relations. Although relations such as similarity and difference seem to be more constant than the diverse terms they relate, they nevertheless depend on these terms and are therefore diverse themselves.)[4] The influence of Bergson and Bradley in their respective countries was considerable in the first decade of the twentieth century, and one measure of their timeliness was the resonance that their ideas found in literature: Bergson's in the writings of Proust, Bradley's in those of T. S. Eliot.

A second way of philosophical synthesis was, as we have already seen, pragmatism. In the hands of such a brilliant stylist as William James, whose lectures on the subject appeared in 1908, pragmatism became a current of philosophy popular in Europe as well as in America.[5] Not only did it win the approval of sophisticated philosophers of science such as Mach, but also intuitive metaphysicians such as Bergson. By being on amicable terms with both men, James had managed to square the philosophical circle. Schools of pragmatism sprouted in England, France, and Italy, where the doctrine drew the interest of Sorel and Mussolini among others. Pragmatism did not take hold in Germany, however, probably because another book appeared in 1911 which seemed to have a position similar to that of James, though cast in a Kantian idiom: *The Philosophy of As-If* by Hans Vaihinger. This book bore the following grandiose subtitle: "System of theoretical, practical, and religious fictions of mankind on the basis of an idealistic positivism." Vaihinger had originally written this work as a young man in 1879, but had failed to complete it then because of ill health.

3. Henri Bergson, *Creative Evolution*, trans. Arthur Mitchell (New York: Henry Holt and Co., 1911), p. 199.

4. F. H. Bradley, *Appearance and Reality*, 2d ed. (Oxford: Oxford University Press, paperback ed., 1969), p. 26.

5. Ralph Barton Perry, *The Thought and Character of William James*, 2 vols. (Boston: Little, Brown and Company, 1936), II, Chs. LXXVIII–LXXIX passim; Hughes, p. 112.

In the meantime, he claimed that many other thinkers such as Mach, the pragmatists, and Nietzsche had become identified with ideas similar to his own.[6] Vaihinger's thesis centered on the concept of "fictions": he maintained that most intellectual activity is based on assumptions which we know to be false but which are nevertheless indispensable for practical purposes. Such an insight was, he asserted, "a common bond which embraces the differentials of mathematics, the atoms of natural science, the ideas of philosophy, and even the dogmas of religion."[7]

The third major form of synthesis was the doctrine of realism, or logical realism, as it is sometimes called. Its principal adherents were Frege, Russell, G. E. Moore, Meinong, and Husserl. These philosophers were motivated by a quest for precision and exactness which put them out of sympathy with metaphysics; at the same time they were repelled by the relativistic implications of pragmatism.[8] Some of them saw the road to such precision in the new symbolic logic, but not all of them, including Meinong and Moore, were logicians themselves. Nor for that matter were all of the new logicians realists. Charles Sanders Peirce, for example, was one of the originators of pragmatism and an innovator in the use of logic. (He found it necessary, however, to distance himself from James's popular version, and renamed his own doctrine "pragmaticism." His letters to James contain admonitions to "think with more exactitude.")[9] In any case, realism was recognized as an established philosophical movement in the years before the war, and even spawned an American counterpart. The American "new realists," who included Edwin Holt and Ralph Barton Perry, looked to Russell, Moore, and Meinong as their "big brothers overseas."[10]

It must be admitted that the standards of this group prevented them from attaining the popularity of the other two. One reason for the influence of figures like James and Vaihinger was undoubtedly their willingness to face the "big questions" of philosophy, the ones

6. Hans Vaihinger, *Die Philosophie des Als Ob*, 10th ed. (Leipzig: Felix Meiner Verlag, 1927), pp. XXVff. Vaihinger's book went through two editions before the war, and six more between 1918 and 1922. Like Spengler, Vaihinger evidently was able to interpret the thought of his time to a broad educated public—a great need following Germany's defeat.

7. *Ibid.*, p. XXXI.

8. Bertrand Russell, *A History of Western Philosophy* (New York: Simon and Schuster, Clarion Books, 1945), p. 834.

9. Perry, p. 437.     10. Findlay, *Meinong's Theory*, p. xii.

that often trouble laymen as well, such as the existence of God or the nature of truth and right. The realists, on the other hand, shared the common conviction that these "big questions" could only be found in the context of a preliminary question: What do we mean when we ask them? The proper definitions of "truth," "knowledge," "right and wrong" could only come from a well-founded theory of meaning. One must ask the question: How is it that symbols, whether in logic or ordinary language, *refer* to something other than themselves? If we know what it is to say that symbols such as "tree," "house," or "$e=mc^2$" mean something, then we can perhaps make some progress on more problematical symbols such as "truth," "knowledge," "power," and "freedom."

It is common today to identify the uniqueness and dignity of man with his capacity for language.[11] The "relevance," then, of this philosophical concern to twentieth-century humanism as a whole should be clear. But it was not always so to the educated public before the First World War, or even necessarily to all philosophers—though it certainly came to be so by the 1920s, if the spate of books on that subject which appeared then is any indication.[12] Nevertheless, the interest in symbols and their meaning was an important theme of the intellectual revolution, if only by virtue of the fact that it was pursued independently by so many leading thinkers. The role of symbols was central to psychoanalysis, to the sociology of Durkheim, to the poetry of Mallarmé—not to mention the work of Karl Kraus, who claimed to practice the proper use of language as an ethical act.

For the logical realists, the linguistic analogy held out the promise of transcending the conflicting claims of empiricism and idealism—that is, of doing justice both to the concreteness of experience and to the role of abstract reasoning, without lapsing into relativism on the one hand, or a teleological view of history (the frequent consequence of idealism) on the other. If such formidable obstacles could be overcome, then the linguistic analogy could possibly hold the key to a philosophical synthesis of the divergent strands of humanistic thought at the turn of the century. This could be done by providing a theory of language that could comprehend both rational and irrational discourse—that is the verbalizations both of human cognition and of our emotions and impulses. Meinong's formulation of these questions and his attempted solutions may be found in his theory of objects, or

11. See Langer, p. 28; Chomsky, pp. 1, 10, 24.
12. See Langer's list, pp. 21f.

Gegenstandstheorie, which he gradually developed out of his notion of objects of a higher order in the last two decades of his life. Not all of this theory is equally well known: Meinong's later works, which address themselves to the intentional objects of irrational experiences (feelings and desires), have been of less interest to Anglo-American philosophers. His reputation rests mainly on his work of 1899–1910, which concerns the objects of cognition. It was this work also that won him the greatest amount of recognition in his own day. We shall examine this phase of his thought in this chapter, placing it within the historical context of logical realism, and shall deal with the later "emotional" Gegenstandstheorie in the next chapter.

It was Russell who first perceived the congruence of Meinong's theories with the logical and linguistic concerns that were taking root in Cambridge. Along with Moore, Russell was "beginning to emerge from the bath of German idealism" that had dominated British philosophy in the 1890s under figures such as Bradley. "It was an intense excitement," he writes, "after having supposed the sensible world unreal, to be able to believe again that there really were such things as tables and chairs."[13] This realism, however, was not simply commonsensical, as the following passage from *The Principles of Mathematics* (1902) reveals:

> *Being* is that which belongs to every conceivable term, to every possible object of thought—in short, to everything that can possibly occur in any proposition, true or false, and to all such propositions themselves. Being belongs to whatever can be counted. If A be any term that can be counted as one, it is plain that A is something, and therefore that A is. . . . "A is not" implies that there is a term A whose being is denied, and hence that A is. Thus unless "A is not" be an empty sound, it must be false—whatever A may be, it certainly is. Numbers, the Homeric gods, relations, chimeras, and four-dimensional spaces all have being, for if they were not entities of a kind, we could make no propositions about them. Thus being is a general attribute of everything, and to mention anything is to show that it is.
>
> *Existence*, on the contrary, is the prerogative of some only amongst beings.[14]

The similarity of this view to that of Plato has often been pointed out, though it must be emphasized that not all realists were as close to Platonism as Russell was at this time. Meinong's realism, for example,

13. Russell, *The Autobiography of Bertrand Russell* (Boston: Little, Brown and Company, 1967), Vol. I, p. 199.

14. Russell, *The Principles of Mathematics*, 2d ed. (New York: W. W. Norton and Co., n.d.), p. 449.

differed from Plato and from Russell's just-quoted doctrine, as we shall see.[15] It was, however, the willingness to conceive of "being" as applicable to more than mere physical objects that characterized realism as a whole, and made it attractive to those concerned with the philosophical foundations of the sciences and the humanities alike.

Two years later, Russell published an extensive review of Meinong's work in the philosophical journal *Mind*, with the dual purpose of presenting Meinong's opinions and of advocating his own, since the "points of agreement [were] so numerous and important." Russell praised Meinong's work in the following way:

> I wish to emphasize the admirable method of Meinong's researches, which, in a brief epitome, it is quite impossible to preserve. Although empiricism as a philosophy does not appear to be tenable, there is an empirical manner of investigating, which should be applied in every subject-matter. This is possessed in a very perfect form by the works we are considering. A frank recognition of the data, as inspection reveals them, precedes all theorising; when a theory is propounded, the greatest skill is shown in the selection of facts favourable or unfavourable, and in eliciting all relevant consequences of the facts adduced. There is thus a rare combination of acute inference with capacity for observation. The method of philosophy is not fundamentally unlike that of other sciences: the differences seem to be only in degree.[16]

Thus despite its Platonistic overtones, realism stood squarely in the empiricist and positivist traditions, though it was markedly different from the Machian version that preceded it, and from that of the logical positivists which followed.

It was through Russell's mediation, then, that Meinong (and Frege too) became identified by contemporaries as a realist. It should be evident, however, that Meinong had arrived at this position by a very different route than Russell: namely, through intentional psychology and epistemology rather than through logic. Nevertheless, Meinong himself had realized the relevance of his theory of "objects of a higher order" to language quite explicitly in his article on the subject: "What a speaker wants to 'say,' or, more exactly, what he wants to speak about, is not that which his words *express*, but that which they *mean*, and that is not the content, but the object of the idea expressed by the

15. Chisholm, *Realism*, p. 8; Richard Routley and Valerie Routley, "Rehabilitating Meinong's Theory of Objects," *Revue Internationale de la Philosophie*, XXVII (1973), 244. On the differences between Meinong and Russell, see Chapter Eight, pt. 1.

16. Russell, "Meinong's Theory of Complexes and Assumptions," in *Essays in Analysis*, ed. Douglas Lackey (New York: George Braziller, 1973), p. 22.

word."[17] There is, then, a triangular relation between experiences, words, and objects. Language is an expression of our experiences, and is in turn directed to the objects that are the meanings of words and sentences. Similarly, experiences are directed to objects through intentionality.[18] After 1899, Meinong increasingly turned to examples from language to illuminate both his psychology and his developing ontology—his views on objects themselves. Though language was by no means identical either with mind or with the objective world, it was possible to draw certain parallels between the three. One can thus talk of a way of philosophizing in which crucial distinctions were made by way of analogy to language. We have seen ample precedents for such analogies in the work of the original empiricists themselves, particularly Locke and Berkeley. Now, in the first decade of the twentieth century, such analogies were revived and reformulated. In this process, Brentano's intentional model played a crucial role, because it conceived the structure of the mind as being similar to that of language. Let us now summarize briefly the main points of contact between language and the intentional model, in order to see how such patterns were used by the realists such as Husserl and Meinong.

    1. The relation between a linguistic symbol and its object is not causal. A horse does not cause the word "horse" to come into existence, as it causes a colt to be born. It is true, of course, that *some* symbols stand in a causal relationship to their objects—for example, a weathervane, which tells us something by the way in which it is affected by the wind. In fact, a Lockean "idea" is such a symbol, because it is both caused by and represents its object (Helmholtz later called these symbols "natural signs," whereas Peirce called them "indices"). But there is no mistaking such "indices" for linguistic symbols.[19] A linguistic symbol can be described only in terms of something outside itself, namely its "reference"; "referring" (Bedeuten) is a directional word, like "intend." One might say, in a more general way, that language is describable in terms of its function in a larger context, the unit of that context being a symbol referring to its object. Indeed, one of the most interesting developments in Meinong's thought after 1900 is the appearance of such "direction" words, which delineated the fine shades of difference in how we are directed to objects: "mean-

    17. Meinong, "Gegenstände höherer Ordnung," *GA*, II, 385.
    18. A similar representation is found in C. K. Ogden and I. A. Richards, *The Meaning of Meaning*, 2d ed., rev. (New York: Harcourt, Brace and Co., 1927), p. 11.
    19. Husserl, *Logical Investigations*, I, 270, 275; see also Langer, pp. 57, 61.

ing" (*meinen*), "grasping" (*ergreifen*), "apprehending" (*erfassen*), and, finally "knowing" (*erkennen*).

2. There is no one-to-one correlation between linguistic symbols and objects. A given object can be referred to by a number of symbols. To give a favorite example of Frege, the planet Venus is known both as "the morning star" and "the evening star." Both these phrases refer to the same object, but they are themselves different. Frege used this example to distinguish between the *sense* of a symbol and its *reference*. Here "the morning star" and "the evening star" have the same reference but different senses.[20] Frege insisted that both the sense and the reference of a word were not subjective—that is, they are not bound to the psychological states of an individual. A sense of a word, according to Frege, "may be the common property of many and is therefore not a part or a mode of the individual mind. For one can hardly deny that mankind has a common store of thoughts which is transmitted from one generation to another."[21] Frege's "sense" was thus a "social fact" in Durkheim's sense of the term. The distinction between sense and idea corresponded approximately to that of the Swiss linguist Ferdinand de Saussure, who in the 1900s was independently formulating the principles which today form the foundation of structural linguistics. Saussure distinguished between *langue* and *parole*, the former being social, the latter individual.[22]

The notions of sense and reference gave Frege a criterion for distinguishing truth from falsity. One can build sentences in which the subject terms have sense but lack reference to existing objects; for example, sentences about Hamlet or Pegasus. He also concluded that language is unable to describe precisely artistic expression. This is because the social nature of sense prevents us from verbalizing our individual psychological responses to a painting or a piece of music. These responses *do* genuinely vary from person to person, Frege thought, and therefore language as social fact is too primitive a tool to express them.[23]

The many-sided relation between symbol and object could also work the other way: a single symbol can have many objects. This is

---

20. Frege, "Function and Concept," in *Philosophical Writings*, p. 29; see also "On Sense and Reference," *ibid.*, pp. 56–78.

21. *Ibid.*, p. 59.

22. Ferdinand de Saussure, *Course in General Linguistics*, ed. Charles Bally and Albert Sechehaye, trans. Wade Baskin (New York: McGraw-Hill, 1966), p. 14.

23. Frege, "Sense and Reference," p. 61.

true of all general names. A passage from Husserl's *Logical Investigations* will illustrate:

> The expression "a horse" has the same meaning in whatever context it occurs. But if on one occasion we saw "Bucephalus is a horse," and on another "That cart-horse is a horse," there has been a plain change in our sense-giving presentation in passing from the one statement to the other.[24]

Twardowski enunciated the same principle in terms of the relation between "content" and "object" in 1894, and it appears in Meinong's writings in 1900. But although there was common agreement between these various thinkers on the principle, there was by no means an agreement on the proper terminology. And differences in labels, as we shall see, were in this case significant, for they led to disagreements on the important question of ambiguity. It is obviously by virtue of this lack of rigorous correspondence between symbol and object that language can be metaphorical, when a single symbol refers to different objects simultaneously. But it was by no means clear how much ambiguity should be allowed into a strictly philosophical interpretation of language. Since this issue is crucial to the question of the broader relevance of realism, we shall return to it.[25]

3. There is no qualitative resemblance between linguistic symbols and objects. The physical shape of the word "Socrates" has nothing to do with the physical shape of Socrates; words are not "pictures" in this straightforward sense. This is, of course, not true of all symbols—Chinese characters may resemble their objects (Peirce also had a name for these: icons).

If many symbols are dissimilar to objects in all these respects, what reasonable basis is there for a linguistic analogy? In what sense *do* objects resemble symbols? The answer given by the logical realists would be that they resemble each other in their structure—that is, in the similarity of relations *between* symbols to those *between* objects. These intramural relations are just as important in describing symbols and objects as their mutual relations. It is true that isolated words have meanings that can be found in dictionaries. But language is more than a list of words, as we recognize when we note the difference between the statements "Horses are white, brown, or black" and "White horses brown are black or." The same words in the first order have meaning, while those in the second do not. In other words, the meaning of a word is characterized not only by its function in a context of

24. Husserl, *Logical Investigations*, I, 288.
25. See below, pp. 159–161.

objects of reference, but also by its place in a context of other words—that is, by its linguistic structure. Language, in short, has a syntax as well as a semantics, and the syntax may often hold the key to understanding the semantics.

To see what philosophical analogies could be drawn from this principle, one has only to consider that the basic unit of syntax is commonly considered to be the sentence, the meaning of which is qualitatively different from the words which constitute it. Sentences have Gestalt-qualities, so to speak: If the structure of the world resembles the structure of language, then, the basic units of the world must be more complex than "things," which are the proper analogues of words. There must also be "states of affairs" of which things are constituents. In this view, for example, the basic elements of the physical universe would not be bodies, but would be the facts pertaining to bodies—such as that they exist, that they attract and repel each other, and so on. Russell called such units "propositions," Husserl and Stumpf called them "states of affairs" (*Sachverhalte*) a usage that Wittgenstein later adopted. Meinong called them "objectives" (*Objektive*). This is not to say that all these philosophers agreed on the proper definition of such entities; it also explains, incidentally, why the father of intentional analysis, Brentano himself, played a relatively peripheral role in the history of logical realism. He was not willing to admit such entities; for him, they were simply "thought contents."[26]

The emphasis on linguistic structure as the key to building analogies for use in other disciplines is still with us today in the form of structuralism, which has many of its roots in Saussure's work of the 1900s. Saussure proposed that linguistics should eventually become part of a larger science of signs (semiology), which would explore the various aspects of social life that behave as language does—that is, as systems of communication using codes that follow regular patterns.[27] In the hands of later structuralists, this notion of social codes has been applied to such phenomena as patterns of dress, cooking, manners, and literature. A given fashion or custom, for instance, is seen as a unit that serves as a sign to other members, and is understood by virtue of shared rules. Structuralism, however, is by no means a contemporary branch of logical realism; for while structuralists would agree

26. Brentano, *Psychology*, pp. 291ff. Brentano's term, Denkinhalt, was adopted by his student Anton Marty, who polemicized vigorously against Meinong on this and other matters. Meinong's response can be found in a general discussion of the proper term for "objectives" in *Über Annahmen*, 2d. ed., *GA*, IV, 97–105.

27. Saussure, p. 16.

with the three characteristics of symbolic relations mentioned above, many of them, including Saussure, saw language primarily as a social product, an arbitrary convention. The fact that there was no one-to-one correspondence between words and objects led Saussure to dismiss this aspect of language as constitutive altogether. He wrote: "The linguistic sign unites, not a thing and a name, but a concept and a sound-image."[28] Both of these elements are psychological, and are defined not in relation to objects, but in relation to other sounds and concepts. For example, there is no natural, given order of colors in the world, but each language orders the color-spectrum on its own. This is done by selecting a certain set of sounds (such as "red," "green," "yellow") and associating these with certain ideas of color. But there is no guarantee that these ideas will be the same for all languages. Put another way, "red" is defined in English not with respect to a set of red objects, but as different from "green" and "yellow." "In language," Saussure wrote, "as in any semiological system, whatever distinguishes one sign from the others constitutes it. Difference makes character just as it makes value and the unit."[29] Saussure thus defined units as *products* of relations rather than as fundamental *presuppositions* of them. For this reason, he might seem to opt for holism as opposed to atomism and analysis, as the Gestalt theorists did. But in Saussure these latter principles are displaced rather than eliminated. For he insists that, for a language to be shared by the members of a social group, there is a need for a set of basic, common, and constant units which are the building blocks of more complex structures. These units are words, not sentences: languages have finite stocks of words, which are part of an individual's social heritage. Sentences, on the other hand, are not shared in the same sense; they can be made in infinite combinations by individuals from the finite stock. Sentences presuppose words, and are a part of *parole*, not *langue*.[30]

Despite these differences, structuralism and logical realism may be

28. *Ibid.*, p. 66.

29. *Ibid.*, p. 121. Not all later structuralists have followed Saussure on this point. Roland Barthes, for example, in his *Elements of Semiology* (trans. Annette Lavers and Colin Smith, New York: Hill and Wang, 1964), claims that Saussure's definition is too psychologistic; in addition to the sound and concept, one must posit an additional dimension: the "something" which is meant by the person using the sign (p. 43). Other commentators have pointed to the existence of both types of relations—those in which the elements are autonomous, and those in which they are shaped by the relations themselves. See Michael Lane, "Introduction," in *Introduction to Structuralism*, ed. Michael Lane (New York: Basic Books, Harper Torchbooks, 1970), p. 24.

30. Saussure, pp. 106, 124.

seen to stem from a common impulse in twentieth-century thought: the desire to use language as a precise tool for the investigation of other areas of human existence in such a way that the traditional dichotomy between the sciences and the humanities—and the rational and the irrational—might be overcome. The logical realists tended to share the assumption that there was a congruence between mind, language, and being, an assumption the structuralists did not share. It may seem naively anthropomorphic to assume that the structure of the world entirely resembles that of a human convention, such as language. But to be able to say precisely in what respects the world does *not* resemble the structure of language, one must be able to formulate such analogies in the first place. Moreover, if one should succeed in drawing such boundaries, one should have an exact idea of the limits of human reason—one of the recurrent concerns of positivists. Part of the historical significance of realism, then, was that it reformulated this concern in terms of the linguistic analogy. By describing the world as analogous to language, and then eventually noting the points where the analogy broke down, they addressed the question of the limits of reason at its most general level. However heretical it may sound, this was a very Kantian strategy—Kant's starting point was the analysis of the structure of human understanding as a basis for determining the applicability of reason. And it is not surprising that Cassirer, a Neo-Kantian, should turn to the philosophy of language as the culmination of his philosophical work in *The Philosophy of Symbolic Forms*.

## 2. The Problem of Ideal versus Natural Languages

In our previous discussion, we have had to consider three different dimensions of language: the psychological, the social, and the philosophical. It is clear that we use language to express certain mental states, albeit in forms which are to a great extent the product of social convention; we may also use language to refer to objects that are neither psychological nor social and perhaps not even physical. As philosophers, the realists did not attempt to do justice to all three dimensions. In drawing linguistic analogies, however, they could scarcely afford to ignore them completely. The continuing importance of psychology in Meinong's formulations should be clear. We must now consider how he and his contemporaries handled the social dimension. For if the realists were to find an answer to relativism through the study of language, the socially conditioned aspects of language posed a real problem. If one is seeking to describe the workings of human reason through the study of meaning, then the fact that the given natural languages of man exhibit a great variety of meanings and rules of usage had to be accounted for. It is in fact the contention of a more recent school of philosophy—the "ordinary language" philosophers such as Ryle and the later Wittgenstein—that there is no common set of meanings underlying this variety, no single ideal language from which the various natural languages could be derived. The issue is by no means closed, however, since the school of Chomsky maintains that there are such universal preconditions, which must correspond to the structure of the human mind. The realists of the prewar period seemed to take it for granted, however, that there *was* such an ideal language, even if they disagreed about what it was. By comparing the approaches that Frege, Husserl, and Meinong took to the question of ideal versus natural languages, we hope to illustrate the particular significance of Meinong's contribution in his Gegenstandstheorie.

Frege had come to the philosophy of language from logic and mathematics, where he had developed his pathbreaking system of notation in 1879. And it was this artificial language that he believed should be the basis for analogies in philosophy, rather than the language of everyday use.[31] For logical language, the distinction between sense and reference was incomplete. One had also to distinguish between two kinds of reference, which Frege called *concept* and *object*. The former was the meaning of a general term, such as "horse" or "planet," and the latter was a particular, that is the meaning of a proper name (such as "Venus"). This meant that the sentence "The morning star is a planet" and "The morning star is Venus" were logically quite different, despite the identity of their syntax in ordinary language.[32] The reason is that the first statement really refers to the

31. Frege, Über die wissenschaftliche Begründung einer Begriffsschrift," in *Funktion, Begriff, Bedeutung*, ed. Günther Patzig (Göttingen: Vandenhoeck and Ruprecht, 1975), p. 94.

32. Frege, "Concept and Object," in *Philosophical Writings*, p. 44. One might explain Frege's reasoning in the following way: if a logical language could get by with numerical symbols alone, then there could be a satisfactory parallel between its meaning and that of ordinary language through the distinction of sense and reference. $2(2)=3+1$ would be equivalent to "the morning star is the evening star." The reference of the first expression would be "4," that of the second "Venus." But symbolic logic needs algebraic symbols as well as numerical ones (such as, x and y). The reference of such symbols is not always clear at first sight: $2x=3+1$ is true only if $x=2$. Thus Frege had to find an

fact that the morning star is something that falls under the concept "planet," whereas "Venus" in the second statement identifies the morning star with a particular object. In other words, the syntax of ordinary language is not to be trusted, and this deceptiveness is full of perils for the person who seeks the maximum use of his or her reason. For it is possible for sentences to be devoid of sense as well as devoid of reference. We recognize nonsense in the case of "White horses brown are black or," but we do not necessarily recognize it in "There *is* Julius Caesar"—a case in which, according to Frege, the word order requires a noun that refers to a concept, whereas "Julius Caesar" refers to an object.[33] Thus for Frege and the philosophers who followed him, "nonsense" became a technical term, and the difference between sense and nonsense served to mark the boundary between rational and irrational discourse. In this way Frege and later the logical positivists found a way of fixing the limits of reason.

The views of Husserl on these questions present a significant contrast. Husserl agreed that natural language should be distrusted, infiltrated as it was with inexactitude. But he did not believe that the alternative lay in a formal, mathematical model:

> The mathematician is not really the pure theoretician, but only the ingenious technician, the constructor, as it were. . . . Philosophical investigation has quite other ends, and therefore presupposes quite other methods and capacities. . . . [The philosopher] wants to clarify the essence of a thing, an event, a cause, an effect, of space, of time, etc., as well as that wonderful affinity which this essence has with the essence of thought.[34]

Symbolic logic, in short, was another linguistic construction, more refined than ordinary language but a social fact nevertheless. The only way to ground such facts was to get behind language to the conscious experiences that words express—because the structure of consciousness was not socially conditioned but universal. Only at this level could one find the "wonderful affinity" that the intentional model reveals. In other words, we can eliminate the deceptiveness of natural language by analyzing the contents of our consciousness and their directedness of contents to objects. Husserl believed that such an analysis would not lead us astray, but would reveal the universally true laws of

---

analogue to ordinary speech for the algebraic symbol, something indeterminate, which could apply to many examples. This he found in the concept, or general term, which (such as "planet") could mean any of the particular planets.

33. Frege, "Concept and Object," p. 50.
34. Husserl, *Logical Investigations*, I, 244f.

logic and could clearly distinguish them from what was relative and contingent. By paying close attention to the relation of the facts of language to the facts of consciousness, we could intuit the elements that form a common denominator for all language—in other words, a universal grammar.[35]

Husserl's *Logical Investigations* reflected his encounter with Frege. He accepted Frege's distinction between sense and reference, though he relabeled them "meaning" and "object." But he did not subscribe to the view that "meaning" was only objective because it was a social fact. An individual's particular response to a work of art was objective too, insofar as it was directed to something other than itself, and thus in principle could be verbalized, though there may be no practical reason for doing so.[36] In addition, Husserl distinguished between sense and nonsense, but he rejected Frege's notion that sentences which appear to be sensible may not be. One can distinguish between the appearances of sense and nonsense by careful inspection; that is, one can tell that the statement "There *is* Julius Caesar" is nonsense by paying careful attention to what one is thinking. And this led Husserl to ascribe "meaning" to certain phrases that Frege said made no sense. One can take a nonsensical phrase such as "the round square" (a favorite of logicians) and make perfectly meaningful sentences with it (such as "A round square is impossible"). Thus it would be wrong to say that the phrase was objectively meaningless.[37] Indeed, this was just the sort of distinction that pure logic would reveal, as it was to be the study of meanings as such. Husserl may thus be said to have allowed human reason a greater scope than did Frege—indeed, he spoke of *"the unbounded range of objective reason*. Everything that is, can be known 'in itself.'"[38] He not only admitted more into the realm of legitimate meaning, but also avowed that reason could be found in appearances directly. Phenomena (appearances), have their own logic— hence the science of phenomenology.

And what of Meinong? At the time he developed his Gegenstands-theorie, he was unfamiliar with Frege but aware of Husserl's position. Meinong agreed with Husserl that objects are first and foremost cor-

35.  *Ibid.*, II, 524f.

36.  *Ibid.*, I, 321. Husserl points out the difference between his terminology and Frege's on p. 292.

37.  *Ibid.*, I, 293; II, 517. Husserl makes a further distinction between "nonsense" and "absurdity." The former would include units such as the round square, which, though meaningless in themselves, can take their place in well-formed sentences; the latter would consist of phrases which cannot—such as "Green is or."

38.  *Ibid.*, I, 321. On logic as a science of meanings, see p. 323.

relates of individual consciousness, not of language itself. But he differed from Husserl in that he made no promises of a universal logical grammar that would spring from this relationship by virtue of some pre-established harmony between the mind and the world. We know that a state of consciousness refers to something other than itself. But we have no right to make any assumptions *in advance* about what sorts of "something" will be referred to. The question of which objects qualify as general meanings, which as particular meanings of the various natural languages, which as social facts, which as facts of biology, literature, or any other specialized discipline—all these categories can only be decided after the observation, analysis, and comparison of a number of cases of referring. If there is any universality in language, it comes not from assuming a universal grammar or pure logic, but from observing carefully the way intentional reference operates in individual cases. The precision of philosophy demands nothing less. As Meinong wrote:

> It is true that when we speak of the meaning of a word, we usually have in mind "the word" in general, not the word spoken by this individual now. We therefore understand the meaning of a word to be not that which this person or that person means by it, but what the totality or majority of speakers mean and thus what the individual "should" reasonably mean. But this is of no consequence for the natural sense of the opposition between expression and meaning. No one hesitates to concede that one and the same word can "mean" different things at different times, at different places, for different social classes, for different families, and in the final analysis for different individuals. So one can say quite generally that a word "means" invariably the object of the idea that it "expresses," and conversely expresses the idea of the object that it means.[39]

There is thus no guarantee of general meaning in Meinong's theory of objects. If there is any level of universal discourse that emerges, it is a posteriori rather than a priori. Indeed, Meinong has been criticized by some philosophers for failing to give a satisfactory account of universals, or of the single, formal objects that are indispensable to any logical enterprise.[40]

39. Meinong, *Über Annahmen*, 2d. ed., *GA*, IV, 25. The footnote reads, "Husserl construes the concept of the object more narrowly than seems natural to me." See also *Über Möglichkeit und Wahrscheinlichkeit*, *GA*, VI, 48, for an even stronger statement that meaning is not primarily a social fact.

40. Bergmann, pp. 22, 364–365; Grossmann, pp. 1f, 180–181. Meinong's lack of interest in a detailed investigation of universals is evident in *Möglichkeit*, *GA*, VI, 207. Findlay, on the other hand, allows that Meinong distinguished a certain type of universal (*Meinong's Theory*, p. 164).

One example of Meinong's approach that points up both his weaknesses and strengths are his views on logic itself. Surprising as it may seem, his definition of logic remained unchanged from his early years, despite the changes that were going on around him. Logic was still in his eyes a practical discipline concerning the rules of proper thinking, and therefore demanded a theoretical discipline as its foundation, namely the theory of objects.[41] While Meinong does not explicitly refer to logic as a type of language, it is clear from his discussion of it that he considers it to be analogous to particular *use* of language rather than to an ideal language. He viewed the traditional rules of inference, as given in syllogisms, as applicable to certain natural contexts only. "Even if one speaks of 'the' syllogism in *modus* Darapti," he wrote, "or of 'the' hypothetical syllogism, and the like, one means an intellectual event or the possible results of such an event, just as one means a physiological event when one speaks of 'the' circulation of the blood."[42] For this reason, Meinong could not identify his theory of objects with Husserl's "pure logic," though he emphasized that Husserl's goals in the *Logical Investigations* were the same as his own.[43]

If Meinong's attitude on this point seems to reflect a failure to keep up with the innovations in his own field, it must be added that the theory of objects itself seemed very close to the newer logic; Russell even wrote to him that he "had become accustomed to use the name 'logic' for what you call the theory of objects."[44] In this respect, Meinong's view on mathematics and the theory of objects is revealing. Meinong definitely saw mathematics as a theoretical discipline and a part of the theory of objects—but only a part, since there are objects which are not measurable. Just as in his earlier thought, mathematics was but a special case of the theory of relations, so now it is but a special case of the successor to that theory. For Meinong's purpose in formulating a theory of objects remains the same as in his earlier thought: to account for the presence of the rational in the empirical—that is, in the appearances given directly to experience. For this reason, Meinong's theory of objects may also be seen as a version of phenomenology.[45]

41. Meinong, "Über Gegenstandstheorie," *GA*, II, 501–502; LTC, p. 93.
42. *Ibid.*, p. 503; LTC, p. 94.
43. *Ibid.*
44. Russell to Meinong, December 12, 1904, *Philosophenbriefe*, p. 150.
45. See Grossmann, p. 106: "Meinong's theory of entities is nothing but Husserl's phenomenology by another name."

The theory of objects, then, may be characterized as analogous to an ideal language which is not logical. All experiences—including emotions and desires—are directed to objects, as are the linguistic terms and phrases which express these experiences. The extraordinarily broad way in which Meinong defined the term "object" is the source of both his greatest weaknesses and his greatest strengths. Unlike Frege and Husserl, he assumes no distinctions between objects or levels of objectivity in advance, such as sense and reference, or meaning and object. On the negative side, this theory offered no easy way to distinguish truth from falsity, sense from nonsense. Trees, golden mountains, round squares—all were objects. It was this aspect of his theory, particularly, which galled the logicians, who made it the butt of such derogatory epithets as "Meinong's jungle."[46] Indeed, such an infinitely broad construction of the term "object" might seem to be utterly uninformative. For if "everything is object," as Meinong explicitly claimed, what possible distinctions could be made with it?[47] Is this not merely another case of an empiricist giving in to the temptation of a single, homogeneous category, like James Mill's "idea" or Mach's "sensation"?[48]

On the positive side, Meinong holds that objects, however infinite their number, are related to each other in certain systematic ways, and thus have certain structural properties in common. There is thus a basis for the classification of objects. This classification, as we shall see, results partly from ontological considerations, and partly from analogies to the structure of consciousness as Meinong sees it. Since these forms of conscious experience are the same for all men, they do form a valid basis for inferring properties of an ideal language. The full picture of this structure will take us some time to present; it cannot be completely understood until we have grasped Meinong's emotional theory of objects, which will be treated in the next chapter. Suffice to say here that the broad use of the term "object" may be justified as a consistent execution of Meinong's premise that valid philosophical insights based on the nature of meaning and reference must be based on the facts of intentionality at the level of individual acts of conscious-

46. Routley and Routley, p. 224.
47. Meinong, *Selbstdarstellung*, *GA*, VII, 14.
48. See Bergmann, p. 358, who claims that Meinong's objects are nothing more than his old ideas "exported" out of the psyche. The persistence of atomism in Meinong is also at the root of Gilbert Ryle's assessment that all objects are "countables"—"Intentionality and the Nature of Thinking," *Revue Internationale de la Philosophie*, XXVII (1973), 257.

ness. Any generalizations based on language as a social fact must be arrived at inductively from this basic level. If, by the same token, we can find patterns and structure at this level, then we have found something that goes beyond social convention. As we shall see, Meinong finds room in this structure for distinctions that correspond to Frege's sense and reference, or Husserl's meaning and object. Finally, the very generality of the term "object" guarantees that the particular subsets of objects that constitute the meanings of the various natural languages or the specialized uses of languages can be defined precisely, as a logical use would require, or metaphorically, as in poetry, or vaguely, as in ordinary language. In this respect, Meinong's theory was particularly well suited to do justice to the variety of rational and irrational discourse that his contemporaries were discovering.

### 3. From Objects of a Higher Order to Gegenstandstheorie, 1899–1904

Meinong's theory of 1904 differed from his views of 1899 in some fundamental respects. While the earlier view may be called a commonsensical realism, in which fictitious objects such as the golden mountain had only a "pseudo-existence," the later view gave such objects a new, less fictitious status: Meinong now held that such objects also had "being" in some sense, though a different sense from physical existence.

As in the 1890s, Meinong was led to this new theory by further considering the problems of wholes and parts and the status of nonexistence. These problems, as we will see, led him to posit several new notions that made Gegenstandstheorie possible: a new category of experience (the assumption), a new sense of being (so-being), and a new kind of object (the objective). It was the psychological category that led to the other two. Meinong took leave of his psychological preoccupations slowly: as late as 1902 he still accepted the term "psychologism" as applied to his work as a whole. Meinong's major work in psychology, and his major opus between 1900 and 1915, was the book *On Assumptions*, which treats of the experience of assuming and its manifold ramifications both in intellectual and emotional life. The book went through two editions; the second, of 1910, was considerably revised, for in the meantime he had developed his theory of objects. It will be necessary first, then, to say something of his mature theory of cognition, which led to it.

As he outgrew psychologism, Meinong moved increasingly away from mental operations as the primary topic in the psychology of thinking. Abstracting and comparing, after all, "operated" on ideas, not on the objects to which they were directed. In order to deal with thinking in an intentional context, Meinong turned to his second class of experiences, judgments. He defined these as follows:

> To my mind there are two things which everyone can admit belong to judgments but not to ideas. One who judges believes something, is convinced of something. . . . furthermore each judgment is by nature subject to the opposition of yes and no, of affirmation and negation. If I have a particular point of view or conviction with regard to A or with regard to its connection with B, then I inevitably mean that A is or that AB is, or that A is not or is not B.[49]

Meinong adds that the linguistic expressions of judgments are sentences. He further maintains that these judgments, or experiences like them, are the basic units of thought. An idea by itself is a mere passive experience, and though it has an object, it is not directed to that object in an authentic sense. A good example is the relation between sensation and perception. The touch sensations from our clothes, or the sensations of peripheral vision, are in consciousness, but we do not perceive them. To do so takes an active intellectual experience, such as making the judgment that they are there. Ideas can grasp objects only through judgments of which they are a part.[50] One can say, then, that judgment represents the lower limit of analysis in the description of thinking: to split a judgment into its components would be to distort thinking.

There is, however, one significant exception to this rule: the assumption. Meinong was led to this unit of experience by the same problems that led him to the theory of objects of a higher order in the first place, and would eventually lead him to the theory of objects itself—namely, the problems of nonexistent objects and the preservation of the analytic approach to Gestalt qualities. *On Assumptions* opens with a discussion of negative ideas, such as "non-smoker," "unextended," "infinite," "hole," "border," and the like.[51] The objects of these presentations seemed to resemble objects of a higher order— "non-smoker" was necessarily founded on "smoker." But the relations and complexes of Meinong's earlier theory required a number of inferiora—at least two, as in "the difference between red and green."

49. Meinong, *Über Annahmen*, 2d. ed., *GA*, IV, 2.
50. *Ibid.*, p. 236.    51. *Ibid.*, p. 9.

What was the second fundament of "non-smoker"? Nor could one point to operations of comparing or abstracting in using the idea. Rather negation had always been a characteristic of judgment, although there was no evidence for our asserting anything to be true or false when we think of a non-smoker. It was here that the assumption came in. An assumption, according to Meinong, was an experience that involved affirmation or negation, but not belief or conviction.[52]

Meinong assures us that the instances of assumptions in psychology are very many, and go beyond the ones we normally express when we use the word "assume." Assumptions play a role in fantasy, in art, in lying, in value judgments, not to mention the purely cognitive sphere. Assumptions thus cut across the entire spectrum of psychic behavior and point the way to the connections between intellectual and emotional experiences (Vaihinger identified them in part with the "conscious fictions" of his philosophy of "As-If").[53]

To give but one example of many that Meinong presents: consider the activity of playing games. However intensely a child may be involved in play, he does not confuse the world of his imagination with the world of reality. In order to set one off from the other, an assumption is necessary. Obviously, the same is true of any game-situation, such as the war-games and military maneuvers of armies.[54] Assumptions also enter into our emotional life through such play-activities. Consider a common adult game: play-acting. The actor must assume that he is the character, and with it all the objects that pertain to the character in the drama. But a good actor never expresses these intellectual assumptions only; he must also convey the feelings built on them, which he is no more prone to confuse with his own personal feelings than we in the audience are likely to confuse a fire in the play with a fire in the theater.[55] The feelings of the actor and the audience may both be labeled "fantasy" feelings:

> That "fear," that "pity," or whatever else it may be that tragedy has the task of "arousing," what are they actually? A fear in which one is basically not at all afraid, a pity in which, on closer inspection, no grief at all is experienced, are these still "feelings" as one usually deals with them at first in psychology? We do not deny that real fear or more easily real pity might now and then come upon some people at the theater, namely those who are still unaccustomed to such things; but likewise one will not easily hesitate to agree

52. *Ibid.*, pp. 4f, 19.
53. Vaihinger to Meinong, April 16, 1911, *Philosophenbriefe*, p. 199.
54. Meinong, *Über Annahmen*, 2d. ed., *GA*, IV, 111ff.
55. *Ibid.*, pp. 113ff.

that such an attitude is neither the normal nor so to speak, the adequate one towards a work of art.[56]

Meinong concludes his book with the notion that, in comparison to judgments, assumptions are "fantasy" experiences as opposed to "serious" ones, and that a similar division can be made among the other basic types of experiences as well (ideas, emotions, and desire).[57]

As far as their role in Meinong's development of the theory of objects was concerned, however, cognitive aspects of assumptions were of prime importance. While assumptions provided a satisfactory description of the experience of nonexistence, they only seemed to bring the question of its objectivity more into the open. For while it is natural to say, from a commonsensical point of view, that nonexistent objects such as the golden mountain are only psychological phenomena (contents), the notion loses much of its plausibility when one adds "non-smoker" or "unextended" to the same category. Moreover, when we talk of fictional or mythical topics, the objects of reference are perfectly distinct from our private experiences concerning them.[58] No one confuses Hamlet with his thought of Hamlet. But what *is* the ontological status of Hamlet?

There were also some problems left outstanding from the theory of objects of a higher order. As long as these objects were conceived on the analogy to ideas, a peculiar problem persisted: how do the three separate ideas of red, green, and difference adequately represent the object "difference between red and green?" Obviously the latter is not simply a collection of three separate objects: red and green stand objectively *in* the relation of difference. But when Meinong attempted to describe how we apprehend this as a whole, he could only say that there must be a further idea of the relation between "red" and "difference" and one of the relation between "difference" and "green." To apprehend *this* relation requires another idea of relation between "red" and "the relation between red and difference," and so on—that is, it involves the multiplication of entities ad infinitum (this was the problem that Bradley had posed in *Appearance and Reality*).[59] In short,

56. *Ibid.*, pp. 309f.
57. Meinong, *Selbstdarstellung*, GA, VII, 30.
58. Meinong, *Über Annahmen*, 2d. ed., GA, IV, 228. This section was reprinted verbatim from the first edition; in a later section of the same chapter, Meinong reformulated the role of assumptions in the light of his theory of objects.
59. Meinong, "Gegenstände höherer Ordnung," GA, II, 390, where Meinong does not view this regress as a problem, and *Über Annahmen*, 2d. ed., GA, IV, 261, where he does.

if we can no longer account for the coherence of our ideas through mental operations, but must rely on some intentional act, what act accounts for this coherence? Obviously judgments or assumptions would enter in here as well.

Meinong's occupation with judgments and assumptions led him to two fundamental insights, which together solved these problems and also led him directly to the theory of objects. The first was a response to a problem that had plagued him since at least 1892. Traditional logic had recognized two types of judgments, the existential (A is) and the categorical (A is B). Brentano had tried to reduce the latter to the former, but Meinong had rejected this attempt. He had claimed, as recently as 1900, that categorical judgments were really relational ones.[60] But in judgments like "the meadow is green," one looks in vain for a relation that corresponds to "similarity" or "difference." Meinong now took the opposite course and subsumed relational judgments under categorical ones. To judge that "difference obtains between red and green" presupposes the judgment that "red is different from green," or vice versa.[61]

The importance of this categorical judgment led Meinong to add one additional sense of "being" to his ontology. In addition to existence and obtaining, there was now so-being (Sosein). Examples of so-being would include facts such as "London is the capital of England," "Red is a color," "Hamlet is indecisive," and even such oddities as "Round squares are round and square." Meinong now sets off such states of affairs from others that he labels simply "being" (Sein), which would include statements such as "There is a red object in the room," "Hamlet does not exist," "Round squares cannot exist," "There is a difference between red and green," or "Newton's laws obtain only within certain limits." To say that something exists is to be able to point to it at a particular place and time; to say that something does not exist is to deny that one can do so. So-being, on the other hand, involved the characteristics of objects that were independent of any such location. Obtaining, as we have said, derives from so-being. Thus so-being came to be one of the most important pillars of Meinong's philosophy, for it bore much of the weight, so to speak, that Meinong had formerly placed on relations.[62] Whereas relations were formerly

60. Meinong, "Abstrahieren und Vergleichen," GA, I, 469.

61. Meinong, Über Annahmen, 1st ed., GA, IV, 422, 441.

62. Meinong, "Über Gegenstandstheorie," GA, II, 494, 520; LTC, pp. 86, 109. It is clear from these passages that the self-evidence of ideal relations was now broadened to include the so-being of objects.

the seat of the self-evidently rational aspects of the world, it is now so-being that is self-evident and known a priori.

The second discovery was in effect the completion of the linguistic analogy. If sentences had their correlates in experience, namely judgments, so too they had their correlates in the realm of objects: the objective. To give Meinong's example:

> Suppose one is talking about . . . a parliamentary election which was preceded by a violent agitation, and says that no disturbance of the peace occurred. First of all, if the given judgment is correct, no one would deny that "something" is apprehended through it. But one could claim at the outset that the "something" would be none other than the object of the judgment "disturbance of the peace." Would a natural speaker say, however, that a disturbance of the peace is apprehended, when the fact in question is that nothing of the sort took place? . . . If we try to specify this "something" more closely, it becomes clear that under normal circumstances there is no single word available for this purpose, if one wants to avoid artificial word-formations. Instead, a [dependent] clause beginning with "that" offers itself as a quite unaffected means of expression. What I apprehend in the case of our example is just this, "that no disturbances of the peace occurred."[63]

It seemed a natural extension of the theory of objects to assign to thinking its own peculiar class of objects. If the hallmark of thinking is affirming and negating, then thinking is directed to objects that have the objective property of being or non-being. In this way, Meinong's old problems of objects of a higher order receive an elegantly simple solution. Complex objects such as "difference between red and green" are derivatives of objectives such as "red and green are different." Similarly, an object of perception to which we apply the concept "black" is apprehended with the help of the objective "this is black."[64]

Just as judgments are built on presentations, so are objectives built on the simple objects of Meinong's earlier theory, which are now called objecta (Objekte). The two hierarchies of mental states and objects correspond to each other.

Meinong had evidently come upon the objective in the midst of writing On Assumptions, for he did not see all of its ramifications for the question of nonexistent objects. This became clear to him within the next two years, and he presents a thorough discussion of it in the

63. Meinong, Über Annahmen, 1st. ed., GA, IV, 428f. In the first edition Meinong treats objectives in chapter VII, following the question of how we apprehend objects of a higher order. In the second edition, he moves the chapter back to III, because he has realized its central importance.

64. Ibid., pp. 456ff.

article that launched the theory of objects in 1904. Meinong presents the paradox in full force. If we admit that all experiences have objective intentions, then we must admit, it seems, that "'There are objects of which it is true that there are no such objects.'"[65] But the objective, properly understood, provides a resolution. For the paradox is based on the illusion that the objective stands in relation to an object as a whole that equals the sum of its parts. In other words, the objective at first glance appears to be an object of a higher order whose parts are homogeneous. But Meinong decisively rejects this analogy:

> Now an Objective, whether it is a Seinsobjektiv or a Nichtseinsobjektiv, tends in relation to its Object (Objekt), albeit *cum grano salis*, as the whole to its parts. But if the whole has being, so must its parts. This seems to mean, when it is extended to the case of the Objective: if the Objective has being (ist), so, in some sense or other, must be the object which belongs to it, even when the Objective is an objective of non-being (Nichtseinsobjektiv) . . . However, no one will deny that this analogy is only an initial expedient in our embarrassment and that there would be no grounds for following this analogy rigorously even for part of the way. Thus, instead of deriving the being of an Object from the being of an Objective, even on the basis of a questionable analogy where the Objective is an Objective of non-being, it would be better to conclude from the facts with which we are concerned that this analogy does not apply to the Objective of non-being—i.e., that the being of the objective is not by any means universally dependent upon the being of its Object.[66]

Thus in the objective, as with the sentence and the judgment, we have the basic unit of ontological analysis. We should only talk of being or non-being in the context of objectives. To ask about the being of the golden mountain or the ontological status of Hamlet is to ask a wrong-headed question: such things no more have being than the oxygen in water has wetness. Meinong says of such objecta that they are "indifferent to being" (*ausserseiend*).[67]

This answer, taken by itself, would seem to solve nothing. For a philosophy of meaning that tells us that Hamlet does not exist would be utterly uninformative. But Meinong proceeds to the notion that is at the heart of the theory of objects: the proper context for such objects are the objectives of so-being. We can and do describe Hamlet in terms of quite definite characteristics, and point to evidence as to why he is irresolute—just as we would about existing persons. This discourse is constituted by categorical judgments and their objectives of

65.  Meinong, "Über Gegenstandstheorie," *GA*, II, p. 490; LTC, p. 83.
66.  *Ibid.*, pp. 492f; LTC, pp. 84f.      67.  *Ibid.*, p. 494; LTC, p. 86.

so-being. Meinong formulates this principle as the "independence of so-being from being," a formulation he derived from one of his best students, Ernst Mally.[68] To ignore this distinction is to give in to a "prejudice in favor of reality," which creates more problems than it solves when used with the linguistic analogy.

In arriving at these new concepts, Meinong succeeded in preserving his commitment to a non-reductionistic type of empiricism. The new theory represented a consistent extension of the assumptions of atomism, analysis, and heterogeneity of parts. This can be seen in two ways. For one thing, Meinong had completed the redefinition of the basic atomic units of his world which he had begun in 1899. The basic congruity of mind, language, and being was no longer at the level of idea-word-objectum, but at the level of judgment-sentence-objective. While the second triads were still classified as objects of a higher order and presupposed the former (just as relations had presupposed fundaments in his earlier theory), the two levels were by no means homogeneous, but had different properties. A second way in which Gegenstandstheorie represented a consistent development of Meinong's earlier views was its insistence on the heterogeneity of the empirical and the rational. Meinong now recognized that this distinction could not be merely psychological, as in his early work, or linguistic, but ontological—the distinction of being and so-being.

Despite these changes, it must be admitted that many vestiges of Meinong's earlier thought remained in his later years, to the detriment of consistency. For example, he did not free himself completely from the old atomism and the view that objecta must have ontological characteristics of their own. Thus he sometimes uses his new term Aussersein to denote an additional *type* of being, along with existing, obtaining, and so-being, and applicable to the objecta.[69] Even more flagrantly, he was unwilling to give up the notion of "objects of a higher order" as a fundamental category. Having carefully explained how such objects presuppose objectives, he turns around to classify objectives as another species of objects of a higher order.[70] Having shown that "obtaining" is really derived from "so-being," he continues to insist that objectives "obtain." These examples show how con-

68. *Ibid.*, p. 489; LTC, p. 82.
69. Meinong, *Über Annahmen*, 2d. ed., *GA*, IV, 79f; "Über emotionale Präsentation," *GA*, III, 353. This work has been translated by Marie-Luise Schubert Kalsi (Evanston: Northwestern University Press, 1972), and will be cited hereafter as "Kalsi" following the reference in the *Gesamtausgabe*. The passage cited here appears on p. 62.
70. Meinong, *Über Annahmen*, 1st ed., *GA*, IV, 465; 2d ed., *ibid.*, pp. 63, 72.

servative Meinong's thought was, how unwilling he was to give up anything established, and also how his phenomenological instincts overshadowed his logical ones. The fact that objects of a higher order did obtain as a matter of careful inspection was much more important to him than the fact that they were logically derivative of something else.

With these concepts at hand, Meinong was at last in a position to complete what he had set out to do in the 1890s: to provide a general theory of the relationships between the rational and the empirical. This was the purpose of Gegenstandstheorie. This new science was to be akin to metaphysics, but distinct from it. For metaphysics was based on being, not so-being. It drew its results from the natural sciences and the Geisteswissenschaften, both of which dealt with existents. But the need for a general science of so-being was demonstrable from the case of mathematics, which was coordinate with neither natural science, the humanities, nor metaphysics. Mathematics was in fact a science of so-being, a part of Gegenstandstheorie.[71] Insofar as so-being was not necessarily quantifiable, a more general science was needed. This may still seem an implausible concept, inasmuch as the subject matter is as infinite as the number of objects we can refer to. Meinong realized this and restricted his theory to those objects which are self-evidently given to experience.[72] Meinong maintained there are many objects which are given in this way without the help of mathematical concepts or symbols and which nevertheless have no clearcut existential status. A good example was those simple sensations he had treated in his article of 1888. On the one hand, elementary colors such as red and yellow did not belong to physics, with its terminology of light-vibrations. On the other hand, color did not belong to physiology, since it was not a neural process, or psychology, since it was not reducible to mental contents. "Red," in Meinong's new terminology, was an example of a "homeless object," and belonged to Gegenstandstheorie.[73] For we can talk with utter precision about the systematic properties (the so-being) of colors, such as the laws of complementarity and mixing, without ever once considering whether these colors exist as light-waves, nerve processes, or ideas. Their existence, in the sense of being at a particular place and time, is irrelevant to the description

---

71. Meinong, "Über Gegenstandstheorie," *GA*, II, 508; LTC, p. 98.

72. *Ibid.*, p. 520; LTC, p. 108.

73. Meinong, *Über die Stellung der Gegenstandstheorie im System der Wissenschaften*, *GA*, V, 214f.

of their properties. Indeed, the situation as Meinong saw it was analogous to the laws of geometry, which apply to figures that have no precise counterpart in the existing world.[74]

One can best appreciate the significance of the theory of objects for Meinong by looking at a particular case: his treatment of perception. It shows Meinong's belief that the self-evident was thoroughly interlaced with ordinary experience:

> Suppose that someone looks out from a window for the first time to a region unknown to him. It can well happen that he says, "The meadows before me are green," and perhaps also, "I see that the meadows are green." But can the greenness of the meadow really be the first thing that falls into his perception? . . . clearly not; the judgment that there are meadows there [outside the window] must be included in that which is experienced in looking out the window. . . . But if it is a matter of testing the judgment "the meadow is green" with some exactitude for its correctness, such a test must inevitably touch on the question: how far is the meadow so constituted to be like that which one normally calls "green"? . . . In no case is one still dealing with a judgment of perception. This is evident from the fact that . . . these judgments are a priori.[75]

Thus, every perception contains within it an objective of so-being. Such a distinction may seem unduly fine, but Meinong draws some important consequences from it regarding language:

> It may be of special importance that even a simple sentence which aims at communicating an act of perception (e.g., "I see a spruce tree") never actually succeeds in expressing just this perception alone—at least for the listener. For it is no longer a matter of perception . . . that what I see is sufficiently similar to that which one calls a spruce tree. . . . For there is naturally no understandable word for that wholly particular thing which I now perceive. The particular in the experiences of individuals cannot account for that which brings about understanding among several individuals.[76]

For Meinong, then, language too is aimed at so-being, by bringing the particular objects of reference into relation with others. At the same time, language is limited in that it cannot describe utterly particular

74. Meinong, "Bemerkungen über den Farbenkörper und das Mischungsgesetz," *GA*, I, 498–499. One may question, of course, as Russell did, whether "being at a particular place and time" is not after all a kind of so-being. See Chapter Eight, pt. 1.

75. Meinong, *Erfahrungsgrundlagen*, *GA*, V, 388f. Meinong goes so far here as to exclude the judgment of so-being from the perception, but retreats from this extreme position in *Möglichkeit*, *GA*, VI, 193.

76. Meinong, *Erfahrungsgrundlagen*, *GA*, V, 390f.

things. This, as we shall see, leads to certain conclusions regarding the extent and limits of reason.

### 4. MEINONG ON TRUTH, APPREHENSION, AND KNOWLEDGE, 1905–1915

It remains to discuss Meinong's application of his new theory to some of the traditional questions of philosophy and to see how it fulfills the requirements of an ideal language. He treated these problems in *On Assumptions, The Foundations of Knowledge in Experience* (1906), and in *On Possibility and Probability* (1915). His treatment of the problem of truth is very straightforward. He defines truth in the following way: "A judgment is true whose objective is a fact."[77] Lest this seem to be mere word-play, it should be noted that Meinong develops a new context in which the term "fact" appears. A factual objective is not merely one of existence or so-being, but includes negative objectives; it is also a fact that centaurs don't exist. Factuality, then, is a distinct property of certain objectives, independent of their being or non-being and is related to such other properties as possibility, probability, and necessity—the so-called modal properties.[78] The statement, "it is a fact that flying saucers don't exist" is along the same lines as "it is possible that flying saucers don't exist." It is to *these* objectives that the terms "true" and "false" should be applied, not the simple objectives of being or so-being. Meinong's definition, it should be noted, does not include a criterion for distinguishing a factual situation from a non-factual one; it is merely an attempt to describe what it is to say that something is true.

Meinong's treatment of modal properties, though an important part of his philosophy, need not concern us further here.[79] More closely related to our questions are his theory of knowledge and especially his views on apprehension, which lead to it. Meinong saw knowledge as an intentional relation between an experiencce and an object, on the same order as apprehension (*erfassen*) and referring (*meinen*). Knowledge is obviously something more than the other two, as it involves the further element of belief; moreover, the objective be-

---

77.  *Ibid.*, pp. 399–400. This should be taken to mean, however, that truth is primarily a property of facts and secondarily one of judgments (see *Möglichkeit, GA*, VI, 440).

78.  *Möglichkeit*, section 15; *Über Annahmen*, 2d. ed., *GA*, IV, 80.

79.  For a full exposition, see Findlay, *Meinong's Theory*, Chs. IV, VII.

lieved would have to be true.[80] Meinong's notion of knowledge may not be properly understood unless his theories on apprehension and referring are presented. In doing so, we may point to the ways in which the theory of objects functions as an ideal language. For Meinong works out the relationships between the mind and objects not primarily at the level of language, but at the level of cognitive experiences, which by virtue of their analogies to language may be transferred to the latter.

In an earlier chapter we said that Meinong preserved his earlier epistemological notions in his later thought. He did not, of course, employ the same terminology: he clearly recognized that mental operations were no more than mental, and that abstraction, comparison, and indirect ideation should really be classified as "idea-production" (Vorstellungsproduktion), rather than as direct means of apprehension.[81] But the functions performed by these operations now find a place in his mature theory. Let us first take the case of indirect ideation—that is, the means of apprehending something unknown through its relations with things known. The ideas employed in such cases now become assumptions of so-being, since the relations now apprehended are now classified as objectives of so-being. To say that John, whom I may not know, is as tall as my friend James presupposes a number of such objectives which apply to James and a number which apply to John, some of which share the same predicate (for example, "James is 5′ 7″"; "John is 5′ 7″"). If I know James's height and the fact that he is as tall as John, I can know something of John as well. Meinong calls this act Soseinsmeinen (reference by way of so-being), which is contrasted to Seinsmeinen (reference by way of being) which he had formerly called a "direct idea."[82] We have already seen how both operate together in the case of perception.

From this theory of apprehension Meinong develops the notion that we may apprehend several levels of objects at the same time. In the example of John and James, the content of my idea of John is also directed to James through the relation of similarity. This idea that a given experience or linguistic unit may be directed to several types of objects is a crucial one for understanding Gegenstandstheorie as analogous to an ideal language—one whose structure can comprehend

80. Meinong, "Über Gegenstandstheorie," GA, II, 485, 499; LTC, pp. 78, 91; Möglichkeit, GA, VI, 414.

81. Meinong, Über Annahmen, 2d. ed., GA, IV, 11.

82. Ibid., pp. 269ff, 284.

the variety of natural and specialized languages, from exact scientific language to poetry. Not surprisingly, this notion has caused some controversy among Meinong's interpreters. Despite his explicit avowal of the principle that a single content may have many objects, a number of commentators have sought to hold him to the notion of a one-to-one correspondence between content and object.[83] There are indeed other passages in Meinong that support this interpretation: those in which he redefines the notion of content in relation to his earlier psychologistic theory. Obviously our mental acts are no longer directed to mental contents, as before, but to transcendent objects. Yet our ideas, judgments, feelings, and so on still have content. What role do these contents now play? Meinong answers that they vary with the objects they represent.[84] Our ideas as ideas of red and of green are different not only by virtue of the objects to which they are directed, but also by virtue of their contents. And the only way to describe this latter difference would seem to be through a one-to-one correspondence.

These passages make it easy to assimilate Meinong to the type of linguistic philosophy held by Russell and the logical positivists, who hold that logic requires a strict correspondence between the terms of a proposition and the objects to which that proposition refers.[85] It leaves open the question, however, of whether these apparently contradictory positions in Meinong can be reconciled. The evidence is clearly that they can be. In one of his later treatises, *On Emotional Presentation*, Meinong addresses himself specifically to the problem. Although contents can indeed be directed to many objects, he claims, the strict correspondence holds in those special circumstances in which an idea is directed to an objectum—the normal case in intellectual experience, insofar as judgments have such ideas as their parts.[86]

83. Meinong, "Abstrahieren und Vergleichen," *GA*, I, 474, 485f; *Über Annahmen*, 2d. ed., *GA*, IV, 277; *Die Erfahrungsgrundlagen unseres Wissens, GA*, V, 464f. Edgar Morscher, in "Meinong's Bedeutungslehre," *Revue Internationale de la Philosophie*, XXVII (1973), 198, claims that Meinong is unclear about this notion and gives an interpretation of his theory of symbolic terms to reconcile it with a one-to-one correspondence (pp. 195, 197). Grossmann points out that whereas Meinong denies this correspondence at the level of ideas, he reestablishes it again at the level of judgments (p. 196). I do not see, however, how this is compatible with Meinong's theory of self-presentation (see Chapter Seven, pt. 3), in which the same content is directed to an object of an external perceptual judgment and *is* the object of an internal perceptual judgment.

84. Meinong, "Gegenstände höherer Ordnung," *GA*, II, 384.

85. See J. O. Urmson, *Philosophical Analysis* (London: Oxford University Press, 1956), p. 190.

86. Meinong, "Emotionale Präsentation," *GA*, III, 342; Kalsi, p. 52.

Thus contents do vary with their particular objects, but it does not follow that these particular objects are the only ones to which they refer in all cases. To give one example: suppose I have a mental image of the color green. According to Meinong, there will be a specific shade of green to which that image refers. But, at the same time, it will also refer less precisely to all other shades of green, and perhaps even to those objects which are questionable borderline cases.[87] This principle seems to apply to all contents, whether they are concrete images or concepts.[88] Thus each mental content has its own particular object, but apprehends many other objects which are more or less similar to the particular one, that is, via Soseinsmeinen. In this way, Meinong can describe both exact reference, such as one would expect in logic, and imprecise reference, such as we might find in ordinary speech, by means of the same theory. We can understand the relations of specialized languages such as those of science to the language of common sense through a given web of similarities and differences between two levels.

Meinong makes an additional and important use of this notion of multiple objects. He distinguishes between phenomena and noumena, or "near" and "remote" objects, in which the former are the objects of immediate, untutored experience, whereas the latter are the objects as they "really are" in the physical world. Thus when we talk about colors, we are also talking about light-waves, albeit indirectly, since our contents refer us to both. The color is for most of us a near object, the light-wave a remote object, of reference. We are justified in establishing such a hierarchy just because the similarities and differences between objects correspond to each other in some lawful way.[89] In this manner, the different levels of objects emerge from the context in which the similarities and differences are defined, rather than being specified in advance, as in Frege.

A good example of how Meinong applies this approach is his revised treatment of concepts, a matter which had occupied him in the first *Hume-Study*. In his later thought, a concept is no longer an idea, but a certain level of object which Meinong calls "incomplete."[90] He derives this from the Lockean notion that an abstract idea of a tri-

---

87. Meinong, "Abstrahieren und Vergleichen," *GA*, I, 484ff.
88. Meinong, *Möglichkeit*, *GA*, VI, 163n.
89. This is a highly condensed account of No. 19–21 of *Erfahrungsgrundlagen*, *GA*, V, 459–469; see also *Über Annahmen*, 2d. ed., *GA*, IV, 277.
90. Meinong, *Möglichkeit*, *GA*, VI, 178.

angle is neither isoceles nor scalene, since it must apply to both. Such an idea, Berkeley had pointed out, contradicted the very notion of "idea" itself as something determinate. But such indeterminate objects, Meinong claims, are indispensable for reference, for it is precisely such an indeterminate triangle which geometers use as a basis for inference. In ascribing a particular shape and size to a triangle, one "completes" an incomplete object by bringing different objectives of so-being to bear on it.[91] Thus a construction of a theory by means of abstract concepts is a process of completion of incomplete objects. The same thing occurs in the common case of perception. To say "The meadow is green" is to apply an incomplete object "green," in which the specific shade of green is unspecified, to a concrete object, meadow, which does have a specific shade. The meadow, then, is complete. But, as said before, we can never apprehend an object in its completeness, we can only approach this goal by bringing in more objectives of so-being.

Meinong's reason for denying that we can ever apprehend concrete objects fully is revealing. Though at first glance it seems most bizarre, it is perfectly consistent with the rest of his thought. A concrete physical object is complete, according to Meinong, not only by virtue of its positive properties, but also by virtue of its negative ones. If properties are described in terms of objectives of so-being, then both positive and negative objectives may apply to any object. A meadow, in other words, is definitely a given shade of green, but equally definitely not another shade. By the same reasoning, it is also not a forest or a building. Since the number of objects of reference is infinite, a complete object has an infinite number of determinations.[92] The number of positive ones would of course be finite, but the number of negative ones would not be. If we are seeking to complete an object, then, we may never be sure that we have exhausted all of its positive properties, since we can never take account of all its negative ones. Incomplete objects, by contrast, are knowable bcause they are not so definite. The concept "green" neither is nor is not a specific shade; thus it is within the reach of our intellect. Meinong thus arrives at a conclusion comparable to that of Kant, though by a very different route: we can never know things in themselves in their determinateness. Nevertheless, unlike Kant, Meinong postulates differences of degree in completion. He speaks at times of the complete physical object as

91. *Ibid.*, pp. 199f.    92. *Ibid.*, pp. 196–197.

the "ultimate object" (Zielgegenstand), and of the incomplete object that we can grasp as the "auxiliary object" (Hilfsgegenstand).[93]

Meinong's distinction of ultimate and auxiliary object, like that of remote and near object of which it is a special case, establishes a hierarchy of levels such as Frege had originally postulated. Meinong recognized the applicability of his distinction to languages also. "The auxiliary object is what words mean, the ultimate object is what they name."[94] For Frege, too, saw that concepts are "incomplete," and that they are the stuff of predication and of the workings of language.[95] At the same time, Frege denied, as did Meinong, that language could fully describe completely particular individual experience. But Meinong claimed that, while this goal is indeed unattainable, one can at least approach it through varying degrees of completion, and thus penetrate into individual experience more deeply than Frege conceded. In this respect he stands between Frege and Husserl, who also invoked the process of "completion" under the name of "fulfillment" (Erfüllung).[96] But as the name implies, Husserl believed that such a process could eventually attain its goal.

This, then, is Meinong's theory of apprehension. We can apprehend reality, but only incompletely. What does this theory contribute to the notion of an ideal language? It gives a satisfactory description of meaning that can be applied to all languages, and it elaborates some rudimentary aspects of structure: languages are intertranslatable insofar as the similarities and differences between their objects of reference can be analyzed in terms of objectives of so-being. At the same time, Meinong's doctrine of the incomplete object precludes the possibility of any one set of objects being elevated as universal "meaning." Because the number of objects is unlimited, no one can ever be sure which ones are germane to human understanding and which ones are not. This approach certainly avoids the dangers of reductionism endemic to most positivistic enterprises: it denies that any one

93. *Ibid.*    94. *Ibid.*, p. 741.

95. Frege, "Function and Concept" (1891), in Geach and Black, pp. 30, 24. Frege identifies a concept as a type of function, and attributes incompleteness to functions.

96. Husserl, *Logical Investigations*, I, 280f, 282; II, 762. See also Findlay, "Einige Hauptpünkte in Meinongs philosophischer Psychologie," in *Jenseits von Sein und Nichtsein*, ed. Rudolf Haller (Graz: Akademische Druck-u. Verlagsanstalt, 1972), p. 21. There is, nevertheless, a certain similarity between Husserl's doctrine of "categorical intuition" and Meinong's theory of evidence outlined below. For a further explanation of *Erfüllung*, see Chapter Ten, pt. 4.

language, be it logical or scientific (or even poetic), is the measuring rod by which all others must be compared. On the other hand, it appears to offer no answer to relativism. If there is no ultimate criterion for selecting what is important from the infinite number of objects and combinations available, then the pragmatic criterion of "what works" would be as valid as any other—a solution with which Meinong appeared to have no sympathy.[97] Moreover, Meinong's theory would seem to be deficient as an analogy to language in one respect: there is no counterpart to the concept of *rule*. In language, one cannot combine words in any odd way to make sentences: combinations are governed by grammatical rules. Thus any language presupposes some kind of criterion to distinguish meaningful sentences from nonsense: "Horses are white, brown, or black" must be distinguished in some way from "White horses brown are black or." The problem of criteria then, enters in at a number of points.

These problems ultimately bear on the adequacy of the empiricist approach to language and meaning in the first place. Atomism and analysis may provide us with a description of what occurs when we refer to something in an isolated instance, but it is by no means self-evident that a satisfactory definition of language emerges from a piling up of such instances. For what distinguishes one language from another seems to depend also on certain choices that are made about the whole of the subject matter, choices which cannot be understood simply by analyzing the parts. These would include choice of rules and choice of what to include as relevant and exclude as irrelevant from the infinite number of possible objects. One of Meinong's most famous critics who took this approach was T. S. Eliot, who was turning to philosophy in the years immediately preceding World War One. Though Eliot had already established himself as a poet through the composition of such works as *The Love Song of J. Alfred Prufrock*, he was evidently attracted to philosophy as a way of stimulating his poetic sense, perhaps to keep it from lapsing into a mere expression of internal experiences.[98] He had heard Bergson in Paris, studied Indian philosophy, and wrote a Ph.D. dissertation at Harvard on F. H.

97. Meinong, *Möglichkeit*, *GA*, VI, 38.

98. See Eric Thompson, *T. S. Eliot, the Metaphysical Perspective* (Carbondale: Southern Illinois University Press, 1963), p. xxi; Herbert Howarth, *Notes on Some Figures Behind T. S. Eliot* (London: Chatto and Windus, 1965), pp. 152–204; John Margolis, *T. S. Eliot's Intellectual Development, 1922–39* (Chicago: University of Chicago Press, 1972), who suggests that Eliot derived the notion that poetry should express something higher than one's own experiences from his teacher Irving Babbitt (p. 7).

Bradley in 1916. Eliot found the idealism of Bradley much to his liking, and in the dissertation he attacked empiricists such as Russell and Meinong, whose ideas he labeled "elaborate superfluities."[99] Although Eliot was willing to defend imaginary and impossible objects against Russell's criticisms, he found Meinong's approach to be excessively analytical. In a manner quite like that of Bradley, Eliot sought to show that Meinong's attempts to overcome the duality of subject and object through the notion of intentionality were bound to fail for this reason. Eliot thus objects to "the drawing and quartering of reality into real and ideal objects."[100] To accept any such divisions will ultimately bar the way to the thing in itself, as it did in Kant.[101] Meinong's admission that such things cannot be known fully amounts to an admission of self-defeat. What is missing, according to Eliot, is a "point of view."[102] Objects are real or ideal not in themselves, but depend on the perspective from which they are apprehended; this perspective will alter the ontological status of the whole. By the same reasoning, there can be no clearcut distinction between judgments and assumptions, or between real and imaginary objects. These distinctions only emerge once a perspective has been defined.[103] In Eliot's case, such a philosophy did find specific application in esthetic criticism. The essay "Tradition and the Individual Talent" of 1919 shows that poetic innovation can take place only within the context of tradition, and yet, by virtue of introducing a new point of view, it alters that tradition as a whole:

> The existing monuments [of art] form an ideal order among themselves, which is modified by the introduction of the new (the really new) work of art among them. The existing order is complete before the new work arrives; for order to persist after the supervention of novelty, the *whole* existing order must be, if ever so slightly, altered.[104]

In both the dissertation and the essay, Eliot studiously avoids identifying this point of view with the personality of the author. Rather, an object of fiction is "a highly complex ideal construction," which must encompass both the author's experiences and the objective properties of the character he has created.[105]

99. T. S. Eliot, *Knowledge and Experience in the Philosophy of F. H. Bradley* (London: Faber and Faber, 1964), p. 91.

100. *Ibid.*, p. 99.    101. *Ibid.*, pp. 95, 100.

102. *Ibid.*, p. 102.    103. *Ibid.*, p. 136.

104. Eliot, "Tradition and the Individual Talent," in *Selected Prose of T. S. Eliot*, ed. Frank Kermode (New York: Harcourt Brace Jovanovich, 1975), p. 38.

105. *Ibid.*, pp. 39f; *Knowledge and Experience*, pp. 124, 136.

While Eliot's critique of Meinong represents a consistent application of the idealistic position, it cannot be said that he read Meinong
too carefully. There are some inaccuracies in translation which make
Meinong appear to be much closer to Kant than he actually was.[106]
Moreover, Eliot does not seem to have been aware of Meinong's theory of values and its relation to experiences of feeling. Yet he does
make the point that some choices about the whole are necessary if
one is to draw satisfactory analogies to language for philosophical
purposes.

Although Meinong was not aware of Eliot's criticism, he does respond to a similar objection in his book *On Possibility and Probability*.
His answer has to do with his theory of knowledge, which was an outgrowth of his views on apprehension.

Knowledge, as we have noted, is like apprehension but contains
something that apprehension does not. Indeed, the difference seems
to lie precisely in the possession of a criterion. In apprehension, we
judge something to be the case, but in knowledge we claim that this
judgment is legitimate. What, then, differentiates knowledge from
apprehension? One thing, certainly, is that the objective in question is
true—that it is a fact. But even this is not sufficient to define knowledge: we may, for example have true opinion about a matter, or we
may make an intelligent guess. In both cases, we will have apprehended a fact, but could not be said to know it was true. To do this, one
additional factor is needed. That factor, Meinong says, is evidence.[107]
The term may connote some sort of additional ground or proof for
saying something is true, but Meinong means something quite different by it. For him, evidence is a state of mind, a subjective factor. It
involves that awareness of insight when something "dawns on us,"
when concepts that were fuzzy suddenly become clear. This definition
may seem a throwback to psychologism, a claim that Meinong denies.[108] In fact, it is descended from Locke's criterion of intuitive
knowledge; for example, in order to "know" a logical proof, one must

---

106. For example, Meinong writes in *Erfahrungsgrundlagen*, p. 57, "Bekanntlich
muss der Gegenstand, den eine Vorstellung erfasst, durchaus nicht existieren; um so
gewisser aber der Inhalt." Eliot translates, "Clearly, the object apprehended in a presentation cannot possibly exist; but still less, then, can the content" (p. 91). On pp. 99–100
of *Erfahrungsgrundlagen*, Meinong writes, "Aber die Gültigkeit dessen, was wir, so wie
wir einmal beschaffen sind, à priori zu erkennen vermögen, wird durch diese Subjec-
tivität in keiner Weise in Frage gestellt." Eliot translates, "But this subjectivity in no way
compromises the validity of what we are able to know *a priori*, once we obtain it" (p. 97).

107. Meinong, *Möglichkeit, GA*, VI, 414ff.

108. *Ibid.*, p. 415.

have insight or understanding of all the steps, rather than simply accepting each one as true. But Locke had identified this intuition with introspection—that is, the awareness of our own ideas. Meinong breaks with the introspective criterion, while retaining the basically subjective character of Locke's definition. Evidence is direct insight into the nature of objects; in the case of so-being, it is rational a priori insight, which is clearly distinguishable from the evidence of inner perception, which is empirical and posteriori. The fact that inner perception is continuous with memory betrays this difference.[109]

One may nevertheless question whether Meinong's transformation of the introspective criterion is adequate as an analogue to linguistic rules. How can we distinguish genuine insight from self-righteous conviction in an individual case? Does the inner certainty that one's utterances are meaningful prevent others from interpreting it as nonsense? The intuitive interpretation of evidence tells us nothing of the circumstances or context in which such an intuition takes place, and this would seem to be crucial for any application of Meinong's theory to problems of language. This gap would seem to be filled only by forsaking the analytical approach—a context could scarcely be defined in terms of its components in isolation. Yet Meinong firmly rejects any appeal to the context or system as an adequate substitute for intuitive evidence of an individual objective.[110] Such appeals ultimately rest on intuition, not the other way around. One can see this by imagining situations in which this intuitive criterion were absent. To give one of Meinong's examples, "the judgment that wood floats on water is doubtless opposed to the judgments that many bodies sink in water: nevertheless no one who has normal experiences at his disposal will let the first be shaken by the second."[111] All testing of knowledge ultimately depends on such untested evidential judgments.

It is to Meinong's credit, however, that his notion of evidence is broad enough to include such circumstantial evidence as well. The criterion we have treated so far is applicable to certain knowledge. But evidence, Meinong claims, admits of degrees, of which certainty is but the highest. There is also evidence for *presumption*, as in the case of judgments of memory.[112] In presuming to know what we remember, we are not justified in claiming infallibility—that is, we may not legitimately assert that the objectives we remember are true. We may

109. Meinong, *Zum Erweise des allgemeinen Kausalgesetzes*, GA, V, 493–494.
110. Meinong, *Möglichkeit*, GA, VI, 455; section 55.
111. *Ibid.*, p. 454.
112. Meinong, *Erfahrungsgrundlagen*, GA, V, 90f.

also legitimately presume (*vermuten*) the objectivity of our judgments of memory, though the evidence involved is only evidence that the objectives are probable rather than true. This is based on the notion that objectives themselves have modal properties that admit of degrees: the factuality of an objective is likewise the upper limit of a series of possibilities, with unfactuality as the lower limit. Furthermore, the legitimacy of such probabilistic evidence does not simply depend on intuition, but on the circumstances: one can arrive at the judgment that something is probable only on the basis of a number of objectives—not on a single one.[113] One of Meinong's commentators, Roderick Chisholm, has called this doctrine of evidence for presumption "one of the most important contributions of the philosophy of the twentieth century."[114] Its innovation is in its denial that the only alternative to certainty is doubt and skepticism. Rather, we may legitimately be said to know something of which we are less than certain. This probabilistic evidence also applies to inductive knowledge of the type based on repeated experience—that is, a posteriori knowledge.

Although Meinong thus does manage to account for circumstantial evidence, it is clear that his account does not really offer any rules for applying it to individual cases. Meinong's efforts rather are directed toward establishing the fact that there *is* knowledge and what it is. He is plainly not interested as much in the question of how to apply or test such knowledge systematically. As Findlay has said, "Meinong's theory of knowledge is therefore the antithesis of any critical theory."[115] The weight of Meinong's argument is to point out how pervasive such evidence is in our experience, so that the alternative of denying it would be chaos and despair.

Does this mean that Meinong has no answer to relativism? Are the criteria for the rules of language ultimately a matter of convention? As we turn to a consideration of Meinong's theory of values and its relation to experiences of feeling, we will find the analogue to the concept of rule that has thus far been lacking.

113. Meinong, *Möglichkeit*, GA, VI, 428. For a fuller treatment, see Kindinger, in Meinong, *Gedenkschrift*, pp. 48ff.
114. Chisholm, "Vorwort zur Neuausgabe," *Möglichkeit*, GA, VI, xi.
115. Findlay, *Meinong's Theory*, p. 254.

# VII

# MEINONG'S THEORY OF VALUE AND THE HERMENEUTICAL TRADITION

In the last decade of his life Meinong turned increasingly to the elaboration of his theory of values, integrating it into Gegenstands-theorie and pursuing its implications for ethics and esthetics. He thereby moved gradually away from the orbit of Anglo-Saxon logical analysis and into that of continental philosophy. Unfortunately, his works in this area were not widely known—his treatise *On Emotional Presentation* of 1916 was published in the proceedings of the Viennese Imperial Academy of the Sciences and languished there until the appearance of the *Gesamtausgabe* in 1967. He completed the systematic revision of his earlier book on value theory just before his death, and it appeared posthumously in 1923 with the financial assistance of his students and his widow (he was working on an additional treatise on ethics when he died, which has been included in the *Gesamtausgabe* as well).[1] By this time, however, the Husserlian brand of intentionality had come to dominate the German philosophical scene, and Meinong's viewpoint was largely ignored. Of the phenomenologists, only Max Scheler seems to have acknowledged Meinong's contributions and their similarity to his own.[2]

1. Meinong, *Ethische Bausteine*, *GA*, III, 659–724.
2. Max Scheler, "Die deutsche Philosophie der Gegenwart," in *Wesen und Formen der Sympathie*, in *Gesammelte Werke*, ed. Manfred S. Frings (Bern: Francke Verlag, 1973), VII, 312.

In his autobiographical sketch of 1920, Meinong gives a remarkable insight into his own isolation from the philosophical trends of the time:

> The continually increasing preoccupation with Kant has made it a tradition to give new thoughts, whenever possible and even beyond this, the form of Kantian conceptions. If one considers, however, how uncertain the interpretation of Kant has become, it seems to me that one can become more than doubtful whether this is a good tradition. In any case, I have thereupon not held it to be indispensable to legitimize a position by way of Kant, but rather detrimental when it involved a detour, and have therefore avoided it. It may be added, perhaps, that he who views the realistic and idealistic conceptions . . . as incompatible opposites can be put off by the *dualism—sit venia verbo—of one who means to be able to approach metaphysics from a realistic, the theory of objects from an idealistic viewpoint.*
>
> Moreover, it may of course have happened that I did not estimate some [intellectual] affinities highly enough, or that I did not bring some to bear sufficiently which I did estimate correctly. For example, I believe it to be beyond doubt that the fundamental intentions of Kant were directed not in the least part to the theory of objects, and that my efforts in this area touch in more than one point those of the Neo-Kantians of the Marburg school on the one hand, and of the representatives of critical value theory [Windelband and Rickert] on the other [italics added].[3]

It is especially unfortunate that Meinong's writings were not better known in Germany, for they touched on some of the crucial issues in the methodological controversy there concerning the status of values in cultural and social studies.

### 1. The German Methodological Controversy and the Concept of Value

The contributions of German intellectuals such as Dilthey, Rickert, and Weber to the philosophy of history and society before the First World War stemmed from very different roots than those of the empiricist tradition we have been studying—and yet they were led to many of the same problems and approaches. These thinkers, too, tended to conceptualize their fundamental problems in terms of the question of meaning. They also took great pains to avoid the ultimate implications of relativism. Admittedly, their starting point had tended to emphasize such relativism: German historicism stressed the diversity and richness of human history and culture, and their views on the

---

3. Meinong, *Selbstdarstellung, GA,* VII, 57.

autonomy of the humanistic studies (Geisteswissenschaften in Dilthey's terminology, Kulturwissenschaften in that of the Neo-Kantians Windelband and Rickert) were part of an attempt to preserve this diversity against the encroachments of positivism. Such an enterprise, moreover, had obvious political and ideological implications in Germany. The middle classes in particular had developed a sense of national identity based on this belief in cultural diversity—that German Kultur was irreducibly different from the rationalistic Zivilisation of the West, where positivism was but one manifestation of the shallow dogma of intellectual and technological progress. At the same time, however, these philosophers realized that a complete absence of universal standards constituted an equally great danger. The relativity of values from one nation or culture to another may have been an undeniable fact, but a surrender to the full implications of this fact would open the way to any and all prophets and creeds, however irrational or destructive. Dilthey expressed this sentiment most poignantly at a speech at his seventieth birthday in 1903:

> The finitude of every historical phenomenon, whether it be a religion, an ideal, or a philosophic system, hence the relativity of every sort of human conception about the connectedness of things, is the last word of the historical world view. All flows in process; nothing remains stable. On the other hand, there arises the need of thought and the striving of philosophy for universally valid cognition. The historical way of looking at things (*die geschichtliche Weltanschauung*) has liberated the human spirit from the last chains which natural science and philosophy have not yet torn asunder. But where are the means for overcoming the anarchy of convictions which threatens to break in on us?
>
> I have worked all my life on problems which link themselves as a long chain to this problem. I see the goal. If I fall by the wayside, I hope that my younger companions and students will go on to the end of this road.[4]

Rickert, too, expressed his abhorrence of a "nihilism" that would result from a complete absence of universals.[5] It was in this sense, then, that the concerns of the philosophers of history touched those of the logical realists. The former were no less divided among themselves than the latter, however; the differences between Dilthey and his followers on the one hand and the Neo-Kantians on the other became known as the methodological controversy.

---

4. Dilthey, "Rede zum 70. Geburtstag," *GS*, V, 9; trans. Georg G. Iggers in *The German Conception of History* (Middletown: Wesleyan University Press, 1968), pp. 143–144. This book contains an extended discussion of the methodological controversy.

5. Iggers, p. 158.

This controversy has been treated extensively by other historians, so I will here indicate only some of its main points.[6] Dilthey's acknowledged position was that of a realist. Although he claimed to have undertaken his epistemological project of a critique of historical reason in the spirit of Kant, he rejected Kant's attempt to pursue such a critique deductively—that is, by inquiring into the a priori conditions of historical knowledge.[7] Rather, Dilthey proceeded inductively, by describing what he believed to be the actual practice of historians, legal theorists, and literary scholars as they apprehended objects in the real world, and drawing out the common features of this practice. We have already seen how he developed this notion from a psychological one in the 1880s to one that involved the interpretation of objective cultural products in his essay on hermeneutics. He continued, however, to emphasize the importance of psychological intuition (*erleben*) in this process, as well as the empathetic apprehension of the experiences of others (*verstehen*) through the interpretation of their cultural expressions.[8] The knowledge that resulted from such a mode of apprehension was obviously different from scientific or logical knowledge, in that its starting point was not a neatly delimited unit of experience such as an isolated sensation or judgment. Dilthey claimed that such states did not occur in the humanistic studies, but that our experiences come in complex wholes, in which thinking, feeling, and willing interact. For example, if one is to understand what a house means to a person, one must note his or her awareness of its physical features, its cost or value, its esthetic features, its sentimental value—all as part of a single relation of "meaning." Only after we can apprehend such wholes may we break them down into parts for classification. Dilthey's work in sorting out the various types of intuition was greatly facilitated by Husserl's *Logical Investigations*—thereafter, he referred to the various types of understanding as relationships between experiences and objects. He distinguished between the objective apprehension (*gegenständliche Auffassen*) and the *having* of objects in thinking and feeling (*gegenständliche Haben*).[9]

Dilthey's approach reflected his awareness of the need for delimit-

6. *Ibid.*, Chs. VI–VII; Ringer, Ch. VI; Hughes, pp. 190–200, 229–248, 296–314.

7. Dilthey, "Studien zur Grundlegung der Geisteswissenschaften," *GS*, VII, 13n.

8. Dilthey, "Der Aufbau der geschichtlichen Welt in den Geisteswissenschaften," *GS*, VII, 143.

9. Dilthey, "Studien zur Grundlegung," *GS*, VII, 10, 24, 45. The relations of feeling and willing give rise to the determination of values and positing of ends and rules (*Wertbestimmung, Zwecksetzung, Regelgebung*).

ing one's subject matter as a whole in defining a particular discipline or area of human inquiry—a delimitation that precedes analysis. At the same time, he realized the potential arbitrariness of such preliminary decisions. How can one tell if the choices one makes in what to include in a study of history, for example, transcend at all the presuppositions of one's own time, place, and upbringing? The problem has become known as that of the hermeneutical circle. Dilthey formulated it in terms of the question of selecting the appropriate level of description. In his essay on hermeneutics he wrote:

> From the individual words and their connections one should understand the whole of a work; but the complete understanding presupposes that of the whole. This circle repeats itself in the relation of the individual work to the mental type (Geistesart) and development of its author.[10]

Thus the problem of relativism was implicit in the hermeneutical method: the unit of description was a matter of subjective choice—the same problem that the scientific philosophers who were committed to the analytical approach had to face.

Dilthey faced the relativistic implications of his views openly. For him, there was no one value-system to be found empirically in history. One could compare and classify the views and assumptions of different periods or groups—Weltanschauungen as he called them—to arrive at a typology. But there was no single, overriding set that applied to all.[11]

Rickert's position was that such methodological dilemmas were endemic to realism as such. There was simply no guarantee of objective knowledge in an empirical approach, and any attempt to pursue it to its end would lead to skepticism and relativism.[12] The only alternative was the way of Kant: to unravel the underlying concepts which the practice of knowing logically presupposes. It was at this conceptual level, Rickert claimed, that the difference between natural science and history could be found: they do not deal with two different sectors of reality, but are two ways of conceptualizing the same reality. Natural science regards empirical reality with reference to general concepts or laws, whereas history uses concepts as a means to portray the individual.[13] But "individual" does not simply mean persons: it rather means

10. Dilthey, "Entstehung der Hermeneutik," *GS*, V, 330.
11. Dilthey, "Das Wesen der Philosophie," *GS*, VI, 402, 405.
12. Heinrich Rickert, *Die Grenzen der naturwissenschaftlichen Begriffsbildung* (Tübingen: Verlag von J. C. B. Mohr, 1902), pp. 659f.
13. *Ibid.*, pp. 212, 251.

the "particular"—that is, something that can be localized in space and time. The individual could thus be a particular event, such as the French Revolution, or a trend, such as capitalism, or even an age or a period. If "individual" is defined so broadly, however, how is one to decide what is "individual" and what is general? It is here that Rickert introduced the idea of value. The criterion for selection of the subject matter of history is that which is relevant to a value—that which is *worth* knowing for some reason. Like Dilthey, Rickert elucidated this notion with reference to the question of wholes and parts: value is that which would be lost if the historical particular were analyzed further. For example, one might want to describe an event such as the King of Prussia's refusal to accept the German crown from the Frankfurt Parliament during the revolution of 1848. Presumably one "part" of that event would be the coat he wore on the occasion. But this component would be irrelevant to any result worth knowing in the context of the political history of Germany. Therefore the coat does not constitute a historical "individual" in Rickert's sense. For him, individual is equivalent to "indivisible." [14] In this sense, Rickert provides a criterion for determining the unit or level of historical analysis.

But Rickert's approach had its own limitations. His critics, both in his own day and more recently, have complained that his notion of value was too formal and abstract to be a useful guide to historians. [15] Moreover, the notion that historians select their material on the basis of value-judgments by no means guarantees that his work will fulfill any standards of objectivity or accuracy. Rickert himself was the first to admit this: value-judgments should not be arbitrary or subjective. A historian should select his material according to what he perceives to be valuable to society in general, not just to himself. Thus objective historical knowledge presupposes that there are such objective standards of value in the first place, an assumption that empirical evidence for cultural diversity tends to refute. Rickert was nothing if not consistent, however, and claimed that all scientific activity, whether in natural science or the historical sciences, presupposes this assumption of objective values. As long as a natural scientist selects and chooses the material from which he draws his general laws, he is guided by the

14.  *Ibid.*, p. 342. Rickert thus disagreed with Windelband's claim that history could portray the particular in concrete fullness. His belief in the limitations of concepts here is close to Meinong's.

15.  See R. G. Collingwood, *The Idea of History* (New York: Oxford University Press, Galaxy Book, 1956), pp. 169ff; Maurice Mandelbaum, *The Problem of Historical Knowledge* (New York: Liveright Publishing Corp., 1938), pp. 144f.

sort of value-judgment that these facts and not others are worth knowing. There is thus no "value-free" analysis in science. As Rickert himself put it, "the logical consciousness is . . . a form of consciousness of duty in general." But this in turn presupposes the notion of an objective order, "that the world is organized in such a manner that cognition is possible in it."[16] In the final analysis, then, Rickert's belief in objective historical knowledge rests on an untested assumption, and thus provided no decisive answer to relativism.

A decisive contribution to the debate was made by Max Weber, who found a way to resolve some of the difficulties raised by Dilthey and Rickert. On the one hand, Weber agreed with his teacher Rickert that value-relevance was the central criterion for the selection of material in the study of man and society. He further agreed that the values of the investigator function as an irreducible presupposition of his method.[17] But these presuppositions were not to be confused with values as the *objects* of empirical study—which are the actual values of a society as they shape and cause institutions and actions in a determinate way.[18] Moreover, the values of the investigator and those of his object may not be compatible—they may not fit into a single value system. But this need not prevent the investigator from doing his work or from doing it well. For however subjective and culture-bound our choice of data may be, the inferences and proofs we draw from that data about the real world should be convincing even to a Chinese.[19] Weber, in short, achieved a peculiar mix of idealism and realism. On the one hand, he fully admitted the importance of values in the selection of data. The best one can do, Weber suggests, is to be as explicit about one's value-judgments as possible. Indeed, the construction of ideal types was directed to just this end. A concept such as the Protestant ethic involved a deliberate abstraction from the concrete and variable circumstances in which Protestantism actually arose. Such concepts, once constructed, were but means to an end, namely the elucidation of those concrete real circumstances themselves.[20]

One key to this solution lay in Weber's notion of causality. The social sciences, including history, were basically directed to causal rela-

16. Rickert, *Grenzen*, p. 737; *Der Gegenstand der Erkenntnis*, 3rd ed. (Tübingen: J. C. B. Mohr, Paul Siebeck, 1915), p. 399.

17. Weber, "'Objectivity' in Social Science," *Methodology*, p. 110.

18. Weber, "The Meaning of 'Ethical Neutrality' in Sociology and Economics," *Methodology*, p. 11.

19. Weber, "Objectivity," *Methodology*, p. 58.

20. *Ibid.*, p. 87.

tionships. Causality, in fact, is a category that bridges natural science and the social sciences. The difference, as Windelband and Rickert had pointed out, was that the natural scientist seeks general causal laws, while the historian or social scientist seeks particular causal relationships. In some of these cases, such as the influence of a great personality on history, one has access to this relationship through *verstehen*.[21] But Weber polemicized strongly against the idea that history was the study of the spontaneous actions of men free from all determining influences. Weber pointed out, as had others before him, that free will and determinism are not incompatible.[22] Rather, whenever one attributes a motive to someone, one assumes that his actions were caused. In his own words:

> The characteristic of "incalculability," equally great but not greater than that of the "blind forces of nature," is the privilege of—the insane. . . . The actions of Czar Paul of Russia in the last stages of his mad reign are treated by us as not meaningfully interpretable [*sic*] and therefore as "incalculable," like the storm which broke upon the Spanish Armada.[23]

To claim this does not involve the further assumption that one could not have acted otherwise. Weber distinguishes sharply between necessity and possibility; causality and freedom are quite compatible so long as one allows for the fact that a particular causal relationship is not the only possible one (Weber's source for this notion of "objective possibility" was the philosopher Johannes von Kries, who also influenced Meinong's work on the subject).[24] Both natural science and social science, then, are directed toward the discovery of causal relationships. In this sense, Weber's theory of science approached the positivist viewpoint, though he was ready to assert the validity of the notion of causality just when others such as Mach were denying it.

If Weber succeeded in overcoming some of the dichotomies between reason and intuition in the social sciences, he did not see these efforts as directed to the overcoming of relativism. On the contrary, it led him to assert the relativity of cultural values even more vehemently than his predecessors. He remained convinced that "the various value spheres of the world stand in irreconcilable conflict with

21. Weber, "Roscher und Knies und die logischen Probleme der historischen Nationalökonomie," *Gesammelte Aufsätze*, p. 116.

22. Weber, "Critical Studies in the Logic of the Cultural Sciences," *Methodology*, p. 119.

23. *Ibid.*, p. 124, and footnote.

24. *Ibid.*, p. 167; see Meinong, *Möglichkeit, GA*, VI, 86.

each other. . . . I do not know how one might wish to decide 'scientifically' the value of French and German culture; for here, too, different gods struggle with one another, now and for all times to come."[25] One might think that this was because Weber was interested less in philosophical foundations of values and more in developing a practical methodology for empirical science itself. But in fact Weber recognized the role of philosophy in working out some common principles of the diversity of values. The scientific discussion of value judgments includes, as he saw it:

> The elaboration and explication of the ultimate, internally "consistent" value-axioms, from which the divergent attitudes are derived. People are often in error, not only about their opponent's evaluations, but also about their own. This procedure is essentially an operation which begins with concrete particular evaluations and analyzes their meanings and then moves to the more general level of irreducible evaluations. It does not use the techniques of an empirical discipline and it produces no new knowledge of facts. Its "validity" is similar to that of logic.[26]

From here, one could go on to deduce the values that follow from the ultimate axioms, and to determine their empirical consequences. In this way, one can understand with complete clarity the values of another nation or culture. But this activity could never lead to any definitive pronouncements that one set of values is better than another. The reason for this is that the types of values that can be derived from such ultimate axioms can themselves be contradictory.[27] One could easily conceive, for example, the United States and the Soviet Union going to war over identical "ultimate" values—say, the greatest good for the greatest number—while being convinced that the derivative values of democracy and communism are irreconcilable. Science cannot decide which of the two is preferable; it can at best point out the empirical consequences of each. The generality of such ultimate values is fatal to their applicability. By the same token, Weber believed that science was misguided in trying to make value judgments on the behavior of individuals. One could predict the consequences that would follow from the actions of an anarchist or terrorist; but one could not conclude scientifically that those actions were wrong.[28] The purpose of science, in brief, was to describe, not to prescribe. It had

---

25. Weber, "Science as a Vocation," in *From Max Weber*, trans. H. H. Gerth and C. Wright Mills (New York: Oxford University Press, 1958), p. 148.

26. Weber, "Ethical Neutrality," *Methodology*, p. 20.

27. *Ibid.*, p. 19.    28. *Ibid.*, pp. 24–25.

no business making ethical judgments, or of providing any sort of spiritual sustenance to people in the wake of ebbing religious faith.

The inability of science to provide meaning in people's lives was one of Weber's most fundamental notions. One finds it not only in his methodological writings, but in his sociology of religion as well—it is but one part of the general process of disenchantment that comes with secularization, mechanization, and rationalization.[29] Weber's pessimism in this respect undoubtedly stems in part from the abuses of scientific authority that he saw around him—his colleagues in the social sciences making pronouncements on policy and on national honor in the name of scientific objectivity. However, it has proven to be one of the most controversial aspects of his thought even today, for it undercuts one of the basic premises of secular humanism as it has developed since the eighteenth century—that man can decisively improve his lot by the use of reason.

### 2. MEINONG AND WEBER ON CAUSALITY

In 1918, the same year that Weber presented his pessimistic views in the lecture "Science as a Vocation," Meinong submitted to the Imperial Academy at Vienna a treatise demonstrating a general causal law. A comparison between Meinong's and Weber's views is instructive, because it bears on the conclusions which Weber drew and which seemed so obviously justified in the light of the political events of that year. Meinong's theory of objects, at least as we have presented it thus far, would seem by implication to agree with Weber's argument concerning values: it is possible to arrive at a general notion of reference and meaning, but this very generality prevents its application to any specific set of meanings that all languages might have in common. But Meinong was nevertheless not led to Weber's pessimistic conclusions about the irrelevance of scientific thought to questions of value. For if there was nothing in Meinong's theory to guarantee the possibility of any such set of universal values, neither was there anything to preclude this possibility once and for all.

The reasons for this difference lie both in Meinong's views on value itself and his notion of causality, and it is in the latter area that the contrast with Weber emerges most sharply. First, let us point out the areas of agreement. Meinong had long held, as did Weber, that free-

---

29. Ernst Topitsch, "Max Weber and Sociology Today," in Otto Stammer, ed., trans. Kathleen Morris, *Max Weber and Sociology Today* (New York: Harper and Row, Torchbooks ed., 1971), p. 13.

dom and determinacy were not incompatible: without some idea of causality it would be impossible to attribute motives to people.[30] Meinong's demonstration in fact is directed to showing that there *must* be a general causal law; otherwise our tracing of individual events backwards in time would make no sense at all. Using an argument derived from Hobbes and Brentano, Meinong asserted that if there were no causality, there would be nothing to prevent us from arguing that an event could begin at any time: nor would there be any obstacle to drawing absurd inferences from that infinite realm of objectives of so-being and applying them to the actual world of existence.[31] The general direction of Meinong's argument is like that of his argument for evidence: to hold consistently to the opposite point of view would lead to chaos. Causality, like evidence, is an indispensable presupposition of our actual cognitive behavior, if not always recognized as such.

All of this resembles Weber's standpoint in many particulars. The difference, however, consists in this: Weber declared that the empirical sciences of fact were absolutely irrelevant to value-laden conclusions because these sciences must select their material from an infinite stream of causal relationships. In his own words:

> The number and type of causes which have influenced any given event are always infinite and there is nothing in the things themselves to set them apart as alone meriting attention. A chaos of "existential judgments" about countless individual events would be the only result of a serious attempt to analyze reality "without presuppositions." And even this result is only seemingly possible, since every single perception discloses on closer examination an infinite number of constituent perceptions which can never be exhaustively expressed in a judgment. Order is brought into this chaos only on the condition that in every case only a *part* of concrete reality is interesting and *significant* to us, because only it is related to the *cultural values* with which we approach reality.[32]

Now this notion might seem to resemble Meinong's, in that he also based his argument against any final standards of meaning on the in-

---

30. Meinong, *Psychologisch-ethische Untersuchungen*, GA, III, 221; *Zum Erweise des allgemeinen Kausalgesetzes*, GA, V, 575.

31. *Ibid.*, p. 514, for the Hobbesian argument, which establishes the probability that an existential objective has a cause. Meinong's terminology in the following demonstration that these objectives must be caused is considerably more involved than I have presented it. It is based on the notion that a factual objective cannot have a merely possible objective as a cause (literally an objective with a possibility less than 1), but must have another existential factual objective. See pp. 526–550, esp. p. 546.

32. Weber, "Objectivity," *Methodology*, p. 78.

finite number of objects. But Meinong's version of infinity is at the level of so-being, not of existence. An object can partake in an infinite number of objectives of so-being, if one is willing to consider all the properties it does and does not have. But it does not follow that the existence of this object has an infinite number and types of causes.[33] On the contrary, the real world is quite finite inasmuch as its objects are complete.

What, then, we might ask, prevents Meinong from lapsing into a rigid determinism that would allow no room for freedom? The answer would lie in epistemological considerations—in our ignorance of what the finite set of causes of a given event actually are.[34] Knowledge of objectives of existence is still a matter of empirical induction, and cannot be certain, but is at best highly probable. This leaves open the possibility that events might have happened otherwise than we believe. If we recall how Meinong developed the notion of so-being from the facts of reference, we can understand the significance of this difference with Weber. For Meinong, the world, insofar as it is analogous to language, is infinite; but this notion is not to be confused with the world insofar as it actually exists. Thus it would seem that the difficulty of arriving at standards of meaning is not due to the chaos of the real world, as Weber seems to think, but due to the peculiarity of our intellectual capacity, which can combine the elements of the real world in an infinite number of ways. This, I believe, is what Meinong meant when he referred to his metaphysics as realistic and his theory of objects (which is primarily concerned with so-being) as idealistic.[35] Whereas Weber, in good Kantian fashion, saw the order in the empirical world as a function of our intellect, Meinong, in good Austrian fashion, saw it as a basic aspect of the world itself. While the mind can never know that order fully because of its own infinite capacity for combination, it can approach that knowledge by degrees of presumption. It is in this approximation of the objective order of things that the basis for some universal meanings and values could conceivably—though never certainly—be found.

This argument, while removing some of Weber's fundamental objections, still does not refute the contention that sciences of fact are irrelevant to decisions based on values. Meinong claimed, however,

33.  Meinong does hold that a chain of causes of a given event stretches infinitely back into time, but not that the types of causes at any one time are infinite. See *Zum Erweise*, *GA*, V, 579–580.

34.  *Ibid.*, pp. 574–575.

35.  Meinong, *Selbstdarstellung*, *GA*, VII, 57.

that such decisions ought to be based on knowledge of facts, so that facts and value are not two incompatible concepts. In order to see why this is so, we may now turn to his theory of value per se.

### 3. MEINONG'S THEORY OF VALUES AS OBJECTS OF EMOTIONAL EXPERIENCES

The first expression of Meinong's mature value theory came in a brief article entitled "For Psychology and Against Psychologism in the General Theory of Values" in 1912. The title shows his general approach and how it represents a consistent extension of his earlier views. His initial task is to establish that there *are* values and to describe what it is to say that we value something. His procedure is once again to approach meaning through experience: values are part of a group of objects to which our feelings are directed—to say that something is valuable is to say that the object has the capacity to arouse certain emotions in us. This theory is not psychologistic, Meinong claims, in that it does not reduce values to those feelings; rather, there are objects of feelings and desires just as there are objects of ideas and judgments. Meinong christens these emotional objects *dignitatives* (objects of feelings) and *desideratives* (objects of desire).[36] Thus each fundamental class of experience has a type of object that corresponds to it. This approach would still probably have seemed all too psychologistic to Weber, who denied that the concept of value in psychology could be translated into that of economics or of other social sciences.[37] But Meinong's basic assumption continues to be that analysis down to the level of the momentary experiences of individuals could provide a common framework for all these different meanings.

Meinong had arrived at this theory of emotional objects between 1905 and 1912 through certain psychological considerations—just as he had done in the case of the original theory of cognitive objects. These considerations centered around two new ideas: the intentional function of *präsentieren* (presenting) and the notion of psychological presuppositions.

The first of these new ideas may be traced by Meinong's reevaluation of the atomistic model and the introspective criterion in the

---

36. Meinong, *Emotionale Präsentation*, GA, III, 397; Kalsi, p. 100. The terms are introduced here for the first time, though the idea of objects of emotional presentation comes in "Für die Psychologie und gegen den Psychologismus in der allgemeinen Werttheorie," GA, III, 280.

37. See Chapter Five, pt. 2.

context of his mature thought. Given Meinong's emphasis on judgments and assumptions from the 1900s onward, the older notion of
the idea might seem to have a merely vestigial function—providing
the building-blocks on which judgments and assumptions were based—
because only the latter could apprehend or know objects. But Meinong
recognized that the older Lockean notion of idea also had a relation
to an object, namely that of "representation" (indeed, the German
word for idea, Vorstellung, is often translated as "presentation"). If,
for example, I have a sensation of a red object in my peripheral vision, there is something in my mind that corresponds to the object. I
may not be actively aware of it, however; the sensation may not be a
part of a judgment or assumption at the moment. Meinong reformu-
lates this situation as follows: the object is presented to my experience.
Rather than our being directed to the object, the object is directed to
us; we remain passive. This relationship Meinong calls *präsentieren*.
Thus, in the case of a judgment or assumption, the idea (Vorstellung)
presents the object to the judgment or assumption.[38] It is important to
note that presenting is never a sufficient function for apprehension:
an idea cannot apprehend its object in itself, but must pass its object
on, so to speak, to another experience.

Meinong developed this interesting notion in the context of our
awareness of our own mental states—those psychic facts which had
originally given rise to the introspective criterion. We have seen how
Meinong came to rely on sources of evidence other than introspection
after 1899, even as far as our own mental states were concerned. Our
recent experiences, for example, were part of memory and therefore
had no claim to certainty. But there remain those momentary flashes
of reflection, when we suddenly catch ourselves in the act of thinking
something, or immediately reflect on our own conscious state, or are
momentarily overwhelmed by joy or sorrow. These momentary experiences, Meinong claims, still deliver certainty, though not the a priori
certainty of insight into so-being. The certainty is derived from the
directness of the experience, which quickly fades as we move away
from it in time. Meinong's analysis of such moments is this: there is
still inner perception, meaning that we have a judgment that we are
thinking or feeling a certain way; but in this case the judgment is not
directed to the object of our thinking or feeling, but to the thinking or
feeling itself. This is a case of *self-presentation*—our experiences pre-

38. Meinong, *Emotionale Präsentation*, GA, III, 287f; Kalsi, 3f; *Über Annahmen*, 2d.
ed., *GA*, IV, 28.

sent themselves, rather than their objects, to our judgment.[39] They are, so to speak "introverted" rather than "extroverted" (Einwärtswendung versus Auswärtswendung).[40]

It is from this nucleus that Meinong gradually elaborated the idea that emotions could present objects on their own. One natural extension of it was in the case of remembering our own feelings on a past occasion. We are likely to recall a traumatic experience with a shudder, or a humorous experience with a smile. In these cases our present emotions are directed to past emotions, just as in the cognitive aspect of memory a present idea is directed to a past one.[41] Another extension was the direction of feelings to those of others through sympathy or empathy.[42] In these cases we do not necessarily need to judge or assume an objective state of affairs involving another person and then feel sympathy; rather, the feeling comes directly through the presenting function of the act of sympathy. In these cases, Meinong's description of intersubjective apprehension resem-

39. *Ibid.*, p. 312; *Emotionale Präsentation, GA,* III, 291; Kalsi, p. 6.

40. Meinong, *Erfahrungsgrundlagen, GA,* V, 426, 440f. These terms are the ancestors of "self-presentation" and "other-presentation," as Meinong's reference on p. 312 of *Über Annahmen* makes clear. The passages in *Erfahrungsgrundlagen* are among the knottiest Meinong ever wrote; perhaps this had led to the fact that Grossmann's analysis of it is misleading. Grossmann claims that the doctrine of "turning inward" and "turning outward" offers "a mystery instead of an analysis" (p. 154)—that is, Meinong does not bother to locate these "activities" in his model. "Meinong's analysis is incomplete as long as he does not tell us whether these acts are, say, presentations, or judgments, or something else." Meinong's diagram on p. 440 shows that Grossmann is in error: these two terms refer not to acts or activities, but to an intentional function on the order of grasping, apprehending, and knowing. Whereas the latter functions are directions of experiences to objects, "presenting," "turning inward" and "turning outward" may be thought of as ways that objects are directed toward experiences. Take the case of perception, which we know as a judgment and an idea. The judgment apprehends an objective; the idea presents the constituent objectum to judgment as a means to that apprehension. In the case of inner perception, the idea that does the presenting is itself the object of apprehension—hence "self-presentation." In the former case ideas are "turned outward" to external objects; in the latter case, they are "turned inward" to judgment. Grossmann, on the other hand, insists on identifying Meinong's doctrine with Brentano's notion that an idea of something and our idea of that idea are identical. But Meinong explicitly denies, on p. 441, that an experience is identical with an inner perception of it. The inner perception consists of the experience *plus* a judgment.

41. Meinong, *Erfahrungsgrundlagen, GA,* V, 444. Meinong adds the stipulation that the present emotion is a fantasy-emotion (analogous to assumptions as fantasy-judgments), as opposed to the past emotion which is "serious."

42. *Ibid.*, p. 445.

bles that of Dilthey's concept of *verstehen*—we not only grasp objects through our intellect, but also "have" them through the intentionality of our emotions.[43]

From these considerations it was but a step to the notion that the objects to which our feelings are directed have qualities which determine these feelings. This would apply not only to the experiences of others or of our own past, but to inanimate objects as well. Thus to say of something that it is delightful or irritating, pleasant or unpleasant, valuable or not valuable, is to attribute qualities to it that are appropriately apprehended by feelings rather than judgments. In Meinong's words:

> The homogeneousness of the predications in "the temperature is pleasant" and, say, "the temperature is high" has so far not been able to come into its own in the face of the strikingly special subjectivity of feeling. Without a doubt, the capacity of feeling as a means of knowledge is far inferior to that of the idea. Our estimation, however, of the subjectivity and general deceptiveness of sensations has . . . long been sufficiently high; we may thus entertain the notion that the distinction between thoughts and feelings in this regard is more a matter of degree than of quality.[44]

Perhaps the most plausible instance of these new entities (*dignitatives*) comes from the subject of esthetics. It seems evident that we use the term "beautiful" to refer to qualities in a work of art or a pleasing aspect of nature that are not identical with the objects and objectives to which our intellectual experiences are directed. Although such properties may be "subjective" in the sense that there is no consensus on what constitutes beauty, they are "objective" in that we normally identify them as properties and not as feelings per se. In a painting, for example, it is the color, line, or expressiveness of the painting itself that we call "beautiful," not the emotions that these properties evoke. The same holds true for values, which are similarly attached to goods primarily, and to our emotions secondarily.

There is one final class of objects, which Meinong posits by extension as belonging to his fourth class of mental states, namely those of desire. His label for these is *desideratives*.[45] Desire may seem to be close to feeling—it is easy to say that what is valuable is also desirable. But

---

43. See Dilthey, "Studien zur Grundlegung," *GS*, VII, 47. Dilthey insists, however, that such emotions occur together with other experiences, so that *Nacherleben* is a preferable term to *Nachfühlen*.

44. Meinong, "Für die Psychologie," *GA*, III, 278.

45. Meinong, *Emotionale Präsentation*, *GA*, III, 397; Kalsi, p. 100.

Meinong has something more specific in mind by "desire": an act of striving or willing something. That such acts may not always be emotional is evident in one linguistic expression of desire that pervades the entire realm of experience: the question.[46] When I pose a question, I am expressing a desire for a certain bit of information. In Meinong's corresponding psychological language, a question expresses a desire based on an assumption: in order to pose a question, I must affirm or negate the content of the question without believing it. In the act of asking, "How is the weather?" I am assuming that the weather is in a certain state of so-being, but rather than expressing my conviction of this objective, I express a desire to apprehend it. The more normal usage of "desire" is subsumed under cases where the experience is based on feelings, as with wishing or wanting. Here, too, we make objective references based on these acts: something is desirable or despicable.[47] Meinong suggests, indeed, any objects that have the sense of "end" or "aim" fall under this category. So do the objectives denoted in sentences involving "should" or "ought."[48] In this way, the emotional experiences are divided into passive and active, just as are the cognitive ones.

The introduction of dignitatives and desideratives still leaves a number of questions unanswered. Are values and beauty simply part of the same category? What is the relationship of values to facts? The answers are provided by Meinong's doctrine of psychological presuppositions. This notion was already present in his early work on value theory in 1894, and probably goes back to Brentano.[49] It suggests that all these types of momentary experiences stand in some definite order to each other, and that this order determines a number of crucial philosophical distinctions. To give a simple example, the feeling that the temperature is pleasant presupposes a sensation of temperature, though it is not reducible to it. In other cases, a feeling might presuppose a judgment as well. If I place a great deal of value on a certain rare collector's item, the value-feeling would be based on the apprehension of certain objectives concerning the item. This judgment would in turn presuppose certain ideas, just as all judgments presuppose the having of ideas to present objecta to them. To put the matter

---

46. Meinong, *Über Annahmen*, 2d. ed., *GA*, IV, 120; *Emotionale Präsentation*, *GA*, III, 382; Kalsi, p. 87.

47. Meinong, *Emotionale Präsentation*, *GA*, III, 323; Kalsi, p. 34.

48. *Ibid.*, pp. 325ff; Kalsi, p. 37.

49. Meinong, *Psychologisch-ethische Untersuchungen*, *GA*, III, 34; *Emotionale Präsentation*, *ibid.*, pp. 314, 351f; Kalsi, pp. 26, 59f; Brentano, *Psychology*, pp. 266f.

slightly differently, all experiences beyond ideas are objects of a higher order, and presuppose certain parts.

It is the type of presupposition that enables us to distinguish between certain types of feelings and their dignitatives. For example, some feelings presuppose presentations directly, without the mediation of judgments; these would include sensual pleasure and pain, which are based on the acts of ideas. Other feelings are based on idea-contents. Meinong assigns esthetic feelings to this category; beauty and ugliness are based on the contents of ideas which present their objects. Still other feelings are based on judgments, such as the pleasure one gets from intellectual discovery or of frustration that stems from the intractability of a problem. These are based on the acts of judgment, whereas value-feelings are based on the content of judgments—whether something exists or not. Thus different types of emotional experience may be specified in terms of the cognitive experiences which they presuppose; this helps us also to classify their objects. We can summarize these relationships schematically:[50]

| Type of feeling | Psychological presupposition | Type of dignitative |
|---|---|---|
| 1. sensual | idea-act | the pleasant |
| 2. esthetic | idea-content | the beautiful |
| 3. knowledge | judgment-act | the true |
| 4. value | judgment-content | the good |

Desires admit of a parallel schematization, though Meinong did not elaborate in much detail. A further ramification of this schema, considerably more awkward, is that judgment-feelings have their opposites; just as judgment can be affirmative or negative, so our feelings can be directed to the existence or nonexistence of an object.[51]

If we pursue the linguistic analogy in conjunction with this principle of psychological presuppositions, it strikes us that we finally have found the counterpart to rules that seemed to be lacking in Meinong's theory. For certainly Meinong would not admit that nonsensical statements like "White horses brown are black or" have the same status as well-formed sentences. The difference would be that such nonsensical examples cannot express units of experiences, since the experiences

---

50.   Meinong, *Emotionale Präsentation*, *GA*, III, 370, 386; Kalsi, pp. 77, 91.

51.   Meinong, *Zur Grundlegung der allgemeinen Werttheorie*, *GA*, III, Ch. IV, No. 3. For a critique, see Findlay, *Meinong's Theory*, pp. 295ff; Chisholm, "Objectives and Intrinsic Value," in *Jenseits von Sein und Nichtsein*, pp. 262f.

involved would violate the order of presuppositions. Thus the principle seems to embody the psychological counterpart of syntactical rules. But Meinong admits that his principle has certain difficulties, centering on the word "presupposition." Does it entail that we must consciously go through each step before we are able to have a value-feeling? Does not the act of writing a nonsensical sentence presuppose the mental act of formulating it? Meinong's response is that the principle stands primarily because the objects they refer to stand in a parallel definite order: objectives presuppose objects, and dignitatives presuppose both of these.[52] Thus the syntactical rules are ultimately based on semantic ones.

Meinong in this way manages to place values within the context of his general theory of objects. Values are among the objects of feeling and desire, though not all feelings and desires are directed to values. That which delimits the notion of value vis-à-vis other objects of emotion is the type of objective it presupposes. Meinong continues to insist, as he had done in his first book on value-theory, that values presuppose the being or non-being of an object.[53] It would be wrong to talk of valuing an object defined purely in terms of so-being, without any consideration of its existence. Thus we do not value colors in themselves, for example; if colors excite certain feelings of pleasure or irritation in us, these are esthetic feelings. Indeed, Meinong writes of works of art in much the same way as he wrotes of colors—their so-being is independent of their existence:

> When and where do we really have to do with Beethoven's Fifth Symphony. . . . What is actually this symphony? Does it consist of the original manuscript of the score, or in every authentic reproduction of the same?—or say the totality of the tone-configurations [Tongestalten] in the broadest sense of the word which are recorded in the notes? If the latter, does it consist of the tones and harmonies which actually sound on the occasion of a performance, so that it ceases to exist as soon as the performance is over? Or is its being rather no existence at all, but a being detached from space

52. Meinong, *Emotionale Präsentation*, GA, III, 369f; Kalsi, pp. 75f. The dignitatives presuppose the objectives as well as the objects, despite the fact that some of the feelings do not presuppose the corresponding judgments. This follows from the point made in the last chapter that objecta can be described only in the context of an objective. Meinong confirms this point here—the esthetic feelings that presuppose the idea-contents can also be called feelings of so-being (Soseinsgefühle), since the particular content of an idea and its objectum have certain properties that are given in the objectives of so-being (*ibid.*, p. 374ff; Kalsi, p. 81).

53. *Ibid.*, p. 373; Kalsi, p. 79.

and time, so that it could be lost to mankind under certain circumstances, but would never so to speak be deprived of its own being?[54]

Although we may respond emotionally to a particular performance of a symphony or drama, it is ultimately the internal structure of properties of the work that determines this response.[55] Values, on the other hand, are related to the joy that comes from the existence of an object, the sorrow that comes from its nonexistence, or our desires for these objects—as in the case of valuing an economic good. Our value-feelings are thus derived from judgments of existence, and the values themselves have objectives of being as their presuppositions.

Meinong's theory of emotional objects bears a brief comparison to the theories of Freud, since both emphasized the intricate interconnections of thinking and feeling in their psychologies. It goes without saying that Meinong cannot touch Freud as a psychologist—the tradition of philosophical psychology in which he worked was extremely narrow in comparison to the new depth psychology that was emerging in Vienna from the study of neuroses. Meinong's theory has none of the dynamic relationships of energy-transfer that Freud postulates, nor does he deal with the unconscious levels of organization. As a result, there is nothing in Meinong's psychology to account for conflict between impulses, either psychic or social, that is so central to Freud. Moreover, Meinong never makes the leap to the concept of "self" or "ego" or "organism," which would seem essential to a complete psychology. Nevertheless, many recent commentators have emphasized that Freudian psychology can be seen as a theory of meaning: the only way of informing ourselves about the mysteries of the unconscious is through the symptoms and symbols that manifest themselves in the conscious and preconscious.[56] The interpretation of dreams, then, is in great degree a hermeneutical exercise: taking the manifest content of dreams and discovering how they point to the level of instincts through their symbolic function. Insofar as our conscious waking life is shaped by these instincts, it presupposes feelings and desires as

54. Meinong, "Über Urteilsgefühle: was sie sind und was sie nicht sind," *GA*, I, 601–602.

55. Meinong, *Emotionale Präsentation*, pp. 374, 453ff; Kalsi, pp. 81, 148ff.

56. Paul Ricoeur, in *Freud and Philosophy*, trans. Denis Savage (New Haven: Yale University Press, 1970) develops this approach fully. Ricoeur stresses particularly that interpretation in psychoanalysis is more than straightforward decoding of references of symbols. Rather it involves uncovering hidden meanings that appear deceptively at first (p. 17). Also, he stresses that psychoanalysis cannot be reduced to hermeneutics; the dynamic aspect of Freud requires us to retain some notion of action and interaction (pp. 393ff).

basic. This is quite clear in the passages where Freud talks of the higher processes. Here is his treatment of judgment, for example:

> The function of judgment is concerned in the main with two sorts of decisions. It affirms or disaffirms the possession by a thing of a particular attribute; and it asserts or disputes that a presentation has an existence in reality. The attribute to be decided about may originally have been good or bad, useful or harmful. Expressed in the language of the oldest—the oral—instinctual impulses, the judgment is: "I should like to eat this," or "I should like to spit it out"; and, put more generally: "I should like to take this into myself and to keep that out." . . . What is bad, what is alien to the ego and what is external are, to being with, identical.[57]

Similarly, ideas are in large part derived from the unconscious, despite the fact that traditionally they were thought to be caused by external stimuli. Although our ideas may have originally come from this source, they remain in the unconscious, as is evident in dreams, and also play a continual role in shaping conscious ideation, interacting with the sensations and thoughts emanating from the external world. Freud explains this relationship as follows:

> What we have permissibly called the conscious presentation [Vorstellung] of the object can now be split into the presentation of the word and the presentation of the *thing*. . . . We now seem to know all at once what the difference is between a conscious and an unconscious presentation. The two are not, as we supposed, different registrations of the same content in different psychical localities . . . but the conscious presentation comprises the presentation of the thing plus the presentation of the word belonging to it, while the unconscious presentation is the presentation of the thing alone.[58]

Thus Freud recognizes the importance of language, but assigns it to the restricted sphere of consciousness.

If we now compare these observations to Meinong's we can see that Freud, too, has a set of psychological presuppositions, but that they are the reverse of Meinong's: ideas and judgments presuppose feelings and desires rather than vice versa. Mental life, insofar as it is governed by the unconscious, can be said to have a similar vocabulary but a different syntax from mental life governed by conscious cognition. Freud recognized this duality also:

> It is a general truth that our mental activity moves in two opposite directions: either it starts from the instincts and passes through the system *Ucs.* [unconscious] to conscious thought-activity; or, beginning with an instiga-

57. Freud, "Negation," *SE*, XIX, 236f.
58. Freud, "The Unconscious," *SE*, XIV, 201.

tion from outside, it passes through the system *Cs*. [conscious] and *Pcs*. [preconscious] till it reaches the *Ucs*. cathexes of the ego and its objects.[59]

Thus it seems that Freud's and Meinong's concepts are to a certain extent intertranslatable and complementary. Whereas Freud emphasizes the aspects of the psyche which are related to the inner instincts, Meinong emphasizes those aspects which are related to the transcendent world. And though Freud by no means ignores the transcendent world to the extent that Meinong ignores the instincts, other phenomenologists and existentialists have noted that psychoanalysis has its own kind of impoverishment in this respect. If two or three basic human drives, such as eros and the death instinct, are universal to all men, then how can they possibly explain the richness and diversity of human consciousness? Sartre, for example, points out that the highly differentiated sensibilities of a writer like Flaubert can never be reduced to the few basic instincts of Freudian theory.[60] Phenomenological psychology and psychoanalysis, then, may be seen as two different uses of the same set of concepts, each based on its own set of assumptions about psychic causation and its own set of rules about how to interpret symbols.

### 4. Meinong on Relative versus Absolute Values

The doctrine of psychological presuppositions is the key to understanding how the theory of objects bridges rational and irrational discourse. According to Meinong, our emotional life, insofar as it is conscious, is not divorced from our verbal capacities. Feelings and desires involve ideas and judgments; the former are more complex than the latter, are irreducible to them, but presuppose them. Moreover, Meinong claims that we can specify what sorts of cognitions underlie what sorts of emotions. But, as we have seen, Meinong justifies his particular hierarchy by an appeal to a parallel hierarchy of objects. What we deem valuable or desirable presupposes what we recognize to be or be so. Inasmuch as our cognitions can approach knowledge of the real order of things, it would seem to follow that there is also an objective order of goodness that is based on the former. Meinong recognized that his theory of dignitatives and desideratives brought him close to the views of Windelband and Rickert, in that he acknowl-

---

59. *Ibid.*, p. 204.
60. Jean-Paul Sartre, *Being and Nothingness*, trans. Hazel E. Barnes (New York: Philosophical Library, 1956), pp. 557ff.

edged values to be objective and independent of a knower.[61] Nevertheless, he was aware of the diversity of actual values which so impressed the philosophers of history and society, though he approached this problem from the standpoint of epistemology. It was easy and tempting to say that the objects of emotion were analogous to the objects of cognition in every respect, but the fact remains that our knowledge of the intrinsically "good" or "valuable" is in a most primitive state compared to knowledge of being or so-being. Emotions are much less reliable than judgments as instruments of knowledge; because of their extreme variability they lack the quality of evidence that enables us to be certain of objective truths.[62] Thus we have no difficulty referring to the so-being and existence of objects in themselves and making inferences in this sphere—every time a scientist uses a mathematical formula to describe an empirical result, he is doing so. But there is no similarly developed axiomatics of value; although such a science is certainly possible—as Weber also admitted—it is more difficult to formulate except in a most formal sense. If one wants to specify the content of values, one must turn to relativism: one can speak of these only in the context of the observable experience that presents the value. Meinong recognizes, however, that in practice economists or philosophers do not always translate their descriptions of value down to this level of analysis; it is thus permissible to talk of value for a subject or person as a whole, provided that value *could* elicit the appropriate emotional response. In brief, Meinong admits that there are personal, relative values which we can apprehend, as well as the impersonal, absolute values which follow from the theory but whose exact nature is far more dubious.[63]

In the last decade of his life Meinong wavered considerably on the question of which type of value, relative or absolute, was more worthy of philosophical study. In 1911 he gave the nod to relative values. Only after further description of the actual values of people could science approach the question of absolute values with any confidence.[64] Ethics, then, was for him a science of the future, and the notion that there are universal ethical standards was still a matter of faith.

By 1916, however, in the midst of World War One, Meinong felt impelled to take a stronger stand in favor of impersonal values, claiming that they were the true object of ethical studies and value theory. Relativism, in other words, was too great a danger:

61. Meinong, *Zur Grundlegung*, *GA*, III, 638.
62. Meinong, "Für die Psychologie," *GA*, III, 281.
63. *Ibid.*, p. 282.      64. *Ibid.*

If the essential attributes of value are in the end constituted through the attitudes of a subject, then the value consequently rises and falls with this subject, and the latter, as the final condition of all values, unites the value in some way in itself. But then the existence of the subject is, as the basis of all values, superior to any special value: life is the highest good. This consequence has actually been drawn now and then, but no age has taken it in this measure practically *ad absurdum*, and has let its inherent frivolity so clearly be felt, as our own.[65]

Meinong's adverse remarks about life as the highest good made in the midst of the Great War may seem like a perverse attachment to the ethics of sacrifice; in reality it was just the opposite—a reaction to the Nietzschean sort of heroic ethics which were so prevalent at that time and which clearly subordinated any set of impersonal moral standards to what was good for the subject. The affirmation of life that Meinong criticizes was not the right of all men to live, but the vital energy that differentiates aristocratic souls from lesser men.

In his last work on the subject, published posthumously, Meinong retreated somewhat from his position of 1916. Though he still maintained that there were impersonal values, he admitted that there was no way to define these except by way of personal ones.[66] Meinong nevertheless insisted throughout these writings that there was nothing self-contradictory in the notion of an absolute ethics. Impersonal values were to personal ones like the "remote" objects of cognition were to the "near" ones; one had to proceed from one to the other, from phenomenon to noumenon.[67]

It remains to be seen how such a projected ethics could be prescriptive in any meaningful sense. How could Weber's objection that such values would be so general as to lead to contradictory applications be refuted—even if philosophy succeeded in such a project? Meinong addresses himself to this problem in his own way, and his solution is most revealing: one can talk of a legitimate or justified value if the objectives which it presupposes are factual.[68] Thus the absolute value of an object, or its usefulness, is a function of the truth of the objectives which pertain to it. And since the objectives which pertain to values are objectives of existence rather than of so-being, one does not have to face the choice of an infinite number of objects and objectives

65.  Meinong, *Emotionale Präsentation*, *GA*, III, 429; Kalsi, p. 127. See also *GA*, III, p. 436; Kalsi, p. 133.

66.  Meinong, *Zur Grundlegung*, *GA*, III, 641f.

67.  Meinong, *Emotionale Präsentation*, *ibid.*, p. 442; Kalsi, p. 138.

68.  Meinong, *Zur Grundlegung*, *GA*, III, 645.

as a basis for such values. Because we can attain knowledge of existence by degrees through presumptive evidence, we can approach—though never completely attain—knowledge of what exists, and the closer we come to this goal, the more clearly the contours of what is ultimately valuable will emerge. In other words, the standards of cognition take precedence over the standards of feeling and desire: "ought" is dependent on "is." Knowledge of human values can become final through knowledge of the natural order of things, so that fact and value are not two separate and incompatible categories. In this way Meinong remains true to the naturalistic assumptions that have supported scientific and much positivistic thought, the protests of positivists against metaphysics notwithstanding. He expresses this allegiance by differing openly with Rickert and the idealists:

> That . . . truth *consists* of value or in "ought," so that an objective is true because it is valid or ought to be, rather than is valid or ought to be because it is true, therein I can only view one of those quasi-Copernican inversions, with which the history of philosophy has tried, more eagerly than fairly, to find what is objectively prior at the point where in the end only the objectively posterior is to be met.[69]

This answer to relativism in ethics thus ultimately stems from his realistic metaphysics; it is buttressed by the notion that objects of meaning stand to each other in definite, hierarchical relationships that could be specified by semantic rules.

Thus in the final analysis Meinong's realism does not succeed in providing a third way of synthesizing the rational and irrational aspects of inquiry, independent of pragmatism and metaphysics. In avoiding the former, he has to invoke the latter. Metaphysics turns out to be a fundamental support for his system, not merely an ornament to it. Yet it seems most likely that precisely such a faith in the real order of existents underlies all positivistic philosophy, however much its adherents seek to deny it.

Meinong's commitment to naturalism does not mean that value-statements are reducible to statements of fact—values are, after all, objects of a higher order, which only presuppose the simpler objects of cognition. Thus the study of values, as well as esthetics, retains autonomy and is not simply another natural science. By the same token, the methodologies of social and historical science, which involve the same types of emotional presentation, are qualitatively distinct from the natural sciences. On the other hand, Meinong would not go as far

69. *Ibid.*, p. 638.

in the direction of idealism as some of the more recent hermeneutical philosophers such as Hans-Georg Gadamer, who claims the reverse of Meinong's order of presuppositions: that scientific discourse is an outgrowth of hermeneutics. Gadamer in particular expounds this view in terms of a philosophy of language which resembles Meinong's in terminology if not in substance. Gadamer emphasizes that hermeneutics is but "a special case of the general relationship between thinking and speaking, the mysterious intimacy of which is bound up with the way speech is contained, in a hidden way, in thinking." [70] In other words, for Gadamer, language and meaning cannot be considered apart from experience—the very stipulation that Meinong applies to objects of emotion as a subset of objects as a whole. Gadamer draws the inference that is diametrically opposed to Meinong's:

> The fundamental relation of language and world does not, then, mean that the world becomes the object of language. Rather, the object of knowledge and statements is already enclosed within the world horizon of language. The linguistic nature of human experience of the world does not include the making the world into an object. [71]

In comparison to these views, the distinctiveness of Meinong's theory of objects can finally be established. Hermeneutics involves a special use of the theory of objects: it delimits a certain set of objects via rules which are not applicable to other objects, namely that the properties of this set can be defined only in relation to the experiences which present it. In this sense, hermeneutics is like logic, in that both represent applications of the theory of objects to certain special cases. The theory of objects itself, with its hierarchies of presuppositions, transcends both of these uses, and thus provides a bridge between the two. It was this achievement that constitutes Meinong's contribution to the intellectual revolution—a commitment to scientific and rigorous philosophy, sufficiently flexible to accommodate less rational modes of discourse, and steering clear of relativism where values and ethics are concerned. In order to understand the uniqueness of his contribution, we must compare his ideas with those of the emerging movements with which he was closely related.

70. Hans-Georg Gadamer, *Truth and Method* (New York: Seabury Press, 1975), p. 351. On Heidegger, see Chapter Ten, pt. 6.
71. *Ibid.*, p. 408.

# PART THREE

*Outcome: The Emergence of Twentieth-Century Philosophy and Experimental Psychology*

# VIII

# MEINONG AND ANALYTICAL PHILOSOPHY

It remains for us to trace the relationships of Meinong's thought to the three major trends of thought in whose origins he shared: analytical philosophy, Gestalt psychology, and phenomenology. All three emerged as distinct movements just before World War One, and played an important part in the intellectual history of the 1920s and 1930s. Meinong's reputation among philosophers today is based mainly on his role in analytical philosophy, an outgrowth of logical realism whose initial protagonists were Russell, Moore, and—somewhat later—Wittgenstein. Together with Frege, they inspired the work of the Vienna Circle in the 1920s, in whose hands the movement became known as "logical positivism." Thus the cross-fertilization of British and Austrian philosophy continued. Although not all members of the analytical movement identified with the specific views of the Vienna group, the movement may be called positivistic in a broader sense, in that its participants looked to science to set the standards of rigorous thinking which they were trying to achieve. The analytical philosophers generally saw themselves as guardians of clear thinking, and as defenders of precision against the obscurities of metaphysics and idealism which were prevalent in Germany and England before the War. In this sense, the closeness of this movement to the earlier empiricist tradition is quite clear. Russell was later to make this point with his usual succinctness:

Modern analytical empiricism . . . differs from that of Locke, Berkeley, and Hume by its incorporation of mathematics and its development of a powerful logical technique. It is thus able, in regard to certain problems, to achieve definite answers, which have the quality of science rather than philosophy. It has the advantage, as compared with the philosophies of the system-builders, of being able to tackle problems one at a time, instead of having to invent at one stroke a block theory of the whole universe. Its methods, in this respect, resemble those of science.[1]

It was analysis, then, as well as experience, to which twentieth-century philosophers have turned in their quest for exactitude. Given the broad significance of the term "analysis," we should distinguish between several uses it came to acquire within the movement. It could mean the general tendency to treat philosophical problems in piecemeal fashion as opposed to system-building, and in this form it has come to dominate British and American philosophy to this day. It could also mean something more specific, namely the reaction of Russell and Moore to idealism as they had learned it from Bradley, who had emphasized the oneness of the philosophical world and the futility of the usual methods of attacking only a part of it.[2] Finally, it could refer to the continuation of the program begun by Frege—that is, the development of a symbolic logic as a model superior to ordinary language for the purpose of philosophical investigations. If one compares this ideal logical language with the less precise languages we actually use, the statements of the latter must be broken down and analyzed in order to find their corresponding expressions in the former. In *this* sense, much of British and American philosophy since the Second World War has broken with logical analysis. There was a reaction to the theories of logical positivism, led mainly by an older Wittgenstein and a school centered in Oxford. The place of this "ordinary language philosophy" in intellectual history is beyond the scope of this book. Suffice to say that many of the main issues that have divided philosophers from each other in the twentieth century—at least in England, Austria, and America—have centered on the proper interpretation of the analytical approach.

The development of analytical philosophy from logical realism may conveniently be divided into three stages. In the first, which dates from 1905 until about 1912, Russell held the center of the stage, thanks to a new technique of analysis he invented partly in response to certain problems posed by Frege and Meinong. He called this tech-

---

1. Russell, *History of Western Philosophy*, p. 834.
2. Morris Weitz, "Analysis, Philosophical," *Encyclopedia of Philosophy*, I, 97.

nique the theory of descriptions, and it led him to modify the logical realism of the *Principles of Mathematics*. Nevertheless, he remained tied to logical realism in many respects and continued to refer to Meinong in his writings. The second stage was dominated by the figure of Wittgenstein, who came to Cambridge in 1912 to study under Russell and soon began to influence the doctrines of his teacher. This phase culminated in Wittgenstein's *Tractatus Logico-Philosophicus* (1921) and continued to characterize British philosophy in the 1920s under the name of "logical atomism." The third stage was marked by the formation of the Vienna Circle under the leadership of Moritz Schlick and Rudolf Carnap in the mid 1920s. While indebted to Frege, Russell, and Wittgenstein, this group developed a distinctive position which in turn influenced British philosophy in the 1930s. Meinong's direct influence on the latter two stages is not detectable, but of his indirect influence there is no doubt: the *Tractatus* in particular mirrors the formulations of Meinong in many passages.[3]

In this development from logical realism to logical positivism, one significant trend emerges: the philosophers involved found it necessary to lower drastically their estimation of human reason and its ability to address significant ethical, social, and metaphysical questions—despite the dizzying heights that reason had itself attained in the *Principia Mathematica*. Given their characterization of reason in terms of language, their sense of its limits was based on their understanding of what a strictly logical language could and could not do. As Wittgenstein expressed it in the introduction to the *Tractatus*:

> The whole sense of the book might be summed up in the following words: what can be said at all can be said clearly, and what we cannot talk about we must pass over in silence.
>
> Thus the aim of the book is to set a limit to thought, or rather—not to thought, but to the expression of thought: for in order to be able to set a limit to thought, we should have to find both sides of the limit thinkable (i.e., we should have to be able to think what cannot be thought).[4]

As the analytical philosophers moved from logical realism to logical positivism, they came to view the province of "what could be said

3. Ludwig Wittgenstein, *Tractatus Logico-Philosophicus*, trans. D. F. Pears and B. G. McGuinness (London: Routledge and Kegan Paul, 1963), 2.01–2.063. References to this work except for the preface will be to the numbers of the individual passages, as is customary. For the similarity of Meinong and Wittgenstein, see Findlay, *Meinong's Theory*, p. xii; Ryle, "Intentionality and the Nature of Thinking," p. 256.

4. Wittgenstein, *Tractatus*, p. 3.

clearly" as narrower and narrower. In this respect the contrast between Meinong and Wittgenstein could hardly be greater. This change arose in large part from the increasing awareness of the discrepancy between logic and ordinary language. Frege had already emphasized this fact, but it found a new support in Russell's innovations of 1905.

To a great extent this process of narrowing coincided with the Great War and its aftermath—events which made a belief in the powers of reason difficult to sustain in any case. The sobering aspect of the development of analytical philosophy, however, was that its adherents mostly claimed it to be independent of political or social considerations. Rather it was seen as a purely internal critique of reason based on the linguistic analogy.

### 1. RUSSELL'S THEORY OF DESCRIPTIONS

The theory of descriptions comes between the two great theoretical works in Russell's output, the *Principles of Mathematics*, written in 1900, and the *Principia Mathematica*, which he and Whitehead completed in 1909. The latter was the completion of the project announced in the former, namely a complete rendering of mathematics in terms of symbolic logic. Russell had hoped to finish this work by 1903, but soon found himself blocked by a number of logical paradoxes which had to be solved if the *Principia* were to be definitive (his communication of one of these paradoxes to Frege had the effect of paralyzing Frege's work for many years, since he realized the edifice he had constructed had weak foundations).[5] Russell spent two summers trying to resolve them, but without results. "Every morning," he wrote, "I would sit down before a blank sheet of paper. Throughout the day, with a brief interval for lunch, I would stare at the blank sheet. Often when the evening came it was still empty."[6] But solutions eventually came, and the *Principia* could be written. Russell published his solutions to the paradoxes in 1906 as the "theory of types." He could not have arrived at this, however, without the theory of descriptions, which had come to him a year earlier and which he published in a short article in *Mind* entitled "On Denoting." Russell later considered it to be one of his greatest works; it is considered by many to be his most important contribution to analytical philosophy.

---

5. Dummett, p. xxiiff.
6. Russell, *Autobiography*, I, 228.

The gist of "On Denoting" is that certain phrases which commonly occur in ordinary language have no counterparts in a well-constructed logical language, and that therefore we have no business inferring that there are objects analogous to them. The phrases in question include any which serve as the subject of a sentence. Russell called these "denoting phrases." Examples would be "a man, some man, any man, every man, all men, the present King of England, the present King of France [a non-existent object], the center of the mass of the solar system at the first instant of the twentieth century." [7] Russell's objections to such phrases may best be understood in the light of his earlier Platonism. His argument for the being of nonexistent objects had been that as long as we can make true statements about them (for example, "The present King of France does not exist"), the parts of our statements must correspond to something in the world. If the world was analogous to language, no other result seemed possible. Indeed, Russell had chided Meinong the year before for not going far enough in this direction; Meinong had not yet fully developed his theory of objects, and, by the time he did, Russell had retreated from a belief in nonexistence. [8] His grounds for doing so were that the parts of statements in ordinary language which seem to correspond to such objects do not occur in logical language.

Russell expounded his theory through polemics against Frege and Meinong. His paraphrasing of their views was none too accurate, but his criticisms were sometimes difficult to refute. [9] He objected to Frege's distinction between sense and reference, partly on the grounds that it was not always possible to distinguish between the two. Russell claimed that there is one area where the distinction between sense and reference does not hold: when we are talking about language itself, that is, when we refer to that which in other contexts would be the sense (the way in which a reference is given). What normally is the sense then becomes the reference. But what is the sense in this case? It was this criticism that led Russell to the theory of types—the paradoxes which Russell later solved all involved this sort of reflexiveness. [10]

Russell's polemic against Meinong bears closer examination. He

7. Russell, "On Denoting," in *Logic and Knowledge*, ed. Robert Charles Marsh (London: George Allen and Unwin Ltd., 1956), p. 41.

8. Russell, "Meinong's Theory," *Essays in Analysis*, pp. 63, 67ff.

9. Dummett, p. 267.

10. See "On Denoting," *Logic and Knowledge*, p. 48f; "Mathematical Logic as based on the Theory of Types," *ibid.*, p. 61.

claimed that Meinong's notion of nonexistent objects led to violations of a basic logical law, the law of contradiction—that is, one must admit that there are objects which do not exist.[11] It will be helpful to review briefly Meinong's views on this subject. In the article "Über Gegenstandstheorie," Meinong raised the paradox that there are objects which do not exist. He resolved it, however, by claiming that the so-being of objects is independent of existence: that any object may have definite qualities even if it does not exist, and that this common occurrence in our thinking and speaking is obscured only by our "prejudice in favor of reality." Thus to say that there are objects which do not exist is to use the terms "are" and "exist" in two completely different senses.[12]

Now this position was different from the one often attributed to Meinong by analytic philosophers, which is simply that Meinong accepted the paradox and carelessly posited a whole implausible realm of fictitious objects—that there were objects which had some sort of being in addition to their properties, even if they did not exist.[13] The responsibility for this interpretation lies partly with Meinong himself, whose cryptic references to Aussersein implied that there was such an additional realm of being, though Meinong's argument in 1904 does not imply this. But the responsibility is shared by Russell, who tended to assimilate Meinong's theory to his own Platonism of the *Principles of Mathematics*. Russell's presentation of Meinong in "On Denoting" makes it appear that he failed to grasp Meinong's distinction between being and so-being. But Russell's reviews of Meinong's publications in *Mind* show the contrary: he clearly rejected the distinction. According to Russell, existence was not a separate category. If one asks when we are entitled to say that something exists, we would have to answer the question in terms of its properties.[14] Meinong, for his part, rejected Russell's criticisms with equally clear sight: the law of contradiction

11. Russell, "On Denoting," *ibid.*, p. 45.

12. Meinong, "Über Gegenstandstheorie," *GA*, II, 490ff; LTC, pp. 83ff.

13. See, for example, Dummett, p. 197; J. O. Urmson, *Philosophical Analysis*, p. 2. (This book contains an excellent history of the analytical movement, to which I am greatly indebted in this chapter.) The consensus among Meinong scholars is that this view is mistaken (see Findlay, *Meinong's Theory*, pp. 46f; Chisholm, "Meinong, Alexius," *Encyclopedia of Philosophy*, V, 261; and Grossmann, pp. 116ff).

14. Russell, "Review of A. Meinong, *Untersuchungen zur Gegenstandstheorie und Psychologie*," *Essays in Analysis*, p. 81. Compare this version with Russell's presentation in "On Denoting," p. 45, or *My Philosophical Development* (London: George Allen and Unwin, 1959), p. 84.

applies only if we use the term "being" univocally—that is, if we admit only objects which exist and exclude so-being.[15]

What was Russell's remedy? It lay in finding a logical construction for such denoting phrases, which may best be illustrated by some examples. Consider the following sentences,

A1. The president of France is mortal.
A2. All men are mortal.
A3. The present king of France is powerless.

According to Russell's theory, the proper logical translations of these statements would be the following,

B1. There is one and only one entity in the universe (x) who is president of France and it (x) is mortal.
B2. It is always true of an entity in the universe (x) that if x is a man, x is mortal.
B3. There is one and only one entity in the universe (x) who is the present king of France and it (x) is powerless.[16]

The advantage of this construction is that it allows us to tell immediately whether it is true or false. The first two cases of ordinary language offer no difficulties in this respect, but the third one (A3) could be construed either as true or false. It could be taken as true *of* the present king of France, just as it is true of Hamlet that he is indecisive or of Pegasus that he has wings. But it could also be taken as false in that there is no such person. In Russell's form, this ambiguity is eliminated: sentence B3 is clearly false—there is no such entity in the universe with the characteristics ascribed to it. Thus there is no reason, from a logical point of view, to require that there be such a nonexistent object as the present king of France. In this sense, too, Russell's theory is closer to common sense than Meinong's—another major advantage, which Russell was later to emphasize:

> One of the difficulties of the study of logic is that it is an exceedingly abstract study dealing with the most abstract things imaginable, and yet you cannot pursue it properly unless you have a vivid instinct as to what is real.

15. Meinong, *Über die Stellung der Gegenstandstheorie im System der Wissenschaften*, *GA*, V, 223. Russell, in his review of this work, rested his case, *Essays in Analysis*, p. 93. The argument concerned an example that Russell saw as a clear violation of the law of contradiction, "the existent round square exists." Meinong claimed that in this case "existent" is a property and thus could be ascribed to an object via an objective of so-being; to say that this object exists is to assert an objective of being.

16. See Russell, "On Denoting," pp. 43ff.

You must have that instinct rather well developed in logic. I think otherwise that you will get into fantastic things. I think Meinong is rather deficient in just that instinct for reality.[17]

The notion that Russell's theory of descriptions effected a reconciliation between linguistic philosophy and common sense is, however, exceedingly difficult to sustain, for the approach to common sense was achieved at considerable cost. While Russell had found a way of analyzing away the names of fictitious entities, the same technique had to be applied to the names of real ones as well. Thus ordinary sentences which appear to be perfectly straightforward had to be translated into a form which rendered them virtually unrecognizable. Consider some examples used by Russell himself. "I met a man" becomes "'I met x, and x is human' is not always false." "'The father of Charles II was executed' becomes 'It is not always false of x that x begat Charles II and that x was executed' and that 'if y begat Charles II, y is identical with x' is always true of y.'"[18] Thus, if denoting phrases are to be analyzed in this way, most of our ordinary references to objects are misleading.

A more telling difference between Russell and Meinong was their respective assumptions about the use of the analytical approach. Russell felt justified in rewriting most ordinary sentences because he tended to equate analysis with a widely accepted principle: economy of formulation. Russell frequently invoked William of Occam's law of parsimony: "entities should not be multiplied beyond necessity," which Russell once called "the supreme methodological maxim in philosophizing."[19] If one can find a common form of logical sentence to replace a number of different forms of ordinary sentences, one no longer needs to make as many initial assumptions about the world in order to proceed with deductive reasoning. Thus, even though the logical versions of statements in ordinary language appear to be bulkier and less economically formulated than the originals, the economy lies in the initial assumptions one is obliged to make in order to test their truth and falsity. In Russell's own formulation, "Wherever possible, logical constructions are to be substituted for inferred entities."[20]

17. Russell, "The Philosophy of Logical Atomism" (1918), *Logic and Knowledge*, p. 223.

18. Russell, "On Denoting," pp. 43f.

19. Russell, "On the Nature of Acquaintance" (1914), *Logic and Knowledge*, p. 145.

20. Russell, "The Relation of Sense-Data to Physics" (1914), in *Mysticism and Logic* (New York: Barnes and Noble, 1963), p. 115.

Meinong, by contrast, with less interest in logic, did not emphasize the law of parsimony; on the contrary, he has been called "perhaps the supreme entity-multiplier in the history of philosophy."[21] While this view is now recognized as an exaggeration, there is one cardinal difference between Meinong's use of analysis and Russell's. Meinong held to the principle of heterogeneity with greater consistency. It was a greater sin to reduce all entities to a single type than to multiply them. Ever since the days of the Gestalt controversy, Meinong had claimed that analysis could be applied to complex wholes without distorting them; this was possible because the parts which resulted were heterogeneous. A melody contained notes and intervals; objects of a higher order included both fundaments and relations. This principle of heterogeneity was later transferred to the objectives: being and so-being constituted two irreducible types. In this sense, Meinong's analyses were never reductionistic: they never involved the assumption that the basic constituents of the world were all of the same sort. For this reason, a choice of units of analysis was possible, as Boltzmann and others had stressed. When Russell questioned the independence of being and so-being, he implicitly paved the way for a reductionistic use of analysis, in which anything that did not fit the pattern was dismissed as illogical and meaningless.

The full implications of the theory of descriptions were by no means immediately exploited or even grasped by Russell, despite their importance for the subsequent development of logical analysis. Through the writing of the *Principia*, Russell continued to believe in a number of different types of objects in addition to existents, including relations, universals, and facts.[22] In this sense, he may still be called a logical realist in this period. Moreover, he retained a sense of the need for the heterogeneity of units in analysis, as is evident from his theory of types, which contains the solutions to the logical paradoxes. While the details of this theory are beyond the scope of this work, it is clear that the paradoxes resulted, in Russell's view, from an attempt to reduce all analysis to the same type of unit. As he himself explained later:

> All words are of the same logical type; a word is a class of series, of noises or shapes according as it is heard or read. But the meanings of words are of various different types; an attribute (expressed by an adjective) is of a dif-

21.  Gilbert Ryle in *Oxford Magazine*, October 26, 1933, quoted in Findlay, *Meinong's Theory*, p. xiii.

22.  Russell, *The Problems of Philosophy* (1912) (Oxford: Oxford University Press, paperback ed., 1959), pp. 97ff, 136.

ferent type from the objects to which it can be . . . attributed; a relation . . . is of a different type from the terms between which it holds or does not hold.[23]

Russell also addressed himself in these years to the philosophical questions of the nature of truth and knowledge. In doing so, he took exception to Meinong in one further respect: he disputed the notion of objectives. Again, Russell sought to bring logical realism closer to common sense, and in this respect, Meinong's contention that there were false or unfactual objectives as well as true ones disturbed him. He had acceded rather reluctantly to Meinong's view before "On Denoting," and in an essay entitled "On the Nature of Truth and Falsehood" (1906), he saw a way to circumvent it. Russell now held that we do not judge objectives, but relations. For example:

> If I judge (say) that Charles I died on the scaffold, is that a relation between me and a single "fact," namely, Charles I's death on the scaffold, or "that Charles I died on the scaffold," or is it a relation between me and Charles I and dying and the scaffold? We shall find that the possibility of false judgments compels us to adopt the latter view.[24]

This view was in fact closer to Meinong's theory of objects of a higher order, which preceded his discovery of objectives. It provided a clear way of distinguishing between truth and falsity. If the relation of "dying" actually subsisted between Charles I and the scaffold, the judgment was true. If the relation did not subsist, it was false. This theory had one further advantage in Russell's eyes: it allowed him to talk of the self or the "I" in a way which had been closed to Meinong. For Russell now defined judgment not as an individual experience but as the intentional relation between myself and another relation (Charles' dying on the scaffold), whereas Meinong talked of judgment as a momentary experience, with an "I" nowhere in sight.[25] On the other hand, Meinong pointed out in response to Russell that the experience of judging normally involves an awareness of a single propositional unit rather than of a multitude of things.[26] To analyze judgment as Russell had done might have been illuminating as far as the question of truth and falsehood was concerned, but it no longer

---

23.  Russell, "Logical Atomism" (1924), *Logic and Knowledge*, p. 332.

24.  Russell, "On the Nature of Truth and Falsehood," in *Philosophical Essays* (New York: Simon and Schuster, 1966), p. 150.

25.  *Ibid.*, p. 155. For this reason, Russell later rejected Meinong's notion of content, in "On Nature of Acquaintance," *Logic and Knowledge*, 171f.

26.  Meinong, *Möglichkeit*, *GA*, VI, 41n.

remained an accurate description of experience. In this instance, as in so many others, Meinong's interests were phenomenological rather than logical.

Russell's concern with truth and falsehood also shaped his epistemology: he was never comfortable with Meinong's version of knowledge as that which is self-evident.[27] The beginnings of an alternative view can already be found in "On Denoting"; Russell soon developed it as the distinction between knowledge by acquaintance and knowledge by description.[28] According to Russell, all knowledge by description—that is, of the indefinite entities of the universe to which his logical propositions referred—must presuppose knowledge by acquaintance. To give an example, if we contrast the statement about the president of France with the one about the present king of France, we are in a position to vouch for the truth of the former because we are acquainted, through some channel of information, with this object, whereas we cannot be acquainted with the king of France in the same way. The most obvious form of acquaintance is sense-data, but this is not the only form: Russell also admitted that we are acquainted with concepts such as "president" or "king" as well. To judge the truth of a statement such as "all men are mortal," we must be acquainted with the concept of mortality.

It will be recognized that this epistemology hearkens back to the old atomistic model of the empiricists. For it bases the knowledge of truths on the knowledge of things.[29] We are acquainted with something when we have an idea in our minds and a name in our vocabulary that corresponds to some object. If such a correspondence is lacking, then the judgment or sentence in which the element occurs is false. This aspect of Russell's philosophy has proved to be one of the most problematical—it has, in a sense, revived all the instabilities of the atomistic model which had plagued the empiricists themselves (such as how one defines the correspondence).[30] On the other hand,

27.   Russell explicitly makes this criticism of Meinong much later, in *The Analysis of Mind* (London: George Allen and Unwin, 1921), pp. 262ff. But it is also implicit, I think, in Russell's review of Meinong's work in 1904. For although he accepts Meinong's theory at this time, he writes: "this theory *seems* to leave our preference for truth a mere unaccountable prejudice. . . . What is truth, what is falsehood, we must merely apprehend, for both seem incapable of analysis" ("Meinong's Theory," pp. 75, 76).

28.   Russell, "On Denoting," pp. 55f; *Problems*, Ch. V.

29.   *Ibid.*, p. 52.

30.   The problem consists of distinguishing cases where we use words to refer to objects and require a proposition to do so, and those cases which are genuinely pre-propositional. In Russell's terminology, how does one distinguish between a definite de-

no other alternative seemed possible if analysis of meaning was to serve directly the quest for truth. For, as Boltzmann had previously maintained, the analytical approach itself involves the presupposition of some stable unit or units.[31] A philosophy that is analytical and yet tolerates ambiguity, as was Meinong's, can afford to allow for a certain heterogeneity of units, so that a whole is not merely reducible to the sum of its parts. But if analysis is to decide between truth and falsehood, without fear of contradiction or ambiguity, then it must provide for a basic unit into which all others can be converted. It was Wittgenstein who brought forth this principle with great clarity: hence it is his name which is associated with logical atomism, a view that Russell then adopted.

## 2. WITTGENSTEIN AND LOGICAL ATOMISM

In 1912, Wittgenstein, following Frege's advice, arrived at Cambridge to study with Russell. The youngest son of a wealthy Viennese industrialist, Wittgenstein's cultural background had been rich and complex. His family had played a prominent role in Viennese musical life; he had read Schopenhauer at an early age, and had fully assimilated his pessimism. Tolstoi and Kierkegaard were among his favorite authors. His interest in science and engineering had also led him to Hertz and Boltzmann, with whom he had been about to study when Boltzmann committed suicide in 1906. From physics he turned to engineering, which he pursued in Berlin and then in Manchester. It was at this time, in 1908, that he discovered Russell's *Principles of Mathematics* and Frege's writings, and became interested in mathematics and philosophy. At Cambridge he became known as a brilliant but eccentric young man; Wittgenstein's behavior there utterly fit the stereotype of the stormy genius.[32] But his work soon transformed the analytic movement, first through conversations with Russell and Moore, and eventually through the great *Tractatus Logico-Philosophicus*, a work begun in 1913 and written for the most part during his wartime service with the Austrian army.

Wittgenstein's position in the *Tractatus* was practically the diametri-

scription and a proper name? On the difficulties, see Urmson, pp. 82ff, 189ff; Dummett, p. 163; Leonard Linsky, *Referring* (London: Routledge and Kegan Paul, 1967), pp. 51ff.

31. Boltzmann, "Unentbehrlichkeit der Atomistik," *Populäre Schriften*, p. 140. For fuller discussion, see Chapter Five, pt. 1, above.

32. See Russell, *Autobiography*, II, 99.

cal opposite of Meinong's: to show how narrow the range of rational discourse is, and to indicate that most significant human problems lie outside it and cannot be meaningfully verbalized. As Janik and Toulmin have suggested, this outlook stemmed largely from his Viennese experience.[33] But his method in elaborating this position was indirect: it consisted in undermining the assumptions of logical analysis from within by carrying them to their ultimate conclusion and by wielding Occam's razor with merciless consistency. If this could be done, the relative insignificance of rational discourse would be demonstrated.

One can best grasp Wittgenstein's strategy by comparing the first and last sections of the work. It begins in the world of logical realism:

1.      The world is all that is the case.
1.1     The world is the totality of facts, not of things.
1.11    The world is determined by the facts, and by their being *all* the facts.
1.12    For the totality of facts determines what is the case, and also whatever is not the case.
1.13    The facts in logical space are the world.

The ending, by contrast, states that all that has preceded is empty talk:

6.54    My propositions serve as elucidations in the following way: anyone who understands me eventually recognizes them as nonsensical, when he has used them—as steps—to climb up beyond them. (He must, so to speak, throw away the ladder after he has climbed up it.)
        He must transcend these propositions, and then he will see the world aright.
7.      What we cannot speak about we must pass over in silence.

Wittgenstein arrives at this conclusion by drawing out the implications of the theory of descriptions, stripped of Russell's efforts to soften it. He emphasizes that the structure of the world must correspond to that of propositions, not things, and further rejects Russell's theory of types, claiming that "all sentences are of equal value."[34] If there is thus no heterogeneity of units either in language or the world, we are perfectly justified in pursuing the analysis of language reductively in order to arrive at truth. There is no choice in the basic units of analysis, because the ultimate constituents of elementary propositions must be simple:

33.  Janik and Toulmin, *Wittgenstein's Vienna*, pp. 29, 169, 190ff.
34.  Wittgenstein, *Tractatus*, 6.4, 3.331–2.

2.02          Objects are simple.

2.0201        Every statement about complexes can be resolved into a state-
              ment about their constituents and into the propositions that de-
              scribe the complexes completely.

2.021         Objects make up the substance of the world. That is why they
              cannot be composite.

2.0211        If the world had no substance, then whether a proposition had
              sense would depend on whether another proposition was true.

2.0212        In that case we could not sketch out any picture of the world
              (true or false).

Thus Wittgenstein accepts both the analytical approach and an atomistic model. These assumptions later enable Wittgenstein, in section
four, to set up his "truth tables," in which any complex sentence could
be broken down into elementary propositions—"atomic facts," as
Russell called them—and the truth or falsity of the whole could be
determined from the truth or falsity of the parts.[35] Thus, for example, the statement "There is one and only one entity in the universe
(x) who is the present king of France and it (x) is powerless" contains
three occurrences of the word "is." According to Wittgenstein's technique, the truth or falsity of each "is" must be tested.

It should be noted that this sort of analysis has no obvious application to the sort of statement that expresses a belief. It is true that "Aristotle believed that the earth is at the center of the universe," but the
proposition "the earth is at the center of the universe" is false. A
proper description of such states of mind was of course at the core of
Meinong's project, and his quest for such a description had led him to
logical realism in the first place. This process, we will recall, involved
rejecting the atomistic model of the mind in favor of a consistent intentional model. Wittgenstein's theory showed, however, that the analytical approach, pursued reductively, was incompatible with the intentional model. At the same time, such analysis was incapable of
describing certain mental states such as judgment.[36]

Wittgenstein's pessimistic view as to the extent of human reason was
further reinforced by his so-called picture theory of language. This

---

35. *Ibid.*, 4.25–4.41.

36. Wittgenstein was aware of the problem, and dealt with it in sections 5.54–
5.5422. The passage is extremely difficult, but seems to be directed mainly against the
view of Russell that belief is a relation between a person and a fact. As far as I can understand the passage, Wittgenstein offers no way of analyzing beliefs so that true beliefs
are necessarily a function of their parts. See Urmson, p. 133.

led him to reject most aspects of realism and turn instead to a sort of nominalism—to the view that most of our rational discourse is in fact about words rather than about objects. The word Wittgenstein uses to describe the relation between language and reality is Bild, which is usually translated "picture." Wittgenstein characterizes a Bild variously as a model of reality, as a mirror image, or as a spatial configuration or arrangement that is analogous to the structure of a state of affairs.[37] Whatever the imagery, it seems clear that at least two factors are involved. First, if the language is to be precise, each element in a proposition must correspond to an element in a state of affairs; when we have fully analyzed our language, this correspondence will be evident, though it may not be at the cruder levels of ordinary discourse:

3.2     In a proposition a thought can be expressed in such a way that elements of the propositional sign correspond to the objects of the thought.

3.201   I call such elements "simple signs," and such a proposition "completely analyzed."

3.202   The simple signs employed in propositions are called names.

Second, the proposition and the state of affairs must share a common form. The arrangement of words in a sentence cannot be a random one: some arrangements, whether in ordinary language or logical language, are nonsensical. This, as we have pointed out, was the core of the linguistic analogy: a parallelism of structure at a certain level of complexity. This notion, as we shall see, was also shared by the Gestalt psychologists, who used the term "isomorphism" to describe it. A specifically logical language requires *both* these conditions, a correspondence of elements and a parallel structure. Wittgenstein gives the following example: a work of music can be represented in a number of ways—by a score, a series of sound-waves, or a configuration of grooves on a gramophone record. These things share a common form, by virtue of which they represent the same piece of music.[38]

Wittgenstein's innovation, his destruction of logical realism, comes from pitting these two conditions against each other. For if all names must correspond to objects, and the arrangements of each are distinct from the names and objects themselves, then *there can be no names for arrangements*. Any label we might use for a complex configuration of things is grammatically incorrect:

37.  Wittgenstein, *Tractatus*, 2.12, 6.13, 3.1431.
38.  *Ibid.*, 4.014–0141.

4.121     Propositions cannot represent logical form: it is mirrored in
          them.
          What finds its reflection in language, language cannot represent.
          What expresses *itself* in language, *we* cannot express by means of
          language.
          Propositions *show* the logical form of reality.
          They display it. . . .
4.1212   What *can* be shown, *cannot* be said.

In the musical example, there is no verbal label or formula to desig-
nate what a score and a recording have in common. One knows *how*
one is related to the other, but one could not put one's finger on what
the relationship is and verbalize it (Meinong, of course, would have
claimed that such a form could in fact be verbalized, and when we talk
of Beethoven's Fifth Symphony, we are doing just that—provided we
do not confuse this object with a physically existing object).[39]
In ordinary language we attempt to label such forms all the time
when we talk of relations or complexes, but logical analysis must reveal the futility of this talk. When we say that A is related to B, we are
really making a statement about the names "A" and "B," rather than
about the objects they represent.[40] Thus any talk of objects of a higher
order is really about nothing in the world; it is simply talk about the
language we use. To say that red is different from green is to say
something about our conventions for labeling rather than about reality. The same applies to our use of abstract concepts. Such statements,
according to Wittgenstein, are not completely nonsensical; but they
are uninformative, since they tell us nothing about the world directly.
He calls such statements tautological.[41] Moreover, it is easy to slip
from tautologies into nonsense, when we mistakenly use abstractions
to refer to the world itself. A good example is the very notion of
Gegenstand itself:

4.1272   Thus the variable name "*x*" is the proper sign for the pseudo-
          concept *object*.
          Wherever the word "object" ("thing," etc.) is correctly used, it is
          expressed in conceptual notation by a variable name. . . .
          Wherever it is used in a different way, that is as a proper con-
          cept-word, nonsensical pseudo-propositions are the result.
          So one cannot say, for example, "There are objects," as one might
          say, "There are books." . . .
          And it is nonsensical to speak of the *total number of objects*.

39.  Meinong, "Über Urteilsgefühle," *GA*, I, 601–602.
40.  Wittgenstein, *Tractatus*, 3.1432.        41.  *Ibid.*, 4.46–462.

The same applies to the words "complex," "fact," "function," "number," etc.

Such a view of abstractions would seem to undermine the whole enterprise of symbolic logic itself. For if the x's and y's of logic can only stand for pseudo-concepts, then logic must at best be tautological— that is, about language rather than about the world. This was precisely Wittgenstein's conclusion.[42] With this assertion, the breach with logical realism was complete. We can only speak rationally about the names of things, not about the things themselves.

Wittgenstein fully realizes that this view nominalizes science, as Mach had done, but he sees the modern faith in the objective truth of science as merely a contemporary brand of hubris:

6.371    The whole modern conception of the world is founded on the illusion that the so-called laws of nature are the explanations of natural phenomena.

6.372    Thus people today stop at the laws of nature, treating them as something inviolable, just as God and Fate were treated in past ages.

And in fact both are right and both wrong: though the view of the ancients is clearer in so far as they have a clear and acknowledged terminus, while the modern system tries to make it look as if *everything* were explained.

Wittgenstein explains that the laws of a given science are not irrelevant to the understanding of the world: they speak of the world indirectly. There is just no compelling reason to believe that Newton or Einstein described the world as it actually was. Both developed a set of tautologies, and if Einstein's was preferable, it was on grounds of simplicity and economy of formulation, rather than because of any realistic criteria.[43] If nature is beyond the ken of reason, it follows that ethics and esthetics are at an even more obscure level. There is no point in trying to put them into words at all. We may be aware of such things as we cannot verbalize, but then we have passed into the mystical.[44]

Perhaps the most significant commentary on this harsh system is Wittgenstein's own later repudiation of it in the 1930s—partly on the grounds that it was wrong to look for a single basic part or atom in language or in the world.[45] In the meantime, however, he had influ-

42. *Ibid.*, 6.1.      43. *Ibid.*, 6.342.      44. *Ibid.*, 6.42–44, 6.522.

45. Wittgenstein, *Philosophical Investigations*, trans. G. E. M. Anscombe, 3rd ed. (New York: Macmillan, 1958), No. 24, 97.

enced Russell to retreat from logical realism. Although Russell never accepted Wittgenstein's mysticism, nor his view that all states of affairs were of the same type, he did gradually abandon many of the compromises with a commonsensical view of analysis he had held before. By 1914, he had to deny that we could speak precisely about the "I," and by 1918 had given up the relational view of judgment in favor of the propositional view.[46] It was in this year also that he first adopted the term "logical atomism" to describe his philosophy. By 1921, he was ready to break with the Meinongian line of thinking completely: In *The Analysis of Mind*, which appeared in that year, he announced his rejection of the intentional model:

> Until very lately I believed . . . that mental phenomena have essential reference to objects, except possibly in the case of pleasure and pain. Now I no longer believe this, even in the case of knowledge. I shall try to make my reasons for this rejection clear as we proceed. It must be evident at first glance that the analysis of knowledge is rendered more difficult by the rejection; but the apparent simplicity of Brentano's view of knowledge will be found, if I am not mistaken, incapable of maintaining itself either against an analytic scrutiny or against a host of facts in psycho-analysis and animal psychology.[47]

The book reveals that Russell was keeping abreast of the changes in psychology of the time, and that his motives for parting company with Brentano and Meinong were more complex than his absorption of Wittgenstein's influence. In his autobiography, Russell tells us of the shock of the War and how it led him to a reevaluation of human reason, rendering him open to the suggestions of Freud.[48]

At the same time, Russell had found an alternative philosophical view of the mind and its relation to objects which was more consistent with his logical doctrines. This was essentially the same version of the atomistic model that Mach had propounded some forty years before: human consciousness and physical objects were both constructions from a single, common body of sense-data. This view had since been

46. Russell, "On the Nature of Acquaintance," p. 164; "The Philosophy of Logical Atomism," p. 226. Russell did not return to Meinong's view that there were nonfactual objectives, however. On his differences with Wittgenstein, see "Logical Positivism" (1950), *ibid.*, p. 370.

47. Russell, *The Analysis of Mind*, p. 15. Russell proceeds to criticize Meinong's notion of the mental act as "the ghost of the subject, or what was once the full-blooded soul" (p. 18)—though this is more reminiscent of Russell's view of 1906 than of Meinong's own ideas.

48. Russell, *Autobiography*, II, 17.

taken up by William James, who had dubbed it "neutral monism." Russell's first encounter with it came in 1914, when it seemed to him a plausible interpretation of the new physics of relativity and quantum mechanics (he later gave credit to Whitehead for turning his thought in this direction).[49] Although he was still far from accepting this view as explaining all phenomena, his writings between 1914 and 1921 reveal a gradual lessening of his resistance to it.[50] The main stumbling block had been the account of thinking, such as acts of belief. But by 1921, Russell was ready to admit that belief was analyzable into a complex of sensations (which included feelings). His argument at this point was admittedly vague: "I, personally, do not profess to be able to analyze the sensations constituting respectively memory, expectation, and assent; but I am not prepared to say that they cannot be analyzed."[51] Both logically and psychologically, then, the description of beliefs was a weak spot in the analytical movement. In retreating from logical realism, the analysts thus reintroduced certain problems that realism had originally been called upon to solve.

### 3. Logical Positivism

Logical atomism continued to dominate the analytical movement in England through the 1920s; but it was soon eclipsed by a new version of analysis that stemmed from the Vienna Circle during the same years: logical positivism itself. Both movements drew much of their inspiration from the *Tractatus*, but with different emphases. Russell and the atomists, for example, admitted they had a "metaphysic"—that they still made assumptions about the structure of the world based on the linguistic analogy—as Wittgenstein had done in the earlier section of the *Tractatus*. The logical positivists, on the other hand, stressed the later sections, where the analysis of language itself had revealed the talk of such a world to be meaningless. The predominant stance of logical positivism was its opposition to metaphysics.[52]

The Vienna Circle grew up around the work of Moritz Schlick and Rudolf Carnap, who came to Vienna from Germany in 1922 and

49. Russell, "The Relation of Sense-Data to Physics," p. 112; *My Philosophical Development*, p. 103.

50. See Russell, "Nature of Acquaintance," pp. 139–159; "Philosophy of Logical Atomism," p. 222; *Analysis of Mind*, pp. 22, 25f.

51. *Analysis of Mind*, p. 250.

52. For a fuller account of the relation between logical atomism and logical positivism, see Urmson, Pt. II.

1926, respectively. Schlick had developed independently some of the same ideas as Wittgenstein, and was invited to occupy the chair in the philosophy of inductive sciences at Vienna that Mach and Boltzmann had held. He found a receptive group of students and colleagues. When the circle published a manifesto in 1929, it sought to identify itself with the prewar positivists such as Mach and with the scientific tradition of Austria in general; in this connection, they also mentioned Brentano as a precursor.[53]

One is struck by the difference in tone between the manifestos of the logical positivists and the pessimism of the *Tractatus*. Schlick, for example, in an article entitled "The Turning Point in Philosophy" confidently proclaimed that the age of divisiveness and inconclusiveness between competing philosophies was over, and that philosophy had discovered a decisive method for solving its outstanding problems.[54] Whereas Wittgenstein had seen the innovations of symbolic logic as rendering philosophy virtually irrelevant to empirical science—it could at best point out to scientists where their statements slipped into metaphysical language—the logical positivists saw the Russell-Whitehead logic as providing a common structure for all science.[55] If the purpose of philosophy for Wittgenstein was to point out the fallacies of science, the purpose for the Vienna Circle was to clarify its achievements. This difference was based on an explicit disagreement with Wittgenstein, at least as far as Carnap was concerned: for him, not *all* logical statements were tautological and without sense, nor were all of the components of scientific language homogeneous.[56] In his first major work, *The Logical Structure of the World*, he distinguished between elements and relations, and proposed a unified language of science on this basis. As he stated his goal:

> Logistics (symbolic logic) has been advanced by Russell and Whitehead to a point where it provides a *theory of relations* which allows almost all problems of pure theory of ordering to be treated without great difficulty. On the other hand, the reduction of "reality" to the "given" has in recent times been considered an important task and has been partially accomplished, for example, by Avenarius, Mach, Poincaré. . . . The present study is an attempt to *apply the theory of relations to the task of analyzing reality.*[57]

53.  A. J. Ayer, "Editor's Introduction," in *Logical Positivism*, p. 4.
54.  Moritz Schlick, "The Turning Point in Philosophy," *ibid.*, p. 54.
55.  See Wittgenstein, *Tractatus*, 6.53, and Carnap, *The Logical Structure of the World*, trans. Rolf A. George, 2d ed. (Berkeley: University of California Press, 1967), pp. 7, 9.
56.  Carnap, "Rejection of Metaphysics," in *The Age of Analysis*, ed. Morton White (New York: New American Library, Mentor ed., 1955), p. 224.
57.  Carnap, *Logical Structure*, p. 7.

Carnap was well aware of the criticisms of Mach's doctrine of sensations that had surfaced since the 1880s; he recognized that the Marburg Neo-Kantians had also stressed the importance of relations, and that this constituted a valid critique of the earlier positivism. He also recognized the problems raised by the Gestalt controversy and the difficulties of ascertaining an ultimate basic unit.[58] Yet Carnap still conserved the combination of analysis and atomism that Mach and the empiricists before him had established—he merely applied it to the level of relations rather than to basic elements. In other words, the relational statements of all sciences could be reduced to a single type, that of similarity.[59] This made it possible to translate the results of one science into another. The result was very much like Mach, despite the changes: one could reduce statements about the physical world and the body to statements about experiences; one could also talk of cultural objects as different combinations of these experiences (Carnap calls the lower level the "autopsychological objects," the intermediate the "physical objects," the upper the "heterospychological and cultural objects").[60]

In many respects, Carnap's system resembles Meinong's: he emphasizes a common structure of natural and social sciences, and insists that *"there is only one domain of objects and therefore only one science."*[61] The possibility of translating results from one special science to another is guaranteed by the common relation of similarity. But the difference between the two systems is central: Meinong denies that this common relation suffices to reduce one science to another because of the principle of presuppositions. Objects of a higher order, including the dignitatives and desideratives of the cultural world, may not be reduced to lower level objects of the physical world, even though they presuppose them. Thus the statements about higher levels cannot simply be translated into lower ones without loss of meaning: each level has its own special structure in addition to the common structure based on the similarity relation. While Meinong and Carnap thus both agreed that complexities presuppose simple elements and common relations, Meinong allowed for a considerably greater degree of heterogeneity in his basic inventory.

The logical positivists had a critical side to their philosophy as well: they were interested not only in describing a common structure of science, but also in erecting criteria for distinguishing good and bad

58. *Ibid.*, pp. 122, 109.
59. More exactly, the relation of "recollection of similarity." See *ibid.*, pp. 127f, 134.
60. *Ibid.*, pp. xxiv, 175–243 passim.    61. *Ibid.*, p. 9.

science, or science from metaphysics. Schlick formulated such a criterion as one of "verifiability," and it was based on the same reductionism assumption we have just pointed out. Statements are meaningful only if they could in principle be translated into experience—that is, if they could be reduced to the psychological level from the higher ones.[62] If this could not be done, then there would be no way of testing the statement empirically, and the statement would be relegated to metaphysics. The logical positivists had in mind such statements as "the essence of the world is mind" or "the essence of the world is matter," claiming that there was no way of deciding between them. In the long run, however, the criterion of verifiability proved to be a great source of embarrassment to the logical positivists, for they could not arrive at a satisfactory formulation of it that would apply in all cases.[63] They refused to recognize, as Meinong had done, that the infinity of objects—and relations that can be made between them—prevents anyone from knowing once and for all what is and is not verifiable in principle.

In the meantime, however, the positivists had anticipated success and confidently banished metaphysics from scientific discourse. Carnap in 1935 had distinguished between the logical and emotional aspects of language, its "representative" from its "expressive" function: the latter included words that were analogous to cries or laughter, expressions such as "Oh!" or "Ha!", as well as poetry, which performed the same function at a higher level. Metaphysics, Carnap claimed, really belonged to this category, in that it expressed some psychological urge without in fact saying anything about the world.[64] Even to say "this object is real" was to make such an expression, in that the statement did not add anything to one's knowledge of the empirical characteristics of the object. It is equally clear, however, that Carnap held that these empirical characteristics (for example the size and shape of an object in space) were independent of the observer, thus affirming his belief in an objective order of things. His objection to realistic metaphysics was against statements that made such affirmations explicit and did not thereby add to any knowledge of the empirical characteristics themselves.[65] In any case, his division of statements into representative and expressive types once again compartmentalized thinking and feeling, rather than seeing them as related. The

62.   Schlick, "Positivism and Realism," pp. 87f.
63.   See Urmson, pp. 168ff; Leszek Kolakowski, *The Alienation of Reason*, pp. 179ff.
64.   Carnap, "Rejection of Metaphysics," pp. 219–220.
65.   Carnap, *Logical Structure*, pp. 333–334.

study of ethics and esthetics was valid only insofar as it could be reduced to statements in the form of science—for example, statements
about psychological or sociological investigations of empirically verifiable responses of individuals. But this was a far cry from the use of
intuition which Dilthey had proposed or which Meinong had sanc-
tioned in his doctrine of emotional presentation (it also involved the
extremely unlikely suggestion that reference of a poem or artistic expression is irrelevant to understanding it).

It was such proclamations, which figured prominently in the initial
statements of the logical positivists, that explain the role of positivism
in the general cultural attitudes of the 1920s and 1930s. It is clear that
the old dichotomy between rational and irrational inquiry had reap-
peared in an even more drastic form than before. For not only was
vitalism in some form winning increasing adherents among educated
people in Germany and Austria, but the upholders of science and reason had voluntarily restricted their interests to a narrow area. The
pessimism of men like Wittgenstein in banishing such a large area
of philosophical concern from the realm of intellect was part of the
same set of attitudes which led other, lesser figures to embrace anti-
intellectualism.

In this context, too, the contrast with the logical realism of the turn
of the century is striking. Meinong's role in the analytical movement
may best be seen in this light. Although none of his successors was
ever tempted to return to nonexistent objects, or to distinguish being
and so-being, their alternative approaches presented problems of
their own. Whereas Meinong had sought to show the continuity of rational discourse and ordinary language by delineating the contexts in
which words and mental contents had an univocal meaning from
those which contained ambiguity, logical analysis had opened an ever-
widening gap between these two.

# IX

# MEINONG AND EXPERIMENTAL PSYCHOLOGY

## 1. Philosophy and Psychology in Germany and Austria

Meinong's reputation in the history of psychology is parallel to that which he long held in the history of analytical philosophy: an important precursor whose ideas were soon superseded. What Russell's theory of descriptions accomplished for analytical philosophy, the theories of the Gestalt psychologists (Wertheimer, Köhler, and Koffka) accomplished for the field of psychology. As far as psychology is concerned, this interpretation contains a good bit of truth. It is reinforced by the fact that Meinong himself showed little interest in the problems of Gestalt phenomena which he and Ehrenfels had raised in the 1890s. To a psychologist, he seems to have wandered off into the ethereal realms of Gegenstandstheorie and value theory, leaving the humbler experimenters behind in their laboratories. Though Meinong did indeed lecture on experimental psychology in the 1900s, his lecture notes reveal that he expected experiments to be limited to questions of sensation and not to address fundamental theoretical problems.[1] Only in this way could the gains in exactness from the experimental method be preserved. Meinong published no experimental monographs himself; the work from his laboratory came from his two most distinguished students, Stephan Witasek and Vittorio Benussi. Of the two, Witasek was closer to Meinong personally. They

---

1. Meinong, *Kolleg über experimentelle Psychologie*, *Nachlass*, Carton 15, folder A., p. 4.

shared a common interest in music, and Witasek's publications, including a book on esthetics, were more closely related to Meinong's own philosophical interests. Benussi, by contrast, was more a specialist, who had little interest in philosophy and who even slept in his laboratory.[2] Yet is it Benussi rather than Witasek who has a greater place in the history of psychology. The experiments he performed at Graz on the perception of optical illusions anticipated the results of the later Gestalt psychologists in many ways. In the light of these facts it is easy to interpret the origins of Gestalt psychology as a process of gradual emancipation from the murky theories of philosophy, a process which other branches of experimental psychology were undergoing at the same time.

Nevertheless, such a unilinear interpretation of the history of psychology during this period has its pitfalls, for it can easily lead to a false picture of the state of psychology in Germany and Austria before the First World War. It is relatively easy to divide experimental psychology after the war into a number of discrete "schools," such as behaviorism, Gestalt psychology, and psychoanalysis. While there were other such schools before the war as well (the Graz school, the functionalist school in America), the situation was generally much more fluid.[3] With the exception of psychoanalysis (which of course dates back to the 1900s), the methods and assumptions of any one particular school were less fixed, and their relations with philosophy much more intimate. This was true in central Europe to an even greater extent than in America, and remained so after the war. A survey of the members of the German Society for Experimental Psychology as late as 1925 shows, for example, that 63 percent of them taught philosophy as well, compared to 21 percent of the members of the American Psychological Association.[4] But even in America, the leading members of that association included William James, John Dewey, and James Mark Baldwin, who wrote a three-volume logic based on

2. Heider, p. 66. On Meinong and Witasek, see Meinong, "Stephen Witasek zum Gedächtnis," *GA*, VII, 257. The single work of Meinong that could be called experimental was published with Witasek: "Zur experimentellen Bestimmung der Tonverschmelzungsgrade," *Zeitschrift für Psychologie*, XV (1897), 189–205.

3. Compare, for example, Robert S. Woodworth's *Contemporary Schools of Psychology* (New York: Ronald Press, 1931), with Boring's account of the earlier period.

4. This was done by comparing the membership list in the society's report of their annual meeting with the data in *Kürschner's deutscher gelehrten-kalender* (Berlin: de Gruyter and Co., 1925) which lists fields for all academics. This in turn was compared with the American Psychological Association Yearbook for the same year, which gives the same information.

functionalist principles. In Germany, the close ties between philosophy and psychology were epitomized by none other than Wundt himself, the founder of the first experimental laboratory and a prolific writer of philosophical works (including a logic, an ethics, and a metaphysics). Wundt emphasized that experimental psychology was only a small part of psychology as a whole, and that any individual empirical study should help to lead to a unified Weltanschauung. At the end of his life, he claimed "that there is no scientific knowledge that is not at the same time philosophical knowledge in some measure, and vice versa."[5] Thus when Meinong claimed that his book *On Assumptions* was a work of psychology, he was by no means standing outside the mainstream of psychological thinking of his day—even though it contained no experimental results.[6]

To understand the role Meinong played in psychology, then, his philosophical writings are by no means irrelevant. By the same token, the changes in psychology and the emergence of experimental psychology as a specialized discipline had a definite effect on the outcome of the intellectual revolution and the transformation of the empiricist tradition. It is these issues that Meinong's psychology illuminates.

We may begin with a sketch of the institutional growth of psychology in Germany. The first laboratory in experimental psychology was founded by Wilhelm Wundt at Leipzig in 1879. By 1913 there were twelve such laboratories and six psychological journals (Graz was still the only Austrian laboratory at this time).[7] The 1890s alone produced a burst of new textbooks, eight in all compared to two in the 1880s.[8] The German laboratories had a great influence abroad: Leipzig in particular, as the birthplace of experimental psychology, became a magnet for students from all countries who wanted to learn the new discipline. A list of students in a seminar in 1888–1889 lists eight students, including two Americans, one Belgian, one Italian, one Swiss, one Russian, and two Germans.[9]

This quantitative growth also involved a great diversification in the

5. Wilhelm Wundt, *Erlebtes und Erkanntes* (Stuttgart: Alfred Kröner Verlag, 1920), p. 124.

6. Meinong, *Über Annahmen*, 2d ed., *GA*, IV, 338, 384. On the general trend, see Ueberweg, p. 486.

7. Rudolf Eisler, *Handwörterbuch der Philosophie* (Berlin: Siegfried Mittler und Sohn, 1913), pp. 519–520.

8. L. William Stern, *Die Psychologische Arbeit des neunzehnten Jahrhunderts* (Berlin: Verlag von Hermann Walther, 1900), p. 26.

9. Oswald Külpe, *Nachlass*, Bayerische Staatsbibliothek, Munich, Carton V, folder 20.

interests and approaches of the psychologists. The original Leipzig experiments had been quite narrow in scope: over half of them were concerned with sensation and perception, based as they were on the Weber-Fechner law.[10] The assumptions about the mind which such an approach entailed were squarely within the empiricist tradition. The model of the mind was atomistic, the basic units being sensations that were caused by physical stimuli. The approach was analytical: one had to begin with these basic elements, investigate their connections, and finally arrive at laws of connections (in the hands of Titchener, one of Wundt's students, this approach became known as "structural psychology"). Wundt also retained the introspective criterion: such experiments were valid because we can know our sensations directly; the controlled conditions of the experiment eliminate any arbitrariness that might otherwise result. Experiment was not seen as an alternative to introspection, but as a complement to it.[11] As psychology grew, these assumptions were increasingly called into question. Wundt himself played a role in this process and devoted increasing amounts of his time to his "psychology of peoples" (Völkerpsychologie) which was more closely related to the Geisteswissenschaften than to natural science. In addition to Wundt's efforts, Dilthey's essay of 1894 on descriptive and analytical psychology as part of the Geisteswissenschaften helped to spark an explicitly humanistic psychology in Germany; one of its proponents was the young Karl Jaspers. While these movements may be seen as part of a "revolt against positivism"—that is, as attempts to establish an alternative psychology to that based on experiment—one can also point to a "transformation of positivism" at the same time, in which other psychologists sought to apply experimental techniques to Gestalt qualities (Benussi), to the higher mental processes such as memory and learning (Hermann Ebbinghaus), and to thinking itself (Oswald Külpe and the Würzburg School). In both cases, the ties between the new psychology and philosophy were maintained rather than dissolved. In addition, others began investigating new areas such as child psychology (Wilhelm Stern), or pathological phenomena (Theodore Ziehen, Emil Kraepelin). In 1906, a society for applied psychology was formed under Stern's leadership.

Though it would be impossible to synthesize these new trends under any single rubric, it is true that one new approach emerged which many of the "new" psychologists shared in common. This outlook is

10.  Boring, p. 340.     11.  Wundt, *Erlebtes und Erkanntes*, p. 197.

often referred to via the concept of "function," and one of its manifestations was a school of psychology in America which called itself
"functionalist" (as opposed to Titchener's "structuralism").[12] The
term implied the rejection of atomism and a turning instead to the
interactions or interrelationships between the psyche and the environment—not only the impact of the environment on the organism,
but the action of the organism on the environment as well. Along with
this model frequently went a commitment to a holistic approach as
opposed to an analytical one: the whole self must be studied in these
relationships, rather than any isolated unit such as a "reflex-arc" of
stimulus-sensation-motor action-response (John Dewey was one of the
first to attack this concept, in 1896).[13] In Germany, the same prompt-
ings found different expression. Dilthey's rejection of experimental
psychology was based on similar grounds—that the classification of
experiences into sensations, feelings, and acts of will must follow
rather than precede the lived experience and understanding (*erleben*
and *verstehen*) in which these components are interwoven. In near-
by Denmark the philosopher Harald Höffding worked out a similar
functional psychology, in which he sought to classify experience as
types of action, rather than as units.[14]

The emphasis on relationships between experience and objects as
the fundamental starting point was, we may recall, a distinguishing
feature of Brentano's intentional model as opposed to the atomistic
one. While the followers of Brentano were more analytical than the
American functionalists, the "act" psychology was in fact viewed at the
time as a European philosophical counterpart to functionalism. One
of Brentano's students, Karl Stumpf, saw fit to label his acts "psychic
functions."[15] In this respect, Meinong's changing psychology of cognition, which led to the formulation of his theory of objects, may be
viewed as part of this trend. Before the 1890s, Meinong's psychology
of thinking was couched primarily in terms of operations such as abstractions and comparisons which took place *within* the mind. One

12. Gardner Murphy, *Historical Introduction to Modern Psychology*, rev. ed. (New
York: Harcourt, Brace and Co., 1949), pp. 222ff.

13. John Dewey, "The Reflex Arc Concept in Psychology," in Wayne Dennis, ed.
*Readings in the History of Psychology* (New York: Appleton Century Crofts, Inc., 1948),
p. 356.

14. Murphy, p. 217.

15. Karl Stumpf, "Erscheinungen und psychische Funktionen," *Abhandlungen der
königlich-preussischen Akademie der Wissenschaften*, 1906, Phil. hist. Klasse, No. 4, p. 4. See
also James R. Angell, "The Relation of Structural and Functional Psychology to Philosophy," *Philosophical Review* XII (1903), 247.

compared contents of ideas and sensations rather than objects. But in the 1900s Meinong's vocabulary became increasingly "functional"— he described thinking in terms of "grasping," "apprehending," "referring," "presenting," which were all relations between experiences and objects. Thus, one might say that assumptions have the function of referring, that judgments have the function of apprehending and knowing objectives, and that ideas have the function of presenting objects to the mind. One of the American functionalists, James Mark Baldwin, found the distinction between assumptions and judgments fruitful, and gave it a central place in his three-volume functional logic.[16]

## 2. MEINONG AND THE WÜRZBURG SCHOOL

Of all the new branches of psychology that developed during his career, Meinong felt the closest affinity to the Würzburg School of Külpe and its investigations of thought processes.[17] Külpe had begun as a student of Wundt and had originally pursued a psychology of sensation, but in the early 1900s, he and his students turned their attention to the experimental study of thinking. The work reflected both the influence of the intentional model and the prevalence of "functionalist" concepts. While the Würzburg experiments showed a greater influence of Husserl's *Logical Investigations* than Meinong's Gegenstandstheorie, Meinong was quick to see that the results confirmed his own ideas and consequently established a correspondence with two of Külpe's students, Karl Bühler and Otto Selz. To Bühler he wrote:

> I do not need to tell you how much that very series of Würzburg investigations interests me. . . . I too was once a follower in the Lockean tradition which you alluded to; but have found less and less satisfaction with it and now welcome with hearty joy all that proves to be suitable in helping to overcome that tradition.[18]

Meinong was eventually to issue invitations to both Bühler and Selz to join the Graz psychological laboratory after Witasek died in 1915.[19]

One of the best known conclusions of the Würzburgers was that

16. James Mark Baldwin, *Thought and Things*, 3 vols. (London: Swan Sonnenschein and Co., 1908), II, 423.

17. Meinong, *Selbstdarstellung*, *GA*, VII, 58.

18. Meinong to Bühler, April 2, 1913. Meinong *Nachlass*, Carton 33, No. 603.

19. Meinong to Bühler, May 5, 1917, *ibid.*, Carton 33, No. 608; Selz to Meinong, May 12, 1917, *ibid.*, Carton 63, No. 6784.

thinking was directed and purposive. In the papers of Henry Watt and Narziss Ach in 1905, for example, the subject was directed to perform a certain mental operation, such as finding a subordinate concept for a number of words (for example, "animal"—"dog").Then a series of words would be given (the stimulus), and the subject would think of the appropriate responses. The experimenters found that the instructions themselves, or the task (Aufgabe) had as much an influence on the response as the stimulus word itself.[20] The subject was thinking about the task he would have to perform ("find a subordinate concept") as well as the word that produced the sensations. These results emerged in even more striking form when Ach performed the experiments under hypnosis. When the Aufgabe was given while the subject was hypnotized, his response upon seeing the stimulus after waking was instantaneous.[21] These results provided independent confirmation of the views of the American functionalists: the isolated sequence of stimulus-sensation-response was insufficient to describe mental activity, which is goal-directed.

In the later Würzburg papers, particularly that of Bühler (1907), the thought processes to be investigated became ever more difficult and intricate. Subjects were expected to give answers of "yes" or "no" to such questions as "Do you consider the detailed presentations of Fichte's psychology a fruitful task?", or "Does monism really mean the negation of personality?"[22] It would often take the subjects ten to twenty seconds to respond to such questions, and the response would be followed by their introspective accounts of what went on in their minds as they were thinking through their answers. Here is an example,

> "Is this correct: 'The future is just as much a condition of the present as of the past'?" Answer: "No." (10 secs.) "First I thought: that sounds like something correct (without words). Then I made the attempt to represent it to myself. The thought came to me: Men are determined by thoughts of the future. Then, however, immediately the thought: *that the thought of the future should not be confounded with the future itself; that such confusions, however, con-*

20.   Henry J. Watt, "Experimental Contribution to a Theory of Thinking," in Jean Matter Mandler and George Mandler, eds., *Thinking: From Association to Gestalt* (New York: John Wiley and Sons, 1964), p. 193. For a full treatment of the Würzburg School, see George Humphrey, *Thinking* (New York: John Wiley and Sons, 1963), chaps. II–IV.

21.   Narziss Ach, "Über die Willenstätigkeit und das Denken," trans. D. Rappaport, in Mandler and Mandler, pp. 202f.

22.   Bühler, "Tatsachen und Probleme der Denkvorgänge I. Über Gedanken," *Archiv für die gesamte Psychologie*, IX (1907), 304; cited in Humphrey, p. 56.

*stitute a frequent dodge in philosophical thought. (Of words or images there was throughout no trace.) Thereupon the answer: No.*"[23]

Such introspective accounts could then furnish material for classifying and ordering the elements of thought; it was clear that such elements were irreducible to sensations or ideas.

Külpe's motives for launching the Würzburg School were philosophical, and reflected an evolution of outlook similar to that of Meinong.[24] Külpe had also become dissatisfied with the attempt to reduce all philosophical questions to states of consciousness; likewise he rejected the Neo-Kantian attempt to cast science and philosophy in purely subjective terms. His alternative was to be "critical realism," and in 1898 he conceived a vast systematic work in order to legitimize the belief in an independent real world in scientific endeavor.[25] In a letter to Meinong, Külpe confessed that this project was indeed the basis for the Würzburg experiments, and his subsequently published lectures on epistemology during the 1900s reveal the connection clearly.[26] Scientists and philosophers had been driven to skepticism, Külpe claimed, because the concept of thinking inherited from the empiricists had been too limited. Thinking is not concerned with sensations or their derivatives and often occurs without the formation of any mental images that resemble sense data—as in the protocol quoted above. Thus, "imageless thought" became another hallmark of the Würzburg work, together with the importance of the Aufgabe. By the same token, Külpe accepted the notion that these imageless thoughts were directed to objects themselves: "The fundamental characteristic of thinking," he wrote, "is for us the *referring* (*meinen*), meaning aiming at something."[27] He, too, saw the necessity of a theory of objects as a foundation of a realistic epistemology, though he preferred Husserl's narrower characterization of objects to the broader one of Meinong. The distinction between "concept" and "object," inherited from Husserl and Frege, runs through the Würzburg

23. *Ibid.*, p. 58.

24. See D. F. Lindenfeld, "Oswald Külpe and the Würzburg School," *Journal of the History of the Behavioral Sciences*, XIV (1978), 132–141.

25. Külpe, *Die Realisierung*, 3 vols. (Leipzig: Verlag von S. Hirzel, 1912–), I, v.

26. Külpe to Meinong, November 5, 1910, Meinong *Nachlass*, Carton 48, No. 3622; *Die Realisierung*, III, 37–45. Külpe never lived to complete his systematic work, but his lectures on epistemology at Würzburg were conceived as first drafts to this end. His students later published these lectures posthumously as volumes II and III.

27. *Ibid.*, p. 10.

work.[28] Bühler also found counterparts to Husserl's distinctions in some of his categories of imageless thought. He distinguished (1) a "consciousness of rule," in which a subject becomes aware of how to solve the complex problem or question at hand, as in the example given above; (2) "consciousness of relation," an awareness that one content is opposite from another, or follows from another; (3) "intention," which involves an awareness of a content in relation to an entire structure, a place within a given order.[29] Such intentions were not always fully worked out, but often occurred as flashes of insight covering a large area of material. For example, one of Bühler's subjects thought in an instant of Pre-Socratic philosophy, its relations to Socrates, and how Plato fought against it—all in a single thought, but unformulated. Bühler also called this a case of "indirect referring," whereby an object is known through its relations to other objects.[30]

Meinong had also grappled with the phenomenon of imageless thought in *On Assumptions*, and came to the rather awkward conclusion that imageless thoughts were a type of assumption—namely the kind that involved reference by so-being. This type he had already discovered in his second *Hume-Study* where he had labeled it indirect ideation, and pointed out that Bühler's third type of imageless thought was an independent confirmation of his own insight.[31] Only

---

28. *Ibid.*, pp. 16–30, esp. p. 28; August Messer, "Experimentell-psychologische Untersuchungen über das Denken," *Archiv für die gesamte Psychologie*, VIII (1906), 148.

29. Bühler, "Tatsachen und Probleme," I, pp. 339–350. The consciousness of rule corresponds to Husserl's categorical intuition, the intention to his "pure significative acts." See *Logical Investigations*, II, 785, 710.

30. Bühler, "Tatsachen und Probleme," I, p. 359.

31. Meinong, *Über Annahmen*, 2d. ed., *GA*, IV, 284. Meinong himself devotes considerable space to imageless thought, though his treatment is unsuccessful; it is a classic example of the inertia that often plagued his thought. In his psychologistic period, Meinong held that all thought derives from sensations, that is, images. Any thinking without images, therefore, must involve the higher mental operations which bring these sensations into complex combinations. In this respect imageless thought is similar to abstract concepts ("Phantasie-Vorstellung und Phantasie," *GA*, I, 234). An imageless thought of a red cross involves the *juxtaposition* of the ideas "red" and "cross," whereas the image of a red cross involves the *combination* of these two. In his mature phase, Meinong defined thinking as directed to objects, and re-defined abstract concepts as incomplete objects (*Möglichkeit*, *GA*, VI, 178). But he never revised his notion of imageless thought accordingly—to think of a red cross without conjuring up an image still involves a complex rather than a unitary mental act, one which juxtaposes two objects "red" and "cross" (*Über Annahmen*, 2d. ed., *GA*, IV, 251). See also Findlay, "Einige Hauptpünkte in Meinong's philosophischer Psychologie," in *Jenseits von Sein und Nichtsein*, p. 18.

after Meinong had pointed out the parallels in the second edition of *On Assumptions* and had opened the correspondence with Bühler and Selz did his work have a greater impact. In the work of Selz particularly, the notion that thinking is directed to objectives or states of affairs is given particular prominence.[32]

The parallel developments of Külpe and Meinong in the early 1900s allow us to see the role that experimental psychology played in the general intellectual revolution. German philosophy is often associated with idealism stemming from Kant and Hegel, but empiricist thinkers were by no means absent in the late nineteenth and early twentieth centuries, and they often found their nesting place in experimental psychology. The philosophical significance of this psychology thus lay in its continuation of the empiricist tradition. Laboratory experiments were simply the most up-to-date method of analyzing and describing experience with the utmost precision.

Nevertheless, these thinkers could not remain insensitive to the revolt against psychologism. They did not wish to deny that empiricism had overreached itself by attempting to reduce all logical and mathematical distinctions to matters of experience, as Mill had done. These aspects of intellectual discourse were indeed free from the whims of circumstance and the contingencies of particular times and places, to which all concrete experience was inevitably subject. At the same time, they could not follow the Neo-Kantians in denigrating such time-bound experiences to such an extent. Conscious experience, accessible through introspection, was not entirely irrelevant to the more abstract realms of logic and mathematics, even if distinct from them. The analysis of experience could still be of use in understanding how such abstract truths are grasped and known, or in providing analogies for classifying and ordering them. But if the relevance of experience was to be maintained, the concept itself would have to be broadened to include more than sensations and ideas. Hence the concern with higher processes and mental acts that were directed to the objects and propositions of logic and mathematics. This program also shows that there were psychologists who were still committed to analysis, and could not follow their American functionalist colleagues in shifting their attention to the self or organism as a whole. Such an approach, while appealing, could nevertheless open the door to a host of imprecisions. In this sense, the psychology of thinking served the same

32. Selz to Meinong, August 23, 1912. Meinong *Nachlass*, Carton 61, No. 6776. See also Humphrey, p. 133.

purpose as the new interest in language: it served as a way of bridging the ideal and the real by modifying atomism but retaining the analytical approach.

Despite the fact that the Würzburg School has won a place in the history of psychology as having made the first attempt to treat thinking experimentally, it failed to have a lasting impact on the development of psychology itself. By the end of the First World War, no more experiments on thinking were conducted in the same way. There were two major reasons for this decline. One of them had to do with methodology: the Würzburg papers soon provoked objections from other psychologists, including Wundt, that the thought experiments had not been rigorous enough.[33] The same few subjects had been used in test after test; the psychologists had been found to exert a suggestive influence on the responses; the conditions surrounding the experiments had not been sufficiently varied, nor had the stimuli been repeated often enough to correct for chance factors. An additional onslaught came from Wundt's student, Edward Bradford Titchener at Cornell, who questioned the very existence of imageless thought. Titchener conducted his own thought experiments to test the Würzburg assumptions, and the introspections of the Cornell subjects failed to uncover any imageless thoughts. He claimed that the Germans had in effect been led astray by the intentional model, and that the focusing on the relations between experience and object had hindered the direct description of experience itself. Titchener called this the "stimulus error"—confusing the objective stimulus with the contents of consciousness.[34] More importantly, the Würzburg-Cornell controversy threw the whole method of experiments-cum-introspection into doubt. If similar experiments could not produce similar results in different places, the whole scientific validity of the experiments had to be rejected. It was this controversy that helped to trigger behaviorism, in which the experiments were conducted only with publicly observable data, with introspection being dispensed with entirely. The writing of John Broadus Watson, the founder of behaviorism, reflects the same impatience with older methods and attitudes that characterized the logical positivists:

> I do not wish unduly to criticize psychology. It has failed signally, I believe, during the fifty-odd years of its existence as an experimental disci-

33. *Ibid.*, pp. 107ff.
34. Edward Bradford Titchener, *Lectures on the Experimental Psychology of the Thought Processes* (New York: Macmillan, 1909), p. 146. See also Humphrey, p. 120.

pline to make its place in the world as an undisputed natural science. Psychology, as it is generally thought of, has something esoteric in its methods. If you fail to reproduce my findings, it is not due to some fault in your apparatus or in the control of your stimulus, but it is due to the fact that your introspection is untrained. . . . The time seems to have come when psychology must discard all reference to consciousness; when it need no longer delude itself into thinking that it is making mental states the object of observation. We have become so enmeshed in speculative questions concerning the elements of mind, the nature of conscious content (for example, imageless thought, attitudes, and Bewusstseinslage, etc.).[35]

Behaviorism, of course, was only one of the several schools to emerge from the multitude of psychologies that existed before the war, one that was taken less seriously in Germany. But the psychology of thinking as practiced by the Würzburgers failed to sustain itself there for another reason: the failure of the thought psychologists to come up with any satisfactory theory about imageless thought. That such thought existed as an empirical fact was beyond doubt, but it proved impossible to integrate it into the existing body of psychological knowledge, whether on the atomistic or the intentional model. For the psychology of sensations had, after all, delivered a considerable amount of knowledge concerning sensation and perception. Were the imageless thoughts simply to be added to sensation and perception as a new element, but obeying different rules? Külpe, for one, was reluctant to embrace the intentional model completely, for he felt that sensations could not faithfully be characterized as being directed toward objects.[36] Bühler and Selz later admitted that imageless thoughts suffered from being treated as isolated entities: in all of Bühler's types, some awareness of a larger structure was involved.[37] What the subjects actually had in mind was rather a certain place in a larger structure of thoughts. So, for example, the response to the question concerning the present and the future involved a number of "imageless thoughts," but none of them made sense without the others. The entire thought process had to be described as a whole. Meinong's conclusion that imageless thought was essentially reference by way of so-being contained fundamentally the same point: to think of something

35. Watson, "Psychology as the Behaviorist Views It," in Dennis, *Readings*, p. 461.
36. Külpe, *Vorlesungen über Psychologie*, ed. Karl Bühler, 2d. ed. (Leipzig: Verlag von S. Hirzel, 1922), p. 131.
37. Bühler, *Die Krise der Psychologie*, 3rd ed. (Stuttgart: Gustav Fischer Verlag, 1965), p. 117. See also Cassirer's criticism of thought psychology, *Substance and Function*, p. 345.

without a concrete mental picture is always to think of it via its relations to other objects.

The outcome of the Würzburg work, then, was to raise once again the whole question of Gestalt: the relation of parts to wholes. How are "lower" mental processes related to "higher" ones? How do individual moments of thought fit into larger structures? It is no coincidence that a spate of publications concerning Gestalt psychology appeared in the years immediately preceding the war. Certainly the best known were the studies of Wertheimer and Köhler in 1911 and 1913. But also in 1913 there appeared a book on the perception of Gestalt by Bühler as well as the first major work by Selz on the laws of ordered thought processes; in 1914 came a paper by Benussi summarizing the researches he had conducted in Graz since 1902.[38] Thus the question raised by Meinong and Ehrenfels came to life once again.

### 3. THE GRAZ SCHOOL AND GESTALT PSYCHOLOGY

In order to trace the relationship between Meinong's work and the new trends in Gestalt psychology, we may briefly review Meinong's role in the Gestalt controversy. With Ehrenfels, he admitted that there were aspects of perceptual complexes that could not be reduced to sensations. Rather than give up the analytical approach, however, he postulated that such wholes contained different orders of parts—fundaments and objects of a higher order. Moreover, it was awkward to assume that we must consciously compare and synthesize these parts to arrive at wholes, as Meinong's earlier psychology had required. Instead, we grasp such wholes through judgments. Judgments, though themselves complex, became the basic units of analysis in Meinongian psychology, parallel to the objectives in his ontology and sentences in linguistics. These units take precedence over the elementary ideas, objects, and words that are contained in them, because the components can be described accurately only in the context of the larger entity.

38. Max Wertheimer, "Experimentelle Studien über das Sehen von Bewegung" (1911), in *Drei Abhandlungen zur Gestalttheorie* (Erlangen: Verlag der Philosophischen Akademie, 1925), pp. 1–105; Köhler, "On Unnoticed Sensations and Errors in Judgment," trans. Helmut E. Adler, in *The Selected Papers of Wolfgang Köhler*, ed. Mary Henle (New York: Liveright, 1971), pp. 13–39; Bühler, *Die Gestaltwahrnehmungen* (Stuttgart: Verlag von W. Spemann, 1913); Selz, *Über die Gesetze des geordneten Denkverlaufs* (Stuttgart: Verlag von W. Spemann, 1913); Vittorio Benussi, "Gesetze der inadäquaten Gestaltauffassung," *Archiv für die gesamte Psychologie*, XXXII (1914), 396–419.

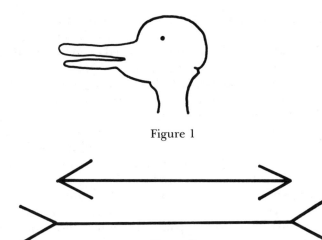

Figure 1

Figure 2

In order to validate Meinong's theories experimentally, Witasek and Benussi set out to observe the effects of ambiguous figures or optical illusions—that is, situations in which the sense-data are given, but different judgments about the objects could ensue.[39] Now Meinong's theory seemed ideally suited for certain types of such figures. For example, the drawing in Figure 1 can be viewed as either a duck or a rabbit.[40] One could describe this situation as a single set of contents directed to two different remote objects, depending on whether I judge it to be one or the other. But there were other figures that did not lend themselves to such an interpretation—such as the Müller-Lyer illusion, shown in Figure 2. One can easily form a judgment that the two horizontal lines are of equal length—in other words, that the figure *is* an illusion. But this conviction will not alter the visual perception itself; we will continue to see the horizontal lines as unequal in length. Here, then, is a case in which the ideas on which a judgment is based are not shaped by the judgment.[41] Surely, moreover, the sensa-

39. Stephen Witasek, "Über die Natur der geometrischen-optischen Tauschungen," *Zeitschrift für Psychologie* XIX (1899), 81–175; Benussi, "Zur Psychologie des Gestalterfassens," in Meinong, ed. *Untersuchungen zur Gegenstandtheorie und Psychologie* (Leipzig: Verlag von Johann Ambrosius Barth, 1904), pp. 303–448.

40. Wittgenstein, *Philosophical Investigations*, p. 194. Wittgenstein derived the figure from I. Jastrow's *Fact and Fable in Psychology*.

41. Witasek, p. 131; Benussi, "Zur Psychologie," pp. 390ff. Meinong in *Erfahrungs-*

tions of the individual parts of the figure—such as the two horizontal lines in isolation—are equal. What, then, produces the illusion? Benussi, in his study of this example, was forced to go back to Meinong's earlier theory: that the idea of the whole is synthesized in some fashion from the ideas of the parts. Following a suggestion of Meinong, Benussi now called this process Vorstellungsproduction, the production of ideas.[42] Benussi sought to prove this by telling his subjects to concentrate alternately on the whole figure and on the individual parts. If we do the latter, we can with practice learn to see the horizontal lines as equal. Thus, Benussi concluded, the analytical attitude reduces illusion; our tendency to produce ideas of objects of a higher order is the source of our illusion.[43] Benussi extended his experiments to other types of illusions, such as a drawing of a cube on a two-dimensional surface, or the apparent motion induced by a stroboscope. In all cases, his experiments were done with the utmost care, and the exact conditions that favor the increase or decrease of a given illusion are worked out. For example, Benussi discovered that if the Müller-Lyer figure and others are illuminated in certain ways, the illusion itself will vary. Later he performed an experiment that showed how colors changed in appearance depending on the background against which they were placed.[44] In all these papers, Benussi won the respect of the later Gestalt psychologists for the thoroughness and accuracy of his observations.[45]

Nevertheless, Benussi's work was plagued by two embarrassing fea-

---

grundlagen admits a similar case in the form of Locke's temperature experiment. If one's hands are of different temperature, and one dips each into the same basin of water, the water will feel a different temperature, though we judge it to be the same. Meinong concludes that such empirical evidence of the senses cannot deliver evidence for certainty, but only evidence for presumption. (Erfahrungsgrundlagen, GA, V, 462). Thus these illusions, which led the Graz school to a psychological dualism between sensation and thinking, also are part of the foundation for epistemological dualism—that we cannot know concrete objects in their fullness with certainty.

42. Meinong, Über Annahmen, 2d. ed., GA, IV, 11n; Benussi, "Gesetze," p. 400n. See also Richard Ameseder, "Über Vorstellungsproduktion," in Untersuchungen zur Gegenstandstheorie und Psychologie, pp. 481–508.

43. Benussi, "Zur Psychologie des Gestalterfassens," p. 403; "Gesetze," p. 409.

44. Benussi, "Zur Psychologie des Gestalterfassens," p. 404; "Versuche zur Analyse taktil erweckter Scheinbewegungen," Archiv für die gesamte Psychologie, XXXVI (1917), 61n. On the experiments with stroboscopic motion, see "Stroboskopische Scheinbewegungen und geometrisch-optische Gestalttäuschungen," ibid., XXIV (1912), 31–62.

45. Köhler, "Unnoticed Sensations," p. 30n; Kurt Koffka, Principles of Gestalt Psychology (New York: Harcourt, Brace and World, Harbinger ed., 1963), p. 134.

tures. First, it gave no account of the processes of "production," an account which was required by the theory. No one was aware of the synthesis which, according to the theory, had to be going on. The perception of wholes seemed to be an immediate act. Benussi was forced to postulate that some unnoticed process of association was taking place.[46] Because the term "production" itself caused so much confusion, Benussi soon changed the name of the experiences of the Gestalt-qualities to "ideas of extrasensory provenance."[47]

A second problem was that it reinforced the dualistic point of view which seemed so unattractive. On the one hand, there were the sensations, for which the governing laws, which were based on the Weber-Fechner principle, were well known. On the other hand were the ideas of extrasensory provenance of the objects of a higher order, which seemed to obey another, mysterious set of rules. Such entities were no better than imageless thought, and proved to be most uncongenial in a period when functional interrelationships were the order of the day. In was in order to avoid such dualisms that Meinong had turned to his theory of judgment in the first place; but the work of his laboratory merely showed that the intentional model was not the solution. It could not account for all the empirical facts of sensation and perception.

It was under these conditions that the work of Wertheimer, Köhler, and Koffka seemed so definitive. In 1913, Köhler published his first major paper, "On Unnoticed Sensations and Errors of Judgment." His thesis was that the vaguenesses which beset most attempts to describe perceptual wholes, such as the unnoticed ideas of Benussi, or the errors of judgment of other psychologists such as Stumpf, all stemmed from a common failing: the notion that one should isolate single relationships between stimuli and sensations (the "constancy hypothesis" in Köhler's terms).[48] If one presumed to be able to break down perceptual wholes into parts without distortion, one could not avoid the assumption that those parts must remain constant—an assumption characteristic of the atomistic model. This would apply even if those parts were heterogeneous, as the Graz school claimed. Thus, according to Köhler, such a psychology cannot avoid a mosaic of sensations, each with a constant set of properties, and each corresponding to a discrete part of a figure. Given this situation, there is no

46. Benussi, "Über die Motive der Scheinkörperlichkeit bei umkehrbaren Zeichnungen," *Archiv für die gesamte Psychologie*, XX (1911), 395.

47. Benussi, "Gesetze," p. 401.

48. Köhler, "Unnoticed Sensations," p. 14.

straightforward way of explaining how those parts should become one single figure, even if we assume a multiplicity of relations and judgments. If, on the other hand, one assumed that the parts interacted with each other and reinforced each other to produce a total stimulus and a total sensation, then these problems evaporated. In other words, the only way to eliminate the problems connected with atomism was to forsake the analytical approach. At the same time, Bühler's book on the perception of Gestalten criticized Benussi's theory along similar lines, and in the following year Koffka's first major article centered on a polemic against Benusssi on the grounds that he had assumed the constancy hypothesis.[49]

Needless to say, these polemics evoked a flurry of counterclaims, particularly on questions of priority of discovery. Benussi published a long article pointing out his own anticipations of Bühler's work; Bühler was later to publish a similar piece against the Berlin School, as Wertheimer, Köhler, and Koffka came to be known.[50] Significantly, however, Benussi made no attempt to defend the constancy hypothesis against the attacks on the Berliners. While he stood by Meinong's theory and announced he would continue to use it, he emphasized that the experimental facts were of much greater consequence than the theories. "As long as there are still moot facts, I find it inappropriate to speak at length of moot ideas," he wrote in 1917.[51] Perhaps this respect for experimental results explains the lack of animosity between Benussi and the Berlin school. During the 1920s they met in Berlin on friendly terms.[52] Meinong, too, felt quite comfortable in his role as predecessor. In response to Bühler's book he wrote to him:

> Many thanks for sending your fine book. You may well imagine how welcome to me is such a notable advance in problems which have provided

49. Bühler, *Gestaltwahrnehmungen*, pp. 28ff; Koffka, "Zur Grundlegung der Wahrnehmungspsychologie—Eine Auseinandersetzung mit V. Benussi," *Zeitschrift für Psychologie*, LXXIII (1915), 19.

50. Benussi, "Die Gestaltwahrnehmungen," *Zeitschrift für Psychologie*, LXIX (1914), 256–292. Benussi sought to show that Bühler had misread him, and that the two were actually closer than Bühler had thought. Meinong also communicated such criticisms to Bühler by letter (letter to Bühler, April 2, 1913, Meinong *Nachlass*, Carton 33, No. 603). Bühler later claimed to have anticipated the Berlin School in "Die 'Neue Psychologie' Koffkas," *Zeitschrift für Psychologie* XCIX (1926), 145, which provoked a response by Koffka, "Bemerkungen zur Denk-Psychologie," *Psychologische Forschung*, IX (1927), 163–183.

51. Benussi, "Über Scheinbewegungskombination," *Archiv für die gesamte Psychologie*, XXXVII (1917), 240n.

52. Heider, p. 69.

such powerful impulses for my own work. These have admittedly pointed me in a somewhat apsychological path; I may take that much greater pleasure in the fact that what could not grow beyond first attempts and sketches for me has been tackled so vigorously by the young generation and has led to such fine results. What matters least is how much or how little of those early concepts may have stood the test: I desire for my scientific activity no better result than to have contributed my part to being quickly antiquated.[53]

Given the presence of Benussi and the interest of Bühler and Selz in coming to Graz, the Graz school could easily have become a major center of Gestalt psychology in the interwar period. This was prevented by the War and by Meinong's death. The Ministry of Education was not ready to fill Witasek's position during the war, and Benussi, as an Italian, left in 1919 for the University of Padua.[54] Presumably the Italo-Austrian hostility made his position in Graz most uncomfortable. After 1920 there was no further attempt to carry on experimental psychology in Graz. Ironically, Vienna finally received a psychological institute of its own, and Bühler himself came to be its director. His interests by that time had diverged in many directions, including child psychology and the psychology of language. He gained a reputation as one of the leading psychologists in Europe in the 1920s and 1930s. He emigrated to the United States in 1939, but was never able to find a position commensurate with his European reputation; he has been called "one of the casualties of the immigration."[55] But his eminence may be judged by the quality of his students, who included Paul Lazarsfeld and Karl Popper.

Meanwhile, the Berlin school became the best known representative of the Gestalt idea. It must not be thought, however, that this predominance was due to chance alone. If anything, it was due to its remarkable ability to combine high scientific standards with a consistent and all-encompassing philosophy. The ambitions of the Gestalt psychologists to be more than mere specialists is evident throughout their writings. Koffka's great textbook of 1935, for example, ends on the following note:

53. Meinong to Bühler, No. 603.
54. Heider, p. 66; Meinong to Bühler, April 19, 1918, Meinong *Nachlass*, Carton 33, No. 612. This reveals the decision of the ministry.
55. Jean Matter Mandler and George Mandler, "The Diaspora of Experimental Psychology: The Gestaltists and Others," in Donald Fleming and Bernard Bailyn, eds., *The Intellectual Migration* (Cambridge: Harvard University Press, Belknap Press, 1969), p. 410.

If there is any polemical spirit in this book, it is directed not against persons but against a strong cultural force in our present civilization for which I have chosen the name positivism. If positivism can be regarded as an integrative philosophy, its integration rests on the dogma that all events are equally unintelligible, irrational, meaningless, purely factual. Such an integration is, however, to my way of thinking, identical with a complete disintegration. Being convinced that such a view is utterly inadequate in the face of the facts, I had to attack it, and that the more since its hold over our generation is strong. . . . I should not have written this book based upon a non-positivistic theory, were it not my deep scientific conviction that truth demands such a philosophy.[56]

Although written in America, such a statement reflected the intellectual atmosphere in Germany in the 1920s, where the concern with "wholeness" had become increasingly pervasive. In addition to the Berlin school and the prevalence of Diltheyan concepts, there was "holistic psychology" (Ganzheitspsychologie), founded by Wundt's successor, Felix Krueger at Leipzig.[57] But the Berlin school stood out because of its claim that positivism was itself unscientific, and that the true science of Gestalt could overcome the antinomies between the natural sciences and the humanistic disciplines. Köhler, in his book *Gestalt Psychology*, arrives at the same point when he attacks both behaviorism and the old introspective method.[58]

The key to such a reconciliation was of course the holistic approach as opposed to the analytical one, and the Gestaltists used such an approach to attack the mind-body problem by substituting the principle of "isomorphism" for the old constancy hypothesis. According to this doctrine, the configuration of a physical whole corresponds to the configuration of the neurophysiological process which registers it, and which in turn is manifest in consciousness as a perception.[59] There was thus still a constant correlation between physical, physiological, and mental events, but at the level of structures rather than elements. Given this premise, it becomes clear that most of the questions that plagued Meinong and his students about the perception of wholes found their solution in the realm of neurophysiology. The initial studies of Wertheimer on stroboscopic motion differed from Benussi's on just this point.[60] Instead of some unnoticed mental pro-

56. Koffka, *Principles*, pp. 684–685.
57. Albert Wellek, "Krueger, Felix," trans. Tessa Byck, in *Encyclopedia of Philosophy*, IV, 366–367; Ringer, p. 381.
58. Köhler, *Gestalt Psychology*, Chs. I, III, esp. pp. 57f.
59. *Ibid.*, p. 89; Koffka, *Principles*, pp. 62f.
60. Wertheimer, "Experimentelle Studien," p. 87.

cess of "production," which creates an idea of motion when there is none, Wertheimer postulated that the quick alterations of parts in the stroboscope lead to a similar alteration and interaction of parts of the brain, which then shapes a whole that is qualitatively different from them—namely, the perceived motion. The physical stroboscope, the brain process, and the perceived motion, then, are themselves simply part of a psycho-physical whole, which has unified structure. Thus the Gestaltists' notion of structure was dynamic: changes in the physical world lead to corresponding changes in brain processes, so that the parts of both brain and world are continually redistributing themselves. The work of the Gestalt psychologists in later years was to study the laws of such distribution—the laws by which parts tend to arrange themselves in certain ways and not others. A "good" Gestalt was one that approximated these laws; for example, a symmetrical figure, which forces itself upon the viewer more easily than an asymmetrical one. In this sense, Koffka could say that Gestalt psychology was the true heir of the functional psychology of the prewar era: it fulfilled Dewey's injunction of forsaking the reflex-arc and concentrating on the interactions of mind, body, and environment.[61]

It was Köhler who was able to expand these examples into a broader framework. He had studied physics with Max Planck, and realized that Wertheimer's hypothesis could be squared with the then-current notion of field physics. "In a sense," Köhler wrote, "Gestalt psychology has since become a kind of application of field physics to essential parts of psychology and brain physiology."[62]

Such an emphasis on physiology and physics may hardly seem to vindicate Koffka's contention that Gestalt psychology was antipositivistic. But the Gestaltists maintained that their laws did equal justice to the humanistic psychology descended from Dilthey, without in the least sacrificing the integrity of experiences in this area. This claim was based on the fact that Dilthey and his successors had always insisted that experience occurred in wholes—that thoughts, feelings, and actions were interwoven and could not be analyzed and classified according to any single scheme, such as Brentano had tried to create. To give an example from Köhler:

> After a long walk, on a hot summer day, I drink a glass of cold beer. While I do so, I feel coolness and a characteristic taste in my mouth. Also there is great enjoyment. Now, is it necessary for me gradually to learn that in such a situation the enjoyment refers to the coolness and the taste? . . . Surely, no

61.  Koffka, "Zur Grundlegung," pp. 56f.
62.  Köhler, "Gestalt Psychology," in *Selected Papers*, p. 115.

such learning is needed. I am no more directly aware of my enjoyment as such, and of the touch and the taste by themselves, than I am of the fact that the enjoyment refers to just this coolness and taste. My pleasure is also felt to be an adequate reaction to these facts. Between the pleasure and its sensory basis I experience what is called in German their "Verständlicher Zusammenhang," which may be expresssed in English as "understandable relationship." [63]

Of course, the same redistributions and interactions of physical and neurological energies take place here as in any "scientific" example, but the living experience we have of such wholes is in no way contradictory to such physical and physiological facts. Thus it was possible for Köhler to translate such common-sense terms as "insight" into "awareness of determination," or to discuss values in terms of "vectors." [64] In one sense, Gestalt psychology was a variation of the project originally conceived by Ernst Mach: to find a common denominator for physics, physiology, and psychology. Whereas Mach sought such a denominator in atomistic elements (the sensations), the Gestaltists sought it in common structures while allowing the elements to vary. [65]

In this sense, the Gestalt theorists addressed themselves to the basic question we have seen posed by the intellectual revolution: to develop a set of concepts that could span both the sciences and the humanities without apparently reducing one to the other. It erased the last traces of dualism that persisted in the model of the Graz and Würzburg schools. In Koffka's words, the higher mental processes of these schools introduced "a dualism between blind mechanical and ordered mental forces. In short, both solutions were vitalistic, and for that reason both are equally unacceptable to us." [66]

Yet it is noteworthy that Gestalt theory had much more success as a limited contribution to experimental psychology than as a consistent Weltanschauung. If the intentional model was inadequate to describe all psychological problems without lapsing into dualism, the Gestalt theory was equally inadequate to deal with certain problems of philosophy and social thought, particularly those which lent themselves to treatment in terms of the linguistic analogy—as Bühler pointed out. [67] For the Gestaltists' synthesis is based on the notion of a perva-

63. Köhler, *Gestalt Psychology*, p. 191.
64. *The Place of Value in a World of Facts* (New York: Liveright Publishing Corp., 1938; reprint ed., New York: Meridian Books, 1959), pp. 73f.
65. Koffka, *Principles*, p. 63.        66. *Ibid.*, p. 560.
67. Bühler, "Die 'Neue Psychologie' Koffkas," p. 155; *Die Krise der Psychologie*, pp. 119f, 123, 59ff.

sive causality; the interactions between physics, physiology, and psychology are ultimately causal. Intentional psychology, on the other hand, with its concentration on reference and meaning, is particularly suited for revealing the relationships between psychology, philosophy, and social thought. Similar objections were raised by phenomenological psychologists such as Aron Gurwitsch and Maurice Merleau-Ponty.[68] Gurwitsch, for example, pointed out that Gestalt theory does not do justice to the different dimensions of being that Meinong and Husserl had probed: there is no distinction between categorical judgment (so-being) and existential judgments.[69]

Thus Gestalt theory, for all its opposition to positivism, still remained true to it in one significant way: its integration was based on physical analogies. It could describe the processes of understanding, meaning, insight, and thinking insofar as these were translatable into physical and physiological processes.[70] The key notion of Gestalt psychology is *action*, which is even more pervasive in its thought than the holistic approach itself. Köhler, for example, claimed that Gestalt psychology did indeed do justice to analysis by recognizing that structures could interact to *segregate* their material into relatively stable units (such as the particles of physics), although these segregated wholes were still explained by causal processes rather than in terms of semantics or methodology.[71] Gestalt psychology also integrated the treatment of values and esthetics by reducing them to physical analogies. In this respect it was similar to the integrating attempt of Carnap, though its route to this conclusion was very different. Logical positivism represented the atomistic model and the analytical approach carried to their limits, applied to the linguistic analogy. Gestalt psychology rejected these assumptions, but retained the physical analogy. Meinong's alternative avoided both these sorts of reductionism by holding that the higher objects of culture were analyzable into the

68. Aron Gurwitsch, "Some Aspects and Developments of Gestalt Psychology," in *Studies in Phenomenology and Psychology* (Evanston: Northwestern University Press, 1966), pp. 54–55; Maurice Merleau-Ponty, *The Structure of Behavior*, trans. Alden L. Fisher (Boston: Beacon Press, paperback ed., 1963), pp. 49, 51, 119–120.

69. Gurwitsch, p. 50.

70. Wertheimer underscores this by attacking traditional logic as a description of what acually takes place while thinking. In its concern for exact criteria of truth, logic removes itself from the actual empirical ways in which we arrive at rational insight (*Productive Thinking*, enlarged ed., ed. Michael Wertheimer [New York: Harper and Row, 1959]), pp. 6, 10. In other words, logic cannot be reduced to causal processes.

71. Köhler, *Gestalt Psychology*, p. 98.

lower objects of physics without being reducible to them. He retained analysis but modified atomism, rejecting the assumption of the homogeneity of parts but accepting the assumption of constancy. For this he paid the price of dualism. It remains to be seen if any intellectual synthesis remained which avoided paying this price. For this, we must turn to Edmund Husserl and phenomenology.

# X

# MEINONG AND PHENOMENOLOGY

The influence of the phenomenological movement in twentieth-century European thought has been tremendous. It led not only to the existentialism of Heidegger and Sartre, but also has had an impact on the social sciences through such thinkers as Alfred Schütz.[1] From the 1920s through the 1950s, phenomenology and analytical philosophy divided the Western philosophical world between them, phenomenology being the dominant movement in Germany and France, and analytical philosophy taking primacy in England, America, and, to a lesser extent, Austria. The currents of thought that were so close in the period before World War One became polarized thereafter. This separation was due not only to the developments within the analytical movement sketched in Chapter Eight, but also to the changing thought of Edmund Husserl, the most influential figure in phenomenology. Between 1903 and his death in 1938, Husserl steered a course further and further away from the empiricist tradition and into the waters of German idealism.

Although Meinong has received far more attention from analytical philosophers than from phenomenologists, it is generally agreed that he properly belongs with the latter movement.[2] Like Husserl, Meinong saw in the intentional relation between consciousness and objects a mode of philosophical analysis that could provide a foundation and common denominator for knowledge in the natural sciences and the

1. The most comprehensive study of phenomenology as a whole is Spiegelberg, *The Phenomenological Movement.*

2. Findlay, "Meinong the Phenomenologist," *Revue Internationale de la Philosophie,* XXVII (1973), 161; Grossmann, p. 106; Guido Küng, "Noema und Gegenstand," in *Jenseits von Sein und Nichtsein,* p. 55.

humanities. Husserl himself acknowledged the similarity of Meinong's researches to his own in a diary entry of 1906:

> Meinong's book [*Über Annahmen*] could not offer me so very much . . . beyond the great stimulation that always comes when a not insignificant man reflects on the same problems that have occupied us for years. . . . Nevertheless a discussion with Meinong will be necessary and unavoidable for evident reasons, quite apart from the fact that it must once be shown that in reality our mutual areas of research and basic findings agree with each other.
>
> We are like two travellers in the same dark continent. Of course we often see the same thing and describe it, but often differently, in accordance with our different masses of apperception.
>
> One can show it paragraph for paragraph, except for the chapters on emotional acts and for the one on hypothetical judgments and deductions from assumptions. The latter I hold at any rate to be quite erroneous.[3]

One can readily find similar acknowledgments in Meinong's writings, as well as in the personal correspondence of the two.[4] And yet Meinong has remained a peripheral figure in the phenomenological movement, overshadowed in reputation by Husserl. The reasons are revealing, for they help to illuminate the origins of the split between Anglo-American and continental philosophy that emerged in the interwar period. One can find such reasons at several levels—the personal relationship of the two men, differences in style which determined their influence, and differences in basic assumptions which became increasingly evident with time.

### 1. MEINONG AND HUSSERL: PERSONAL CONTACTS AND RELATIONSHIPS

Meinong and Husserl never met, but they corresponded with each other periodically between 1891 and 1904. The correspondence and other archival material shows that each was familiar with the other's work, at least through 1902 on Husserl's part, and through 1913 on Meinong's.[5] Yet not only did they apparently fail to exert a

3. Husserl, "Persönliche Aufzeichnungen," ed. Walter Biemel, *Philosophy and Phenomenological Research*, XVI (1956), 295–296.

4. Meinong, "Über Gegenstandstheorie," *GA*, II, 503; LTC, 94; *Selbstdarstellung*, *GA*, VII, pp. 57–58; letter of Husserl to Meinong, August 27, 1900, *Philosophenbriefe*, p. 102; Meinong to Husserl (draft), April 10, 1902, *ibid.*, p. 108.

5. The contacts and influences of Husserl and Meinong on each other have been fully discussed by Hans Schermann in *Meinong und Husserl*. Husserl's notes on the phenomenology of time consciousness reveal a familiarity with Meinong's writings of the

strong influence on each other, but both actually went to great lengths to guard against such influence. Both were highly possessive about their own ideas and were extremely sensitive to the issue of proper citation. The correspondence bristles with innuendo as to the other's lack of originality. Meinong, we may recall, responded in such a manner to Husserl's early *Philosophy of Arithmetic* in 1891.[6] With the publication of *On Assumptions* in 1902, it was Husserl's turn to be sensitive—the book appeared shortly after his own *Logical Investigations* but contained only a few references to it.[7] By the time of his announcement of Gegenstandstheorie in 1904, Meinong had assimilated the *Investigations*, and admitted that his aim was close to that of Husserl's "pure logic." But Meinong preferred to fashion his own terminology, partly because his own conception of logic was quite different from Husserl's.[8]

Such tensions are understandable in the light of Meinong's and Husserl's respective personalities, which seemed to be as similar as their ideas. Both preferred to work in solitude, and each presumably liked to view their own achievements as original. Husserl went much further in this direction than Meinong: his writings convey the unmistakable image he had of himself as a lonely prophet, struggling with the most profound issues of his day without recognition (he once referred to phenomenology as the "promised land" on which he himself would never set foot; at another time he compares himself to the knight in Dürer's engraving "Knight, Death, and Devil," carrying on a noble mission in the face of temptation).[9] The thought that a contemporary could be arriving at the same result independently was undoubtedly threatening to him. In addition, Husserl for a long time felt that his contributions had not received proper recognition from his academic colleagues. Husserl was reluctant to publish his findings prematurely—he had been working on the *Logical Investigations* throughout the 1890s, and his lack of publications led him to remain a Privatdozent for fourteen years (from 1887 to 1901), at a time when

---

1890s (*Phänomenologie des inneren Zeitbewusstseins*, pp. 217n, 219n). Meinong's papers contain a set of notes on Husserl's *Ideas for a Pure Phenomenology* of 1913.

6.   Meinong to Husserl (draft), May 20, 1891, *Philosophenbriefe*, p. 96. Schermann cites the letter actually sent on p. 13, in which the accusation is subdued, but still present. It is also Schermann's considered opinion that Meinong and Husserl developed their ideas independently (p. 48).

7.   Husserl to Meinong, April 5, 1902, *Philosophenbriefe*, p. 103.

8.   Meinong, "Über Gegenstandstheorie," *GA*, II, 501–502; LTC, p. 93.

9.   Husserl, *Ideas*, trans. W. R. Boyce Gibson (London: George Allen and Unwin, 1931), p. 29; "Persönliche Aufzeichnungen," p. 300. See Spiegelberg, I, 90f.

Meinong's works were receiving much recognition.[10] While the *Investigations* brought him a promotion and a move from Halle to Göttingen, the faculty there rejected a further promotion to Professor Ordinarius in 1905 on the grounds that Husserl's work was "scientifically insignificant."[11] Success soon followed, however: Husserl received an offer from the University of Freiburg in 1906, and remained there for the rest of his career. It is possible that these difficult years left a lasting mark on Husserl's attitudes, as they did on Meinong's, long after he had in fact achieved academic success.

Whatever the reasons, Husserl's attitude towards Meinong became increasingly antagonistic after 1905. Not only did he come to view the theory of objects as borrowed from his own *Investigations*—the phrase "theory of objects" does admittedly appear in that work—but he also regarded Meinong's work as more superficial than his own.[12] Husserl's next major publication, the *Ideas for a Pure Phenomenology* in 1913, contained the statement that Meinong's work "has not made any real advance on my own attempts, whether in respect of substance or method."[13] Meinong was stung by this remark, and responded that Husserl had now made any rapprochement between phenomenology and the theory of objects impossible.[14] Such antagonisms help explain why Meinong was excluded from the mainstream of phenomenological thought, which followed Husserl.[15]

## 2. DIFFERENCES IN STYLE AND BASIC IDEAS

More important than these personal tensions were undoubtedly the stylistic differences between the two. Not that Husserl's prose is more accessible than Meinong's—if anything, it is less so. But Husserl had a way of communicating the relevance and even the urgency of his philosophical concerns vis-à-vis the intellectual needs of his day. Whereas Meinong rarely succeeded in presenting his theory of objects as more than a new topic for philosophical specialists, Husserl

10.  *Ibid.*, pp. 90, 98.

11.  Husserl, "Persönliche Aufzeichnungen," pp. 293–294.

12.  Schermann, p. 45.

13.  Husserl, *Ideas*, p. 313n. See a similar remark in the second edition of the *Investigations*, II, 480.

14.  Meinong, *Möglichkeit*, *GA*, VI, xx; *Selbstdarstellung*, *GA*, VII, 57–58.

15.  Farber, for example, follows Husserl in his evaluation of Meinong in *The Foundation of Phenomenology*, p. 206. Spiegelberg claims that Meinong had not analyzed consciousness sufficiently (p. 101).

presented his corresponding views as the key to resolving the spiritual crisis of the twentieth century. In this respect he acquired Brentano's sense of mission in a way unmatched by Meinong. That mission, by Husserl's own confession, was positivistic: to render philosophy a "rigorous science," free from all the inconclusiveness which had plagued it in the past.[16] At the same time, Husserl increasingly emphasized that such a goal could not be achieved by slavishly imitating the established methods and assumptions of natural science, but by providing the critical foundations for such methods and assumptions, thereby eliminating the traces of inconsistency and naiveté that still plagued the practitioners of science. Phenomenology, in other words, was to save science from itself. In one of his best known programmatic works, "Philosophy as a Rigorous Science" (1911), he wrote:

> He who is capable of awakening faith in, of inspiring understanding of and enthusiasm for the greatness of a goal, will easily find the forces that are applied to this goal. I mean, our age is according to its vocation a great age—only it suffers from the scepticism that has disintegrated the old, unclarified ideals. And for that very reason it suffers from the too negligible development and force of philosophy, which has not yet progressed enough, is not scientific enough to overcome sceptical negativism (which calls itself positivism) by means of true positivism. Our age wants to believe only in "realities." Now, its strongest reality is science, and thus what our age most needs is philosophical science.[17]

Husserl wrote this passage in 1910. As he later experienced the widespread disillusionment with rational values that followed the war, he adhered to the same interpretation—but now he saw this disillusionment as a crisis of Western thought. In one of his last works, *The Crisis of European Sciences and Transcendental Phenomenology* (1936), he attributed this lack of faith to the same false positivism that scientists had in fact pursued. The remoteness of mathematical formulas, their apparent lack of relation to ordinary life, their inaccessibility to the non-specialist, were all traceable to a lack of proper philosophical foundation:

> The change in public evaluation was unavoidable, especially after the war, and we know that it has gradually become a feeling of hostility among the younger generation. In our vital need—so we are told—this science has

16. Husserl, "Erinnerungen an Franz Brentano," p. 154; "Philosophy as a Rigorous Science," trans. Quentin Lauer, in *Phenomenology and the Crisis of Philosophy* (New York: Harper and Row, Torchbook edition, 1965), pp. 74f.

17. *Ibid.*, p. 145.

nothing to say to us. It excludes in principle precisely the questions which man, given over in our unhappy times to the most portentous upheavals, finds the most burning: questions of the meaning or meaninglessness of the whole of this human existence. Do not these questions, universal and necessary for all men, demand universal reflections and answers based on rational insight? The mere science of bodies clearly has nothing to say; it abstracts from everything subjective. As for the humanistic sciences, on the other hand, all the special and general disciplines of which treat of man's spiritual existence [*sic*] . . . their rigorous scientific character requires, we are told, that the scholar carefully exclude all valuative positions, all questions of the reason or unreason of their human subject matter and its cultural configurations.[18]

It was phenomenology that provided this foundation by showing that science and life could both be interpreted in terms of objects which appear to individual consciousness, just as Meinong had held.[19] Husserl and Meinong also agreed that while such a synthesis could also come about through the study of language and its meanings, the prelinguistic relations between consciousness and objects offered a more secure and certain ground for philosophical analysis.

While Husserl's appeal to "relevance" also helps to explain his greater reputation, it cannot be said that his own writing was suited to win over masses of non-specialists. If Meinong's philosophy has been compared to a formal garden containing some intricate mazes, Husserl's has been compared to a labyrinth.[20] While the *Logical Investigations* of 1900–1901 are relatively easy to follow, Husserl's later writings take on new layers of imposing and forbidding terms: phenomenology becomes "transcendental," "pure," involves a certain operation known as *epoché*, contains within it a self-discipline called "hyletics," and yields such distinctions as that between "noesis" and "noema." Such terms have been the bane of those who have tried to understand Husserl and his significance, and have doubtless helped sustain the distance between phenomenology and Anglo-American philosophy. At the same time, some of these distinctions were based on Kantian terminology, which made them more accessible to German audiences.

18. Husserl, *Crisis of the European Sciences*, p. 6. In Part II of this work Husserl traces this irrelevance back to Galilean physics and its separation of the "objective" mathematically defined world from the "subjective" world of sense qualities.

19. Husserl, "Philosophy as a Rigorous Science," pp. 89, 91, 147.

20. Findlay, *Meinong's Theory*, p. xi; Paul Ricoeur, *Husserl: an Analysis of His Phenomenology*, trans. Edward G. Ballard and Lester E. Embree (Evanston: Northwestern University Press, 1967), p. 29.

Husserl's entire academic career, it should be noted, was spent in Germany.

These terminological changes were symptomatic of the more profound change in Husserl's thought after the *Investigations*, a change that distanced him further from Meinong and from logical realism. By the time of his next major work, the *Ideas for a Pure Phenomenology* of 1913, Husserl had altered his conception of phenomenology significantly. Unfortunately, the known scholarship on Husserl is not sufficiently advanced to give a complete chronological account of this change. Husserl left behind some 45,000 pages of notes and manuscripts, and much has yet to be studied, though much of this material suggests that the change occurred in 1906–1907.[21] There is also some question among Husserl scholars as to how drastic this new conception was in comparison to the old—whether it marked a completely new direction or simply carried the projects of the *Investigations* further.[22] Whatever the genesis, we can see that certain differences between Husserl's and Meinong's approach to intentionality were evident at the time of the *Investigations*, and this fact may possibly help to clarify Husserl's later development.

One major difference between Husserl and Meinong was Husserl's greater drive for systematic coherence in philosophy. For Meinong, the theory of objects was to be *a* philosophical discipline, but not *the* philosophical discipline; he remained true until the end of his life to his early notion that philosophy was a group of disciplines which admitted of no single definition.[23] Husserl, on the other hand, sought to establish a hierarchy of philosophical disciplines, each of which would be logically prior to the next, leading eventually to a philosophy that would be "free of presuppositions." He sketches this hierarchy in the first volume of the *Investigations*. Empirical science presupposed theoretical science, which in turn presupposed a unity of theories; this unity was based on certain conditions that could be called a theory of theories or a science of sciences, namely pure logic.[24] Within pure logic, phenomenology served a preliminary role, that of showing how logical objects were evident to consciousness.[25] With the development of "pure" phenomenology, however, this discipline eclipsed logic as

21. Küng, "The Phenomenological Reduction as Epoche and as Explication," *The Monist*, LIX (1975), 63, 67; Ricoeur, *Husserl*, p. 30; Spiegelberg, I, 74.

22. Ricoeur, *Husserl*, pp. 24f.

23. Meinong, *Selbstdarstellung*, *GA*, VII, 12–13.

24. Husserl, *Logical Investigations*, I, 227ff, 236.

25. *Ibid.*, pp. 237f.

the fundamental philosophical science. It not only provided the foundations of the Geisteswissenschaften as well as the strict sciences, but also came to provide the framework for logic itself.[26]

Along with this hierarchical sense went a search for certainty—a final permanent answer to skepticism and relativism.[27] For this reason Husserl did not emphasize probability and evidence for presumption to the extent that Meinong did. Nor could he tolerate the dualistic elements that Meinong's realism allowed. One consistent motive throughout Husserl's thought, early and late, is the quest to know objects in their fullness, free from the limits that both Meinong and Kant imposed upon our knowledge of the "thing in itself."[28] In the *Investigations*, Husserl admitted that we can achieve this perceptual adequacy only in inner perception—that is, we can be certain of what we ourselves are sensing or thinking about.[29] He defined phenomenology as a description of our experiences of thinking and knowing, the analysis of consciousness on the intentional model. By reflecting on our own experiences and the objects to which they were directed, one could find the clarity and distinctness that could guarantee the certainty needed for the rigorous science of philosophy.[30]

Husserl in the *Investigations* in fact hewed closer to the old introspective criterion of Locke and Brentano than Meinong did in the *Foundations of Knowledge in Experience*, where he introduced the notion of evidence for presumption. We may not be sure whether the physical object of perception really exists, but we are sure that we are perceiving and that our perception is directed to that object and to no other. Like Meinong, Husserl insisted that the question of whether

26. Husserl, *Formale und Transcendentale Logik I, Husserliana*, XVII (The Hague: Martinus Nijhoff, 1974), pp. 274, 296; *Ideas*, p. 188.

27. Spiegelberg, p. 85; Maurice Natanson, *Edmund Husserl* (Evanston: Northwestern University Press, 1973), p. 5. Both of these commentators present this aspect of Husserl's thought as a quest rather than as an achievement. It seems to me, from a reading of the primary sources, that this certitude was to be achieved by phenomenology and logic together. In the *Ideas*, pp. 399f, Husserl makes it clear that pure phenomenology describes more than the insight into rational truth and self-evidence itself, but also with the less rational aspects of intentionality. It is the application of such insights to ontological questions that delivers this final certainty, this freedom from presuppositions (*Formale und Transcendentale Logik*, p. 279, 296ff).

28. On Meinong, see above, Chapter Six, pt. 4, concerning incomplete objects. On a comparison of Kant and Husserl on this point, see Gurwitsch, "The Kantian and Husserlian Conceptions of Consciousness," in *Studies in Phenomenology and Psychology*, pp. 154f, 158.

29. Husserl, *Logical Investigations*, II, 542.

30. *Ibid.*, I, 249, 255. The reference to "pure" phenomenology is missing in the first edition.

the object existed or not was irrelevant—our thoughts may be directed, just as surely to golden mountains as to physical trees and houses.[31]

Nevertheless, Husserl realized that the introspection had its problems—it was hardly the infallible source of certainty that Locke and Brentano had made it out to be. Introspection may be a necessary condition of certainty, but is by no means a sufficient one, for not all aspects of our experience are equally reliable as intentional material. Not only are there the disturbing circumstances such as our emotional state, or distractions that disturb concentration, or self-consciousness that clouds our introspection (Brentano had realized these problems as well). But even under ideal conditions, the material of experience that is needed as the source of logical distinctions is not simply "there"; we must abstract the cognitive aspects of experience from the emotional to arrive at the appropriate momentary acts. We must isolate it from the other parts of experience—for example, we must disregard the emotional momentary acts and focus on the cognitive ones; we must ignore the fact that these acts are empirically interwoven and unified in a "self" or "ego." Introspection can thus furnish certainty only under proper conditions of analysis, by taking the acts, contents, and objects out of empirical context.[32] Husserl emphasized, even in the first edition of the *Investigations*, that this analysis is different from that of experimental psychology.[33] By so qualifying the introspective criterion of the empiricists, Husserl believed he had salvaged its main contribution: the achievement of epistemological certainty through the analysis of experience.

### 3. IDEALISM AND THE ANALYTICAL APPROACH

However careful Husserl had been to avoid the pitfalls of the earlier empiricist tradition, he later came to the conclusion that he had not been careful enough. The key to his revision of phenomenol-

31. *Ibid.*, II, 558f. These passages also reveal a characteristic difference from Meinong's use of the term "object," which is broader; Husserl does not consider objects in the context of objectives. For Meinong, perceptual adequacy is ultimately a matter of an existential judgment directed to an objective. For Husserl, the object is still a thing.

32. *Ibid.*, II, 542f. The first stage, according to Husserl's terminology here, gives us the "real" content of the experience; it gives us the ideal conditions for inner perception. Brentano had the same thing in mind when he distinguished inner perception from introspection (Selbstbeobachtung) as a method. The second stage, the abstraction from the real contents of consciousness, yields the intentional content. This passage clearly anticipated Husserl's later talk of "phenomenological reduction."

33. *Ibid.*, I, 256.

ogy probably lay in the need to avoid any possibility of skepticism. The empiricists, after all, had fallen into the trap of skepticism time and time again; the problem seemed endemic to any kind of dualism between experience and physical nature. It was obvious in the case of any kind of psychology that allowed physical entities to cause and shape non-physical entities. But it persisted, somewhat more subtly, in the intentional psychology of Brentano. Here the problem was the reverse: how could a real, existing person have experiences that were directed to objects that were not real? One could claim, of course, that such unreal objects were but figments of the individual imagination. But the arguments against this view had been persuasively raised in the critique of psychologism. How, then, were unreal objects "transcendent"? Meinong's answer was to posit two different senses of being, but even he admitted that our ability to apprehend and know such transcendent objects was a mystery, an ultimate fact of epistemology that could not be proven.[34] Husserl, with his search for ultimate presuppositions, could not accept this alternative; the "mystery" had to be solved. The solution, and the key to "pure" phenomenology, was this: to avoid making any assumptions about the real, existing mind in which intentional experience occurs.[35] If one is willing to ignore the question of the existence of the object, one should also be able to ignore the question of the existence of the mind. In this way, the analysis of acts, contents, and objects would be ontologically on all fours, so to speak. As long as the momentary experiences had been viewed as part of our actual minds, the mysteries and unbridgeable gaps between knower and known would remain, even under ideal conditions. The dualists had separated psychological existence from physical existence; pure phenomenology separates psychological and physical objects together *from* existence. This is why it was "pure":

> Consciousness, considered in its "purity," must be reckoned as a *self-contained system of Being*, as a system of *Absolute Being*, into which nothing can penetrate, and from which nothing can escape; which has no spatio-temporal exterior, and can be inside no spatio-temporal system; which cannot experience causality from anything nor exert causality upon anything.[36]

This phenomenology was also "transcendental" in that all other certain statements about the physical and psychological world presup-

---

34.  Meinong, "Über Gegenstandstheorie," *GA*, II, 485; LTC, p. 78.

35.  Husserl, *Crisis*, p. 79, 81f, where Husserl criticizes Descartes' failure to do this. "Philosophy as a Rigorous Science," p. 101.

36.  Husserl, *Ideas*, p. 153.

posed it. Husserl did not *deny* that the world existed for a moment; he merely insisted that one must initially isolate phenomenology from this context in order eventually to be able to make rigorous pronouncements about it.[37]

Husserl's transition to idealism, then, may be viewed as a reevaluation of the analytical approach, of deciding what needed to be left out in order to arrive at precision. This is clear in his use of the term *epoché*, which is Greek for "abstention." *Epoché* is a procedure of isolation and "reduction," in which belief in the natural world is suspended. The notion shares some similarities with Descartes' systematic doubt, though Husserl makes it clear that *epoché* is not synonymous with doubt:

> It is ... not a transformation into presumption, suggestion, indecision, doubt. ... *Rather it is something quite unique. We do not abandon the thesis we have adopted, we make no change in our conviction. ... We set it as it were "out of action," we "disconnect it," "bracket it."*[38]

Husserl envisages *epoché* as consisting of several steps. First we disconnect the parts of the natural world that vary with space and time, the disturbing features that ordinarily blur analysis of any sort. This is the "eidetic reduction," and is common to any theoretical enterprise. When a scientist talks of an atom or an electron, a chromosome or a conditioned reflex, he is abstracting from the specific spatio-temporal conditions in which these objects occur—that is, the "here" and "now." Husserl's early phenomenology, like Brentano's descriptive psychology or Meinong's, was of this sort. Indeed, any "model" is eidetic in this sense, including mathematical models. But it is necessary to bracket still further. In the second stage, the "phenomenological reduction," objects and consciousness are stripped of any further assumptions about their existence; we view them purely as "data." With this step, any vestiges of empiricism are erased; references to actual experience are eliminated.[39]

It was on this basis that Husserl's critique of psychologism became more vigorous and radical after 1907. Psychologism, like empiricism, was just a manifestation of the deeper error of "naturalism"—of assuming that reference to the natural world will deliver certainty and rigor.[40] Here was the basis for distinguishing the true positivism from the false; here, too, was the reason that science seemed "irrelevant" to the rest of thought. As long as scientific objects were idealized and the

37. *Ibid.*, pp. 168f.    38. *Ibid.*, p. 108.
39. These stages of reduction are treated in *Ideas*, pp. 175–182.

world of experience was not, their relation would remain a mystery. Because of this gap, Husserl claimed in the *Crisis*, one could see how specialists in science and technology could operate with and manipulate theoretical concepts without understanding them—without seeing their relationship to the rest of the world.[41] As long as such relationships were not clarified, the temptation of irrationalism in thought and society could never be erased.

A comparison of Husserl's phenomenology with Meinong's theory of objects yields a fundamental paradox: Husserl sought to unite science and ordinary discourse by abstracting both from their empirical context, while Meinong sought to show the minute interconnections between the rational and the empirical in both science and ordinary language, all the while maintaining a dualism between subject and object which left the door open to skepticism. In Husserl's terms, Meinong's philosophy remained at the "eidetic" level.[42] Meinong's overcoming of psychologism had been based on the view that psychology could not be made independent of ontology, that one must consider content and object. Likewise his theory of objects, though distinct from his psychology, paralleled that psychology at every point—the four basic classes of experience matched the classes of objects. Meinong continued to insist that psychology and philosophy belonged naturally together, and that the analytical approach should illuminate this relationship rather than obscure it.

Meinong's continuing commitment to psychology as part of philosophy was revealed in an incident concerning academic politics in 1912. In that year Hermann Cohen, the leading Marburg Neo-Kantian retired and was replaced by a psychologist, Ernst Jaensch. This appointment spurred a number of philosophers, including Husserl, Natorp, Rickert, and Windelband, to draft a "declaration" calling for the separation of philosophical and psychological teaching positions, so that philosophy would not be impeded by this new specialty. In a sense, the declaration marked the recognition of experimental psychology as an autonomous discipline. The declaration received over one hundred signatures, but among those who refused to sign were Wundt, Külpe, and Meinong.[43] Meinong stated his position in his autobiographical sketch:

40. Husserl, "Philosophy as a Rigorous Science," pp. 79f, 86.
41. Husserl, *Crisis*, pp. 46ff.     42. Husserl, *Ideas*, pp. 67f.
43. Rickert to Meinong, December 7, 1912, December 19, 1912, Meinong *Nachlass*, Carton 60, Nos. 6224, 6225; Meinong to Rickert (draft), December 10, 1912, *ibid.*, Carton 67, unnumbered; see also Wilhelm Wundt, "Die Psychologie im Kampf ums Da-

The experimental direction of modern psychology . . . has actually given to some the impulse simply to deny this science the right to the name of a philosophical discipline. If I see things correctly, however, every attempt to carry out such a departure from the psychic in philosophical practice convinces one that such a beginning is basically unnatural. It attempts to divide that which by nature belongs together, whether or not we have at present a concept available to cover it. As with all other sciences, the deciding factor is ultimately the naturalness of the relations and of what is brought together, both with respect to the material and with respect to the way it is treated. The metaphysician and epistemologist will never be able to get out of touch with psychological working-methods or results without loss to himself, regardless of the division of labor. Likewise, the psychologist can afford to lose familiarity with epistemology and the theory of objects only to the disadvantage of his own achievements, however much he may still give priority to the experimental method.[44]

It may seem that this nostalgia for a dying philosophical psychology is an example of Meinong's deficient sense of system, and that his actual definition of the theory of objects as concerned with so-being contradicted his own practice. The theory of objects, Meinong had said, was the general science of so-being and was distinct from metaphysics, the general science of being.[45] But a close reading of Meinong's programmatic work on the theory of objects shows that the distinction is more subtle, and quite consistent with Meinong's practice:

> If the theory of Objects chose to make one of its fundamental principles that of indifference to being, then it would have to renounce all claims to be a science, and even the knowledge of Sosein would thereby be excluded. As we know, it is completely unnecessary that the Object of knowledge should have being. However, all knowledge must have an Objective which has being; and if the theory of Objects concerns itself with a Sosein which did not have being itself, then . . . it no longer has any claim to be a theory. . . .
>
> What can be known about an object in virtue of its nature, hence a priori, belongs to the theory of Objects. This involves, in the first place, the Sosein of the "given." *But it also involves its being (Sein) insofar as that can be known from its Sosein.* On the other hand, that which is to be determined about Objects only a posteriori belongs to metaphysics, provided that the knowledge is of a sufficiently general character. . . . There are, therefore, precisely two sciences of highest generality: an a priori science which concerns everything which is given, and an a posteriori one which includes in its investigations

sein," in *Kleine Schriften*, III (Stuttgart: Alfred Kröner Verlag, 1921), pp. 518ff; the declaration itself appears in *Logos* IV (1913), 115f.

44. Meinong, *Selbstdarstellung, GA*, VII, 13–14.
45. Meinong, "Über Gegenstandstheorie," *GA*, II, 519; LTC, p. 108.

everything which can be considered by empirical knowledge, i.e., reality in
general. The latter science is metaphysics, the former is the theory of Objects [Italics added].[46]

This passage shows that Meinong never intended the theory of objects to be a "pure" theory in Husserl's sense; the separation of existence and so-being is artificial beyond a certain point. Meinong retains
this position in his unpublished notes on Husserl's *Ideas*, a book that
he used in his seminar at Graz. Not only did he find that existence and
so-being were intertwined, but he was unimpressed by Husserl's terminology. "The remarkable *epoché*," he writes, "is nothing more than
ordinary disregarding, leaving unexamined, and such."[47] Nor did he
believe that Husserl's reflection on the data of consciousness, even
when "reduced" in Husserl's way, avoided psychologism. Meinong
also noted that Husserl did not give the notion of the objective as central a place in his writings as it deserved.[48] Meinong's practice confirms his theory: the works in which he uses the theory of objects, such
as the *On Possibility and Probability* and the *Demonstration of the General
Causal Law*, shift back and forth between being and so-being, and to
a lesser extent between psychology and ontology—which all remain
perfectly distinct in definition, although the "natural" relationships
between them are fully exploited. In this way, Meinong remained true
to the empiricist tradition, as he admitted in his autobiographical
sketch.[49]

### 4. THE REJECTION OF ATOMISM AND THE PURE EGO

One major difference, then, between Husserl's and Meinong's
phenomenologies had to do with the level of analysis at which each
chose to operate. But there was another difference as well, one which
concerned the atomistic model. Husserl in fact emancipated himself
from the atomistic model to a far greater degree than Meinong; in
this respect his use of intentionality was more "natural" than Meinong's. If Meinong's description of the relations between consciousness
and objects were less artificial than Husserl's, Husserl's description of
the relations and patterns *within* consciousness was less artificial than

46. *Ibid.*, *GA*, II, 519–521; LTC, 108–109.
47. Meinong, notes on Husserl's *Ideas*, Meinong *Nachlass*, Carton 22, p. 4. On the
implications of existence and so-being for each other, see pp. 1, 3.
48. *Ibid.*, pp. 14–15, on psychologism; p. 28 on the objective.
49. Meinong, *Selbstdarstellung*, *GA*, VII, 4.

Meinong's. Husserl's rejection of atomism also provides some insight into his later elaboration of idealism, particularly during the 1920s and 1930s.

Husserl could not hold that consciousness was divided into units of discrete, static experiences. We have already seen how Husserl's views on the consciousness of time were more flexible than Meinong's in this respect.[50] The influence of James' notion of the stream of consciousness is apparent throughout Husserl's works. According to Husserl, our perception of what is just past can be as "adequate" as our perception of what we are now thinking.[51] In his diary of 1906, Husserl wrote that he found Meinong's concept of the idea (Vorstellung) to be "incomprehensible."[52] Husserl's lectures on internal time-consciousness, dating from 1904–1905, reveal a much richer portrayal of the temporal aspects of consciousness than Meinong's analyses—as, for example, how immediate memory is distinct from long-term recollection, and how the structures of memory and anticipation are related ("retention" and "protention" in Husserl's terminology). The further he developed this view of consciousness, the further he moved away from the linguistic analogy: consciousness was no longer a hierarchy of experiences that resembled a grammatical diagram, and the meaning or reference of any such stream of consciousness was much less clearcut.

Husserl's instinct for the dynamic aspects of awareness was also evident in his description in the *Investigations* of the act of knowing. As with Meinong's theory of evidence, Husserl insisted that knowledge contains an intuitive element, that *adequatio rei et intellectus* that constitutes the core of knowledge. Unlike Meinong, however, Husserl used the same word to convey both the intuition of thought and the intuition of sense—Anschauung.[53] Husserl did not share the fascination with "imageless" thought which the Würzburg school and Meinong possessed, and he sought to show the parallels between the vivid insight that constitutes knowledge and the vividness of full sense perception. Husserl preferred to portray knowledge as a process rather than as a static state. He elaborated this in his famous doctrine of "fulfillment" (Erfüllung). One gets to know an object, according to Husserl, by examining it from all perspectives—from close-up, from

50. See Chapter Five, pt. 4, above.
51. Husserl, *Phänomenologie des Inneren Zeitbewusstseins*, p. 38.
52. Husserl, "Persönliche Aufzeichnungen," p. 296.
53. Husserl, *Logical Investigations*, II, 773ff, 787.

a distance, from one side, then another.[54] Before one has done this, one cannot be said to have perceived or known the object in itself, and each individual act of apprehension is performed in expectation of approaching this goal. Thus knowledge is a process of approximating an object as it is in itself, whether through perception or through judgments. An analogy that Husserl gives is "the transition from a rough drawing to a more exact pencil-sketch, then from the latter to the completed picture, and from this to the living finish of the painting, all of which present the same, visibly the same object."[55]

This doctrine is close to Meinong's notion of "completion" of a remote object, and it anticipates Meinong's version by fifteen years. Yet even in the *Investigations*, Husserl realized that for a real physical object, the goal of fulfillment was unattainable.[56] Perhaps this admission of the limits of our knowledge—itself a path to skepticism—led him as well to forsake realism. Certainly Husserl insisted in the *Ideas* also that the object could not be completely apprehended through perspectival variation. But there was a compensation: the realm of pure consciousness allows us to exercise our fantasy, to vary the object in our imagination, as a geometer might do in formulating a proof.[57]

We have noted that most positivistic thinkers who remained committed to analysis felt it necessary to retain some form of atomism—at the very least the assumption that the basic units of analysis must remain constant over time. Husserl was an exception. Yet the problem of sustaining rigor in the absence of such units confronted him too—it is evident in his writings on time-consciousness that followed the lectures of 1905–1906. For if the data of consciousness, which are to provide the foundations of all philosophy and science, are continually in flux, how can we be certain of them? Is not the act of reflecting on these data itself a part of a stream of consciousness continually changing as well? What way is there of knowing that the intentional data and the act of reflection belong to the same stream?[58]

54. *Ibid.*, p. 714.    55. *Ibid.*, p. 721.

56. *Ibid.*, p. 747. I would take issue with Findlay's translation here: Husserl speaks of an idea which is "adequate" to its object, even though "objectively mutilated." Husserl's word for "adequate" is *angemessen*, which he distinguishes from *adäquat*: the latter is clearly the stronger term, and Findlay's translation of both by the same English word seems misleading to me.

57. Husserl, *Ideas*, pp. 199f, 57; on the incompleteness of realistic perception, see p. 138.

58. Husserl, *Phänomenologie des Inneren Zeitbewusstseins*, pp. 114f. For a further discussion of the role of time-perception in the origin of Husserl's idealism, see Findlay, "Husserl's Analysis of the Inner Time-Consciousness," *The Monist*, LIX (1975), 13–20.

It was in connection with such problems that Husserl introduced a further Kantian concept: the "pure ego." There must be some unity to the stream of consciousness, some constant bond that holds it together. If there were no such unity, then our time-bound awareness would indeed be fragmentary and uncertain; but they are not. Thus the "self" or "ego" is a necessary foundation of the conscious stream:

> In principle, at any rate, every *cogitatio* can change, can come and go. . . . But in contrast the pure Ego appears to be *necessary* in principle, and as that which remains absolutely self-identical in all real and possible changes of experience, it can *in no sense* be reckoned as a real part or phase of the experiences themselves. . . . In the words of Kant, *"The 'I think' must be able to accompany all my presentations."*[59]

The "pure ego" was thus not the concrete self we naturally find in our introspections. Rather, it was an expression of the requirement that analysis needs some constant unit, though not necessarily the smallest or the simplest. In fact, the doctrine of the pure ego represents Husserl's complete dissociation of the analytical approach from the atomistic model. One attains rigor by isolation, by taking one's subject-matter deliberately out of context. But the constancy of that subject matter is not guaranteed by any of its *parts*, as in the atomistic model, but by the whole. Needless to say, Meinong found such a pure ego to be as "incomprehensible" as Husserl found Meinong's concept of the idea.[60]

This aspect of Husserl's thought represents the influence of the Marburg Neo-Kantian school on Husserl. He had read the work of one of the Marburgers, Paul Natorp, one of the earliest critics of psychologism. Natorp had already expressed the need for such an ego as a unifying factor in 1883, and Husserl had polemicized against it in the *Logical Investigations*, claiming that he simply could not find such a pure ego in his consciousness. In the 1913 edition of the *Untersuchungen*, however, he added a footnote: "I have since managed to find it."[61] Like Natorp, Husserl emphasized that this ego was not a part of experience, but a presupposition of it. Natorp's way of expressing this concept was that experience was there *for* a subject—in other words, without a subject, consciousness would not be what it was. Husserl's later writings increasingly emphasize this expression, contrasting it to the realistic viewpoint of experience as being part of, or *in* a

59. Husserl, *Ideas*, pp. 172–173.
60. Meinong, notes on *Ideas*, Meinong *Nachlass*, Carton 22, p. 17.
61. Husserl, *Logical Investigations*, II, 549.

world. Here, for example, is a passage from the preface to the 1931 edition of the *Ideas*:

> If we now perform this transcendental-phenomenological reduction . . . this psychological subjectivity loses just that which makes it something real in the world that lies before us; it loses the meaning of the soul as belonging to a body that exists in an objective, spatio-temporal Nature. . . . I am now no longer a human Ego *in* the universal, existentially posited world, but exclusively a subject *for* which this world has being . . . so that the real being of the world thereby remains unconsidered, unquestioned, and its validity left out of account.[62]

With such language, Husserl placed himself completely outside the positivistic tradition and within the hermeneutical one. For the attitudes of Dilthey who preceded Husserl, and of Heidegger and Gadamer who followed him, coincided in this respect: one must examine "objective" knowledge, such as that given in science, in the light of its meaning for the subjects of the society in which it arises. And Husserl's last major works, the *Cartesian Meditations* and the *Crisis of the European Sciences* both elaborated this very point of view. The certainty derived from the analysis of consciousness can only lead back to knowledge of the world if we view that world in the context of subjectivity. Science, whether natural science or the Geisteswissenschaften, presupposes a subject; they are part of a "life-world" rather than part of a world that exists independently. "The true nature in its proper scientific sense," Husserl wrote, "is a product of the spirit that investigates nature, and thus the science of nature presupposes the science of the spirit."[63]

Such an extension of idealism would seem to go squarely against Husserl's earlier impulse to create a truly universal and certain philosophy. Here, too, scholars are divided as to Husserl's motives and consistency.[64] Certainly the evidence indicates that Husserl in the 1920s and 1930s was no more of a relativist than in the earlier period. Indeed, the *Crisis* indicates that he had found the same answer to relativism that so many other post-Kantians had found, including Hegel, Marx, and the Marburg Neo-Kantians: a belief in the teleology of history. If the world is there for a subject in any significant sense, and yet

---

62. Husserl, *Ideas*, p. 14.

63. Husserl, "Philosophy and the Crisis of European Man," in *Phenomenology and the Crisis of Philosophy*, p. 189. On the concept of a "life-world," see *Crisis*, pp. 124ff.

64. James C. Morrison, "Husserl's *Crisis*: Reflections on the Relationship of Philosophy and History," *Philosophy and Phenomenological Research*, XXXVII (1976), 312f.

all human subjects participate in a common order, that order must be found in history. In the final works of Husserl, this conviction is explicit:

> The spiritual *telos* of European Man, in which is included the particular *telos* of separate nations and of individual human beings, lies in infinity; it is an infinite idea, toward which in secret the collective spiritual becoming, so to speak, strives.[65]

Whether or not Husserl's later thought represents a deliberate and consistent extension of his earlier ideas, one thing is clear: his faith in the unlimited bounds of reason, explicitly stated in the *Investigations*, guided him through to the end. The assumption that one could conceptualize workings of human society in a single, rational framework bespeaks the same optimism and confidence—an impulse utterly alien to Meinong's humbler empiricism. Meinong's version of intentionality showed both the extent and the limits of reason. Husserl, on the other hand, has rightly been called a "philosopher of infinite tasks."[66]

### 5. MEINONG, PHENOMENOLOGY, AND EXISTENTIALISM

It is a remarkable fact that Husserl's most distinguished followers took a position that was closer to Meinong's realism than to his own idealism. Phenomenology was valuable in that it viewed the world as it appeared to consciousness, but not necessarily at the expense of assumptions about the world itself. For example, Max Scheler and Alfred Schütz, who both pioneered in applying phenomenology to social thought, found it unnecessary to perform Husserl's phenomenological reduction.[67] The same can be said of Heidegger, Sartre, and Merleau-Ponty. Indeed, Scheler, writing in 1922 on the state of philosophy in Germany, noted that none of Husserl's contemporaries in the phenomenological movement were following him in this path.[68] Apart from Scheler, however, none of these phenomenologists turned to Meinong as a source. Why was this true?

If we examine the works of two leading existentialists, Heidegger and Sartre, in the light of their relationship to phenomenology, the

---

65. Husserl, "Philosophy and the Crisis of European Man," p. 158. See also *Crisis*, pp. 71f.

66. This is the subtitle of Natanson's book.

67. Spiegelberg, I, 230, 242; Natanson, p. 118.

68. Scheler, "Die deutsche Philosophie der Gegenwart," p. 311.

similarities and differences to Meinongian realism become evident. Heidegger, in *Being and Time*, for example, was explicit in claiming that phenomenology and ontology could not be divorced. "Ontology and phenomenology," he wrote, "are not two different disciplines which belong among others to philosophy. Both labels characterize philosophy itself according to object and method of treatment."[69] The investigation of being must further begin with existence, which Heidegger analyzed as "being-in-the-world." Heidegger's language was deliberately structured to avoid thinking of such topics in terms of entities such as "self" or "thing," but in terms of states, such as "being-there" (Dasein), being "present at hand" (Vorhandenes) or "ready at hand" (Zuhandenes).

Having studied at Freiburg in the years before the war under Rickert and later Husserl, Heidegger had certainly been in a position to acquaint himself with Meinong's ideas. He was familiar with Brentano and had written his dissertation on the problem of psychologism.[70] Yet Heidegger remained in many respects tied to the idealistic framework. Although he emphasized the concrete reality of the world, the structure of the world itself was not something independent of ourselves, but was there for us. For example, we normally think of objects in terms of their practical use, not their intrinsic being: objects are not simply "present at hand," but primarily "ready at hand" for use as tools for some human purpose. Objects belong primarily to the "environment" (Umwelt) rather than to "nature" (Natur):

> Hammer, tongs, nail in themselves refer to—they consist of—steel, iron, ore, stone, wood. "Nature" is co-discovered in the tool that is used, through the use—"nature" in the light of the products of nature.[71]

One might say that Heidegger's epistemology was realistic but his metaphysics were idealistic. The Cartesian belief in the reality of extended substance was a generalization from a very limited region of being; natural sciences and mathematics could not be the road to ontology, but rather the hermeneutical sciences pointed the way.[72] Thus Heidegger's existentialism reinforced the split between scientific and

---

69. Martin Heidegger, *Sein und Zeit* (Tübingen: Max Niemeyer Verlag, 1967), p. 38.

70. Spiegelberg, I, 292f.

71. Heidegger, *Sein und Zeit*, p. 70. On the proper role of idealism, see *ibid.*, p. 208.

72. *Ibid.*, pp. 37, 97.

humanistic thought which Meinong and the prewar generation had sought to heal.

The French followers of Husserl broke with idealism to an even greater degree than Heidegger did. Sartre, in one of his earliest works, *The Transcendence of the Ego*, proclaimed the relevance of phenomenology to the time:

> The theorists of the extreme Left have sometimes reproached phenomenology for being an idealism and for drowning reality in the stream of ideas. . . . On the contrary, for centuries we have not felt in philosophy so realistic a current. The phenomenologists have plunged man back into the world; they have given full measure to man's agonies and sufferings, and also to his rebellions. Unfortunately, as long as the *I* remains a structure of absolute consciousness, one will still be able to reproach phenomenology for being an escapist doctrine, for again pulling a part of man out of the world and, in that way, turning our attention from the real problems.[73]

But Sartre goes on to say that some form of unity to the objective world is necessary: one must be able to talk of the person or self as an objective "me" rather than the subjective "I."[74] One cannot simply dwell on a series of disjointed objects. This aversion to the atomistic model is evident also in Sartre's *The Psychology of Imagination*. There are passages in this work that are reminiscent of Meinong, especially those concerning the interplay of fantasy and reality.[75] But Sartre's purpose in this work is to deny the efficacy of describing momentary psychological states as Meinong would do. To fix on a single "image" or thought may appear to resemble our perception of the world, but in fact it constitutes a very different sort of cognition. Sartre quotes the work of the Würzburg school in showing the futility of trying to isolate such units of experience.[76] Not that such fixations are confined to academic psychology—Sartre finds them also in dreams, which are

73. Sartre, *The Transcendence of the Ego*, trans. Forrest Williams and Robert Kirkpatrick (New York: Farrar, Straus and Giroux, The Noonday Press, 1957), pp. 104–105.

74. *Ibid.*

75. See Sartre, *The Psychology of Imagination* (New York: Philosophical Library, 1948), Conclusion. Here Sartre discusses the closeness of imagining and negating. His statement, "That which is denied must be imagined" (p. 273), duplicates Meinong's position that a negative judgment presupposes a fantasy-judgment—that is, an assumption (*Über Annahmen*, 2d. ed., *GA*, IV, No. 2). Also, compare Sartre's description of a symphony as something other than real (pp. 278ff) with Meinong's ("Über Urteilsgefühle," *GA*, I, 601f).

76. Sartre, *Imagination*, pp. 82–85.

often pervaded by such static images. In waking life, too, we can become obsessed with a single idea over an extended period, so much so that it can condition our body reflexes. A pervasive feeling of disgust, for example, can lead to nausea. But such fixations, according to Sartre, are just the opposite of authentic existence. Being in the world involves immersion in its complexities and uncertainties, whereas the atomistic model is a form of escape.[77]

A similar comparison could be made between Meinong and Merleau-Ponty. The author of two books on philosophical psychology, *The Structure of Behavior* and *The Phenomenology of Perception*, Merleau-Ponty attempts to synthesize the findings of Gestalt psychology with the phenomenological method and to interpret these findings in terms of an intentional model rather than a causal one. He, too, finds the merit of phenomenology to be its descriptive powers of the world as it actually appears, free from any theoretical preconceptions. Yet such preconceptions include precisely the attempt to analyze and atomize perception into discrete separate units.[78]

Thus the distance between Meinong and the rest of the phenomenological movement remained a great one, and stemmed from Meinong's commitment to analysis and atomism. Whereas Meinong talked of objects and objectives of being and non-being, Heidegger and Sartre talked about Being as a whole. Whereas Meinong talked of individual acts of perception and imagination, Merleau-Ponty talked of the self, the body, and the natural world. What Meinong gained in clarity, he sacrificed in immediate relevance and appeal. For this reason, he continues to be read by the more specialized Anglo-American philosophers, the heirs of Russell and Wittgenstein, rather than by his fellow phenomenologists.

---

77. *Ibid.*, pp. 193–197.
78. Merleau-Ponty, *Phenomenology of Perception*, trans. Colin Smith (London: Routledge and Kegan Paul, 1962), pp. viii, x.

# CONCLUSION

Although Meinong's influence on European thought as a whole has not been great, his reputation among philosophers is currently on the rise. There is less and less inclination to see him as a mere precursor of Russell, a man whose work was rendered obsolete by the theory of descriptions. This trend is undoubtedly due to the fact that the theory of descriptions itself has come into increasing disrepute: ever since P. F. Strawson's paper "On Referring" (1950), ordinary-language philosophers and logicians have become aware that the gap between Russell's logical constructions and natural language has been embarrassingly great. A good example is a book by Leonard Linsky entitled *Referring* (1967), which both criticizes Russell's argument as being circular and praises Meinong's theory of objects as "an ontologizing of the logic of our ordinary use of referring expressions."[1] It has thus been Meinong's ability to combine empirical observation of how we actually employ experience with rigorous and detailed argument—the qualities that first elicited Russell's admiration in 1904—which have attracted Linsky and others. Some logicians are now arguing that there is nothing *logically* suspect about dissociating being and so-being, and that to expect all logical statements to refer to actual existing objects is in fact a prejudice.[2] Some have sought to recover the lost ties between analytical philosophy and phenomenology in Meinong, and others have sought to reformulate the theory of objects in terms of modern set theory—and have even found a niche in their systems for the round square.[3]

1. Linsky, pp. 16, 53.
2. Karel Lambert, "Being and Being So,' in *Jenseits von Sein und Nichtsein*, pp. 37–38; Routley and Routley, p. 248.
3. Chisholm, *Realism*; Findlay, "Meinong the Phenomenologist," *Revue Internationale de Philosophie*, XXVII (1973), 161–177; Terrence Parsons, "A Prolegomenon to Meinongian Semantics," *Journal of Philosophy*, LXXI (1974), 529.

As a work of intellectual history, the task of this book has been a different one: to present Meinong's significance with respect to his own age—to the thought of the early twentieth century. We may say that Meinong was representative of a type of positivism that was broader and more flexible than both the evolutionary positivism that preceded it and the logical positivism that followed it. It was based on the notion that the intentional model in philosophy was compatible with the strictest standards of reasoning such as those used in the hard sciences; by virtue of the parallelism between this model and the current theories of language, it could link the new advances in logic with the humanistic concerns of Dilthey, the Baden Neo-Kantians, and others. In Meinong's case, this link was his theory of objects, which, in its fully developed form, presented a world in which the objects of reason and intuition—and by analogy the languages of the sciences and the humanities—were interrelated, though distinct and irreducible to each other. It was this interrelationship that made it possible for Meinong to speak of facts, values, and esthetic objects within a common conceptual framework, unlike the divorce which the later positivists effected or the reduction to biological or mechanical principles which the earlier ones had sought to carry out.

Meinong was able to achieve this kind of synthesis because of a more fundamental commitment: to reveal the presence of the self-evident a priori aspect of discourse in both these realms, not just in the realm of the sciences. This was his purpose in framing the theory of objects, of which mathematics was but a part and logic but a special application. A priori knowledge and knowledge of contingencies were interwoven at every level of discourse and experience—whether the topic be perception, fantasy, or esthetics. Here also, Meinong sought to emphasize the interrelatedness of heterogeneous dimensions, to which he gave the labels being and so-being. In this respect Meinong's theory was distinct from others that sought the same kind of synthesis. The Gestalt psychologists sought to overcome the narrow aspects of positivism by subsuming the data of science and the humanities under their laws of organization. But these laws were derived from empirical investigations in psychology; thus considerations of ethics and esthetics could be drawn only by analogy from these a posteriori principles. The Gestalt view, then, reintroduced a reductionism of the same order as that of the evolutionary positivists—generalizing about the humanities on the basis of the results of the natural sciences. Husserl's phenomenology, on the other hand, stressed the a priori aspect of knowledge; the phenomenological reductions were aimed at distinguishing the self-evident from the contingent. But Husserl's consistent pursuit of this aim led him further into idealism and consequently to the opposite kind of reduction from that of the Gestalt psychologists: he made experience of the natural world—and hence the natural sciences—dependent on the a priori categories imposed on that experience. Science, then, should be understood as a human creation, a part of human history, rather than as an enterprise whose epistemological value is independent of its origin. Meinong avoided both these kinds of reduction by adhering to a dualism—a realistic metaphysics and an idealistic theory of objects. It was this choice that enabled him to achieve a balance which eluded others.

In this respect, Meinong's position represented a significant restatement of secular humanism, in that it defined both the possibilities of reason and the autonomy of the irrational within a single framework. Unlike the existentialists, who were also concerned with articulating a form of humanism, Meinong remained within the positivist, analytical tradition and would not have accepted the rejection of science which existentialism required. However, the very factors that contributed to this synthesis undermined Meinong's influence on European thought. His analysis was not concerned with man directly, but with isolated aspects of human life. At the same time, the fact that he successfully avoided reducing the humanities to the sciences or vice versa precluded any formulation of ultimate criteria for meaning and truth which could guide the non-specialist through the immediate problems of life. If there is any hope that emanates from Meinong's philosophy, it is a highly abstract one: that the results of the various disciplines are intertranslatable, that specialization need not mean fragmentation, and that the plurality of values does not necessarily imply that human conflict and violence are eternal. Yet Meinong's lack of contact with popular thought was hardly unique to him. The thinkers in the social sciences who were also concerned with linking the rational and the irrational—such as Dilthey and Weber—were, if not ignored, equally misunderstood.[4] One wonders whether Meinong's fate of benign neglect was any worse than the simplifications that befell his better-known contemporaries.

It would certainly be presumptuous and false to claim that the twistings and turnings of European thought which we have traced in this

4. Hughes writes, for example, in *Consciousness and Society*, that the work of the social thinkers "encouraged an anti-intellectualism to which the vast majority of them were intensely hostile" (p. 17).

book played a dominant role in shaping the great convulsions of European society between 1914 and 1945. Yet it would also be presumptuous, it seems to me, to deny them any role at all, particularly in explaining the rise of movements such as Fascism and Communism. We must remember that the spokesmen of these movements often expressed themselves in terms of the issues we have raised here. Mussolini referred to Fascism as "arising from the general reaction of the century against the flaccid materialistic positivism of the nineteenth century." [5] One does not have to look far in the writings of Communists for the word "scientific." Fascism and Communism appealed, after all, not only to the dispossessed and unemployed, but also to the educated and economically secure. The dictators would not have used such terminology in their speeches and writings if they had assumed that it would fall on deaf ears. Nor is it too much to say that the opposition between these two ideologies rested in part on their estimation of reason. The Fascists gloried in the irrational unity of the nation, and the Communists justified themselves in terms of the idealist logic of history—the belief that reason would govern human events.

Positivism, with its concern for defining the limits of reason while maintaining a faith in it, might have been expected to provide the foundations for an alternative to these extremes in social and political theory—just as empiricism had once provided the basis for liberalism. Yet positivism is surely no less compatible with political oppression or totalitarianism than Fascism or Communism. The traditional positivists' account of the limits of reason provided no necessary check to a belief in the right of scientific experts to dictate policy—as Comte's sketch of a positivist religion proves. Indeed, the anti-humanistic implications of a society based on purely scientific principles have never been far from the modern European imagination. One thinks of Dickens' opposition to Utilitarianism in *Hard Times*, or the anti-utopian literature of Huxley, Orwell, and others.

It is with respect to such dilemmas that the ideological import of the philosophical issues discussed in this book suggests itself—however remote these issues may seem from the more urgent questions of political and social thought. For a number of commentators have suggested that the most innovative, and most dangerous, aspects of twentieth-century thought have been in the ability of intellectuals and ideologists to extinguish or ignore questions—the "big" questions such as the meaning or purposiveness of human life, or the com-

5.    Benito Mussolini, *The Doctrine of Fascism* (Florence: Vallechi Editore, 1936), p. 9.

patibility of freedom and authority. Sir Isaiah Berlin pointed out in an essay on political thought that Fascism and Communism both had this in common: by reducing such issues to matters which admitted of technical, straightforward solutions, both ideologies eliminated the need to pose such questions within their respective frameworks.[6] Herbert Marcuse, in his book *One-Dimensional Man*, made essentially the same point about liberal democracy, and pointed an accusatory finger at analytical philosophy as an expression of this mindlessness.[7] Certainly if we equate positivism with the rejection of metaphysics and phenomenalism—and many traditional definitions of positivism would do so—Marcuse's objections are unanswerable. For by eliminating reference to transcendent objects, be they deities or things-in-themselves, phenomenalists have restricted the sphere of human inquiry to the knowable and have drawn the further conclusion that what is unknowable is not worth inquiring about. In this way, the limits of reason are formulated in such a way as to remove a basic philosophical support for the liberty of individuals to inquire. For it is in the nature of "big" questions to admit of no permanent or definite answers, and yet somehow to seem continually worth asking—if only to provide a sense of alternatives to a very imperfect status quo. Such questions seem necessarily to involve a sense of transcendence—the belief that there are objects which are at least partially unknowable, yet significant by virtue of their very inexhaustibility.

The realism at the turn of the century, of which Meinong was a representative, presented an alternative form of positivism. While maintaining its commitment to scientific philosophy, it admitted the need for transcendent objects, however metaphysical such an assumption may be. In Meinong's case, his rejection of psychologism and turn to realism stemmed from the view that phenomenalism was too confining for a strictly scientific treatment of the problems he faced; only by explicitly accepting the metaphysics of a natural order of things could the complexities of Gestalt phenomena and the descriptions of value be satisfactorily dealt with. We may know this natural order through empirical or probabilistic knowledge, though we may never achieve complete certainty of its properties. At the same time, Meinong's treatment of the capacities and limits of human reason, through his use of intentionality and the linguistic analogy, provided a guaran-

6. Isaiah Berlin, "Political Ideas in the Twentieth Century," in *Four Essays on Liberty* (New York: Oxford University Press, 1970), pp. 21–24.

7. Herbert Marcuse, *One-Dimensional Man* (Boston: Beacon Press, paperback edition, 1966), Chs. I, VII, p. 232.

tee that the "big" questions would always be worth posing, because they admitted an infinite variety of answers. For although the objects of the real world have a finite number of properties, our minds can view them in an infinite variety of ways. In terms of the linguistic analogy, these objects could be the terms of an infinite number of true statements, corresponding to Meinong's infinite number of objectives of so-being. Though the object is "complete," we ourselves may never complete it. Our ability to link one object to any other prevents us from selecting once and for all what particular links to make. This is the basis of our ignorance of the object as well as of our freedom to transform it. For we may always presume that objects might be other than they seem to be, and no amount of progress will ever completely eliminate our right to make that presumption. It is our very ignorance which is the foundation of this right. Thus the optimistic view of the Enlightenment is justified: human suffering is due to human ignorance rather than to any divine agency. But at the same time, the view that this suffering could ever be completely eliminated is rejected: the permanent possibility of ignorance should guard us against scientific hubris. We may improve the world, but we may never perfect it. In this sense, Meinong's philosophy may be seen as the basis for a strictly *secular* form of humanism, one which sees the greatness and the weakness of man in the light of his own gifts, and which interprets the tragedies and disasters which he suffers as being of his own making.

# BIBLIOGRAPHY

I. WORKS BY MEINONG

## A. Published Sources

1. Collections
   a. *Gesamtausgabe.* Edited by Rudolf Haller, Rudolf Kindinger, and Roderick M. Chisholm. 7 vols. Graz: Akademische Druck-u. Verlagsanstalt, 1968—.
   b. *Philosophenbriefe.* Edited by Rudolf Kindinger. Graz: Akademische Druck-u. Verlagsanstalt, 1965.

2. Individual Works (in chronological order)
   *Hume-Studien I. Zur Geschichte und Kritik des modernen Nominalismus* (1877); *Gesamtausgabe* I, 1–76.
   "Modern Nominalism" (1879), *Gesamtausgabe* VII, 118.
   *Hume-Studien II. Zur Relationstheorie* (1882). *Gesamtausgabe* II, 1–184.
   *Über philosophische Wissenschaft und ihre Propädeutik* (1885). *Gesamtausgabe* V, 1–196.
   "Zur erkenntnistheoretischen Würdigung des Gedächtnisses" (1886). *Gesamtausgabe* II, 185–214.
   "Über Begriff und Eigenschaften der Empfindung" (1888). *Gesamtausgabe* I, 109–192.
   "Über Phantasievorstellung und Phantasie" (1889). *Gesamtausgabe* I, 193–278.
   "Zur Psychologie der Komplexionen und Relationen" (1891). *Gesamtausgabe* I, 279–304.
   Review of Hillebrand's *Die neuen Theorien der kategorischen Schlüsse,* (1892). *Gesamtausgabe* VII, 197–222.

"Beiträge zur Theorie der psychischen Analyse" (1893). *Gesamtausgabe* I, 305–396.

*Psychologisch-ethische Untersuchungen zur Werttheorie* (1894). *Gesamtausgabe* III, 1–244.

"Über Werthaltung und Wert" (1895). *Gesamtausgabe* III, 245–267.

"Über die Bedeutung des Weberschen Gesetzes" (1896). *Gesamtausgabe* II, 215–376.

"Zur experimentellen Bestimmung der Tonverschmelzungsgrade," *Zeitschrift für Psychologie* XV (1897), 189–205 (with Stephen Witasek).

"Über Gegenstände höherer Ordnung und deren Verhältnis zur inneren Wahrnehmung" (1899). *Gesamtausgabe* II, 377–480.

"Abstrahieren und Vergleichen" (1900). *Gesamtausgabe* I, 443–494.

*Über Annahmen*, 1st ed. *Ergänzungsband II der Zeitschrift für Psychologie und Physiologie der Sinnesorgane.* Leipzig: Verlag von J. A. Barth, 1902. The *Gesamtausgabe* contains Nos. 18–20, 31–45 in VI, 385–489.

"Bemerkungen über den Farbenkörper und das Mischungsgesetz" (1903). *Gesamtausgabe* I, 495–576.

"Über Gegenstandstheorie" (1904). *Gesamtausgabe* II, 481–536.

"Über Urteilsgefühle; was sie sind und was sie nicht sind" (1905). *Gesamtausgabe* I, 577–616.

*Über die Erfahrungsgrundlagen unseres Wissens* (1906). *Gesamtausgabe* V, 367–481.

*Über die Stellung der Gegenstandstheorie im System der Wissenschaften* (1907). *Gesamtausgabe* V, 197–365.

*Über Annahmen*, 2nd revised ed., (1910). *Gesamtausgabe* IV, 1–384.

"Für die Psychologie und gegen den Psychologismus in der allgemeinen Werttheorie" (1912). *Gesamtausgabe* III, 267–282.

"Stephan Witasek zum Gedächtnis" (1915). *Gesamtausgabe* VII, 255–261.

"Über die Wiederaufnahme der internationalen wissenschaftlichen Zusammenarbeit nach dem 1. Weltkrieg" (1915). *Gesamtausgabe* VII, 273–276.

*Über Möglichkeit und Wahrscheinlichkeit* (1915). *Gesamtausgabe* VI, 1–728.

*Über emotionale Präsentation* (1917). *Gesamtausgabe* III, 283–467.

*Zum Erweise des allgemeinen Kausalgesetzes* (1918). *Gesamtausgabe* V, 483–602.

"Allgemeines zur Lehre von den Dispositionen." *Gesamtausgabe* VII, 287–310.

*Selbstdarstellung* (1921). *Gesamtausgabe* VII, 1–62.

*Zur Grundlegung der allgemeinen Werttheorie* (1923, posth.). Edited by Ernst Mally. *Gesamtausgabe* III, 469–656.

*Ethische Bausteine* (posthumous fragment). *Gesamtausgabe* III, 657–724.

3. Works in Translation
    1. "The Theory of Objects" (1904). In *Realism and the Background of Phenomenology*, pp. 76–117. Edited by Roderick M. Chisholm, translated by Isaac Levi, D. B. Terrell, and Roderick M. Chisholm. Glencoe: The Free Press, 1960.
    2. *On Emotional Presentation* (1917). Translated by Marie-Luise Schubert Kalsi. Evanston: Northwestern University Press, 1972.*
    3. "Meinong's Ontology" and "Meinong's Life and Work," translations of pp. 112–120 and 102–110 of the *Selbstdarstellung*, in Reinhardt Grossmann, *Meinong*, pp. 224–236. London: Routledge & Kegan Paul, 1974.

## B. Unpublished Sources

1. Meinong *Nachlass*. Universitätsbibliothek Graz. The book draws particularly on Meinong's notes on Husserl's *Ideas* (Carton 22), his letters (Cartons 31–67), and his lecture notes on Psychology (Cartons 13–15). Additional material from the *Nachlass* concerning Meinong's published works has been included as appendixes in the pertinent volumes of the *Gesamtausgabe*.

---

*As this book goes to press, another set of translations by Kalsi has come to my attention, entitled *Alexius Meinong On Objects of Higher Order and Husserl's Phenomenology* (The Hague: Martinus Nijhoff, 1978). It includes "On the Psychology of Complexions and Relations," "An Essay Concerning the Theory of Psychic Analysis," "On Objects of Higher Order," and "Critical Notes on E. Husserl's *Ideas*" from the *Nachlass*.

II. OTHER WORKS

## A. Published Sources

1. Ach, Narziss. *Über die Willenstätigkeit und das Denken*. Translated in part by D. Rappaport. In *Thinking: From Association to Gestalt*, pp. 152–162, 201–206. Edited by Jean Matter Mandler and George Mandler. New York: John Wiley and Sons, 1964.
2. American Psychological Association. *Yearbook*, 1925.
3. Ameseder, Richard. "Über Vorstellungsproduktion." In *Untersuchungen zur Gegenstandstheorie und Psychologie*, pp. 481–508. Edited by Alexius Meinong. Leipzig: Verlag von Johann Ambrosius Barth, 1904.
4. Angell, James R. "The Relation of Structural and Functional Psychology to Philosophy." *Philosophical Review* XII (1903), 243–271.
5. Avenarius, Richard. *Kritik der reinen Erfahrung*. Leipzig: Fues's Verlag, 1888.
6. Ayer, A. J. "Editor's Introduction." In *Logical Positivism*, pp. 3–28. Edited by A. J. Ayer. New York: The Free Press, 1959.
7. Baldwin, James Mark. *Thought and Things*. 3 Vols. London: Swan Sonnenschein and Co., 1908.
8. Barber, Kenneth. "Meinong's Hume-Studies." *Philosophy and Phenomenological Research*, XXX (1970), 550–567; XXXI (1971), 564–584.
9. Barthes, Roland. *Elements of Semiology*. Translated by Annette Lavers and Colin Smith. New York: Hill and Wang, 1964.
10. Bauer, Roger. *Der Idealismus und seine Gegner in Österreich*. Heidelberg: Carl Winter Universitätsverlag, 1966.
11. Ben-David, Joseph, and Randall Collins. "Social Factors in the Origins of a New Science: the Case of Psychology." *American Sociological Review*, XXXI (1966), 451–465.
12. Benussi, Vittorio. "Gesetze der inadäquaten Gestaltauffassung." *Archiv für die gesamte Psychologie*, XXXII (1914), 396–419.
13. ———. "Die Gestaltwahrnehmungen." *Zeitschrift für Psychologie*, LXIX (1914), 259–292.
14. ———. "Über die Motive der Scheinkörperlichkeit bei umkehrbaren Zeichnungen." *Archiv für die gesamte Psychologie*, XX (1911), 366–396.
15. ———. "Zur Psychologie des Gestalterfassens." In *Untersuchun-*

*gen zur Gegenstandstheorie und Psychologie*, pp. 303–448. Edited by Alexius Meinong. Leipzig: Verlag von Johann Ambrosius Barth, 1904.

16. ———. "Stroboskopische Scheinbewegungen und geometrisch-optische Gestalttäuschungen." *Archiv für die gesamte Psychologie*, XXIV (1912), 31–62.

17. ———. "Versuche zur Analyse taktil erweckter Scheinbewegungen." *Archiv für die gesamte Psychologie*, XXXVI (1917), 59–135.

18. Bergmann, Gustav. *Realism. A Critique of Brentano and Meinong.* Madison: University of Wisconsin Press, 1967.

19. Bergson, Henri. *Creative Evolution.* Translated by Arthur Mitchell. New York: Henry Holt and Co., 1911.

20. ———. *Time and Free Will.* Translated by F. L. Pogson. London: Swan Sonnenschein, 1910. Reprint ed., New York: Harper and Row, Torchbooks ed., 1960.

21. Berkeley, George. *A Treatise Concerning the Principles of Human Knowledge.* Edited by Colin M. Turbayne. Indianapolis: The Liberal Arts Press, 1972.

22. Berlin, Isaiah. "Political Ideas in the Twentieth Century." In *Four Essays on Liberty.* New York: Oxford University Press, 1970.

23. Blackmore, John T. *Ernst Mach.* Berkeley: University of California Press, 1972.

24. Bodmershof, Imma. "Christian von Ehrenfels, Eine Skizze." In *Gestalthaftes Sehen*, pp. 427–435. Edited by Ferdinand Weinhandl. Darmstadt: Wissenschaftliche Buchgesellschaft, 1960.

25. Boltzmann, Ludwig. "Über die Frage nach der objektiven Existenz der Vorgänge in der unbelebten Natur." In *Populäre Schriften*, pp. 162–187. Leipzig: Verlag von Johann Ambrosius Barth, 1905.

26. ———. "Theories as Representations." Translated in part by Rudolph Weingartner. In *Philosophy of Science*, pp. 245–252. Edited by Arthur Danto and Sidney Morgenbesser. Cleveland: World Publishing Co., Meridian ed., 1960.

27. ———. "Über die Unentbehrlichkeit der Atomistik in der Naturwissenschaft." In *Populäre Schriften*, pp. 141–157.

28. ———. "Ein Wort der Mathematik an die Energetik." In *Populäre Schriften*, pp. 104–136.

29. Boring, Edwin G. *A History of Experimental Psychology.* 2nd ed. New York: Appleton Century Crofts, 1950.

30. Bradley, Francis Herbert. *Appearance and Reality*. 2nd ed. Oxford: Oxford University Press; paperback ed., 1969.

31. Brentano, Franz. *The Origin of Our Knowledge of Right and Wrong*. Translated by Roderick M. Chisholm and Elizabeth H. Schneewind. New York: Humanities Press, 1969.

32. ———. *Meine letzten Wünsche für Österreich*. Stuttgart: Verlag der J. G. Cotta'schen Buchhandlung, 1895.

33. ———. *Psychology from an Empirical Standpoint*. Translated by Antos C. Rancurello, D. B. Terrell, and Linda McAlister. New York: Humanities Press, 1973.

34. ———. *Die vier Phasen der Philosophie und ihr augenblicklicher Stand*. Stuttgart: Verlag der G. G. Cotta'schen Buchandlung, 1895.

35. ———. *Über die Zukunft der Philosophie*. Edited by Oskar Kraus. Leipzig: Felix Meiner Verlag, 1929.

36. Büchner, Ludwig. *Kraft und Stoff*. 15th ed. Leipzig: T. Thomas, 1883.

37. Bühler, Karl. *Die Gestaltwahrnehmung*. Stuttgart: W. Sperrmann, 1913.

38. ———. *Die Krise der Psychologie*. 3rd ed. Stuttgart: Gustav Fischer Verlag, 1965.

39. ———. "Die 'Neue Psychologie' Koffkas." *Zeitschrift für Psychologie*, XCIX (1926), 145–160.

40. ———. "Tatsachen und Probleme zu einer Psychologie der Denkvorgänge." *Archiv für die gesamte Psychologie* IX (1907), 297-365; XII (1908), 1–124.

41. Carnap, Rudolf. *The Logical Structure of the World*. Translated by Rolf A. George. 2nd ed. Berkeley: University of California Press, 1967.

42. ———. "The Rejection of Metaphysics." In *The Age of Analysis*, pp. 209–225. Edited by Morton White. New York: New American Library, Mentor ed., 1955.

43. Cassirer, Ernst. *The Problem of Knowledge*. Translated by William H. Woglom and Charles W. Hendel. New Haven: Yale University Press, 1950.

44. ———. *Substance and Function*. Translated by William Curtis Swabey and Marie Collins Swabey. Chicago: Open Court Publishing Co., 1923. Reprint ed., New York: Dover Publications, 1953.

45. Chisholm, Roderick M. "Beyond Being and Nonbeing." In *Jen-*

*seits von Sein und Nichtsein*, pp. 25–36. Edited by Rudolf Haller. Graz: Akademische Druck-u. Verlagsanstalt, 1972.

46. ———. "Brentano on Descriptive Psychology and the Intentional." In *Phenomenology and Existentialism*, pp. 2–23. Edited by Edward N. Lee and Maurice Mandelbaum. Baltimore: Johns Hopkins Press, 1967.

47. ———. "Brentano's Descriptive Psychology." In *Acten des XIV internationalen Kongresses für Philosophie*, pp. 164–174. Vienna: Herder Verlag, 1968.

48. ———. "Objectives and Intrinsic Value." In *Jenseits von Sein und Nichtsein*, pp. 261–269. Edited by Rudolf Haller. Graz: Akademische Druck-u. Verlagsanstalt, 1972.

49. ———, ed. *Realism and the Background of Phenomenology*. Glencoe: The Free Press, 1960.

50. ———. *Theory of Knowledge*. 1st ed. Englewood Cliffs, N.J.: Prentice-Hall, 1966.

51. ———. "Vorwort zur Neuausgabe." In *Über Möglichkeit und Wahrscheinlichkeit* by Alexius Meinong. *Gesamtausgabe* V, ix–xii. Graz: Akademische Druck-u. Verlagsanstalt, 1972.

52. Chomsky, Noam. *Language and Mind*. New York: Harcourt, Brace and World, 1968.

53. Cohen, Hermann. *Logik der reinen Erkenntniss*. Berlin: Bruno Cassirer, 1902.

54. Comte, Auguste. *The Positive Philosophy of Auguste Comte*. Translated by Harriet Martineau. 2 vols. London: John Chapman, 1853.

55. Cornelius, Hans. *Psychologie als Erfahrungswissenschaft*. Leipzig: Druck und Verlag von G. B. Teubner, 1897.

56. ———. "Über Verschmelzung und Analyse." *Vierteljahrsschrift für wissenschaftliche Philosophie*, XVI (1892), 404–446; XVII (1893), 30–75.

57. Descartes, René. *Meditations on First Philosophy*. In *The Philosophical Works of Descartes*, I, 131–299. Translated by Elizabeth S. Haldane and G. R. T. Ross. Cambridge: Cambridge University Press; paperback ed., 1968.

58. ———. *Rules for the Direction of the Mind*. In *The Philosophical Works of Descartes*, I, 1–77.

59. Deutsche Gesellschaft für Psychologie. *Bericht über den IX en Kongress für experimentelle Psychologie*. Leipzig: Verlag von Johann Ambrosius Barth, 1925.

60. Dewey, John. "The Reflex Arc Concept in Psychology." In *Readings in the History of Psychology*, pp. 355–365. Edited by Wayne Dennis. New York: Appleton Century Crofts, 1948.

61. Dilthey, Wilhelm. *Der Aufbau der geschichtlichen Welt in den Geisteswissenschaften*. In *Gesammelte Schriften* VII, 79–291. Berlin: Verlag von B. G. Teubner, 1927.

62. ———. "Ausarbeitung der deskriptiven Psychologie." In *Gesammelte Schriften*, XVIII, 112–185. Göttingen: Vandenhoeck und Ruprecht, 1977.

63. ———. "Die Einbildungskraft des Dichters." In *Gesammelte Schriften* VI, 103–241. Stuttgart: B. G. Teubner, 1958.

64. ———. *Einleitung in die Geisteswissenschaften*. *Gesammelte Schriften*, I. Stuttgart: B. G. Teubner, 1959.

65. ———. "Die Entstehung der Hermeneutik." In *Gesammelte Schriften* V, 317–338. Stuttgart: B. G. Teubner, 1957.

66. ———. "Ideen über eine beschreibende und zergliedernde Psychologie." In *Gesammelte Schriften* V, 139–316.

67. ———. "Rede zum 70. Geburtstag." In *Gesammelte Schriften* V, 7–9.

68. ———. "Studien zur Grundlegung der Geisteswissenschaften." In *Gesammelte Schriften* VII, 1–75.

69. ———. "Das Wesen der Philosophie." In *Gesammelte Schriften* V, 339–416.

70. Du Bois Reymond, Emil. *Über die Grenzen des Naturerkennens: Die Sieben Welträtsel*. Leipzig: Verlag von Veit. and Comp., 1891.

71. Dummett, Michael. *Frege*. London: Duckworth, 1973.

72. Durkheim, Emile. "Individual and Collective Representations." In *Sociology and Philosophy*, pp. 1–34. Translated by D. F. Pocock. New York: Macmillan, Free Press ed., 1974.

73. Ehrenfels, Christian von. "Über Gestaltqualitäten." *Vierteljahrsschrift für wissenschaftliche Philosophie*, XIV (1890), 249–292.

74. ———. "Sexualethik." *Grenzfragen des Nerven-und Seelenlebens*, IX (1908), 1–95.

75. ———. "Wahrheit und Irrtum im Naturalismus." *Freie Bühne*, II (1891), 737–742.

76. Einstein, Albert. "Ernst Mach." *Physikalische Zeitschrift* XVII (1916). Quoted in John T. Blackmore, *Ernst Mach*, p. 255. Berkeley: University of California Press, 1972.

77. ———. *Ideas and Opinions*. New York: Crown Publishers, 1954.

78. Eisler, Rudolf. *Handwörterbuch der Philosophie*. Berlin: Siegfried Mittler und Sohn, 1913.

79. Eliot, T. S. *Knowledge and Experience in the Philosophy of F. H. Bradley*. London: Faber and Faber, 1964.

80. ———. "Tradition and the Individual Talent." In *Selected Prose of T. S. Eliot*, pp. 37–44. Edited by Frank Kermode. New York: Harcourt, Brace Jovanovich, 1975.

81. *Encyclopedia of Philosophy*. S.v. "Analysis, Philosophical," by Morris Weitz.

82. ———. S.v. "Duhem, Pierre Maurice Marie," by Peter Alexander.

83. ———. S.v. "Intuition," by Richard Rorty.

84. ———. S.v. "Krueger, Felix," by Albert Wellek.

85. ———. S.v. "Meinong, Alexius," by Roderick M. Chisholm.

86. ———. S.v. "Positivism," by Nicola Abbagnano.

87. ———. S.v. "Psychologism," by Nicola Abbagnano.

88. Farber, Marvin. *The Foundation of Phenomenology*. Cambridge: Harvard University Press, 1943.

89. Findlay, John N. "Einige Hauptpünkte in Meinongs philosophischer Psychologie." In *Jenseits von Sein und Nichtsein*, pp. 15–24. Edited by Rudolf Haller. Graz: Akademische Druck-u. Verlagsanstalt, 1972.

90. ———. "Husserl's Analysis of the Inner Time-Consciousness." *The Monist* LIX (1975), 3–21.

91. ———. "The Influence of Meinong in Anglo-Saxon Countries." In *Meinong Gedenkschrift*, pp. 9–19. Edited by the Philosophical Seminar of the [Graz] University. Graz: "Styria" Verlagsanstalt, 1952.

92. ———. "Meinong the Phenomenologist." *Revue Internationale de la Philosophie* XXVII (1973), 161–177.

93. ———. *Meinong's Theory of Objects and Values*. 2nd ed. Oxford: Clarendon Press, 1963.

94. Foucault, Michel. *The Order of Things*. New York: Random House, Vintage ed., 1973.

95. Frege, Gottlob. "On Concept and Object." In *Translations from the Philosophical Writings of Gottlob Frege*, pp. 42–55. Edited by Peter Geach and Max Black. Oxford: Basil Blackwell, 1966.

96. ———. *The Foundations of Arithmetic*. Translated by J. L. Austin. Oxford: Basil Blackwell, 1950.

97. ———. "Function and Concept." In *Translations from the Philosophical Writings of Gottlob Frege*, pp. 21–41.

98. ———. Review of Husserl's *Philosophie der Arithmetik*, excerpts. In *Translations from the Philosophical Writings of Gottlob Frege*, pp. 79–85.

99. ———. "On Sense and Reference." In *Translations from the Philosophical Writings of Gottlob Frege*, pp. 56–78.

100. ———. "Über die wissenschaftliche Begründung einer Begriffsschrift." In *Funktion, Begriff, Bedeutung*, pp. 91–97. Edited by Günther Patzig. Göttingen: Vandenhoeck and Ruprecht, 1975.

101. Freud, Sigmund. *Civilization and its Discontents*. In *The Standard Edition of the Complete Psychological Works of Sigmund Freud* XXI, 59–145. Edited by James Strachey, Anna Freud, et al. London: Hogarth Press, 1966–74.

102. ———. "A Difficulty in the Path of Psycho-Analysis." In *The Standard Edition*, XVII, 135–44.

103. ———. *The Future of an Illusion*. In *The Standard Edition*, XXI, 1–56.

104. ———. *Introductory Lectures on Psycho-Analysis*. In *The Standard Edition*, XV–XVI.

105. ———. "Negation." In *The Standard Edition*, XIX, 235–239.

106. ———. "The Unconscious." In *The Standard Edition*, XIV, 159–215.

107. Fuchs, Albert. *Geistige Strömungen in Österreich, 1867–1918*. Vienna: Globus Verlag, 1949.

108. Gadamer, Hans-Georg. *Truth and Method*. New York: Seabury Press, 1975.

109. Gasman, Daniel. *The Scientific Origins of National Socialism*. London: Macdonald, 1971.

110. Gawronsky, Dimitri. "Cassirer, His Life and Work." In *The Philosophy of Ernst Cassirer*, pp. 1–27. Edited by Paul Arthur Schilpp. La Salle, Ill.: Open Court Publishing Co., 1949.

111. Grossmann, Reinhardt. *Meinong*. London: Routledge and Kegan Paul, 1974.

112. Gurwitsch, Aron. "Husserl's Theory of Intentionality of Consciousness in Historical Perspective." In *Phenomenology and Existentialism*, pp. 25–57. Edited by Edward N. Lee and Maurice Mandelbaum. Baltimore: The Johns Hopkins Press, 1967.

113. ———. "The Kantian and Husserlian Conceptions of Con-

sciousness." In *Studies in Phenomenology and Psychology*, pp. 148–174. Evanston: Northwestern University Press, 1966.

114. ———. "Some Aspects and Developments of Gestalt Psychology." In *Studies in Phenomenology and Psychology*, pp. 3–55.

115. Habermas, Jürgen. *Knowledge and Human Interests*. Translated by Jeremy Shapiro. London: Heinemann Educational Books, 1972.

116. Haller, Rudolf. "Ludwig Wittgenstein und die Österreichische Philosophie." *Wissenschaft und Weltbild* XXI (1968), 76–87.

117. Heidegger, Martin. *Sein und Zeit*. Tübingen: Max Niemeyer Verlag, 1967.

118. Heider, Fritz. "Gestalt Theory: Early History and Reminiscences." In *Historical Conceptions of Psychology*, pp. 63–73. Edited by Mary Henle, Julian Jaynes, and John J. Sullivan. New York: Springer Publishing Co., 1973.

119. Helmholtz, Hermann von. "Einleitung." In *Über die Erhaltung der Kraft. Ostwald's Klassiker der exakten Wissenschaften*, I, 6f. Leipzig: W. Engelmann, 1889. Cited in Ernst Cassirer, *The Problem of Knowledge*, p. 86. Translated by William Woglom and Charles Hendel. New Haven: Yale University Press, 1950.

120. Höfler, Alois. "Franz Brentano in Wien." *Süddeutsche Monatshefte*. May 1917, 319–325.

121. ———. *Logik*. Unter Mitwirkung von Alexius Meinong. Vienna: F. Tempsky, 1890.

122. ———. *Psychologie*. Vienna: F. Tempsky, 1894.

123. ———. *Selbstdarstellung*. In *Die Philosophie der Gegenwart in Selbstdarstellungen*. Edited by Raymund Schmidt. II, 117–166. Leipzig: Felix Meiner Verlag, 1921.

124. ——— and Stephan Witasek. *Hundert psychologische Schulversuche*. Leipzig: Verlag von Johann Ambrosius Barth, 1899.

125. Holborn, Hajo. "Wilhelm Dilthey and the Critique of Historical Reason." *Journal of the History of Ideas* XI (1950), 93–118.

126. Holtzmann, H. "Der Religionsbegriff der Schule Herbarts." *Zeitschrift für wissenschaftliche Theologie*, XXV (1882), 66–92.

127. Howarth, Herbert. *Notes on Some Figures Behind T. S. Eliot*. London: Chatto and Windus, 1965.

128. Hughes, H. Stuart. *Consciousness and Society*. New York: Random House, Vintage ed., 1958.

129. Hume, David. *A Treatise on Human Nature*. Edited by L. A. Shelby-Bigge. Oxford: The Clarendon Press, 1896.

130. Humphrey, George. *Thinking*. New York: John Wiley and Sons, 1963.

131. Husserl, Edmund. *The Crisis of the European Sciences and Transcendental Phenomenology*. Translated by David Carr. Evanston: Northwestern University Press, 1970.

132. ———. "Erinnerungen an Franz Brentano." In *Franz Brentano*, pp. 153–167. Edited by Oskar Kraus. München: Oskar Beck, 1919.

133. ———. *Formale und Transcendentale Logik*. In *Husserliana* XVII. The Hague: Martinus Nijhoff, 1974.

134. ———. *Ideas. General Introduction to Pure Phenomenology*. Translated by W. R. Boyce Gibson. London: George Allen and Unwin, 1931.

135. ———. *Logical Investigations*. 2nd ed. 2 vols. Translated by J. N. Findlay. New York: Humanities Press, 1970. 1st ed., Tübingen: Max Niemeyer Verlag, 1900–01.

136. ———. "Persönliche Aufzeichnungen." Edited by Walter Biemel. *Philosophy and Phenomenological Research*, XVI (1956), 293–302.

137. ———. *Zur Phänomenologie des inneren Zeitbewusstseins (1893–1917)*. Edited by Rudolf Boehm. *Husserliana* X. The Hague: Martinus Nijhoff, 1966.

138. ———. "Philosophy and the Crisis of European Man." In *Phenomenology and the Crisis of Philosophy*, pp. 149–192. Translated by Quentin Lauer. New York: Harper and Row, Torchbooks ed., 1965.

139. ———. "Philosophy as a Rigorous Science." In *Phenomenology and the Crisis of Philosophy*, pp. 71–147.

140. Iggers, Georg G. *The German Conception of History*. Middletown, Conn.: Wesleyan University Press, 1968.

141. Izenberg, Gerald. *The Existentialist Critique of Freud*. Princeton: Princeton University Press, 1976.

142. James, William. *Pragmatism*. New York: Longmans, Green and Co., 1931.

143. ———. *The Principles of Psychology*. 2 Vols. New York: Henry Holt and Co., 1890; reprint ed., New York: Dover Publications, 1950.

144. Janik, Alan, and Stephen Toulmin. *Wittgenstein's Vienna*. New York: Simon and Schuster, Touchstone ed., 1973.

145. Johnston, William M. *The Austrian Mind*. Berkeley: University of California Press, 1972.

146. Jones, Ernest. *Sigmund Freud: Life and Work.* 3 Vols. London: The Hogarth Press, 1953.

147. Kafka, Franz. *The Diaries of Franz Kafka, 1910–1913.* Edited by Max Brod. Translated by Joseph Kresh. New York: Schocken Books, 1965.

148. Kant, Immanuel. *Critique of Pure Reason.* Translated by Norman Kemp Smith. 2nd ed. New York: St. Martin's Press, 1964.

149. Kindinger, Rudolf. "Das Problem der unvollkommenen Erkenntnisleistung in der Meinongschen Wahrnehmungslehre." In *Meinong Gedenkschrift.* Edited by the Philosophical Seminar of the [Graz] University. Graz: "Styria" Verlagsanstalt, 1952.

150. Kirchhoff, Gustav. *Vorlesungen über mathematische Physik.* 2nd ed. Leipzig: B. G. Teubner, 1877.

151. Köhler, Wolfgang. *Gestalt Psychology.* New York: Horace Liveright, 1947. Reprint ed., New American Library, Mentor ed., 1954.

152. ———. "Gestalt Psychology." In *The Selected Papers of Wolfgang Köhler*, pp. 108–122. Edited by Mary Henle. New York: Liveright, 1971.

153. ———. *The Place of Value in a World of Facts.* New York: Liveright Publishing Corp., 1938. Reprint ed., New York: Meridian Books, 1959.

154. ———. "On Unnoticed Sensations and Errors of Judgment." Translated by Helmut E. Adler. In *The Selected Papers of Wolfgang Köhler*, pp. 13–39.

155. Koffka, Kurt, "Bemerkungen zur Denk-Psychologie." *Psychologische Forschung* IX (1927), 163–183.

156. ———. "Zur Grundlegung der Wahrnehmungspsychologie— Eine Auseinandersetzung mit V. Benussi." *Zeitschrift für Psychologie* LXXIII (1915), 11–91.

157. ———. *Principles of Gestalt Psychology.* New York: Harcourt, Brace and World, Harbinger ed., 1963.

158. Kolakowski, Leszek. *The Alienation of Reason.* Translated by Norbert Guterman. Garden City, N.Y.: Doubleday, 1968.

159. Kraus, Oskar, ed. *Franz Brentano.* München: Oskar Beck, 1919.

160. Külpe, Oswald. *Die Realisierung.* 3 vols. Leipzig: Verlag von S. Hirzel, 1912–1923.

161. ———. *Vorlesungen über Psychologie.* Edited by Karl Bühler. 2nd ed. Leipzig: Verlag von S. Hirzel, 1922.

162. Küng, Guido. "Noema und Gegenstand." In *Jenseits von Sein und Nichtsein*, pp. 55–62. Edited by Rudolf Haller. Graz: Akademische Druck-u. Verlagsanstalt, 1972.

163. ———. "The Phenomenological Reduction as Epoché and as Explication." *The Monist* LIX (1975), 63–80.

164. *Kürschner's deutscher gelehrten-kalender*. Berlin: W. de Gruyter and Co., 1925.

165. Kuhn, Thomas. *The Structure of Scientific Revolutions*. 2nd ed. Chicago: The University of Chicago Press, 1970.

166. Lambert, Karel. "Being and Being So." In *Jenseits von Sein und Nichtsein*, pp. 37–46. Edited by Rudolf Haller. Graz: Akademische Druck-u. Verlagsanstalt, 1972.

167. Lane, Michael, ed. *Introduction to Structuralism*. New York: Basic Books, Harper Torchbook ed., 1970.

168. Langer, Suzanne K. *Philosophy in a New Key*. Cambridge: Harvard University Press, 1942.

169. Lichtheim, George. *Marxism*. 2nd ed. New York: Praeger Publishers, 1965.

170. Lindenfeld, David. "Oswald Külpe and the Würzburg School." *Journal of the History of the Behavioral Sciences* XIV (1978), 132–141.

171. Linsky, Leonard. *Referring*. London: Routledge and Kegan Paul, 1967.

172. Locke, John. *An Essay Concerning Human Understanding*. Edited by Peter H. Nidditch. Oxford: Clarendon Press, 1975.

173. Mach, Ernst. *The Analysis of Sensations*. Translated by C. M. Williams and Sydney Waterlow. 5th ed. Chicago: Open Court Publishing Co., 1914. Reprint ed., New York: Dover Publishers, 1959.

174. ———. *Populärwissenschaftliche Vorlesungen*. 4th ed. Leipzig: Verlag von Johann Ambrosius Barth, 1910.

175. Mackie, J. L. *Problems from Locke*. Oxford: Clarendon Press, 1976.

176. Mally, Ernst. "Alexius Meinong." In *Neue österreichische Biographie* VIII, 90–100. Edited by Anton Bettelheim et al. Vienna: Almathea Verlag, 1935.

177. Mandelbaum, Maurice. *History, Man and Reason*. Baltimore: Johns Hopkins Press, 1971.

178. ———. "Locke's Realism." In *Philosophy, Science and Sense Perception*, pp. 1–60. Baltimore: Johns Hopkins Press, 1964.

179. ———. *The Problem of Historical Knowledge*. New York: Liveright, 1938.

180. Mandler, Jean Matter, and George Mandler. "The Diaspora of Experimental Psychology: The Gestaltists and Others." In *The Intellectual Migration*, pp. 371–419. Edited by Donald Fleming and Bernard Bailyn. Cambridge: Harvard University Press, Belknap ed., 1969.

181. ———. *Thinking: From Association to Gestalt*. New York: John Wiley and Sons, 1964.

182. Marcuse, Herbert. *One-Dimensional Man*. Boston: Beacon Press, paperback ed., 1966.

183. Margolis, John. *T. S. Eliot's Intellectual Development, 1922–1939*. Chicago: University of Chicago Press, 1972.

184. Martinak, Eduard. *Psychologische und pädagogische Abhandlungen*. Graz: Leykam-Verlag, 1929.

185. Masur, Gerhard. *Prophets of Yesterday*. New York: Macmillan Co., 1961.

186. McGrath, William J. *Dionysian Art and Populist Politics in Austria*. New Haven: Yale University Press, 1974.

187. ———. "Student Radicalism in Vienna." *Journal of Contemporary History* II (1967), 183–202.

188. Menger, Carl. *Grundsätze der Volkswirtschaftslehre*. In *The Collected Works of Carl Menger*. London: London School of Economics and Political Science, 1934.

189. Merlan, Philip. "Brentano and Freud—A Sequel." *Journal of the History of Ideas* X (1949), 451.

190. Merleau-Ponty, Maurice. *Phenomenology of Perception*. Translated by Colin Smith. London: Routledge and Kegan Paul, 1962.

191. ———. *The Structure of Behavior*. Translated by Alden L. Fisher. Boston: Beacon Press, paperback ed., 1963.

192. Merz, John Theodore. *A History of European Thought in the Nineteenth Century*. 4 vols. William Blackwood and Sons, 1904–12. Reprint ed., New York: Dover Publications, 1965.

193. Messer, August. *Empfinden und Denken*. 2nd ed. Leipzig: Verlag von Quelle und Meyer, 1924.

194. ———. "Experimentell-psychologische Untersuchungen über das Denken." *Archiv für die gesamte Psychologie* VIII (1906), 1–224.

195. Metzger, Wolfgang. "The Historical Background for National

Trends in Psychology: German Psychology." *Journal of the History of the Behavioral Sciences* I (1965), 109–115.

196. Mill, James. *Analysis of the Phenomena of the Human Mind*. 2nd ed. 2 vols. London: Longmans, Green, Reader and Dyer, 1878. Reprint ed., New York: Augustus M. Kelley, 1967.

197. Mill, John Stuart. *Autobiography*. Indianapolis: Bobbs-Merrill Co, Library of Liberal Arts ed., 1957.

198. ———. *An Examination of Sir William Hamilton's Philosophy*. 3rd ed. London: Longmans, Green, Reader and Dyer, 1867.

199. ———. *A System of Logic*. 3rd ed. 2 vols. London: John W. Parker, 1851.

200. Miller, Eugene F. "Hume's Contribution to Behavioral Science." *Journal of the History of the Behavioral Sciences* VII (1971), 154–168.

201. Mischel, Theodore. "Kant and the Possibility of a Science of Psychology." *The Monist* LI (1967), 599–622.

202. Molisch, Paul. *Politische Geschichte der deutschen Hochschulen in Österreich*. 2nd ed. Vienna: Wilhelm Braumüller, 1939.

203. Morscher, Edgar. "Meinong's Bedeutungslehre." *Revue Internationale de la Philosophie* XXVII (1973), 178–206.

204. Murphy, Gardner. *Historical Introduction to Modern Psychology*. Revised ed. New York: Harcourt, Brace and Co., 1949.

205. Musil, Robert. *The Man Without Qualities*. Translated by Eithne Wilkins and Ernst Kaiser. 2 vols. New York: Capricorn Books, 1965.

206. Mussolini, Benito. *The Doctrine of Fascism*. Florence: Vallechi Editore, 1936.

207. Nagel, Ernest. *The Structure of Science*. New York: Harcourt, Brace and World, 1961.

208. Natanson, Maurice. *Edmund Husserl. Philosopher of Infinite Tasks*. Evanston: Northwestern University Press, 1973.

209. Natorp, Paul. *Allgemeine Psychologie*. Tübingen: J. C. B. Mohr, 1912.

210. Neesen, Peter. *Vom Louvrezirkel zum Prozess*. Göppingen: Verlag Alfred Kümmerle, 1972.

211. *Österreichisches statistisches Handbuch*. Vienna: Verlag der K. K. statistischen-centralcommission. Published yearly.

212. Ogden, C. K. and I. A. Richards. *The Meaning of Meaning*. 2nd ed., revised. New York: Harcourt, Brace and Co., 1927.

213. Ostwald, Wilhelm. *Die Überwindung des wissenschaftlichen Materialismus*. Leipzig: Verlag von Veit and Comp., 1895.

214. Pachter, Henry M. *The Fall and Rise of Europe*. New York: Praeger Publishers, 1976.

215. Parsons, Terrence. "A Prolegomenon to Meinongian Semantics." *Journal of Philosophy* LXXI (1974), 561–580.

216. Passmore, John. *A Hundred Years of Philosophy*. London: Duckworth, 1966.

217. Paulsen, Friedrich. *Geschichte des gelehrten Unterrichts*. 3rd ed. 2 vols. Berlin: Vereinigung wissenschaftlicher Verleger, 1921.

218. Perry, Ralph Barton. *The Thought and Character of William James*. 2 vols. Boston: Little, Brown and Co., 1936.

219. Planck, Max. "The Unity of the Physical World-Picture." Translated by Ann Toulmin. In *Physical Reality*, pp. 1–27, edited by Stephen Toulmin. New York: Harper and Row, Torchbooks ed., 1970.

220. Pulzer, Peter J. *The Rise of Political Anti-Semitism in Germany and Austria*. New York: John Wiley and Sons, 1964.

221. Rancurello, Antos. *A Study of Franz Brentano*. New York: Academic Press, 1968.

222. Randall, John Hermann. "The Development of English Thought From J. S. Mill to F. H. Bradley." *Journal of the History of Ideas* XXVII (1966), 217–244.

223. Rickert, Heinrich. *Der Gegenstand der Erkenntnis*. 3rd ed. Tübingen: J. C. B. Mohr (Paul Siebeck), 1915.

224. ———. *Die Grenzen der naturwissenschaftlichen Begriffsbildung*. Tübingen: J. C. B. Mohr, 1902.

225. Ricoeur, Paul. *Freud and Philosophy*. Translated by Denis Savage. New Haven: Yale University Press, 1970.

226. ———. *Husserl: An Analysis of His Phenomenology*. Translated by Edward G. Ballard and Lester E. Embree. Evanston: Northwestern University Press, 1967.

227. Ringer, Fritz K. *The Decline of the German Mandarins: The German Academic Community 1890–1933*. Cambridge: Harvard University Press, 1969.

228. Routley, Richard, and Valerie Routley. "Rehabilitating Meinong's Theory of Objects." *Revue Internationale de la Philosophie* XXVII (1973), 224–254.

229. Russell, Bertrand. *The Analysis of Mind*. London: George Allen and Unwin Ltd., 1921.

230. ———. *The Autobiography of Bertrand Russell*. 3 vols. Boston: Little, Brown and Co., 1967–69.

231. ———. "On Denoting." In *Logic and Knowledge*, pp. 39–56.

Edited by Robert Charles Marsh. London: George Allen and Unwin Ltd., 1956.

232. ———. *A History of Western Philosophy*. New York: Simon and Schuster, 1945.

233. ———. "Logical Atomism." In *Logical Positivism*, pp. 31–50. Edited by A. J. Ayer. New York: The Free Press, 1959.

234. ———. "Mathematical Logic as based on the Theory of Types." In *Logic and Knowledge*, pp. 57–102.

235. ———. "Meinong's Theory of Complexes and Assumptions." In *Essays in Analysis*, pp. 21–76. Edited by Douglas Lackey. New York: George Braziller, 1973.

236. ———. *My Philosophical Development*. London: George Allen and Unwin Ltd., 1959.

237. ———. "On the Nature of Acquaintance." In *Logic and Knowledge*, pp. 125–174.

238. ———. "On the Nature of Truth and Falsehood." In *Philosophical Essays*. New York: Simon and Schuster, 1966.

239. ———. "The Philosophy of Logical Atomism." In *Logic and Knowledge*, pp. 175–281.

240. ———. *Portraits from Memory*. New York: Simon and Schuster, Clarion ed., 1956.

241. ———. *The Principles of Mathematics*. 2nd ed. New York: W. W. Norton and Co., n.d.

242. ———. *The Problems of Philosophy*. Oxford: Oxford University Press, paperback ed., 1959.

243. ———. "The Relation of Sense-Data to Physics." In *Mysticism and Logic*, pp. 108–131. New York: Barnes and Noble, 1963.

244. ———. Review of Meinong's *Die Stellung der Gegenstandstheorie im System der Wissenschaften*. In *Essays in Analysis*, pp. 83–93.

245. ———. Review of Meinong's *Untersuchungen zur Gegenstandstheorie und Psychologie*. In *Essays in Analysis*, pp. 77–88.

246. Ryle, Gilbert. *The Concept of Mind*. New York: Barnes and Noble, 1949.

247. ———. "Intentionality and the Nature of Thinking." *Revue Internationale de la Philosophie* XXVII (1973), 255–265.

248. Sartre, Jean-Paul. *Being and Nothingness*. Translated by Hazel E. Barnes. New York: Philosophical Library, 1956.

249. ———. *The Psychology of Imagination*. New York: Philosophical Library, 1948.

250. ———. *The Transcendence of the Ego*. Translated by Forrest

Williams and Robert Kirkpatrick. New York: Farrar, Straus and Giroux, Noonday press ed., 1957.

251. De Saussure, Ferdinand. *Course in General Linguistics*. Edited by Charles Bally and Albert Sechehaye. Translated by Wade Baskin. New York: McGraw-Hill, 1966.

252. Schlick, Moritz. "Positivism and Realism." Translated by David Rynin. In *Logical Positivism*, pp. 82–107. Edited by A. J. Ayer. New York: The Free Press, 1959.

253. ———. "The Turning Point in Philosophy." Translated by David Rynin. In *Logical Positivism*, pp. 53–59.

254. Schnitzler, Henry. "Gay Vienna—Myth and Reality." *Journal of the History of Ideas* XV (1954), 84–118.

255. Schorske, Carl E. "The Transformation of the Garden: Ideal and Society in Austrian Literature." *American Historical Review* LXXII (1967), 1283–1320.

256. Schumann, Friedrich. "Zur Psychologie der Zeitanschauung." *Zeitschrift für Psychologie* XVII (1898), 106–148.

257. Selz, Otto. *Über die Gesetze des geordneten Denkverlaufs*. Stuttgart: Verlag von W. Spemann, 1913.

258. Spencer, Herbert. *First Principles*. 4th ed. New York: D. Appleton and Co., 1896.

259. ———. *The Principles of Psychology*. 2 vols. New York: D. Appleton and Co., 1896.

260. Spiegelberg, Herbert. *The Phenomenological Movement*. 2nd ed. 2 vols. The Hague: Martinus Nijhoff, 1969.

261. Stern, Fritz. *The Politics of Cultural Despair*. Garden City, N.Y.: Doubleday; Anchor ed., 1965.

262. Stern, L. William. *Die psychologische Arbeit des neunzehnten Jahrhunderts*. Berlin: Verlag von Hermann Walther, 1900.

263. Stumpf, Karl. "Erscheinungen und psychische Funktionen." In *Abhandlungen der königlich-preussischen Akademie der Wissenschaften*. 1906.

264. ———. "Franz Brentano." In *Franz Brentano*, pp. 85–149. Edited by Oskar Kraus. München: Oskar Beck, 1919.

265. Tannenbaum, Edward. *1900*. Garden City, N.Y.: Doubleday, Anchor Press ed., 1976.

266. Thompson, Eric. *T. S. Eliot, The Metaphysical Perspective*. Carbondale, Ill.: Southern Illinois University Press, 1963.

267. Titchener, Edward Bradford. *Lectures on the Experimental Psychology of the Thought Processes*. New York: Macmillan, 1909.

268. ———. *Systematic Psychology: Prolegomena.* New York: Macmillan, 1929. Reprint ed., Ithaca: Cornell University Press, 1972.

269. Topitsch, Ernst. "Max Weber and Sociology Today." In *Max Weber and Sociology Today*, pp. 8–25. Edited by Otto Stammer, translated by Kathleen Morris. New York: Harper and Row, Torchbooks ed., 1971.

270. Twardowski, Kasimir. *Zur Lehre vom Inhalt und Gegenstand der Vorstellungen.* Vienna: Alfred Holder, 1894.

271. Ueberweg, Friedrich. *Ueberwegs Grundriss der Geschichte der Philosophie.* Edited by T. K. Oesterreich. 13th ed. Basel: Benno Schwage and Co., 1951.

272. Urmson, J. O. *Philosophical Analysis. Its Development Between the Two World Wars.* Oxford: Oxford University Press, 1967.

273. Vaihinger, Hans. *Die Philosophie des Als Ob.* 10th ed. Leipzig: Felix Meiner Verlag, 1927.

274. Valjavec, Fritz. *Der Josephinismus.* Munich: Verlag von R. Oldenbourg, 1945.

275. Watson, John B. "Psychology as the Behaviorist Views It." In *Readings in the History of Psychology*, pp. 457–471. Edited by Wayne Dennis. New York: Appleton Century Crofts, 1948.

276. Watt, Henry J. "Experimental Contribution to a Theory of Thinking." In *Thinking: From Association to Gestalt*, pp. 189–200. Edited by Jean Matter Mandler and George Mandler. New York: John Wiley and Sons, 1963.

277. Weber, Max. "Critical Studies in the Logic of the Cultural Sciences." In *Max Weber on the Methodology of the Social Sciences*, pp. 113–188. Translated and edited by Edward A. Shils and Henry A. Finch. Glencoe, Ill.: The Free Press, 1949.

278. ———. "Die Grenznutzlehre und das 'psychophysische Grundgesetz.'" In *Gesammelte Aufsätze zur Wissenschaftslehre*, pp. 384–399. Edited by Johannes Winckelmann. 3rd ed. Tübingen: J. C. B. Mohr, 1968.

279. ———. "Über einige Kategorien der verstehenden Soziologie." In *Gesammelte Aufsätze zur Wissenschaftslehre*, pp. 427–474.

280. ———. "The Meaning of 'Ethical Neutrality' in Sociology and Economics." In *Max Weber on the Methodology of the Social Sciences*, pp. 1–47.

281. ———. "'Objectivity' in Social Science and Social Policy." In *Max Weber on the Methodology of the Social Sciences*, pp. 50–112.

282. ———. "Roscher und Knies und die logischen Probleme 'der historischen Nationalökonomie." In *Gesammelte Aufsätze zur Wissenschaftslehre*, pp. 1–145.

283. ———. "Science as a Vocation." In *From Max Weber*, pp. 129–156. Translated by H. H. Gerth and C. Wright Mills. New York: Oxford University Press, 1958.

284. ———. *The Theory of Social and Economic Organization*. Translated by A. M. Henderson and Talcott Parsons. New York: The Free Press, 1964.

285. Wertheimer, Max. "Experimentelle Studien über das Sehen von Bewegung." In *Drei Abhandlungen zur Gestalttheorie*. Erlangen: Verlag der Philosophischen Akademie, 1925.

286. ———. *Productive Thinking*. Edited by Michael Wertheimer. Enlarged ed. New York: Harper and Row, 1959.

287. Wesley, Frank. "Masters and Pupils among the German Psychologists." *Journal of the History of the Behavioral Sciences* I (1965), 252–261.

288. Windelband, Wilhelm. "Geschichte und Naturwissenschaft." In *Präludien* II, pp. 136–160. 5th ed. Tübingen: J. C. B. Mohr, 1915.

289. Winter, Eduard. *Der Josefinismus und seine Geschichte*. Brünn: Rudolf M. Rohrer Verlag, 1943.

290. Witasek, Stephan. "Beiträge zur Psychologie der Komplexionen." *Zeitschrift für Psychologie* XIV (1897), 401–435.

291. ———. "Über die Natur der geometrischen-optischen Täuschungen." *Zeitschrift für Psychologie* XIX (1899), 81–175.

292. Wittgenstein, Ludwig. *Philosophical Investigations*. Translated by G. E. M. Anscombe. 3rd ed. New York: Macmillan, 1958.

293. ———. *Tractatus Logico-Philosophicus*. Translated by D. F. Pears and B. F. McGuinness. London: Routledge and Kegan Paul, 1963.

294. Woodworth, Robert S. *Contemporary Schools of Psychology*. New York: Ronald Press, 1931.

295. Woolhouse, R. S. *Locke's Philosophy of Science and Knowledge*. New York: Barnes and Noble, 1976.

296. Woozley, A. D. Introduction to *Essay on Human Understanding* by John Locke. Cleveland: The World Publishing Co., Meridian ed., 1964.

297. Wundt, Wilhelm. *Erlebtes und Erkanntes*. Stuttgart: Alfred Kröner Verlag, 1921.

298.    ———. "Über psychische Causalität und das Princip des psychophysischen Parallelismus." *Philosophische Studien* X (1894), 1–124.

299.    ———. "Die Psychologie im Kampf ums Dasein." In *Kleine Schriften* III, 515–543. Stuttgart: Alfred Kröner Verlag, 1921.


### B.   Unpublished Sources.

1.   Archival Material
    a.   Records of the *K. K. Ministerium für Cultus und Unterricht.* Files on Brentano and Meinong. Österreichisches Staatsarchiv, Vienna.
    b.   Külpe, Oswald, *Nachlass.* Bayerische Staatsbibliothek, Munich.


2.   Dissertation
    a.   Schermann, Hans. *Meinong und Husserl. Eine Vergleichende Studie.* Ph.D. Dissertation. Université Catholique de Louvain, 1970.

# Index

Compositor: G&S Typesetters
Printer: Thomson-Shore
Binder: Thomson-Shore
Text: VIP Baskerville
Display: VIP Baskerville
Cloth: Kivar 5 Cocoa
Paper: 50 lb. P&S offset